Clinical Management
of Sex Addiction

Clinical Management
of
Sex Addiction

Edited by
Patrick J. Carnes, PhD
Kenneth M. Adams, PhD

Brunner-Routledge
New York and Hove

Published in 2002 by
Brunner-Routledge
29 West 35th Street
New York, NY 10001
www.brunner-routledge.com

Published in Great Britain by
Brunner-Routledge
27 Church Rd.
Hove, East Sussex
BN3 2FA
www.brunner-routledge.co.uk

Brunner-Routledge is an imprint of the Taylor & Francis Group.
Printed in the United States of America on acid-free paper.

Cover Design: Jen Crisp

10 9 8 7 6 5 4 3 2 1

Library of Congress Cataloging-in-Publication Data
Clinical management of sex addiction / edited by Patrick J. Carnes, Kenneth M. Adams.
    p. cm.
    Includes bibliographical references and index.
       ISBN 1-58391-361-0
    1. Sex addiction. I. Carnes, Patrick, 1944–   II. Adams, Kenneth, M.
    RC560 .S43 C56 2002
    616.85'8306—dc21

                                                              2002003956

To our friends,
Richard Irons and James Fearing

Contents

Section IV: Clinical Practice and Resources

Preface

Only a few decades ago compulsive sexual behavior was seen primarily as a matter of values and character. There was no conceptualization of sex addiction or compulsion as an illness. Sex had not emerged as a legitimate area of scientific inquiry, despite the efforts of courageous pioneers. The addiction field was still focused on alcoholism and had not even integrated drug dependence as a viable component to most treatment programs. To suggest that sex could be part of the addiction process was far beyond most professionals' paradigms. Even further beyond was how to treat the problem.

Today a growing body of medical literature documents the existence of sexually compulsive behavior that has all the features of addictive illness. There is a coordinated effort involving psychiatry, psychology, addiction medicine, trauma medicine, sexology, and those providing services in a criminal justice setting to have a workable diagnostic framework or nosology around the disorder. Our growing conceptualization has sharply clarified our understanding of major societal issues, including child abuse, sex offending, prostitution, and anonymous sex. Advances in addiction medicine have created a paradigm of understanding that addictions also coexist and interact with one another. Furthermore, the phenomenon of cybersex addiction has underscored how people can literally experience a loss of control over their sexual choices. Finally, the explosion of knowledge from the field of neurochemistry has helped integrate the different conceptual frameworks.

During this time, a group of clinicians has steadily been working out ways to help people who suffer with the disorder. Over the years these clinicians have presented papers at professional conferences, participated in the National Council on Sex Addiction and Compulsion, and contributed to the medical journal *Sexual Addiction and Compulsion: The Journal of Treatment and Prevention*. We felt that it was time to gather together the knowledge of these dedicated clinicians. There are plenty of books and papers on theory, case examples, and research. But no book collects the experience of clinicians who have worked with this problem and have clinical wisdom about it. Our intent was to create a book that would answer the basic questions of the clinician who has no experience with this problem, as well as serve as a reference for the veteran therapist whose work focuses on this population.

This book contains chapters not previously published that are certain to become classics in the field. Some chapters have been completely rewritten from their previously published form in *Sexual Addiction and Compulsivity: The Journal of Treatment and Prevention* and updated with the clinicians' current experience and knowledge. Other chapters have been reprinted in their original form, as we considered them classics that are able to stand the test of time. Together, they form a collection of wisdom, techniques, and proven methods to assist clinicians in their treatment of sexual addiction. In essence, this book is like having a group of expert clinicians at your disposal for consultation regarding clinical management of this disorder.

The book is structured in four parts. Section I is "The Early Stages." It begins with "The Sexual Addiction Assessment Process," by Pat Carnes and Marie Wilson, to assist the clinician with the process of early assessment and diagnosis. Chapter 2 is "Intervention and the Sexually Addicted Patient" by James Fearing, in which intervention is strategically outlined. "Breaking Through Defenses," by Maureen Canning—chapter 3—gives practical guidelines on how to deal with the defensive structure of sex addicts. Chapter 4 is an important contribution regarding families of sex addicts entitled "Strategies for Assessment and Early Treatment with Sexually Addicted Families" by Judith C. Heaton Matheny.

Section II is "Treatment and Therapy." Ken Adams and Don Robinson begin in chapter 5 by describing necessary considerations of treatment in "Shame Reduction, Affect Regulation, and Sexual Boundary Development: Essential Building Blocks in Sexual Addiction Treatment." Chapter 6, "Manifestations of Damaged Development of the Human Affectional Systems and Developmentally Based Psychotherapies" by Mark F. Schwartz and Stephen Southern, is an important contribution regarding the need to treat early developmental issues associated with sex addiction. Boundary issues that are invariably encountered during treatment are addressed in chapter 7, "Clinical Boundary Issues With Sexually Addicted Clients," by Tim Tays, Brenda Garett, and Ralph Earle. "The Integration of Psychotherapy and 12-Step Programs in Sexual Addiction Treatment," by Jan Parker and Diana Guest, is the next chapter, which helps the reader understand the importance of the 12 steps in treatment. Mark R. Laaser in chapter 9, "Recovery for Couples," takes the reader through important guidelines for helping couples who have been betrayed by the addiction. Chapter 10, by Jennifer P. Schneider and M. Deborah Corley, follows by revealing additional issues for couples in "Disclosure of Extramarital Sexual Activities by Persons With Addictive or Compulsive Disorders: Results of a Study and Implications for Therapists." Marie Wilson offers helpful guidelines for art therapy in chapter 11, "Art Therapy: Treating the Invisible Sex Addict." "The Value of Group Psychotherapy for Sexual Addicts," by Alyson Nerenberg, offers critical considerations for therapists in chapter 12. Chapters 13 and 14 are both important offerings by John Sealy. Chapter 13, "Psychopharmacologic Intervention in Addictive Sexual Behavior" thoroughly outlines the use of medication. And chapter 14, "Dual and Triple Diagnoses: Addictions, Mental Illness, and HIV Infection Guidelines for Outpatient Therapists," is a comprehensive analysis of critical treatment considerations.

Section III is "Special Populations." David Delmonico begins chapter 15 by describing the importance of addressing cybersex, in "Sex on the Superhighway: Understanding and Treating Cybersex Addiction." An important contribution on women sex addicts by Marnie Ferree is found in chapter 16. "Females: The Forgotten Sexual Addicts." In a good complement to the preceeding chapter, Shannae Rickards and Mark R. Laaser offer sound clinical considerations in chapter 17, "Sexual Acting Out in Borderline Women: Impulsive Self-Destructiveness or Sexual Addiction/Compulsivity?" Chapter 18, "Pastors and Sexual Addiction," by Mark R. Laaser and Ken Adams, undertakes the special considerations of the clergy. "Sexually Addicted Health-Care Professionals" is expertly handled by Richard Irons in chapter 19. Chapter 20 discusses the often-overlooked group of the homeless in Ken McGill's "The Homeless and Sex Addiction." Robert Weiss deals with the unique treatment considerations of gays in "Treatment Concerns for Gay Male Sexual Addicts," chapter 21. "Adolescent Sex and Love Addicts," by Eric Griffin-Shelley, addresses the special treatment and assessment issues of adolescents in the chapter 22. David Delmonico and Elizabeth Griffin deal with the importance of sex offender issues in chapter 23, "Classifying Problematic Sexual Behavior: A Working Model Revisited."

Section IV is "Clinical Practice and Resources," which focuses on helping clinicians deal with the business of treatment. In chapter 24 Martha Turner outlines needed components of a successful practice in "How to Build a Sex Addiction Practice." This is followed by a "Resources" section, which provides quick access to important information that the clinician will need for referrals to 12-step programs.

We want to thank all the contributors. We hope this book succeeds as a testimony to their dedication and years of service. We wish to thank our colleagues who have put up with our deadlines and requirements—and sometimes our crankiness. The good people at Taylor and Francis have been more than helpful. Their patience has been tested, but we are grateful they have continued their support. Both of us wish to thank our wives, Suzanne and Cheryl, respectively, and our families for their ongoing love and support.

SECTION I

The Early Stages

CHAPTER 1

The Sexual Addiction Assessment Process

PATRICK J. CARNES
MARIE WILSON

Therapists working in mental health clinics, drug and alcohol treatment programs, forensic settings, community hospitals, and private practice are frequently confronted with clients whose problematic sexual behavior fits the parameters of addictive/compulsive illness. When these cases present themselves, professionals need to know how to take the necessary steps to make an appropriate assessment in order to determine whether an addictive process is present. An accurate assessment will help with decisions about appropriate interventions, clinical approaches, and the level of care necessary for each client. These scenarios represent typical cases that you may encounter:

- A 45-year-old postal employee, with 6 years of recovery from drugs and alcohol, spends hours every night on the Internet, checking out pornography websites and chat rooms. He frequently loses track of time and arrives at work late, disheveled, and exhausted. His supervisor suspects that he is drinking again and sends him to the Employee Assistant Program at the post office, where you work as a counselor.
- A minister in his 50s has a compulsive prostitution problem. He has gone through his family inheritance and now finances his habit from parish funds. When the money is discovered missing and he is confronted by his wife, he takes an overdose of pills and ends up in the local hospital emergency room, where you are employed as a social worker.
- You are a marital therapist in private practice and have been working with a couple for 2 months on communication issues, when the wife reveals to you

in a private session that she has had serial, extramarital affairs for the entire length of her 20-year marriage. Her last affair was with her husband's best friend and business partner. Her husband, she says, doesn't know a thing.

The cases all represent examples of sexual behavior where loss of control and excess seem evident and clear. However, many times therapists experience situations that are far less clear. Sexually addictive patterns are not always easily identified in the clinical setting. Clinical assessment of sexual addiction may be either overlooked or misdiagnosed by even the best clinician. For example, the therapist may have little initial data from which to draw an assessment. The sexual addiction may be obscured by convoluted marriages or job situations, or the sex addict may simply have successfully avoided all the consequences thus far. Initial contact with clients may be shadowed by their seductive or flirtatious behavior or inappropriate disclosures. Hints about affairs, a history of relationship struggles, or conflicts about intimacy and jealousy may all signal the possibility of addiction (Fossum & Mason, 1986).

Typically, individuals in trouble for their sexual behaviors are not candid about what has taken place, nor are they likely to reveal that the specific behavior actually is part of a consistent, self-destructive pattern. If clients hold any type of leadership position (such as in the church, business, community, or politics), there may be an even greater desire to withhold information from the therapist. A wide range of behaviors can be problematic, including compulsive masturbation, affairs, pornographic magazines or videos, Internet pornography (cybersex), prostitution, voyeurism, exhibitionism, sexual harassment, and sex offending. Seldom do clients engage in just one behavior, but rather in a collection of behaviors. For instance, in addition to multiple affairs, there might also be problems with prostitution, pornography, cybersex, and compulsive masturbation (Carnes & Schneider, 2000). Assessment may be further complicated by clients who deliberately deceive the therapist by telling only part of their story. Sometimes spouses or partners may collude in that deception or mistrust, although they may still want help desperately.

PROBLEMATIC SEXUAL BEHAVIOR AS AN ADDICTIVE DISORDER

Many behaviors can be defined as normal in some people, but addictive in others. *Addiction* is a term traditionally associated with compulsive and out-of-control use of alcohol or drugs. The term, however, has grown in popularity in the past decade and is now used to diagnose and describe other compulsive behaviors such as gambling, overeating, and sex, when these behaviors are also out of control. Compulsivity is the loss of the ability to choose whether or not to stop or continue a particular behavior. The continuation of sexual behaviors that have resulted in adverse consequences such as arrests, divorce, and loss of health, job, or freedom clearly define behavior that is compulsive and out of control. When sexual behavior is compulsive and yet continues despite adverse consequences, it is called *sex addiction*.

Often professionals who specialize in the treatment of sexual addiction are asked, How does one discriminate between behaviors considered to be within the norms of sexual experience and those behaviors that indicate that an addiction is present? The discovery of an inappropriate sexual incident does not make for an addictive illness. To have a long-term affair, for example, may be a problem for the spouse, but might not involve a compulsive pattern. Also, it is possible for individuals to engage in sexual behaviors that seem excessive for a period of time, such as experimenting sexually after a divorce or the sexual excesses usually associated with college life, for instance. Nonaddicted individuals have the ability to stop the excessive behaviors and pull back, reestablishing control. Addicted individuals can maintain control or stop problematic behaviors for only brief periods of time and are unable to regain balance in their lives without treatment, or involvement in a 12-step fellowship, or both.

Presently, the *DSM-IV* does not recognize sex addiction as a disorder. Sexual activity clearly works as a mood enhancer and mood alterator. Behavior-induced mood alteration is well documented and closely associated with other *process addictions* such as compulsive gambling and binge eating (Schneider & Irons, 1997). In addition, consistent patterns of sexual addiction closely resemble the patterns of alcoholics and drug-addicted clients, as well as of compulsive gamblers. Patterns that describe (1) a *loss of control*, as exhibited by a persistent desire or unsuccessful efforts to control or stop behaviors; (2) a *continuation of the behavior despite adverse consequences* such as arrests, broken marriages, financial problems; and, (3) an obsession or *preoccupation* with obtaining, using, or recovering from the behaviors, all represent the probable existence of an addictive process. When problematic sexual behaviors fulfill these same three criteria, the process is considered to be an addiction (Carnes & Schneider, 2000).

There is further cause to examine these behaviors from an addiction perspective, given that more than 83% of sex addicts report multiple addictions, including chemical dependency (42%), eating disorders (38%), compulsive working (28%), compulsive spending (26%), and compulsive gambling (5%). Studies of alcoholism treatment find sexual compulsion in 42 to 73% of patients (Carnes, 1998). One assumption often made incorrectly is that addiction to drugs or alcohol decreases inhibition and therefore causes or is substituted with sex addiction. The truth is that alcoholism is a concurrent illness and not the cause of sex addiction. Treatment centers that miss the diagnosis of sex addiction may unintentionally contribute to relapse and to the recidivism factor of alcoholism and drug addiction (Carnes, 1992).

GOALS FOR ASSESSMENT

Because assessment and treatment of sexual addiction remain relatively new to the mental health arena and are still being challenged on the grounds of their overlap with other fields such as sexology, psychiatry, addiction medicine, and the criminal justice system, a comprehensive approach to assessment of sex addiction clearly enhances diagnostic credibility. In addition, a comprehensive assessment provides information to support a differential diagnosis and identify an accurate baseline for each client. Therapeutically, the assessment process can help educate and normalize the experience for the sex addict, who has experienced great frustration and anxiety in trying to stop behaviors that he or she does not understand and cannot control.

Ideally, assessment for sex addiction should include (1) a semistructured clinical interview, (2) self-report screening tests, and (3) collateral assessment information. A semistructured interview offers both formality and flexibility and allows interviewees to discuss their experiences using their own descriptive words and metaphors. Clinicians can make interventions when appropriate by interpreting, clarifying, reflecting on, and listening to responses. Attention can be paid to behaviors such as avoidance, emotional detachment, or minimization. This valuable information can help clinicians assess the client's readiness for treatment, as well as the level of care necessary at this juncture. For instance, will individual therapy and regular involvement in a 12-step community be sufficient, or does the client require additional support, such an outpatient or residential setting that specializes in the treatment of sexual addiction? This process of decision making, as well as treatment options, will be reviewed in greater detail later in this chapter. Self-report assessment tools can be a time- and cost-efficient means for collecting data, providing the respondents' views of their symptoms in a context that is not influenced by direct interaction with an interviewer. Collateral assessment information, such as reports from spouses, family, and friends, can provide valuable information. Prior medical records or court documents may also help to support your initial assessment. Collateral reports as well can provide data that may not be observable under assessment conditions.

THE CLINICAL INTERVIEW

In the initial interview for assessment of sex addiction, it is important to acquire as much information as possible about the person's acting-out behaviors. Therapists should ask questions about a client's sexual history, as well as obtain information about the person's family of origin and experiences growing up. These may all offer valuable clues to assist with evaluation. As you listen to their histories and descriptions of their families of origin, consider the following:

- Sex addicts typically inherit a genetic structure that disposes them to addictions in general. Ask if either of their caregivers had a history of affairs or if there were family patterns of unwanted pregnancies, multiple marriages, sexually transmitted diseases, or unexplained job losses.
- Many sex addicts come from families in which there are already addictions of all varieties. Parents, siblings, and extended family often will have addictive or compulsive disorders or both.
- There is a history of failure to sustain intimacy in relationships. This represents a fundamental failure to trust others enough to bond with them. Addiction is often described as an intimacy disorder.
- Sex addicts also come from families that are rigid and authoritarian. This often results in a resistance to being accountable.
- Excesses in religiosity, or extreme sexual negativity, or both, most likely will intensify sexual curiosity and obsession.
- Childhood abuse is a factor for many, leading to extreme reactivity.
- Significant losses, such as those brought about by a parent's death during childhood or mental or physical illness in the family, can contribute to the problem.
- Evidence may exist of an overly enmeshed relationship with a primary caregiver. Although there may be an absence of physical sexual contact, frequently the child's role was to meet the companionship needs of the parent, similar to that of a surrogate spouse. This is referred to as covert incest (Adams, 1991).
- Other contributing factors may include being exposed to sexually explicit information, such as stories with sexual content, pornography, or sexual acts as a child or parents or adults frequently walking around the house in the nude.

THE DISCLOSURE PROCESS

Acquiring an accurate history of acting-out behaviors can often be difficult, due to the sex addict's issues with trust and accountability. The therapist's expectation for intimacy and truthfulness may be experienced as a tremendous risk for the client. Therefore, disclosure can be slow and you can safely assume that you may not get the whole story in the initial session. Like alcoholics and drug addicts, sex addicts engage in distorted thinking, defending, justifying, and blaming others for their problems. Many deny that they have a problem at all and believe that they are in your office only to appease an angry spouse or to avoid criminal prosecution. In addition, the sex addict's shame and secrecy limit the therapist's access to information. Sex-addicted individuals are quite adept at presenting themselves in favorable ways, without fully disclosing problematic behaviors or faulty thinking. Clients may disclose past behavior, but be secretive about current problems. In other words, the fact that they have disclosed does not mean that problematic behavior has stopped. Typical beliefs that addicted persons may have at this stage of engagement are:

- Thinking that nothing will help
- Thinking that you, the therapist, and others are overreacting to "normal" things
- Thinking that their problems will blow over
- Thinking that they can stop by trying harder, as opposed to undertaking therapy or recovery
- Thinking that they will be okay if only they cut down
- Thinking that the reason they do this is because of their spouse or some external scenario

It may be useful to normalize a client's difficulty with disclosure by saying that it is common to hold back information. Many clients do not fully realize the impact that their addiction has had on their lives until they see the connections with all their behaviors. Asking for more specific details, such as how many times a day they masturbate or how large their collection is of pornographic videos, can help clients recognize patterns of minimization.

Many times, defenses such as denial operate out of clients' unconscious processes, with clients largely or entirely unaware of the entirety of their maladaptive patterns. Such clients live reactively and operate via automatic thinking processes, rarely aware of what motivates their behaviors. Second, addicted individuals tend to compartmentalize their thinking and indeed may not fully recognize problematic behaviors. Compartmentalizing is the act of separating one's life into various compartments. These compartments function separately from one another, and information from one compartment is not shared with another. Third, sometimes clients are so anxious about consequences, such as an impending court date or a divorce, that they may not remember some details due to their anxiety level being so high. As clients feel safe enough to tell their stories and begin to disclose their secrets, it is hoped that their full stories will be revealed.

Disclosure is often a process and not an event that takes place in one session. The events between President Bill Clinton and Monica Lewinsky that recently occupied our country provided an example of the process of disclosure. Initially, during the election primaries, when questioned about Jennifer Flowers, Clinton denied any kind of relationship with her. Later, in a court testimony, he admitted to having had sex with her once; meanwhile, Flowers described a 12-year ongoing relationship with Clinton. When the news of Monica broke, Clinton appeared on national TV and adamantly denied the allegations. Later, he qualified his statements and called their relationship "inappropriate"; however, he still maintained that he did not have sex with her because oral sex was not sex. It would not be appropriate to make the determination that Clinton's behaviors indicate the presence of addiction; however, we are using this chain of events to illustrate an almost textbook example of one individual's complex process of denial and gradual disclosure. Clinton displayed a remarkable ability to compartmentalize, despite an intense ongoing examination by both our country and the impeachment hearings. He concealed his inappropriate sexual activities while continuing to do a good job of running our country. The Disclosure Testing Process (figure 1.1) provides a way of looking at this complex process with your clients.

As clients begin to share their history, certain patterns of behavior will begin to emerge. Based on research and clinical experience, 10 signs indicate the presence of sexual addiction. A minimum of 3 criteria must be met; however, most addicts have 5, and over half have 7 or more.

1. Recurrent failure to resist sexual impulses in order to engage in specific sexual behaviors
2. Frequently engaging in those behaviors to a greater extent or over a longer period of time than intended
3. Persistent desire or unsuccessful efforts to stop, reduce, or control those behaviors
4. Inordinate amounts of time spent in obtaining sex, being sexual, or recovering from sexual experiences

Client Activity	Patient Affect	Patient Behavior
Initial Discourse	Despair	Revealing hidden behavior, usually under stress or duress
Admission of Details	Relief	Details of what happened and how bad it is
Retraction Phase	Fear, what will the therapist think of me, embarrassment/shame that there were more details	Efforts to look good; seeks assurance that no one will find out
Further Disclosure	Embarrassment/shame that there were more detials	Modifying statements
Further Details	More relief, maybe even euphoria	Understands links with earlier disclosure
Retraction Phase	Fear of spouse, boss, or others finding out	Everything is under control. Now that I understand, I am fine.

FIGURE 1.1. Disclosure Testing Process

5. Preoccupation with sexual behavior or preparatory activities
6. Frequently engaging in the behavior when expected to fulfill occupational, academic, domestic, or social obligations
7. Continuation of the behavior despite knowledge of having a persistent or recurrent social, financial, psychological, or physical problem that is caused or exacerbated by the behavior
8. The need to increase the intensity, frequency, number, or risk level of behaviors in order to achieve the desired effect; or diminished effect with continued behaviors at the same level of intensity, frequency, number, or risk
9. Giving up or limiting social, occupational, or recreational activities because of the behavior
10. Distress, anxiety, restlessness, or irritability if unable to engage in the behavior

Preliminary studies have indicated (Carnes, 1998; Wines, 1997) that addicts in recovery for longer than 2 years will have much more clarity about their illness than those in the initial 48 hours of treatment. This is based on the review of the previous 10 criteria with clients within 48 hours of admission to residential treatment for sex addiction, compared with a group of 57 participants in a Sex Addicts Anonymous group who had been in recovery, on average, 2½ years. Both studies indicated a discrepancy between the initial and long-term figures, with the long-term figure always being a larger percentage. The argument can be made that this reflects denial. Even so, 80% of those initial assessments yielded at least 3 of the criteria, which is the standard in the *DSM-IV* for gambling, alcoholism, and substance abuse. Wines (1997) found that 94% had at least 5 criteria, and over 50% had at least 7 criteria. So, despite the inherent challenges of an accurate initial assessment, it would appear that agreement exists between what clients typically experience in their addiction and clinical assessment criteria. In other words, the patient's experiences actually fit the criteria.

SEXUAL ADDICTION SCREENING TOOLS

Although there is really no substitute for clinical judgment, structured screening questions or tests provide clinicians and clients alike with a tangible format for reviewing and evaluating problematic sexual behaviors. To date, a wealth of literature exists on the usefulness of screening instruments to assist in diagnosing alcoholism. Historically, these instruments have proved valuable as adjuncts to the therapist's assessment process.

This kind of tool—called the Sexual Addiction Screening Test, or SAST— has been developed for sex addiction (Carnes, 1989). Developed in conjunction with hospitals, treatment programs, private therapists, and community groups, the SAST provides a profile of responses that helps professionals to discriminate between addictive and nonaddictive behavior. To complete the test, patients are asked to answer a total of 25 questions by placing a check in the appropriate *yes* or *no* column (figure 1.2). It is fairly easy to administer and evaluate. Variations of the SAST were especially developed for women and homosexual men. All three versions of the SAST are available on the website www.Sexhelp.com

The Sexual Addiction Screening Test

The Sexual Addiction Screening Test (SAST) is designed to assist in the assessment of sexually compulsive or "addictive" behavior. Developed in cooperation with hospitals, treatment programs, private therapists, and community groups, the SAST provides a profile of responses that help professionals discriminate between addictive and nonaddictive behavior. To complete the test, answer each question by placing a check in the appropriate *yes* or *no* column.

Yes   No

1. Were you sexually abused as a child or adolescent?
2. Have you subscribed to or regularly purchased sexually explicit magazines like *Playboy* or *Penthouse*?
3. Do you feel that your sexual behavior is not normal?
4. Do you often find yourself preoccupied with sexual thoughts?
5. Did your parents have trouble with sexual behavior?
6. Does your spouse (or significant other[s]) ever worry or complain about your sexual behavior?
7. Do you have trouble stopping your sexual behavior when you know it is inappropriate?
8. Do you ever feel bad about your sexual behavior?
9. Has your sexual behavior ever created problems for you and for your family?
10. Have you ever sought help for sexual behavior your did not like?
11. Have you ever worried about people finding out about your sexual behavior?
12. Has anyone been hurt emotionally because of your sexual behavior?
13. Are any of your sexual activities against the law?
14. Have you made promises to yourself to quit some aspect of your sexual behavior?
15. Have you made efforts to quit a type of sexual activity and failed?
16. Do you hid some of your sexual behavior from others?
17. Have you attempted to stop some parts of your sexual activity?
18. Have you ever felt degraded by your sexual behavior?
19. Has sex been a way for you to escape from your problems?
20. When you have sex, do you feel depressed afterward?
21. Have you felt the need to discontinue a certain form of sexual activity?
22. Has your sexual activity interfered with your family life?
23. Have your been sexual with minors?
24. Do you feel controlled by your sexual desire?
25. Do you ever think your sexual desire is stronger than you are?

FIGURE 1.2.

The next step in the evolution of sexual addiction assessment tools is the Sexual Dependency Inventory (SDI; Carnes, 1989). This is a longer and more comprehensive assessment device, designed to help researchers investigate the theoretical concept that sexual addiction can be divided into distinct categories (Delmonico, Bubenzer, & West, 1998). The SDI consists of six sections that not only evaluate the presence of specific behaviors but also ask for information about clients' sexual history and the development of their disorders. The SDI has been edited and expanded into the Sexual Dependency Inventory—Revised (SDI-R; Carnes & Delmonico, 1996). The SDI and SDI-R are both available to clinicians and can be purchased through the Meadows by contacting 1-800-MEADOWS.

COLLATERAL INDICATORS

One of the most reliable and helpful clues to the presence of any addiction is the information obtained from concerned family members (Carnes & Schneider, 2000). In addition to information gathered from family and friends or from previous medical or court records, there are 20 collateral indicators that assist in the assessment of sexual addiction. These may be useful in helping to firm up an initial diagnostic impression. A minimum of 6 criteria must be met:

- Patient has severe consequences because of sexual behavior.
- Patient meets the criteria for depression and it appears related to sexual acting out.
- Patient meets the criteria for depression and it appears related to sexual aversion.
- Patient reports history of sexual abuse.
- Patient reports history of physical abuse.
- Patient reports emotional abuse.
- Patient describes sexual life in self-medicating terms (intoxicating, tension-relief, pain-reliever, sleeping pills).
- Patient reports persistent pursuit of high-risk or self-destructive behavior.
- Patient reports that sexual arousal for high-risk or self-destructive behavior is extremely high, compared to that for safe sexual behavior.
- Patient meets diagnostic criteria for other addictive disorders.
- Patient simultaneously uses sexual behavior in concert with other addictions (gambling, eating disorders, substance abuse, alcoholism, compulsive spending), to the extent that the desired effect is not achieved without sexual activity and other addiction present.
- Patient has a history of deception around sexual behavior.
- Patient reports that other members of the family are addicts.

- Patient expresses extreme self-loathing because of sexual behavior.
- Patient has few intimate relationships that are not sexual.
- Patient is in crisis because of sexual matters.
- Patient has a history of crisis around sexual matters.
- Patient experiences anhedonia in the form of diminished pleasure for same experiences.
- Patient comes from a "rigid" family.
- Patient comes from a "disengaged" family.

GUIDELINES FOR CONDUCTING ASSESSMENTS

There are some important guidelines to remember when doing assessments.

- Be aware that there are women sex addicts. A tendency exists to see this as only a male problem. For every three male sex addicts, there is one woman. This ratio of men to women is an exact parallel to the gender ratios found in compulsive gambling and alcoholism.
- Sex addiction is seldom isolated. It is wise to remember that sex addiction has a high comorbidity for other substance-related disorders, as well as for post-traumatic stress disorder (PTSD). The development of sexual addiction and compulsivity has been discussed in relation to PTSD, in particular, by many authors (Carnes, 1991; Robinson, 1999; Sealy, 1999). In addition, it is not unlikely for sex-addicted clients to also suffer from mood disorders, other anxiety disorders, and personality disorders. Given the complexity of this clinical picture, clinicians may also want to administer other assessments relevant to PTSD, substance-related disorders, depression, and the like. This will help to rule in or rule out disorders that may require medication, other treatment regimes, or both. Sex addicts who also experience symptoms related to PTSD, such as hyper-reactivity or intrusive thoughts or who are also trying to cope with symptoms of depression such as constant fatigue or dysphoria, may find it difficult to remain engaged in treatment for their sex addiction. It is also not unusual for sets of symptoms to appear differently across the lifespan, further complicating the clinical picture.
- Another consideration when doing an assessment is the necessity of providing psychological safety during the evaluation process. Clients who have experienced childhood abuse or who have never fully experienced the emotions related to traumatic events from their past may become triggered and experience flashbacks or dissociation during the assessment. Descriptions of traumatic memories and feelings may be accompanied by other strong emotional reactions, such as anger at the therapist, memory blocking, or the urge to leave. When undergoing assessments, clients should be in a physically safe

environment in order not to be placed under any additional stress. Individuals should understand the goal of the assessment and the roles and responsibilities of both the evaluator and the person being assessed. It may also be helpful to normalize these responses if they occur, in order to reassure clients that what they are experiencing is a normal reaction to an abnormal situation from the past.

- Problematic sexual behavior can be viewed on a continuum. Sex addicts in more advanced stages of the disorder may cross personal boundaries and engage in sex-offending behaviors such as inappropriate touching (frotteurism), obscene phone calls, or exhibitionism. This can often be a result of the progressive nature of the addiction. Individuals who initially begin with masturbation may eventually turn to exhibitionism in an attempt to sustain their sexual high. This, however, can go both ways. Often, the compulsive behavior of sex offenders includes nonoffending behavior as well. Individuals who begin primarily with sex offending may, in an attempt to control their behavior, go to less offensive forms of acting out, such as visits to adult book stores or prostitutes.

- About 72% of sex addicts also evidence symptoms of sexual aversion–desire disorder or, as it is sometimes called, sexual anorexia (aversion–desire disorder, *DSM-IV* 302.797). Similar to those with eating disorders, patients will flip from being out of control into a super "in control" period. Or there will be a binge/purge pattern. Also, it is not unusual to see simultaneous binge/purge, as in a patient who is out of control outside of the marriage and compulsively nonsexual with his or her spouse. There are different criteria for assessing sexual anorexia (Carnes, 1997, 1998).

- High-stress situations such as medical school or work or dangerous situations such as warfare can create addictive behaviors where there were no predisposing factors.

- Finally, clinicians should also be aware of the possibility for secondary gain experienced by the client in the telling of his or her story. Part of the arousal template for some forms of sexual acting out is the reaction of shock or repulsion by the viewer. Some clients may intentionally review details of their acting out in order to provoke a response from the therapist. This can be considered offending behavior, because it is a violation of the therapist's boundaries, and should be confronted.

DIAGNOSIS AND TREATMENT PATH

Once the assessment is complete, the clinician is faced with decisions about treatment options and recommendations. Figure 1.3 provides a schematic overview of the diagnosis and treatment path involved in therapy with the sexually

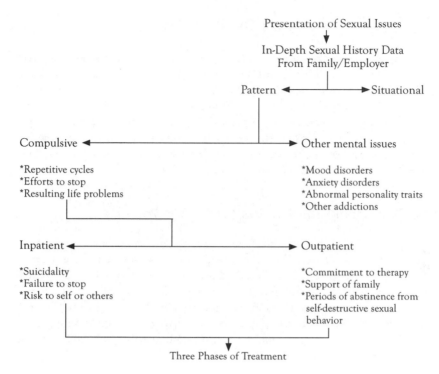

FIGURE 1.3. Diagnosis and Treatment Pattern for Compulsive Sexual Behavior

addicted person. When the person presents sexual issues involving a loss of control, the clinician conducts an in-depth sexual history. If the situation has escalated to the point where the family, employer, or legal system is involved, then all relevant data must be gathered. To rely on the client alone around such sensitive issues is not helpful because of the characteristic issues of denial. Interviewing family members or obtaining copies of lawsuits, legal charges, or company complaints is vital to escalated cases. At this point, the clinician must decide whether the sexually excessive behavior is situational or part of a pattern, based on the assessment criteria. The next decision is the level of intervention. A number of treatment options are available to clients. Although many sex addicts do well in outpatient settings, clients who are suicidal or at risk to themselves or others should be encouraged to seek residential treatment. Failure at an outpatient level or continuation of high-risk, life-threatening sexual practices despite all outpatient efforts would be an indication for inpatient treatment. Signs of good prognosis on an outpatient basis would be a significant commitment to therapy; an involved, intact supportive family; and significant periods of time in which the patient was able to abstain from self-destructive behavior.

THE RECOVERY PROCESS

In an effort to understand recovery from sexual addiction, data were gathered from a study of sex addicts and their families over a 5-year period. This data included a month-by-month history of clients' recovery process and an extensive life status inventory. A series of content analyses helped discern six phases in which recovery changes occur. Awareness of this recovery process will help therapists assess what level of intervention may be necessary at a particular stage because clients may appear for treatment at different stages of this process. The following overview represents a summary of this data:

The Developing Stage (Lasts Up to Two Years)

During this period, the sex addict's problems mount and create an awareness that something will have to be done. The person may even seek therapy or attend a 12-step group, then drop out. At this time, therapists often fail to see the problem of sexual acting out, or if they do, fail to follow through on it. Research shows that no matter what therapists try at this time, clients might not be ready for treatment. Persons with compulsive sexual behavior have a growing appreciation of the reality of the problem, but tend to minimize the problem or believe they can handle it themselves.

The Crisis/Decision Stage (1 Day to 3 Months)

At some point, the addict crosses over a line and experiences a fundamental commitment to change. This is often precipitated by a personal crisis. This crisis might include events like arrests, diagnosis of a sexually transmitted disease, a spouse or partner leaving, facing a sexual harassment lawsuit, loss of a professional license, a car accident, or a suicide attempt. For some of the respondents, the commitment to change was not about crisis but rather was about choice, and they simply were no longer willing to exist in the old way.

The Shock Stage (First 6 to 8 Months)

Once they admit the problem, addicts enter a stage that parallels what happens to anyone who has experienced deep loss and change. Disbelief and numbness alternate with anger and feelings of separation. Addicts describe physical symptoms of withdrawal that are at times agonizing. They report disorientation, confusion, and an inability to concentrate. Feelings of hopelessness and despair become more intense as their sense of reality grows. They may become reactive to limits set by therapists, sponsors, or family members. If they belong to a recovery group, they can experience a sense of belonging and a realization that recovery was the right decision for them. They report feelings of relief and acceptance once the double life is over.

The Grief Stage (6 Months)

As clients emerge from their shock, they become aware of the emotional pain. Their suffering has several components. First, there is awareness of all the losses they have experienced due to sexual addiction, which include jobs, relationships, children, time, money, and physical well-being. Second, there is a sense of loss of the addiction because it ceases to serve as friend, comforter, and emotional high. Third, the addiction has masked deeper hurts that usually stem from early childhood abuse or neglect. Without the cover of the addictive process, memories return and clarity about those early wounds emerges. Understanding the level of suffering at this point helps explain why the relapse rate is so high during this period.

The Repair Stage (18 to 36 Months)

Sex addicts who were successful in negotiating the rigors of the previous stage move from pain into a deep, internal restructuring. Belief systems about self, sex, family, and values are overhauled and new patterns of behavior develop. Systems theory would describe this as a "paradigm shift." Sex addicts take responsibility for themselves in all areas of life, including career, finances, and health.

The Growth Stage (2 Years Plus)

As sexually compulsive persons achieve more balance in their lives and develop a greater sense of themselves, they become more available to others. Relationships with partners, friends, children, and family members go through a period of renewal. Sex addicts report feeling more compassion for themselves and others. They develop a new trust for their own boundaries and integrity in relationships.

In terms of the assessment process, it is useful for therapists to consider at what stage of this process clients present themselves for treatment. Clearly, a sex addict in the Developing Stage may not be ready for treatment, and the best that a therapist can offer is information, educational materials, and a list of 12-step meetings in the area. Contrast this with someone in the Crisis/Decision Stage, who is beginning to experience the profound effects and consequences of his or her addiction. This situation may require that the therapist move quickly to mobilize supports, which include the possibility of residential treatment.

CLOSING REMARKS

In the last 2 decades, professional researchers and clinicians have made extraordinary progress in understanding both the etiology and the assessment of sex addiction. In 1999, the American Foundation for Addiction Research (AFAR) funded the Addiction Psychiatry Department of the medical school at Vanderbilt University in collaboration with the University of Iowa, to initiate a project that would result in establishing the protocol for the inclusion of sexual addiction as a diagnosis in the next edition of the *Diagnostic & Statistical Manual of Mental Disorders*, the *DSM-V*. One of the overriding concerns for this project is that there is no nosology or commonly agreed-upon set of criteria for assessing sexual addiction. Without a set of criteria for assessment, epidemiological studies could not be conducted to empirically show the prevalence and characteristics of the disorder. This points to an area of research of strategic importance in the field of sex addiction. If we have accurate descriptors of the patient's condition, it will help us legitimize the field and the work that we do with our clients. Sex addiction has emerged as a clinical entity. With the hard work of many people, this information makes the shadow of sex addiction less elusive now than it was 20 years ago.

REFERENCES

Adams, K. (1991). *Silently seduced: When parents make their children partners: Understanding covert incest.* Deerfield Beach, FL: Health Communications.

American Psychiatric Association. (1994). *Diagnostic and Statistical Manual of Mental Disorders* (4th ed.). Washington, DC: American Psychiatric Association.

Carnes, P. (1989). *Contrary to love: Helping the sexual addict.* Center City, MN: Hazelden.

Carnes, P. (1991). *Don't call it love: Recovery from sexual addiction.* New York: Bantam Books.

Carnes, P. (1992). *Out of the shadows.* Center City, MN: Hazelden.

Carnes, P. (1997). *The betrayal bond: Breaking free of exploitive relationships.* Deerfield Beach, FL: Health Communications.

Carnes, P. (1997). *Sexual anorexia: Overcoming sexual self-hatred.* Center City, MN: Hazelden.

Carnes, P. (1998). The case for sexual anorexia: An interim report on 144 patients with sexual disorders. *Sexual Addiction & Compulsivity, 5*(4), 293–309.

Carnes, P. (1998). The obsessive shadow: Profiles in sexual addiction. *Professional Counselor, 13*(1), 15–17, 40–41.

Carnes, P. (1998). The presidential diagnosis. *Sexual Addiction & Compulsivity, 5*(3), 153–158.

Carnes, P., & Delmonico, D. (1996). *Sexual dependency inventory-revised.* Mineapolis, MN: Positive Living Press.

Carnes, P., & Schneider, J. (2000). Recognition and management of addictive sexual disorders: Guide for the primary care clinician. *Primary Care Practice, 4*(3), 302–318.

Delmonico, D., Bubenzer, D., & West, J. (1998). Assessing sexual addiction with the sexual dependency inventory-Revised. *Sexual Addiction & Compulsivity, 5*(3), 179–187.

Robinson, D. (1999). Sexual addiction as an adaptive response to post-traumatic stress disorder in the African American community. *Sexual Addiction & Compulsivity, 6*(1), 11–22.

Schneider, J., & Irons, R. (1997). In Miller, N., Gold, M., & Smith, D. (Eds.), *Treatment of gambling, eating, and sex addictions. Manual of therapeutics for addictions*. New York: Wiley-Liss.

Sealy, J. (1999). Dual and triple diagnoses: Addictions, mental illness, and HIV infection guidelines for outpatient therapists. *Sexual Addiction & Compulsivity, 6*(3), 195–219.

Wines, D. (1997). Exploring the applicability of criteria for substance dependence to sexual addiction. *Sexual Addiction & Compulsivity, 4*(3), 195–220.

CHAPTER 2

Intervention and the Sexually Addicted Patient

JAMES FEARING

Intervention: A collective, professionally guided effort by the significant people in an addict/alcoholic's life to precipitate a crisis through gentle confrontation and thereby to remove the patient's defensive obstructions to recovery. In preparing for such a confrontation, the family and friends of the alcoholic/addict also deal with their lack of knowledge about, and prior mismanagement of, the disease (Twerski, 1983).

In the history of treating sexual addiction in the United States, the inception of crisis intervention is very recent. In general terms, it has been commonplace to hear friends, families, and employers respond to the addict's destructive chemical use or pathological behaviors in frustration, stating, "they cannot be helped until they ask for help themselves or hit rock bottom. The previously mentioned intervention process allows individuals to receive treatment for their alcoholism or addiction in spite of the denial factor.

The clinical concept of intervention was pioneered and developed in the late 1970s and early 1980s in Minneapolis, Minnesota, by Vernon Johnson, founder of the Johnson Institute. His book *I'll Quit Tomorrow* (1980) remains one of the primary works in print today that pertains to crisis intervention in the field of treating addictions. Johnson describes *intervention* as "a design for a cohesive group of friends and family to take a stand with the alcoholic, and present the specific facts of his/her drinking and behavior in a loving and caring way, coupled with an offer of immediate help." Although many of the original techniques presented by Dr. Johnson have been refined, professionals throughout the United States refer to the "Johnson Institute Model" (Faber & Keating-O'Connor, 1991) of intervention as the model used in their clinical framework for facilitating crisis interventions (Johnson, 1986).

The intervention process for the sexually compulsive patient normally requires two or more meetings. The first meeting is scheduled to assist the intervention team in its members' preliminary education and preparation for the actual intervention. In many instances, the participants involved in the crisis intervention know little or nothing about addiction, recovery, intervention, or treatment. What they do know is that someone they love and care about is hurting, and possibly hurting them, through his or her actions. Professionals who facilitate interventions agree that it is extremely important to establish a solid foundation through education for the intervention team to work from. This ensures that everyone involved is properly prepared. It is essential that all team members access the appropriate information needed for themselves. As clinicians around the country acknowledged many years ago, addiction affects the whole family or system. Sexual addiction can also be called a family illness.

When the clinician addresses these family issues in the intervention preparation, strategic planning or scripting may take place in order to assist the team in setting appropriate boundaries with the identified patient. In most cases, this plan is written out using worksheets or a letter, which can be used as a reference during the actual intervention meeting. The vital information gathered may be forwarded to the patient's treatment team to assist its members in their assessment process. A key factor in facilitating a successful intervention is the ability of the facilitator to contain the entire process, keeping everyone focused on the objective.

To date, very little information is available regarding intervention and its success rate. This is due to the difficulty in identifying the providers of intervention services, as well as the challenges in distinguishing which patients have been intervened once they reach treatment. In an attempt to accumulate important information regarding intervention, in 1994 members of the Association of Intervention Specialists (AIS) group took a poll regarding the percentage of patients admitted into recovery programs via interventions attempted (Fearing, 1994). The national success rate presented in this informal poll for professionally facilitated interventions was estimated to be 90% (AIS, 1994). This poll was subjective, and there was not any follow-up to the cases involved. The definition of *success* used for this informal poll was as follows:

> Interventions professionally facilitated in which the identified patient was admitted into treatment. This admission was the direct result of the professional intervention. (Fearing, 1994)

It is important to provide an accurate understanding of what is often described as the denial factor in order to facilitate understanding of the need for crisis intervention. The manifestation of denial can, in many cases, prevent addicts or alcoholics from asking for help themselves. Amodeo and Liftik (1990) referred to the denial factor in the treatment of addictions "as very often the barrier to effective diagnosis, referral, and treatment." On the basis of the limited information that is available, clinicians working in this field may benefit from accessing information pertaining to this complex component of the disease (i.e., denial). As witnessed in treating sexual addiction, this denial factor is also mentioned in the approved definition of alcoholism by the Board of Directors of the National Council on Alcoholism and Drug Dependence (February 3, 1990) and the American Society of Addiction Medicine (February 25, 1990). Their definition is as follows:

> Alcoholism: Alcoholism is a primary, chronic disease with genetic, psychosocial, and environmental factors influencing its development and manifestation. The disease is often progressive and fatal. It is characterized by continuous or periodically impaired control over drinking, preoccupation with the drug alcohol, use of alcohol despite adverse consequence, and distortions in thinking, most notably denial. (O'Neill & O'Neill, 1993)

The denial factor can reach far beyond the individual who is suffering from this illness. Throughout the past century, a combined familial and societal level of denial has contributed to the attitude that alcoholism is not really a problem. This is a socially constructed solution to a problem that is being avoided (Brissett, 1988). In other words, if it is not acknowledged, it is not happening, and therefore it cannot be a problem. This dynamic is even more prevalent today in regard to sexual addiction and the overall denial in both personal and professional arenas. The current status and lack of acceptance of sexual addiction as a disease today are not unlike the status of alcoholism or drug addiction from 1950 to 1970.

This issue of denial is addressed by Larkin (1986):

> It is suggested that an alcoholic and those intimately involved with him or her, develop a complex network of psychological defenses, particularly that of denial, protecting them from their emotional pain. Professionals who attempt to diagnose and treat alcoholics many times find it frustrating and confusing to hear alcoholics' repeated statements that they do not need help, despite evidence to the contrary. For caregivers who work with alcoholics and addicts, denial is a significant impediment to treatment. In order to have a positive impact on someone's drinking behavior, caregivers need strategies for working through the client's denial. The possibility of successful intervention is enhanced if caregivers understand the nature of denial and have a plan for getting the alcoholic to accept the diagnosis and become involved in treatment.

In his book *Addiction the High Low Trap*, Cohen (1995) states, "The addict's denial is a basic psychological defense mechanism that is often present."

Individuals who suffer from sexual compulsivity/sexual addiction may display many symptoms similar to those of people affected with other addictions.

Until recently, this disorder remained in the background for many health-care providers, as well as for as the general public. Today greater numbers of people, both professionals and laymen, are becoming familiar with this disorder. People are understanding the extreme emotional pain, physical health risks, and deep shame associated with sexually addictive behavior. There has also been a heightened awareness of successful treatment options that are available for the sexually compulsive client. Unfortunately, it has taken high-profile cases of the entertainer/celebrity, professional athlete, or national politician to gain this attention and amplify this hidden addiction in the media.

In comparing a variety of features often found in sexual addictive behaviors with those in the more commonly treated addictions, we find many similarities. The number one commonality seen in all addictive behavior is an attitude of denial, combined with the continuous demonstration of a "loss of control." This loss of control is present regardless of the potentially painful, negative consequences that are experienced when the client acts out the compulsive behavior. At a deep emotional level the affected person often experiences this inability to self-regulate, which sets up a dynamic of feeling total powerlessness, dramatic mood swings, and painful isolation.

Another predominant feature witnessed by the sexually addicted person is the presence of overwhelming shame. To some degree, shame is a common characteristic found in all addictions, yet this specific disorder is fully grounded in shame. Sexual addiction has been called a shame-based disease. Addicts are typically very uncomfortable about their dependency needs and tend to regard them with either deep shame or denial (Carnes, 1991). At a deep emotional level, sexually addicted people experience inner conflict with society's well-defined moral codes. This turmoil, combined with the acting out or behavioral inconsistencies with their own core belief system regarding "normal sexual behaviors," produces shame and internal conflicts. It is important for the clinician working with this type of patient to understand the strong connection between shame and sexually compulsive behaviors. Based on the presence of denial, shame, and isolation, the process of intervention can be very appropriate and successful in "helping the sex addict get help." It is not uncommon for the sexually addicted patient to state what a relief it is after the intervention has taken place. In many cases the person comments, "I knew I was sick, but I did not know what to do or where to go. I felt so alone and hopeless."

Sexual addiction oftentimes coexists with other addictive disorders, such as drug addiction, alcoholism, or eating disorders (Carnes, 1991; Schneider & Schneider, 1991). In a 1994 published study, obtained from interviewing 137 health-care professionals who were board-directed to be assessed because of sexually inappropriate behaviors with patients, 38% of those diagnosed with sexual addiction were found to be chemically dependent as well (Irons & Schneider, 1994). It is essential to provide an accurate clinical assessment for each patient. This assessment will assist the treatment team in creating the proper treatment plan to address the spectrum of clinical needs identified. If a patient is diagnosed with multiple addictions or is dual-diagnosed with a personality disorder, mood disorder, and so on, and it is not treated simultaneously with the addiction, the patient will be set up for relapse and failure.

INTERVENTION STRATEGIES

For an intervention in which the primary diagnosis is sexual compulsivity/sexual addiction, the appropriate preparation is critical. This includes gathering key information prior to assembling the "team." This preliminary, informal assessment will help determine the feasibility and appropriateness of providing an intervention prior to starting the process. The "point person" who initiated the first call would typically have the insight needed to provide this profile. The six main components of the initial intervention screening profile are as follows:

1. *Identified patient profile* (including past consequences, pending legal action, prior treatments, family knowledge and involvement, physical health issues, psychological overview, etc.).
2. *Screening of potential intervention team members.* Who are the appropriate people to engage in this sensitive process?
3. *Disclosure.* How much do you disclose at this stage? What if the identified patient's wife/husband/partner is not aware of his or her partner's acting out?
4. *Geographic location and timing.* When is the best time and where is the best location to plan the intervention?
5. *Discussion of appropriate treatment provider, insurance, and general financial information.*
6. *Establishment of schedules for the pre-intervention meeting.*

It is critical for the professional to include in his or her pre-intervention training that all team members understand that this is an illness and not a lack of willpower or a moral issue. Upon the identified patient being intervened, that person will most likely admit to having tremendous levels of shame; therefore, attempts should be made not to shame the patient because of a lack of understanding the illness. This will only create more obstacles for the patient to move forward in his or her treatment.

As mentioned earlier, it is not uncommon to find that a large percentage of people suffering from sexual addiction are professionals who hold responsible positions in their workplace and community. In an effort to include real-life scenarios, we will look at case studies that involved a doctor and a lawyer as the "identified patient." In this depiction, a key point that emerges is the complete powerlessness and denial of the addict, a total inability to self-regulate his or her behavior when the addiction goes untreated. It is evident from the dynamics in both of the following complex cases that many identified issues are not found in the "normal" alcohol or drug abuse intervention. Based on these complexities, the need for a solid clinical base is enhanced for any professional facilitating this type of intervention.

Case Example: Dr. John Doe

The initial call came from a health-care consultant who facilitiates strategic retreats for small and medium-sized clinics and hospitals. This outside consultant called from an off-site, 3-day retreat hosted by the identified patient's clinic. The identified patient is Dr. John Doe, owner and CEO of this midwestern clinic. The precipitant to this call was a female member of the clinical staff who stepped forward and discussed with this consultant a litany of sexually inappropriate behaviors acted out by Dr. John Doe. These behaviors ranged from making lewd sexual jokes out in the open; to forcing his hand down the pants of a nurse in a darkened examination room, with a patient present; to a series of forced sexual contacts with other staff members. This report triggered a series of confidential one-on-one meetings with the entire female staff. The consultant identified seven women who had been sexually harassed, inappropriately touched, talked to inappropriately, or some combination of these by Dr. John Doe. At this point, steps were taken to begin the intervention process.

The following list is a sample of the key points that were obtained through questions prior to setting up a formal intervention:

1. Dr. John Doe presented himself as a great boss who was in complete denial of this addiction.
2. Dr. John Doe's spouse was totally unaware of this behavior.
3. Dr. John Doe had received treatment for alcoholism more than 5 years ago and was still, in his mind, "working a program" and was abstinent from alcohol.
4. Dr. John Doe was in good physical health and prided himself on his commitment to a daily exercise routine.
5. To the consultant's and clinical staff's knowledge, no legal charges were pending from any of his behaviors.
6. The women involved had developed a collective foundation for emotional support to each other and were now willing to act on these violations. Independently, they had been unwilling or unable to step forward prior to this time.
7. The consultant was disengaging completely from the process at this point.

8. Two objectives were defined in doing a professionally facilitated intervention: (1) interrupt this painful pattern and attempt to help Dr. John Doe receive the appropriate help, and (2) empower these women to take care of themselves in the most appropriate way possible.

9. Action needed to be taken right away because of the seriousness of the infractions and the impact this was having on the staff members and their families. Definition of reporting responsibilities needed to be addressed as soon as possible.

10. Not all of the women who had been violated felt completely dedicated to the intervention process. There was an underlying fear of facing this problem, which included fear of losing jobs and incomes.

Each one of these sensitive concerns needed to be understood and properly dealt with as vital components of facilitating this intervention. The appropriate boundaries were essential here, in the knowledge that more than one patient was emerging from this dysfunctional system. Understanding that one interventionist could not provide help for everyone was very important, so two female therapists were enlisted to help assess the women postintervention and develop treatment plans where needed. The interventionist guarded against giving legal advice to anyone and instead supported everyone in securing the appropriate legal answers from professionals who specialized in this area. At the entry point of such a damaged system, the interventionist must self-regulate and discipline himself or herself to not become enmeshed into the system (playing the hero role and providing all the answers). This opportunity did present itself, being driven by the high degree of pain and confusion everyone experienced during the crisis. Staying focused on the original objective, yet helping to facilitate other mini-interventions, is key.

Case Example: Lawyer John Doe

This intervention was initiated by Lawyer John Doe's wife, who was also a working professional. She had suspected her husband of some unusual sexual behavior over the last 2 years, but had never found any specifics. Through a series of circumstances, she was alerted to the fact that her husband was involved in some kind of sexual acting out on his computer via the Internet. Upon becoming aware of this initial situation, she investigated in more detail the reality of her husband's "cybersex" activities. Through these efforts, she was to find out that it involved nightly communication with gay or bisexual men around the country. The amount of time he spent on this activity each day added up to many hours. She also found a "stash" of gay pornography hidden at their residence. She reported feelings that ranged from confusion, to shame, anger, and hurt. At this point she contacted the interventionist for a recommendation. It was apparent that the status quo was not acceptable, and something had to be done quickly to address this crisis situation. The key points to consider in planning this professionally facilitated intervention were as follows:

1. What was the day-to-day status of their marriage?
2. Had she been concerned about her husband's sexual activity, sexuality, or both prior to this 2-year time period?
3. Were there any pending professional or legal problems with the bar association, police, and so on?
4. Was there reason to believe that her husband had been involved physically with any of his sexual partners on the Internet?
5. Who else was aware of what she had discovered? Who would she feel comfortable in bringing to the intervention process as a team member?
6. What funding/insurance monies were available for his treatment? Who would be the most appropriate provider for this complex scenario?
7. Did she want to continue working on the marriage if he went into treatment? Was she willing to set clear boundaries for herself via the intervention?
8. Was she willing to accept her husband's sexuality if he engaged in treatment and quit acting out inappropriately?
9. To what level should the children be involved and at what point?
10. Is anyone aware of John Doe being sexually abused as a child?

CONCLUSION

The following checklist contains major points that should be addressed in the preparation and execution of an intervention for the sexually addicted patient. A successful intervention always contains a well-prepared, thought-out plan for everyone involved:

- Identification of an experienced, clinically trained interventionist
- A clear definition of perceived sexually compulsive behaviors and associated problems
- Discussion of potential intervention team members
- Completion of the six-point intervention screening profile (see the "Intervention Strategies" section)
- Identification and discussion of any pending legal issues
- Exploration of conditions surrounding the children, if involved
- Discussion of reporting procedures, if appropriate
- Identification of any physical health-related concerns (e.g., HIV, etc.)
- A well-designed "Plan B" is essential to have in place for both the identified patient and participants from the affected system. The difficult question must

be answered; "What happens if he doesn't get help via this intervention?" Everyone involved needs to feel safe and understand the plan to move forward, regardless of the identified patient's decision to receive help or not.

   This intervention program was used in both of the previous case examples. The identified patients entered into treatment using this intervention process. An appropriate program of recovery was developed and implemented for other members of these dysfunctional systems. In both cases, a professionally guided intervention may have been the only vehicle available to break through the layers of denial successfully and allow everyone to receive the appropriate help he or she needed. Professional intervention offers a respectful way to raise the bottom, prior to patients having an irreversible crisis that may change their lives forever.

REFERENCES

Amodeo, M., & Liftik, J. (1990). Working through denial and alcoholism. *Families in Society* 7(3), 131–135.

Association of Intervention Specialists. (1994). Unpublished informal poll.

Brisset, D. (1988). Denial in alcoholism: A sociological interpretation. *Journal of Drug Issues, 18*(3), 385–402.

Carnes, P. (1991) *Don't call it love.* New York: Bantam.

Cohen, I. (1995). *Addiction the high low trap.* Santa Fe, NM: Health Press.

Faber, E., & Keating-O'Connor, B. (1991). Planned family intervention. *Johnson Institute Method. Special Issue: Chemical dependency: Theoretical approaches and strategies working with individuals and families.*

Fearing, J. (1994). Comparative research comparing the inpatient chemical dependency treatment experience between the self-referred patient and the intervened patient. *Treatment Today* 8(2), 10–11.

Irons, R. J., & Schneider, J. P. (1994). Sexual addiction: Significant factors in sexual exploitation of health care professionals. *Sexual Addiction & Compulsivity: Journal of Treatment and Prevention, 1*(3), 198–214.

Johnson, V. E. (1980). *I'll quit tomorrow. A practical guide to alcoholism treatment.* New York: Harper-Collins.

Johnson, V. E. (1986). *Intervention. How to help someone who doesn't want help.* Minneapolis, MN: Johnson Institute.

Larkin, C. (1986). Identifying and treating the alcoholic client. *Social Casework, 67*(2), 67–73.

O'Neill, J., & O'Neill, P. (1993). *Concerned intervention. When your loved one won't quit alcohol or drugs.* Oakland, CA: New Harbinger.

Schneider, J., & Schneider, B. (1991). *Sex, lies, and forgiveness: Couples speaking out on healing from sex addiction.* Center City, MN: Hazelden.

Twerski, A. J. (1983). Early intervention in alcoholism: Confrontational techniques. *Hospital & Community Psychiatry, 34*(11), 1027–1030.

CHAPTER 3

Breaking Through Defenses

MAUREEN CANNING FULTON

Treating the resistant or defended sexually addicted client can be challenging. The most skilled clinicians may know that the client is in a state of denial, and yet the relentless challenge of confronting his or her resistant tactics can leave even the clinicians doubting their own reality or, worse, finding themselves colluding with the client's reality. The intention of this chapter is to provide a framework for working with the defended sexually addicted client and to give specific interventions that can facilitate the healing process.

Defenses are thought patterns that protect us from our pain. Because these defenses operate from the unconscious, the individual is often unaware of these patterns until his or her beliefs and attitudes are challenged in regard to change. The irony is that even though defenses protect the addict from his or her pain, these same defenses are the obstacles that stand in the way of recovery. For addicts even to consider discarding their defenses is extremely frightening, because in so doing they leave themselves vulnerable to feeling pain. Any clinician who challenges these defenses will surely be met with great resistance.

CLINICAL CASE EXAMPLE

To avoid pain and shame, a client may exhibit total denial despite overwhelming evidence to the contrary. (See chapter 5 for more discussion regarding defenses against shame.) Take, for example, the case of Bill. Bill came into treatment stating that he was codependent and depressed and that he had a history of chemical abuse. In the beginning of treatment Bill was in total denial of his sexual addiction, despite overwhelming evidence. Bill owned several strip clubs. He had sex with the strippers on a regular basis and often became involved with them in ongoing relationships. A committed relationship on Bill's part involved him supporting the strippers financially, which enabled them to quit working in his clubs. They would move into his house and would receive an allowance from Bill. Bill saw his behavior of rescuing these "poor strippers" as codependent, which was true. However, Bill also was addicted to sex.

Bill was able to justify his sex addiction by "saving" these women, which masked the guilt and shame he felt in using them for his own sexual purpose. Once he became committed to these women, he would grew disinterested in them sexually. Bill would then begin to act out through a series of one-night stands with other strippers in his clubs. Bill's girlfriends would discover his infidelities and ultimately leave him. He would then go into a sexually anorexic state where work would replace the guilt and shame he felt about losing his girlfriend because of his sexual acting out outside of his "committed" relationship. This pattern would repeat itself, with Bill returning to a series of one-night stands until he found someone new to rescue.

Bill's sexually addictive patterns began early in his life. His mother was a prostitute during Bill's formative years. When Bill was 4, his mother married a man who "saved" her from her livelihood of pain and shame. However, Bill's new stepfather beat both him and his mother unmercifully. Sometimes Bill's mother would call out to Bill to save her from the beatings. He felt protective of both his sisters and his mother, often sacrificing himself to save his mother from physical and emotional abuse. Bill learned early that women are the objects of abuse and disrespect and that it was his job to rescue them. Bill's defenses toward his sexual addiction were an unconscious attempt to cover the pain and shame of his early childhood trauma. For him to acknowledge his sexual addiction meant that he would have to deal with the pain of his past.

Moving away from pain and shame is the motivation for the addictive behaviors. Addicts will risk anything to distract them from their pain. This can include the following types of behaviors:

- Risk of safety—including going into dangerous neighborhoods, having unprotected sex, or having sexual encounters in which there is the risk of getting caught by a jealous lover.
- Financial risks—spending money on prostitutes, pornography, strip clubs, clothing, sex toys, videos, trips to meet sexual partners, and legal costs if arrests are involved.
- Risk of relationships—betrayals of primary partners and family members, loss of responsibility in parenting children, and isolation from friendships or community.

To a healthy individual these behaviors may seem unfathomable, but to the addict they have become normalized through the addict's defense structure. Most often, these defenses are not conscious; they are automatic thought patterns whose roots lie buried deep beneath the surface of reality. The first step in treatment is the addict's acknowledging that these behaviors are a problem. The second is to break through the defense that allows the addict to continue these behaviors. The task of the clinician often becomes to guide the client through the process of challenging the unconscious beliefs, wherein the unconscious then becomes conscious. This awareness enables clients to become empowered to make choices about their behavior. Through creating awareness, the client can make the first steps toward change.

SURRENDER/CONVERSION

Working with the unconscious becomes key to breaking through the client's defenses, but it can often be the most difficult aspect of treatment. With Bill, the patterns of his childhood and the messages he received—that is, his belief that women are the objects of abuse and disrespect and that it was his job to rescue them—were unconscious. Yet Bill played the unconscious beliefs out in his addiction. The goal in treatment was to establish a bridge between the unconscious and the conscious mind and move Bill to the point of awareness of his sexually addictive behaviors and, ultimately, to recognition or admission of the problem.

The goal is to convert unconscious material to consciousness through the act of exploration and emotional maturation. This can be challenging. The client will often demonstrate willfulness or control as a means to maintain their current reality. This often yields the illusion of security. This becomes all the more reason to resist change and maintain the status quo. The treatment goal then is helping the individual stretch through the process of surrender so as to awaken or open to a new and more functional reality.

Milton Erickson's (1977) approach to conversion and surrender stated that

> The patient doesn't consciously know what the problems are no matter how good a story he tells you, because that's a conscious story. What are the unconscious factors? You want to deal with the unconscious mind, bring about therapy at that level and then translate it to the conscious mind.

Bill's conversion took place, first, when he was able to disclose the trauma of his childhood and, second, when he could feel the pain and shame his acts of perpetration caused. The feelings of pain and shame were the catalyst to bridge the gap between the unconscious pain of his past and his conscious reality.

In the book *Pathways to Reality* (1991), Dr. John Lovern mentioned that the patient has to have motivation in order to change and that there has to be enough pain and guilt in order to move forward with treatment. Lovern stated that "It is proposed that the addicts' awareness of their pain and their willingness to do something to alleviate it constitutes adequate motivation to recover. That is impossible, at least in the beginning" (p. 33).

It is impossible for the addict in the beginning of treatment to have adequate motivation because of the addict's unwillingness to let down his or her defenses. What is possible is using the patient's consequences as motivation for change. Such consequences may include an arrest for solicitation of prostitutes, contracting AIDS, a pending divorce, or incarceration for lewd acts. Each of these consequences can bring about the motivation for alleviating the pain. When the addict is in enough pain, he or she becomes willing to change. Often the change in treatment will take place in stages. As the levels of denial are lifted, the progress in treatment advances.

CLINICAL CASE EXAMPLE: UTILIZATION

Mary came into treatment because she was about to lose a lucrative job opportunity due to her drinking and promiscuous sexual behavior. Her boss sent her to treatment to "get these things under control." Mary's motivation for treatment was the consequences of losing her job. Her goal in treatment was to secure her livelihood. Mary had not only slept with her boss, complicating the present situation, but also had had a string of one-night stands with more than 300 men. In addition, Mary had been warned by her boss of her sexually revealing and inappropriate work attire.

Applying Erickson's (1977) theory of utilization in relation to the case of Mary demonstrates how to motivate the client to change. According to this theory, the therapist's goal is to find the greatest form of resistance and utilize it as leverage to accomplish a state of change. Focusing on Mary's career goals became the leverage needed to motivate her changes. Once the motivation was in place, it was possible to explore Mary's deeper issue of her low sense of self-worth. Mary had been sexualized since she was 12, when she was prostituted by her uncle. Mary's self-worth came from her sexual identity. Like Mary, sex addicts have many forms of resistance. Lovern (1991) stated that some of the traits of sexually addicted people are self-hate, low self-esteem, pain, need for excitement, guilt, rebelliousness, and defiance. When the clinician identifies the greatest source of the client's resistance in one of these areas, he or she can go to work. Examples are given in the following sections that identify how to utilize each one of these traits.

Self-Hate and Low Self-Esteem

Sex addicts don't respect or trust themselves, so they are unlikely to trust the therapist. They will see the therapist's warm personal regard for them as manipulation. The client will see the therapist as someone who is getting paid to like the client or will think that the therapist needs to feel needed or successful in his or her work. The techniques of building trust and empathic connections, as well as disclosing personal history of his or her own pain and life challenges, can help the clinician create a bond with a client who suffers from low self-esteem. A therapist who discloses his or her process of self-nurturing and love mirrors hope for the client and the possibilities of the client's own recovery. Use your experience to lend hope, insight, and understanding to the client. This does not mean that you lose your sense of therapeutic boundaries, but, rather, you deepen the client–therapist bond to diminish the client's defenses.

With Mary, as with many clients, the clinical goal became moving the client beyond the initial motivation into the deeper issues of the self-destructive behavior patterns. In working with Mary, the therapist needed to mirror Mary's low sense of self-worth related to her sexuality. The therapist, by aligning herself with Mary's belief system, established a therapeutic alliance, and the next level of work was begun: exploring Mary's core beliefs.

In Dr. Patrick Carnes's model of addiction (1997), the client's sense of low self-esteem and self-loathing is based in the client's sense of core beliefs. In this model we can see that the client's sense of self originates from these core beliefs. In the place of a healthy sense of self, clients see themselves from the perspective of three basic beliefs: I am basically a bad, unworthy person; no one could love me as I am; my needs are never going to be met if I depend on others. To block these painful feelings of low self-worth, the addict uses compulsive sexual behaviors to block the pain. The addict's motivation is compounded by the belief that "sex is my most important need." It is the addict's most important need because it blocks the pain of his or her feelings of worthlessness. The addict's sense of survival is motivated by the need to move away from the core belief of a low sense of self.

When Mary was able to identify her core beliefs—that sex was her most important need—she was then able to identify that sex was the only means she knew to sate her hunger for love, acceptance, and nurturance. She was unable to feed this hunger in a healthy way because of her low self-worth. The only way Mary had learned to feed this hunger was by sexualizing herself.

With Mary, as with other clients, an ego split occurs between the presenting client and the addict aspect of the personality. The split may be so severe that the client is unaware of the separation. The client's unconscious organizing and defensive thought becomes "Bringing these two parts of myself together would threaten my survival; I could die if I do this." This is because, if clients allowed themselves to see the "addict" aspect of their personalities, they would then be forced to verify and be vulnerable to the original core belief that "I am basically a bad, unworthy person."

Mary began working with her ego split. The addict believes that "I am valuable only if I am sexualized," and the presenting ego believes that "I deserve to be loved in healthy, loving ways." In doing so, Mary began to empower herself to change her beliefs and her behaviors. This shift provided the catalyst for Mary to begin to respect herself and to find healthy ways to validate, nurture, and love herself. This is not to say that Mary did not frequently regress, especially when she became fearful, but she was able to regain the progress she made toward the integration of her newly established core beliefs.

Pain

Most addicts will seek help when the pain of the addiction is worse than the rewards of the addictive behavior. Using the consequences of the client's addictive pain can be the catalyst that moves the client into treatment. When a client is resistant to change, reinforcing the reality of his or her pain can be a powerful tool for motivation. Here are some examples of such intervention strategies:

- *Consequences:* Remind clients of the consequences of their behavior: sexually transmitted diseases, unwanted pregnancies, suspension from work, possible divorce.
- *Prophesy:* List what the realities may be if clients return to their compulsive behavior: "You will never get better, you may lose it all, you will have pain, it will get worse, you may die."
- *Challenge:* Challenge clients to return to their behavior; remind clients that their addiction is their greatest teacher, the addict will always be ready for action, the addict will never disappoint. Ask clients if they are ready for more pain.

It is important to acknowledge not only the pain associated with the addict, but also the grief related to letting go of the addiction. It has been the client's friend, the one constant in his or her life. But also remind clients where the addict has led and will lead them—and keep reminding clients until they are ready to surrender the addict.

Need for Excitement

Most addicts like to live on the edge, where taking risks becomes a way of life. Excitement and risk taking are the ways in which they relate to themselves and are often in relationship to others. Thus, the prospect of addicts losing the excitement and the adrenaline rush in their lives of recovery becomes terrifying. Acknowledging the client's terror is crucial. Addressing his or her fears and then continuing to challenge this client in treatment will maintain the client's interest. This may be accomplished by varying clinical techniques, allowing the therapist's own personal style to play out and enticing the client's involvement in the therapeutic process. Personal style may include flamboyance and methodical or cognitive challenges.

Challenging the Client

To create excitement in the therapeutic process, challenge the client by pushing his or her comfort zone. One way to accomplish this is with behavioral contracts. In a primary care treatment center, these contracts are easily facilitated due to the containment and accountability found in this environment. However, they can be just as effective in outpatient treatment, if they hold the client accountable. Sexually addicted clients demonstrate several behavioral patterns that lend themselves to behavioral contracts. First, sex addicts have difficulty being vulnerable; two, they isolate; three, they use a wall of words to mask feelings; four, they seek perfection and attention through external gratification; and five, they do not know how to have healthy fun.

Vulnerability. The *Help Me Contract* assists the client in beginning to trust and reach out to others. In the Help Me Contract, clients are encouraged to ask someone to open the door, ask their spouse to make dinner, ask a friend to drive them to the store. If addicts can learn to ask for help, they will begin to bond with a recovery community and thus enhance their chances of remaining in sobriety. Have clients ask for help five times a day, then invite them to keep a journal of the feelings, thoughts, and reactions they are having in relation to the contract.

Isolation. The *Self-Nurturing Contract* challenges the client to participate in 10 self-nurturing acts throughout the day. They can include simple tasks, such as taking a walk, indulging in a warm bath, or watching the sunset. The second phase of this contract is for the client to report his or her activities to a friend or 12-step sponsor. Integrating the positive attributions of the self and sharing them with a healthy, supportive person are the beginning of healthy bonding.

Wall of Words. The *Six Sentence Contract* can assist clients in first becoming aware of the wall of words they use to mask underlying anxiety and fear of feelings. Assign clients to verbally respond to others using only six sentences.

Enabling clients to slow down their process by becoming quiet will assist you in assessing their feelings. Helping clients connect with feelings is one of the most important aspects of treatment. Feelings are what the addict has been avoiding, especially shame and fear.

Perfectionism-Attention. The *Scruffy Contract* challenges the client to drop the mask that protects the sense of deep self-loathing and fear. External gratification is often what holds the sex addict's ego intact.

Jack came into treatment wearing a suit and tie. His boots were shined, his hair was immaculately groomed, and he smelled of expensive aftershave. The second day of treatment Jack removed the tie, but remained in suit coat and rigidly "perfect." Jack was invited to participate in a Scruffy Contract.

It was explained to Jack that the idea was to dress casually and not to comb his hair or wear expensive aftershave. Despite the therapist's encouragement and explanations of the purpose of the contract, Jack refused to participate. After several days of the therapist's working with Jack, Jack relinquished control and agreed to the contract. New levels of healing then became possible.

This contract is difficult in an outpatient setting, but some suggestions can include asking the clients not to add accessories to their wardrobes, to come scruffy to therapy, or to leave a room or the house scruffy. Remember, addicts are creative, so invite their suggestions to alter the contracts to fit the healing environment.

Playtime.   The *Playtime Contract* is designed for the overly responsible, perfectionistic client. The client finds other recovering friends (again, this is a much easier contract in an inpatient setting because of the bonding and trust already developed) and invites them to play a child's game. The game can include hopscotch, freeze tag, four square, musical chairs, or leapfrog. When therapists make these game suggestions in a group setting, the clients' faces will often light up as if they are filled with fond memories of childhood play.

The next time the group meets, the client briefs the others about the feelings he or she experienced with this contract. The client is then encouraged to repeat the contract for several group meetings. With this contract, the client's inhibitions and rigid defenses can begin to dissolve.

The instant gratification of these contracts is often what entices the client to participate. Clients also enjoy the challenge and attention associated with this work. Keeping the client engaged in the therapeutic process is often half the therapeutic battle. Using this tool can be one source of support in winning the fight.

Use Varied Techniques

A therapist working in an inpatient setting has the added advantage of observing the disorientation that clients experience on admission. The setting is new, there are unfamiliar rules, they have been stripped of their outside identities, and they are fearful and often confused as they experience withdrawal. This set of experiences is often an aid in itself. Capitalize on this reality by keeping the client guessing.

The client's anxiety related to the process in the first few days of treatment can enhance his or her interest in the therapeutic process. If you are working in a group, limit the time for this client to share. This will raise anxiety and make that person much more willing to work when it is his or her turn. Addicts are often the center of their universe, and by delaying gratification one enables them to experience a sense of powerlessness and supports their process of surrender.

Manipulation of the therapeutic interventions by the clinician can create anxiety for the client, thus keeping the client interested in the therapeutic process. Interventions may include narrative therapy, gestalt techniques, psychodrama, art therapy, movement exercises, visualizations, and psychoeducational components.

CLINICAL CASE EXAMPLE

Roger was enmeshed with his mother. He was in his 30s and still lived at home, was unable to keep a primary relationship, and did not work. As a result, he had no money. Roger's failure to have a manageable adult life stemmed from the fact that he was unwilling to individuate from his mother. His mother unconsciously seduced him into believing that she needed him for emotional survival. Roger's sexual addiction included having sex with prostitutes, use of pornography, and compulsive masturbation. Roger had explored this issue through talk therapy and psychoeducation, yet he was unable to break through his denial related to his relationship with his mother. During a family session, Roger participated in a psychodrama, attempting to depict the enmeshed dynamic. However, during the process Roger dissociated and could not continue the process.

Roger was unable to see how he was unconsciously protecting his mother from the realities of their relationship. Roger then participated in a family sculpture with his group members. Roger directed the scene and began by having his father stand in the corner of the room, blocked off by chairs. Roger lay on the floor, and his mother knelt on the ground and leaned over his body. The group held these positions for a period of time until Roger began to weep. He was finally able to feel the pain and grief of the overpowering relationship with his mother.

Not only did Roger benefit from these techniques, but the group members also remained interested in the dynamic and deepened their knowledge and subsequent healing of their own pathologies.

THERAPEUTIC STYLES

Clinical styles are as varied as therapists are. Whatever your style may be, capitalize on it to motivate your client to move through resistance. An example of this is a husband and wife who are on the opposite ends of the spectrum in their therapeutic approaches. The husband is very cognitive-behavioral, and the wife is quite flamboyant in her clinical approach. Both have great success in their caseloads because they are able to use their personal clinical styles to motivate their clients. The husband, who is methodical and cognitive-based, uses mental challenges to keep the interest of his clients engaged in the therapeutic process. He includes constant communication wherein the client is challenged and encouraged to walk through the communication and processing of feelings in a safe way. His methodical approach creates a nurturing environment that allows affirmation and containment of the client's process. He communicates each step of the process, beginning with assisting the client in identifying his or her agenda for the treatment. This agenda may be identified as the clinician never sitting in judgment of the client, giving honest feedback, and never being dismissive of or negating the client's reality. In addition, he entices clients to stay present in the process by constantly challenging and reinforcing them to reclaim their personal power. He helps clients identify the ways in which they give away their personal power. The discussion may include identifying the reaction to, rather than the control of, a situation. Clients are often enticed by the dialogue of gaining personal power and control, because these have been the addicts' goals all along: control and power. This style reframes the concept of control as clients finding their own personal power, rather than giving it away to the addiction. It continues by challenging the client, by creating awareness and offering solutions through behavioral changes. Part of this style is to be consistent in feedback and to reinforce the positive behavioral changes. It is this mental challenge, reinforcement, containment, and safety that can facilitate and maintain the client's interest in treatment.

On the other end of the continuum is the wife, who uses her flamboyance to entice the addict to stay focused on recovery. It is no coincidence that therapists, like the wife, who work with sexual addicts, are often flamboyant. They speak, dress, carry themselves, and react in dramatic terms. Often the client sees the therapist as being "larger than life." These therapists have magnetic personalities and often bring a passion and intensity to their work that are enticing to the client. This magnetism often draws the client into the therapeutic process and can even create a reputation and a following for the therapist.

The wife is a great storyteller; she avails herself of humor and is fearless in her quest to wrestle with the demons of her clients. Through her flamboyance, she passionately conveys the life-and-death issues surrounding the nature of recovery. She radically emotes in a safe and engaging way, allowing the client to enter her emotional world, which mirrors her client's reality. She allows the clients to be a part of her life's journey, sharing the universal pain and joy of growth. Through her self-disclosure, she creates hope and vision for her clients. Her clients are able to connect to her process and reality until they are able to do so for themselves. She shares her own emotional intensity and passion, which align and provide confinement and containment for the client.

Each of these styles provides a level of mirroring, protection, safety, and nurturance that produces the therapeutic alliance for recovery. This husband and wife, though radically different, use their therapeutic styles to engage the client and sustain their exploration and growth in treatment.

USING DEFIANCE

Therapists meeting clients in their rebelliousness and mirroring this behavior can be disturbing enough for clients to motivate them to change. Some risk is involved in this intervention, and the therapist needs to assess the situation before making the choice to use this therapeutic technique. The risks include clients becoming so agitated that they leave therapy and never return, which, for some clients, could spiral them into a sense of hopelessness and despair that could lead to a serious relapse or even death. It is important to use caution with this intervention. First use your intuition in assessing the situation. Check in with your own countertransference and make sure that this decision is made from a place of therapeutic integrity. Always remind yourself that the focus is on the clients' consequential behaviors of their disease and not their worth as people. The intervention needs to be made in a place of dignity and respect for the client.

CLINICAL CASE EXAMPLE

Bob came into treatment unwilling to believe he had a problem with sex. While in group, he stated, "I am sick of all you perverts and want to change to a different group. All I am here for is my depression." Bob had already lost a 25-year marriage because of a string of affairs. His last affair had progressed into sexually offending behaviors when he engaged in sexual relations with his student aide in a department at the university where he worked. Bob went on to say that he was "in love" with her and she with him. He became quite indignant when confronted, stating, "I think you have the problem, and that you are jealous of the happiness that I have with my girlfriend."

The approach when utilizing defiance is the implementation of the "bad cop, good cop" technique. In this intervention the "bad cop" attacks the addict's defenses. The bad cop states the truth, often using a judgmental, dismissive role. The goal is to agitate the client enough to facilite change. In other words, the client might become angry enough to recover in spite of him- or herself. The "good cop" aligns with the client. The alignment is designed to give the structure necessary to establish safety and trust. Juxtaposition of these clinical characters can create enough tension to motivate the client to change. An intervention may proceed as follows: First, the cofacilators stop talking to the client and turn to each other and begin a dialogue about the client. The bad cop states, "Well, I think Bob is about the most hopeless case I have seen. I mean, we see a lot of really sick cases, but this one takes the prize."

The good cop responds with "Oh, I don't think it's all that bad.

Many people come in here with the same thoughts."

Bad cop: "Not in this bad shape. In fact, I don't think I want to work with someone who already has it figured out."

At this point the client begins to feel defensive—"Hey, why am I paying you so much money? If I had it figured out, I wouldn't be here."

The clinicians ignore Bob's response; the bad cop continues by stating, "I don't think this one is going to make it. He is going to relapse, and his relationship will be the last thing he has to worry about. In fact, I don't think he will have the guts to complete this program or even come to group tomorrow."

"I don't know," the good-cop cofacilitator says.

"Well, OK, then, I will bet you a lunch he doesn't come back."

"I'll take that bet, because I believe he wants this."

"Well, this will be the easiest free lunch I have ever won!"

The focus then moves to the other patients and their work for the day. The client is allowed to sit with his anger, confusion, and fear. The hope is that the client will return, ready to work.

COGNITIVE DISTORTIONS

For the sex addict, cognitive distortions involve not only perceptions of reality but also entire ways of thinking. The sex addict has a wide variety of cognitive distortions that protect his or her world. The predominant form of cognitive distortions is denial. As discussed earlier, the addict will deny any problems, despite overwhelming evidence to the contrary. Cognitive distortions then allow the addict to continue the addictive behavior and justify the consequences.

If the client has either a great deal of energy or is excessively passive around the subject of sexuality, this suggests denial of sexual issues. Questioning the client about sexuality will undoubtedly lead to uncovering the clients' distorted cognition. It is in this discovery that a prognosis can begin to emerge. The following list may help in identifying the thought patterns and responses that are clues to the underlying pathology.

- *Absolute thinking*: "No problem whatsoever"—despite glaring consequences to the client's sexual behaviors.
- *Rationalization*: "People are sexually inhibited"; "I am just liberated"; "You are an addict yourself and just deluded; I can't trust your perceptions."
- *Minimization*: "I see prostitutes only once in awhile."
- *Comparison*: "I am not as bad as [name]. If you think I am a sex addict, you ought to check out the numbers my old roommate had going."
- *Uniqueness*: "I have a high libido"; "My situation is different"; "They are not in recovery so they do not understand."

- *Avoidance*: Behaviors that include laughing, joking, angry outbursts, threats, shocking behavior, canceling appointments.
- *Intellectualization*: Looking for answers in "why" questions, getting lost in details and rationalization.
- *Manipulation*: Using charm or lies, withholding information, seductive behavior, and dishonesty with self.
- *Scapegoating*: "If you were on the road all week, you would cruise, too"; "If you had a spouse like mine, you would take up sexual distractions, too"; "But the gay community is small; of course, I've slept with all my friends and their lovers, too."

When you hear clients make statements like the ones mentioned here, the first goal is to identify the statement as a cognitive distortion. The second is to educate the client. An excellent tool to aid in the educational process is David Burns's (1980) book *Feeling Good*. Burns gives clinicians effective methods for integrating the concept of cognitive distortions by first defining what cognitive distortions are, followed by a test.

12-STEP MODEL

The addict who is involved in individual and group therapy, as well as participating in a 12-step program, has a better chance of maintaining sobriety. One of the reasons for this success rate is the enormous impact that 12-step meetings can have on challenging the addict's cognitive distortions. Chapter 8, "The Integration of Psychotherapy and 12-Step Programs in Sexual Addiction Treatment," guides the clinician through the use of the 12-step program.

The 12-step model also can challenge sex addicts' core beliefs, hold addicts accountable by requiring them to work the 12 steps, and can function as addicts' first "healthy family" by accepting and supporting them unconditionally. Such groups help addicts by mirroring, supporting, and affirming them as they move toward sober and healthy sexuality. Built into the 12-step model is shame reduction. For example, when an individual says, "Hi, my name is John, and I am a sex addict," those in attendance do not get up and leave the room, nor do they condemn the person. The addict is welcomed, understood, and accepted, thus reducing the shame of the disease. When addicts share their experience, strength, and hope, individuals do not sit in judgment or call them "perverts"—rather, people say, "I identify with you." As shame is lifted, individuals are now in a better position—a less defended one—to begin to look at their cognitive distortions and other coping mechanisms. Self-esteem will undo addiction, for just as abandonment fuels shame, and shame fuels addiction, healthy self-love fuels connection, which is the base or glue of spirituality. Step 12 points out that this healthy self-love is the basis of recovery. "Having had a spiritual awakening as a result of these steps," addicts learn that they are not terminally unique, and this reduces the sense of shame that is at the core of all sex addicts. It is the gift of humility and recognizing their own humanness that allow the emergence of the true self.

At the heart of the 12-step model is spirituality. Addicts are challenged by the 12 steps to admit their powerlessness, to develop a relationship with a power greater than themselves, and to turn their will and life over to this higher power. The goal of the steps is to allow addicts to see how their choices about their behavior are not working, that addicts are not in control, that they need help.

SUMMARY

In treatment of the defended sexually addictive client, it is of primary importance to explore the client's core beliefs. The core beliefs are the source of the client's shame and pain. This shame and pain ignite the need to stay defended, because most clients believe they are worthless, unwanted, and unlovable. Treatment is meant to displace the feelings of shame with healthy self-esteem. This challenge is terrifying to sex addicts because, at their very core, they believe they are unworthy of self-love. Clients who are vulnerable and who divulge the truth of their pain and shame fear rejection. Acceptance by the clinician becomes paramount to the healing process. So that the client can develop the trust in the therapeutic relationship, clinicians are encouraged to use their clinical style to create safety, containment, trust, and acceptance. In so doing, the clinician will help the client explore the shame and fear that are at the core of the addictive behaviors. Once an alliance is established, the clinician supports the client by addressing cognitive distortions, providing behavioral contracts, challenging unconscious processing, and holding the client accountable. The client's interest in treatment can be maintained by varying clinical techniques. This may be accomplished through myriad clinical applications, depending on the client's form of defense. Finally, clients need the adjunct support of a 12-step program that supports the client in recognizing the humanness of his or her disease and offers the compassion and acceptance that characterize the 12-step groups.

REFERENCES

Burns, D. (1980). *Feeling good: The new mood therapy*. New York: Avon.

Carnes, P. (1997). *Sexual anorexia: Overcoming sexual self-hatred*. Center City, MN: Hazelden.

Erikson, M. H. (1977). Hypnotic approaches to therapy. *American Journal of Clinical Hypnosis, 20*.

Lovern, J. D. (1991). *Pathways to reality*. New York: Brunner/Mazel.

CHAPTER 4

Strategies for Assessment and Early Treatment With Sexually Addicted Families

JUDITH C. HEATON MATHENY

Although there has been recent growth in research and treatment approaches in the sexual addiction/compulsivity field, assessment and early treatment of the family members has received less attention. This chapter addresses the significance of including assessment of family members in the early treatment stage. Numerous family of origin histories make apparent the strong link from early childhood on through adulthood between family events that created conflict, turmoil, misunderstanding, and troubled concepts of personal sexuality. Addressing family of origin factors without involving the addict's current family unit, however, provides only an understanding of the addictive/compulsive behavior, not the tools to change it. The addict's family members must involve themselves from the earliest stages of recovery, both to provide support and to allow the addict and themselves to break what can be a familial cycle of addictive behaviors. We are fortunate to have research and knowledge from the chemical dependency field to validate the need for early intervention in detecting the impact of addiction on each person in the family system. This chapter provides a suggested blueprint for the therapist in the assessment and early treatment stages for sexual addicts, their partners, and their children. The primary focus is on families without overt sexual perpetration with the children—situations involving incest need the full attention of a chapter written to address specifically intervention with both the incested child and other family members. The discussion here focuses on the necessity of family involvement for successful treatment of addicts and the emotional well-being of their children and partners. It then outlines techniques for initial assessment of both the addict and the co-addict, as well as their children. Finally, it presents a two-phase model for early treatment, one that stresses family involvement over exclusive attention to the individual addict.

INTRODUCTION

It is in the family that children learn their core beliefs about sense of the self. Co-addict parents share common core beliefs with their addict partners that keep the family system dysfunctional in beliefs, attitudes, and actions. Because "the most fundamental characteristic of codependency is looking outward for one's self-worth" (Schneider, 1988, p. 45), the effects of the addiction on the sexual addict's family are often unspoken and unrecognized within the family home.

Sexual addiction brings with it a long history of secrecy and maintenance of a double life. The undercurrents of this life often have hidden effects on both addicts and their families. These effects can go undetected for years—particularly in families where the secret/double life has not yet been exposed—while silently eroding the self-confidence, security, emotional well-being, and healthy sense of sexuality of the partner and the children, as well as that of the addict.

Because of the dire consequences of these undercurrents, the therapist must have a heightened awareness of the effects of the addiction on each family member. Early inclusion of the family in intervention and recovery can assist all members in finding ways to dispel the lies and secrecy inherent to sexual compulsivity. The family must learn effective life skills to transition from shame and enabling behaviors to a life with less oppressive expectations.

THE CRUCIAL NATURE OF FAMILY INVOLVEMENT

The family unit is fundamental in teaching rules and attitudes about self and others. Consequently, family assessment and treatment need to be a part of the ongoing and vital therapeutic process necessary to evaluate the effects of sexual dependency on family members. The chemical dependency field has made a great contribution in heightening awareness of the necessity of outreach to and involvement of family members.

In a therapist's first meeting with an individual, it is important to determine if that person is single or part of a family. The family of origin plays a significant role in the development of compulsive behaviors. The therapist should continue to note information to provide an increased understanding of the family system and dynamics as the assessment and early treatment processes evolve. The opportunity to have a window into some aspects of the family of origin often presents itself during the evaluation or assessment time. Issues and events that will help address the healing of childhood wounds, teaching of unlearned life skills, or both are useful later in the therapeutic process.

Therapists should gather as much information about the present family members and how to best intervene and stop further destruction, while they learn about the family of origin's impact throughout this procedure. During the initial interview, when questions are raised with the addict and co-addict to determine their potential for self-harm or harm to others, is an important opportunity for therapists to learn if there has been a familial history of violence to others, self-harming behaviors, or completed suicides. This is key knowledge that will assist therapists in determining the client's personal vulnerability and developmental wounding.

Research has shown that genetic predisposition leads to the creation of neurochemical deficits. These deficits make a person particularly vulnerable to situational and environmental stress (Carnes, 1991, p. 72). In the addictive home, family members will be particularly at risk to the effects of addictive process. There are generations of families with addictions among family members, which substantiate that addiction is a part of familial systems.

The resulting devastation of addiction on the lives of the children and the adults in families must be limited. Jean Piaget notes that the child is "but as an organism which assimilates things to itself, selects them and digests them according to its own structure. In this way even what is influenced by the adult may still be original" (Cruise & Cruise, 1989, p. 185).

Intervention in assessing the differences in developmental strengths and limitations of any given individual is a complex and extensive process. Using psychological tests to aid in the assessment process is one possibility. Another is family members' reports of their experiences of the imprint of being part of an addictive family system. The assessment process itself becomes an early treatment tool—first, by establishing empathy and understanding that what has happened was the way individuals devised to survive pain and confusion. Furthermore, assessment gives insight into what behavioral areas the addiction has found expression and how this has affected and possibly targeted particular family members. Assessment further offers therapists the opportunity to begin to analyze how the co-addict partner and the children have organized their behaviors and thinking around the addict's behavior and moods, to the detriment of their experience of life.

This opportunity offers individuals in the family encouragement to change and the hope that recovery can bring, as they explore treatment and resource possibilities.

Areas to Cover in Early Assessment of the Addict

(Be aware of your state's laws regarding the practitioner's legal responsibilities to report to authorities any acting-out behaviors involving persons under 18 years of age and laws requiring reports of physical and sexual abuse to adults. The clinician should explain the process and support the client through this process.)

1. Explore the potential harm to self or others.
2. Assess the patient using Sexual Addiction Screening Test (SAST; Carnes, 1989, pp. 219–220), Gay Assessment Screening Test (GAST), or Women's Assessment Screening Test (WAST).
3. Give the self-assessment survey (Carnes, 1991, pp. 395–406) for homework.
4. Ask about clients' awareness of the most obvious effects of the acting-out sexual behaviors on their partners (e.g., sexual problems, sexually transmitted diseases, trust issues, increased tension).
5. Evaluate the most immediate effects of the addiction on the family.
6. Check out clients' readiness to involve their partners in the assessment and early treatment process.
7. Evaluate and sensitively probe clients' reasons for resistance or openness to including their partners; use a denial pattern outline to listen more effectively (Carnes, 1989, pp. 208–209; Gorski, 1989, pp. 20–25).
8. Ask about the consequences of clients' acting-out behaviors on their lives, in spite of attempts to stop.
9. Explore the frequency of behaviors and any resulting self-harm or harm to others.
10. Review the 11 types of acting-out behaviors and have clients identify the ones in which they have been participants (Carnes, 1991, pp. 41–67).
11. Evaluate the effects of unstructured time on the ability to have acting-out time—"a double life."
12. Evaluate depressive symptoms and any plans for self-harm or harm to others.
13. Check out clients' interest in or openness to connecting with a 12-step meeting (Salmon, 1995, pp. 193–213).
14. Determine, if possible, the need for Axis II, *DSM-IV* (American Psychiatric Association, 1994) evaluation. The differential diagnosis of addictive sexual disorders and how to use the *DSM-IV* are addressed in Irons and Schneider (1996, pp. 7–24). Keep in mind that the diagnostic process is also an ongoing one and that addictive sexual disorders do not fit into standardized *DSM-IV* categories. This will likely need revisitation in treatment.

EARLY ASSESSMENT OF ADDICTS

In the preceding list, the time frame to cover these various queries will take three to four sessions, depending on the state of anxiety or desperation of the new client. In the early stage of assessment, addicts need assistance to "step into ownership," and they need to recognize their powerlessness over their addiction and the unmanageability of their lives. It is vital to encourage them to recognize the necessity of including their partners. Often, addicts' fear of desertion/abandonment by partners is great, and addicts persist in the irrational belief that they can face their problem alone. This mind-set needs persistent reality testing.

Usually, a specific event(s) has precipitated enough anxiety about the acting-out behaviors that the individual is to the point of self-identifying as being sexually compulsive. The precipating event may be the diagnosis of an STD, a near-arrest, the loss of a job, gross debt, or a distraught partner threatening to separate or divorce. A therapist can often weave the pieces of events into a more complete agreement of the individual's need and situation, though this requires very close listening.

In taking the SAST/GAST/WAST, individuals begin to react to the quantity of yes answers they find themselves providing. The question may arise whether the questions pertain to now or the past. The therapist can answer either and then explain he or she will go over their answers with them. This offers clients an opportunity to talk further about their questions, concerns, anxiety, and shame.

The homework assignment of the self-assessment survey gives clients an opportunity to deepen their reflection on the addictive process. The client receives an anonymous number and returns the survey by mail, to be read over by the therapist before the next session.

Sometime during the first three sessions, it is important to introduce the partner's role. The partner's involvement is key, and addicts will need to learn what their partners know about the acting-out behaviors. Frequently, addicts are fearful their partners will leave them or "could not take it" if the partner knew about the acting-out behaviors. This presents an opportunity for therapists to explain minimally the complexity of addiction and co-addiction and to introduce the reality of the process of establishing sobriety and recovery. It is important that the new client understands that fear of the repercussions of our actions is natural and is given assurance that part of treatment is confronting the fear of consequences and shame about behavior.

Resistance to involving the partner has at its base the delusion that the addict can become cured and keep the partner from experiencing pain. This can be the first of numerous educational opportunities about the need for the co-addicted partner to enter into couple's assessment, in order to address enabling and controlling behaviors.

Listening to addicts' fears about self-disclosure to their partners often gives the therapist an opportunity to acknowledge that the addict's fear validates the destructive core belief that "no one would love me as I am" (Carnes, 1983, p. 87). For successful treatment, the therapist must challenge this belief. In addition, it can be helpful to draw from treatment histories and emphasize that the best achivements in recovery happen when the partner is also involved in treatment.

By the fourth session, the therapist may need to submit some diagnostic evaluation formulation for insurance coverage (Irons & Schneider, 1996, pp. 7–21) and address the differential diagnosis of addictive sexual disorders and how to use the DSM-IV.

Treatment is also about getting support in successfully addressing the addiction and getting relief from the heavy burden of a double life. If clients are ready to make contact with someone in a sexual addiction 12-step group, make sure there is a plan they can initiate to do this. Establish a time that they will check in and let you know if they have completed contact with a 12-step person. This is often an exceedingly difficult step for an addict to take and any hitch in the process can be very discouraging.

When the suggested areas for the fourth session have been covered, clients have more clearly identified their powerlessness to control the addiction and the unmanageability of their lives. There is a deepened recognition of the isolation and withdrawal that have occurred in their lives and the need for a connection with others to give support, hope, and lessen the shame. Plans to include the partner in the near future are possible to make at this point, as the addict has begun to see more clearly the need for the partner's involvement in the change.

ASSESSING THE CO-ADDICT

The partner is "co-addicted" because the partner's addiction is to the relationship with the addict. Most often, partners carry resentment and anger, even when they do not consciously know about the sexually addictive behaviors. The emotional unavailability and hurtful behavior of the addict are confusing, and an atmosphere of blame is often the result of the co-addict's and addict's dissatisfaction with life. The partner may have noticed or questioned observable symptoms, which can facilitate the partner's conscious recognition of the effects on his or her own life (Laaser, 1992, pp. 56–57).

It is understandable that this person will frequently come to the session demonstrating guardedness, anger, and hurt. The addict has either asked the partner to come, or the partner has arranged for the initial meeting. Partners have sought meaning for their lives in the world of people, places, and things outside themselves (De Busk & Weiss, p. 10), and this is particularly true in their relationships with addicts. Therefore, a partner's ambivalence about what may happen in these early encounters with the therapist is understandable.

Later sessions will uncover the partner's own family history and patterns of past abuses. For these assessment sessions and in early treatment, however, the partners' major focus is on learning how to recognize that there is work to do to restore themselves to some sense of sanity. Their lives have increasingly become about making up for the emotional and behavioral deprivations of the family, often taking on more and more tasks to keep the family going. These can include financial, parental, and scheduling responsibilities.

The partner has confused the intensity of the relationship and the resulting turmoil with the way life has to be. The partner's level of involvement in "keeping things going" and the focus on the addict's actions and nonactions mean a loss of sense of self. This can be different when the co-addict is in control of his or her thoughts, feelings, and behaviors. This will require partners at the beginning of the assessment process to shift the focus back to awareness of the effects and consequences of their own thinking and their own behavior process in their recovery.

Steps for Assessing the Co-Addict

Areas to cover in the early assessment of the co-addict:

1. Learn how co-addicts made the discovery that the addict was acting out (noting the levels of their shock and denial).
2. Explore the extent of co-addicts' knowledge of the kinds of acting-out behaviors and their feelings and reactions to these.
3. Inquire how co-addicts see that their family life has been affected, what they have done to make up for absences, and so on.
4. Learn what awareness co-addicts have of how (and to what extent) their children's lives have been affected.
5. Assign the self-assessment survey for co-addicts (Carnes, 1991, pp. 407–413).
6. Explore what co-addicts need to learn about how to assist themselves in addressing their own help.
7. Evaluate if there is dysthymia, depression, or any ideation of self-harm or of hurting others.
8. Explore the potential of harm to self or others.
9. Assess co-addicts' ability to identify which of their own behaviors are reactive to the addict's acting out.
10. Aid co-addicts in assessing their support system and their available confidants.
11. Evaluate and ask if they are ready for and interested in contact from someone in a 12-step program.
12. Ask about their awareness of their own compulsive behaviors and how these impact their lives.
13. Encourage them to evaluate how ready they are for support and participation in a 12-step group.

How the discovery happens often has a direct influence on the motivation to get help. It can take a great deal of time to come to terms with the shock and denial that result. If there is little or no knowledge of the acting-out behaviors, it will take time for the partner to assimilate this painful information. Typically, this will not be forthcoming all at once, as addicts often hold back telling about all the variations of their behaviors. Partially, this is due to their own denial that some of these actually are acting-out behaviors.

There is often specific recognition of the effects on the family. The depth to which this has happened, however, is a more difficult awareness to integrate. The partner's filling in for the absences of the addict has helped to enable the addiction but has been such a part of the family's life that it often goes unnoticed.

Focusing on the impact on the children's lives usually brings up the most apparent ways the addict has affected the family, such as missed activities. The addict's more general lack of a parental relationship with his or her child and the partner's filling in for the addict with the child can also be very subtle. Discussion of the more in-depth impact of the behaviors will come as the children feel safe enough to talk openly.

Information about how co-addiction and addiction fit within the relationship system helps. This can be most effective after the addicted client has relayed an acting-out event that follows some negative couple interaction. Emphasizing that the partner does not cause the client to act out is vital. It is also important to help the addict see how a partner's behavior may trigger the addictive cycle. This can be a key factor in breaking through some self-invested protectiveness of the co-addict. An example would be the partner's control issues.

Case Illustration

Charles had dated his present wife for 3 years before their marriage 2 years ago. During that time, he had numerous phone and in-person sexual encounters, spent thousands of dollars on pornography and topless-bottomless shows, and was increasingly more in a euphoria-seeking addictive state that interfered with the completion of his deadlines. Charles was a cartoonist for a national magazine that had demanding deadlines. The stress would cause a high adrenaline flow, his performance anxiety would increasingly heighten, and he would begin to think that he was no good; fear of exposure of his inadequacies and his spiraling self-depreciation would soar, culminating in a total production block.

During this process, his partner began by being encouraging and then took on more and more family and household responsibilities, attempting to help him feel less pressure. She also made frequent remarks to remind him of his deadline when he was having downtime. Her own family background, in which the women took on more and more to avoid her father's wrath, was already a pattern that fit into Charlie's core belief that he was an unworthy, inadequate person. His consuming fears of rejection, failure, abandonment, and wanting to protect himself from feeling responsible for his wife's hurt were deterrents to including her in the assessment and early treatment process. His modus operandi of feeling that he had to be in control and fix things continued to feed his belief that his needs could not be met if he had to depend on another person. The dynamics kept replaying, with his fear and loneliness so engulfing him that he would act out to relieve the greatly magnified pain and savor the satisfied sense of his conquest. His investment in keeping his wife out of treatment so that she would continue to work hard to accommodate him and he could maintain his control was complex and well hidden, even to himself. What did bring his wife into treatment were his repeated relapses in spite of his surface sobriety.

This case is an example of how not including the partner early on undermines sobriety efforts. The partner's part in the system can unwittingly be a key influence in the treatment of the addictive cycle (Carnes, 1991, pp. 147–157). Education about couples and family systems plants early seeds in the addict's mind; this, along with the necessity for early assessment of honesty, can defuse other elaborate plans to act out.

There are two common scenarios for introduction of the partner into the assessment situation. In the first, the partner comes with the addict because the acting-out behaviors have somehow invaded the partner's world (e.g., finding the secret credit card stash and the brutal reckoning of thousands of dollars of debt; a call in the night from an irate partner of someone with whom the addict had an affair). Another common scenario is dissatisfaction with the sexual relationship for either partner, the couple entering routine sex therapy, or both. Whatever initiates the partner's call or presence at the session, it will be imperative for the therapist to begin to listen to the partner's pain. It is most helpful if the therapist verbalizes for the person, "This has been painful for you," to help partners shift the focus to themselves. This assists partners in bolstering their recognition of the relevance of setting firm personal behavioral and emotional boundaries. This will include making the connection between their painful feelings and the addict's behavior and acknowledging the information they have given as facts about the addiction.

Case Illustration

Ann had become increasingly depressed and sexually shut down. While cleaning, she had found a note from one of her husband's patients, telling him of how their time together had rekindled what she thought had been her inability to feel sexual. When Ann discussed her history with depression, her first incident did occur after 6 months into her relationship with Al, who needed a lot of support and encouragement, which she felt she could give. In reviewing their relationship, she began to relate how she had dropped out of more activities and relationships with others as Al's dependence on her became greater. Though committed to not having sexual intercourse before marriage, she allowed Al to convince her that this act would be an expression of her true love for him, to give him what he needed and wanted most—a testimony that love for other is greater than love for self. This became a theme for Ann throughout their relationship. She succumbed to fulfilling more and more of Al's requests to make their sexual experiences more special than he had had with anyone else. Meanwhile, Ann sank further into shame and low self-regard, as she allowed him to snap nude shots of her and videotape their sexual encounters, while she gave up more outside activities that had been gratifying to her.

Coming to terms with the early realization of a partner's addictions is a painful process that takes time and timing. Often, the best orchestration of this happening is a combination of individual and couple sessions. In a joint session, it becomes clear what central issues are paramount in the relationship. Chapter 10 discusses in detail the issue of disclosure.

In joint sessions, the co-addict can begin to learn the important lesson of how to be a part of a support system, rather than of a control system. Co-addicts can also learn that attempts at outside control will likely encourage an addict's sense of noncompliance. It is vital that the system not become organized around the co-addict's control issues instead of around the take-charge efforts of the addict.

Case Illustration

Susan found herself exhausted with her daily life and with her frequent thoughts of what Mike might be doing during his growing number of absences during the evenings and even during the day when he was at work. She had discovered a note among his papers, with a woman's telephone number and the quickly scribbled question, "Why haven't you called me?"

She found herself calling him at work more frequently, thinking more about what he might be doing when he wasn't there, what she could say to him, how to say it, how to keep him from getting angry, their previous night's fight about being sexual (she did not want to wear that teddy and wiggle the way he pressured her to do), and much more. Her mind had been so full of thoughts that she had missed her expressway exit, run a red light, and had not supervised the children when they got ready for school (which resulted in missed belongings that they needed when she dropped them off that morning). Lack of sleep from arguing about sex with Mike last night really affected her. Finally, at lunch she talked to her best friend, Gayle. With tears flowing, she heard herself describe how her life was becoming more chaotic; she was getting less sleep and felt physically down and emotionally overwhelmed. Preoccupied with how to please Mike sexually and avoid his anger, she was felt terribly inadequate about herself and her life in general.

When Gayle told Susan how Mike had made a pass at her at the Saturday cookout, Susan was crushed and angry. She had organized her entire Saturday around doing what he wanted to do, having sex in the early morning hours and then in the afternoon when the girls were out playing (she was anxious the whole time for fear they would come inside), and then she had worn that tight outfit, with a low neckline, to please him. She felt awkward and embarrassed. She had made excuses and apologies for him, explained his behavior as misunderstandings, covered bounced checks, and now agonized over whether she should talk to him about what she had learned. She was furious, but scared he would leave. What could she do? She began thinking about what she could do to bring his attention back to her: Change her hair color? Buy him that new golf club he had wanted? Give in and let him try that new sexual technique he'd read about in *Hustler?*

The previous is only one example of how the co-addict partner will work hard to accommodate the addict, unwittingly enabling his or her addiction and undermining any sobriety efforts. The co-addict's involvement in the relationship then becomes more clear: by mistaking intensity for intimacy, the partner helps to create chaos and drama (Schneider, 1988, p. 28). Both the addict and the co-addict must address this if there is to be change. The partner's wellness or continuing investment in the addict's sobriety greatly influences the addict's recovery.

Through learning about the origin of their codependency, the husband and wife can learn about being responsible for themselves. Schneider (1988) emphasized the need for intervention with both the co-addict and in the couple system. Factors in the family of origin and early experiences influence the co-addict's core belief that sex is the best way to get love (p. 55). How the couple has lived out this belief has far-reaching effects for the co-addict and in the functioning of the relationship. Often, behavior is at one of two extremes: the performing of sexual acts that violate one's internal sense of what is right, or withholding sex out of punishment or anger. Whatever the reason the partner comes to a session, it is imperative to listen to his or her pain. Layers of anger and resentment may cover this. Eventually, assisting partners in bolstering their recognition of the relevance of setting firm personal behavioral and emotional boundaries, after helping them define what these need to be for them, is an early treatment task. COSA (Co-Sex Addicts Anonymous) attendance can greatly assist this.

Beginning with assessment and throughout treatment, acknowledging the addict's acting-out behaviors and the intertwining of the addictive and co-addictive processes are imperative to recovery issues. Often, the most effective orchestration of this happening is a combination of individual and couple sessions. Couple sessions are not marital therapy. Instead, in the joint sessions it becomes clearer what central issues are paramount to the successful recovery relationship. It also becomes clearer when the co-addict wants to dictate the addict's recovery program. Both partners need to be clear that each of them must be in charge of his or her own recovery program. They both must focus on improving their own emotional, physical, sexual, and spiritual health. It must be pointed out that attempts at controlling the other person's treatment and recovery will result in noncompliance.

The inclusion of assessment of the children ideally occurs shortly after the addict and co-addict have made inroads into their own denial about the addictive system and the repercussions on their lives. The recognition of the breadth and depth of the feelings of shame and responsibility they have likely developed is often covert. This can be different if the child was the focus in the addiction process of the addict's acting out. The fact that repercussions are not as apparent often results in the assessment of the children occurring later in the process. This is especially true if the parents are not emotionally ready to include them. When the parent can acknowledge the systemic nature of this disease, the children can become a part of the dynamic of assessment.

ASSESSMENT OF THE CHILDREN

In the assessment of the children, the first step is to discover their level of awareness about the addiction and how it is acted out. Parents can be resources in this if they think the child overheard them planning or executing acting-out behaviors, arguing about the addiction, or otherwise "discovered" the parent's stash (whether that be a person, pornography, or paraphernalia). How the child found out about the addiction, behavior, or both is important because the circumstances themselves can shock and traumatize.

Areas to Cover in Early Meetings With Children

1. Educate in simple terms about the purpose of family counseling and point out that every family member's idea is important about what is going on and the effects on that person.
2. Talk with children about how they see their family at this time—talk through the fact that their parents have come to counseling because the parents recognize that there are problems in their relationships.
3. Meet with the children to gain understanding of their level of awareness of the addiction (do they know about acting-out behaviors?).
4. Explore with children what questions they may have about their family coming to counseling and the observations they have of any recent changes in the family.
5. Explore the children's understanding of boundaries and what their family boundaries are.

6. Explain the importance of asking questions: This is how we learn information and check out with other people what they are thinking and feeling.
7. Educate by engaging the children's life experience; let them know that sometimes the people we question do not have the answers or may be uncomfortable talking about something. It is important to find a safe person and place to talk and ask questions.
8. Educate about the family as a system—when one person has a problem, it will have some effect on others in the family. Use stories and drawings to help develop this idea.
9. Use "checking out" and "active listening" with the children to gain better clarity about what they are thinking and experiencing.
10. Consider the child's exposure to the addiction and his or her age when educating about sexual addiction.
11. Keep it simple but clear when differentiating between healthy sexuality and people experiencing problems with sexuality.
12. Emphasize to the children that people may act out feelings of anger toward them, but that children are not responsible for how others express anger, frustration, and so on.
13. Check out the possibility of depression or whether the child is experiencing thoughts of self-harm or harm to others.
14. Talk about a future meeting to gain better understanding of how everyone in the family is doing.

Children with a sexually addicted parent have learned to keep secrets—to not ask certain questions or not ask for specific information. For the therapist who is cultivating a relationship with each child, it is important to educate about the harmfulness of keeping secrets and to let the child know that asking questions is okay, even healthy.

The age of the child and his or her developmental stage are important considerations when you decide how much to educate about addictions and sexual addictions in particular. The child's direct exposure to the behaviors is very significant. In cases of the child's involvement in the parent's acting-out behaviors, there is serious damage to repair.

The following case illustrates the father's involvement of his teenage daughter in his addiction.

Case Illustration

Bob had an insatiable voyeuristic interest in young women, so when his daughter Linda became an adolescent, it seemed very easy and natural to encourage her to have her friends over for overnights and swim parties. Linda felt uncomfortable and increasingly embarrassed by her father's sexualized remarks toward her friends, particularly when he began drinking. Her own sense of trust and self-worth were greatly impacted by her and her friends being sexually objectified by her father in very subtle ways. She found a collection of candid photos he had taken of her and her friends when they were sunbathing and in their nighties at slumber parties. One can only imagine her shock and horror when she discovered peepholes her father had bored through the walls in the bathrooms to view her and her friends as they bathed.

The ways of using children in the acting-out cycle can seem limitless. Some addicts use children's activities to get out of the house; are openly voyeuristic in malls while shopping with the children; take children along to lure or meet conquests; and use the children or their friends to objectify sexually through sexual remarks, voyeurism, and exhibitionism.

Children in families of sexual addicts/co-addicts learn early on not to feel the confusion, insecurity, and self-doubt that result from their parents' secretiveness. They have a driving need to block out the negative feelings they have toward their parents (Crow & Earle, 1989, p. 196). When a parent maintains a secret life, his or her children pick up on even subtle inconsistencies of what the parent says and what that person actually does. Meanwhile, the other parent is likely to be experiencing anxiety and distrust at some level. That parent may act out unpredictably through the expression of anger, impatience, criticism, or compulsive behavior.

There are "lost children" who perform well academically, have outstanding natural achievements, and look good outwardly. Inwardly, however, these children can be developing deeper coping mechanisms of denial, distrust, and their own ways of deceiving themselves and others.

In the assessment and early treatment period, it is unlikely that even older children will talk much about the addiction. They will likely have little understanding of how it has affected them or the family. An exception is the child who has learned to referee the arguments between his or her parents. However, it is important to create an opportunity for the family to come in to talk about the effect that early recovery is having on them. Family life in assessment and early treatment is changing in ways that affect the children's lives: a parent may be absent due to therapy or meetings; parents may (for the first time) begin to actually talk about problems; or a parent may monopolize the phone, talking to 12-step program people. Better follow-through with parenting may change what behaviors the child can hide or get away with. The children may now hear words of encouragement that they talk about what is on their mind, but may feel uncomfortable and untrusting.

In the family of an addict, feelings have so frequently been pushed under or glossed over that it is difficult for children to believe that they will be heard or that it is safe to ask questions or make observations. There will need to be hard work and a great deal of consistency in parental honesty before any movement occurs. For a time, things get worse before they get better. This situation also needs acknowledgment and support from other sources. No one way will fit everyone. Each child is an individual with a complex internal, cognitive, emotional, spiritual, and biological makeup, affected in different ways and degrees. What is traumatic for one person has fewer and lesser consequences for another. It is only by really listening, observing, and acknowledging what therapists hear that children can begin to experience themselves.

Children of a sexually compulsive parent often confuse sexual boundaries and behaviors. Similar to the homes in which most addicts and co-addicts grew up, the families of the sexually compulsive seldom discuss sexuality. The view of sexual experience is negative, or at least something not related to natural, healthy, loving, intimate, giving, and receiving experiences. Particularly during the teen years, defining or redefining sexual boundaries for the child is confusing and difficult. The extremes can be that the relationship is sexual or that defined limits are rigid. The idea that sexuality is an unfolding process and that teens need the opportunity to talk to others to explore what is and is not okay for them is totally foreign in the homes of most sex addicts.

In assessment and early treatment it is important to talk, educate, and encourage all family members to work on establishing healthier boundaries. Because the earliest stage of assessment seldom involves children, it is vital to keep working with the parents (who need to redefine their own boundaries and need to talk about this process with their children). There may be indications for children to have their own treatment in this early stage. Indications that a child needs individual therapy are most likely if the child has experienced harassment or sexual, physical, or emotional abuse. An example is when children have witnessed a parent's acting out. Treatment should begin with the child (or children) as soon as possible, but it is absolutely necessary that the parents stay in their own treatment and recovery programs.

Many families address family counseling later in the recovery stage. Knowing what they want and what is healthy for them is not apparent. For co-addicts, there is much work to be done on defining the self separately from their addict partners. Their thinking and behavior vacillates between old ways of focusing on their own actions and feelings such as sadness, anger, and fear. Concurrently, addicts need support and genuine recognition of their struggle and the hard work it takes to be accountable for their actions/reactions. It can be helpful for the therapist to review with both members of the couple the results/cost of their reactive behaviors to each other.

When there is a better understanding of the individual's and couple's relationships, the therapist can begin the assessment of family strengths and disturbances. Parents will need to be able to listen empathetically as children address their experiences in the family. Parents need to have worked on stabilizing themselves and developing more skills before they are ready to hear and purposefully work on altering the family dynamics.

EARLY TREATMENT

By the time they complete the individual assessment process, both partners have engaged in learning more about their particular roles in this complex system, and the assessment has turned to the effects on the coupleship. The resulting focus has often included financial and job problems, difficulties in their sexual relationship, and the emotional features of depression, anger, resentment, confusion, guilt, and even physical symptoms (Schneider, 1988, p. 96). Both parties will be trying to make behavioral and cognitive changes and at this stage are likely sorting out which changes to focus on first. At this point, the couple sessions are not for the purpose of marital therapy per se, but are a time to prepare a treatment plan for the next few months. Putting the treatment plan together with both members of the coupleship present helps to validate the fact that both individuals have personal work and change on their agendas.

As the therapist assists addicts in becoming as honest as they can be and supports partners in breaking through their denial, this phase is comparable to the careful and intense dismantling of a bomb. It is important for the therapist to approach this task with compassion for each partner, checking out what that person's thoughts and feelings are during the joint session. Each individual is usually in a different reference place and knowledge space. Most likely, the addict has confessed some of his or her behaviors, but left out some others. In direct relation to the dependent role, the partner's reactivity serves as some sense of self-protection. The destruction of the addict's and co-addict's world and relationship, as they have known these, means that things can never be the same again. Being sensitive to the individuals, the therapist can use this opportunity to tell them that sobriety and recovery offer a reconstruction period for each of them separately and as a couple. The therapist's careful interjection of stories of others in recovery—and the resultant sense of renewal after those experiences—can offer some light in what can seem total darkness.

The Couple's Tasks During Early Treatment

1. Recognize their powerlessness and the unmanageability of their situation.
2. Understand the importance of honesty in identifying the types of behavior participated in, but *not* the details.
3. Identify the unsuccessful efforts the addict and the co-addict have made to control their behavior.

4. Work on being aware of and beginning to reconnect to their emotions.
5. Further their understanding of addictive and co-addictive recovery by attending educational sessions and reading.
6. Attend 12-step meetings, including Recovering Couples Anonymous meetings, if available.
7. Pursue support and affirmation for the work they are doing from program people, family members, and treatment group members.

To understand the couple's focus in early treatment work and the therapist's enhancing presence, it is helpful to keep the treatment plan and the following tasks in mind.

The Therapist's Tasks in Early Treatment

1. Support the addict's and co-addict's honesty and courage in self-accountability.
2. Support the partners in identifying and becoming aware of their feelings.
3. Offer hope and ways to get sobriety and recovery actualized.
4. Supply or find community resources for the couple to get education about sexual addiction and co-addiction.
5. Encourage attendance in 12-step programs; assist in finding resources for this.
6. Help each family member to focus primarily on his or her own recovery, *not* on the other person's.
7. Listen to and recognize with them how painful this is for each person in his or her different ways to do this work.
8. Tell them empathetically what they have acknowledged in the joint sessions about their self-defeating behaviors.
9. Reference how difficult it is for the partner to begin to shift his or her focus from addict to self. This lets both know again that the treatment will be for themselves and that they should focus on self, not each other.
10. Recognize with addicts that their partners' shift will bring up some feelings and concerns, and they will need to address this in their treatment.

At our center, we ask the couple to attend a two-phase program that focuses on education. It requires homework assignments, which provide the opportunity to develop deeper realization of the origins and patterns of addictive and co-addictive behaviors. Phase II, which focuses on relapse prevention, is described here. The focus is to deepen understanding of the patterns of behavior and the beliefs driving these behaviors. At the same time, the couple and therapist identify areas for targeted treatment and for life-skills enhancement. Both partners attend these classes to learn and experience that there are others who are working for sobriety and how they are coping. It is also an occasion for therapists to educate partners on using a 12-step program to get support and learn life skills, both for themselves and to help them experience their lives differently. This period of re-education can break through the denial. Partners can also learn how sexual addiction might present itself differently—for example, when a husband acts out addictively and his preoccupation is with his wife.

In deference to being rigid, factual observations help to develop clear behavioral boundaries, particularly regarding each partner's own sexuality. This is particularly important, given the level of shame involved. These guidelines are also helpful with parents in relating to their children. This models behavior and stimulates thinking about what boundaries they are setting for their children to see, to hear, and to pattern their behavior on. Boundaries give guidelines and offer the safety to explore new ways of behaving within given limits, and everyone is clear what the boundaries are. The family needs to clearly establish boundaries for four areas of behavior: sexual, physical, emotional, and mental.

It is extremely important for the therapist to encourage and model methods of addressing difficult issues in a nonblaming, respectful way. The therapist's questions alone can trigger issues with family members, so it is important to continue to check out what each person is hearing and how they are reacting.

Each person needs affirmation that his or her needs, thoughts, and feelings are important and deserve attention. Therapists should reiterate that family members need to focus on themselves and on their own thoughts and behaviors. Continuing to tease out the enmeshment is another ongoing therapeutic probe. In later treatment phases, when the addict and co-addict have better clarity and groundedness in their own recovery, family members will explore the areas in the system that need deeper attention.

The Therapist's Task With Family Members in Ongoing Treatment

1. Assess where each family member is in his or her awareness of the addiction: how it is acted out.
2. Develop a relationship with each family member.
3. Gain an understanding of each person's relationship with the addict.
4. Develop insight into what role each person has in the family and how that individual may have been used or neglected in the acting-out cycle.
5. Clarify how each child is reacting behaviorally and emotionally.
6. Check out what feelings are triggered, especially fear and anger.
7. Encourage children to talk about these feelings (Crow & Earle, pp. 188, 190).
8. Remind the partner and children that they adapted to situations and behaviors to survive. Learn about their survival techniques.

9. Explore and respect each individual child's unique developmental stage, coping mechanisms, and place in the family.
10. Remember that much shock and grief exists at this stage.
11. Begin to teach about sexuality and boundaries and affirm boundary setting.

CONCLUSION

It is important to include family members in the process of assessing and treating sexual addiction. Intervention often follows the path of exploring the life-altering effects on the sexually dependent person and the necessity of including family members if there is to be an opportunity for recovery for all. Sexual addiction directly affects family members, and each member has his or her own set of symptoms and behaviors that require treatment and recovery.

This proposed framework for organizing an assessment and early treatment approach is sensitive to the importance of including partners as soon as possible and to aid them in gaining understanding of their own dynamics in this system. Once the addict and co-addict have begun to identify their addictive thinking and behaviors, the therapist needs to include the children in this phase of early treatment. The goal is to begin to gain an understanding of how the disease affects each child. This is accomplished through developing insight into the depth of the effects of the addiction and how this has manifested itself in the child's place in the addictive family system.

In the sexually addicted family system, the cumulative effect of the two very different standards of behavior being exposed and acted on have many repercussions for everyone impacted by this often baffling compulsion. This process takes patience, skill, and sensitivity to peel away the denial, fear, shame, and resistance to giving up a cultivated way of thinking and behaving that has affected all family members. This is an ongoing process and one that is an investment in each family member's future health.

NOTE

Special gratitude to Martha Turner, MD, creator of the STAR Program in Bryn Mawr, PA, for her inspiration, mentoring, and outstanding dedication to treatment in this field. Appreciation to Jeffrey Mercer for his valuable assistance and feedback.

REFERENCES

American Psychiatric Association. (1994). *Diagnostic and statistical manual of mental disorders* (4th ed.). Washington, DC: Author.
Carnes, P. (1983). *Out of the shadows: Understanding sexual addiction.* New York: Bantam.

Carnes, P. (1989). *Contrary to love: Helping the sexual addict*. Minneapolis, MN: Compcare.

Carnes, P. (1991). *Don't call it love: Recovery from sexual addiction*. New York: Bantam.

Carnes, P. (1993). *A gentle path through the twelve steps*. Center City, MN: Hazelden Educational Materials.

Crow, G., & Earle, R. (1989). *Lonely all the time*. New York: Pocket.

Cruise, J., & Cruise, R. L. (1989). *Children in recovery* (1st ed.). New York: W. W. Norton.

De Busk, D., & Weiss, D. (1993). *Women who love sex addicts*. Fort Worth, TX: Discovery.

Gorski, T. (1989). *Passages through recovery*. San Francisco: Hazelden.

Irons, R., & Schneider, J. (1996). Differential diagnosis of addictive sexual disorders using the *DSM-IV*. *Sexual Addiction and Compulsivity: Journal of Treatment and Prevention, 3*, 7–21.

Laaser, M. (1992). *The secret sin*. Grand Rapids, MI: Zondervan.

Salmon, R. (1995). Therapist's guide to 12 step meetings for sexual dependencies. *Sexual Addiction & Compulsivity: The Journal of Treatment and Prevention, 1*, 3.

Schneider, J. (1988). *Back from betrayal*. Center City, MN: Hazelden Educational Materials.

Treatment and Therapy

CHAPTER 5

Shame Reduction, Affect Regulation, and Sexual Boundary Development

Essential Building Blocks in Sexual Addiction Treatment

KENNETH M. ADAMS
DONALD W. ROBINSON

Sexual addiction can best be conceptualized as an intimacy disorder (Schwartz & Masters, 1994) manifested as a compulsive cycle of preoccupation, ritualization, sexual behavior (or anorexia—excessive control over sexual behavior), and despair (Carnes, 1983). Central to the disorder is the inability of the individual to adequately bond and attach in intimate relationships. The origin of the disorder is rooted in early developmental attachment failure with primary caregivers (Schwartz, 1996: Carnes, 1983, 1991). Sexual addiction becomes a way to compensate for this early attachment failure. The ultimate treatment goal for sex addicts is mastering the experience of bonding and attaching in enduring and trusting intimate connections with others. The treatment challenge for clinicians is to find specific strategies to assist these individuals to reach this objective.

Three key barriers prevent addicts from breaking the compulsive cycle and establishing successful intimacy: shame, affect dysregulation, and an inability to maintain adequate sexual boundaries. Shame is a feeling that alienates the self from the self and others (Kaufman, 1980); see figure 5.1. It is experienced as self-contempt, feeling inadequate, and painful disapproval of the self. It originates from inadequate early developmental caretaking and is reproduced with painful intensity by the compulsive cycle of sexual addiction. Many feelings, self-appraisals, and life experiences are filtered through the lens of shame, further alienating the individual from herself or himself and others. Intimate connections are lost, and further reliance on the addiction occurs. Strategies to reduce shame and alter the subsequent belief system are paramount to sexual addiction treatment.

The ability to successfully master affective states—that is, feelings, moods, impulses, cravings—to achieve intimacy and other successful life experiences can be traced to *good enough* parenting (Winnicott, 1965). When there is a failure in early developmental caretaking, the child is unable to soothe feelings of loneliness, sadness, anger, and fear. Strong affects that the individual is unable to regulate may be linked to rituals around the natural function of sexuality (Schwartz, 1996). Here, pleasure and orgasm are used to soothe and comfort states of internal distress. Sexual feelings merge with shame, sadness, anger, and loneliness, which then become triggers for the addictive cycle. The addiction causes further shame and affect dysregulation. In turn, the individual uses the addictive system again to soothe and reproduces a new layer of shame and dysregulation. Strategies to assist individuals in finding alternate ways to discharge painful feelings and regulate affect are crucial to treatment.

One of the hallmarks of sexual addiction is the sexualizing of feelings and experiences that are not meant to be sexual (Adams, 1996). The addict presents with an absence or a poor set of clearly defined sexual boundaries. Without

FIGURE 5.1. A Depiction of Shame by a Sexually Addicted Client

boundaries, the sexually addictive system progresses, thereby causing more shame and affect dysregulation. Central to the addiction model of treatment is the development of sexual boundaries that are designed to preempt the addictive cycle (Carnes, 1989). By disrupting the early phases of the addiction, sexual boundaries become a safeguard against engaging in sexually compulsive behaviors. Treatment requires specific boundaries unique to the rituals each addict uses to heighten the early arousal phases of the addiction. Clinicians will benefit from an understanding of the need for delineating specific sexual boundaries for their clients.

Shame, affect regulation, and sexual boundary development are essential building blocks to successful treatment of sexual addiction. Strategies for achieving necessary objectives in these areas will be outlined.

SHAME REDUCTION

In order to assist the sex addict to reduce shame, the clinician will need to

1. Understand the origin of the shame and its function in the addictive system;
2. Differentiate between shame and guilt;
3. Identify the defenses utilized to deny the painful feelings created by the shame;
4. Utilize specific shame reduction strategies at critical points in the treatment process; and
5. Change negative core beliefs that reinforce shame.

In conceptualizing a treatment program for a sexually addicted client, understanding the function of shame in the addictive cycle of preoccupation, ritual, compulsive sexual behavior, and despair (Carnes, 1983) is a crucial first step. Shame and guilt make up the feelings of despair and, when overwhelmed by these emotions, the addict will use the compulsive behavior again until the cycle is intervened on and alternative coping strategies are established. Treatment designed to reduce the shame associated with the cycle is necessary with this population.

In addition, shame is part of the core identity of sex addicts and affects how they view their needs, feelings, and sexuality. Shame has become merged with arousal in the template or love map (Mooney, 1986) of the individual during critical developmental periods. The addict seeks sexual experiences that are shamed-based and unique to his or her trauma history. Here, the addiction can be conceptualized as a metaphor for the unconscious trauma (Adams, 1996). Treatment strategies must also include shame reduction that is associated with the original trauma in the addict's life.

Differentiating between guilt and shame is important in assessing an addict's shame core and its role in the addiction. A common clinical error is the assumption that the addict's shame is primarily guilt from an overly repressive, moralistic, and punitive superego (or governing self), and that the addict should let go of the guilt and become sexually set free. Here, it is assumed that the guilt will reduce and eliminate the need for a compulsive or perverse compensation. This does not work with sex addicts. In fact, it may free the addict to do more of what he is driven to do, thereby increasing his sense of shame and engulfing him further in the addictive cycle.

Shame, not guilt, is what drives the addictive system. Although guilt ("I have done bad things") is present, shame ("I am bad, unworthy") is the primary feeling the addict is trying to medicate, rework, compensate for, or any combination of these. The arousal associated with the preoccupation and ritual phases of the addiction provide the escape the addict is searching for. During the "high," shame is not felt. In fact, omnipotence, grandiosity, and a false sense of esteem rise up and cover the painful experience of shame. However, once the cycle is complete, the individual has intensified his feeling of shame ("See, I really am a bad, unworthy person") and falls into more despair. Once again, the addictive system is returned to, in an attempt to escape and rework the painful self-appraisals. The addictive system is strengthened, not reduced.

Defenses Against Shame

Shame is painful and causes individuals to deny its presence to self and others. Consequently, addicts frequently will not admit their feelings of shame or the behavior that caused the shame. Clinicians will need to provide a caring framework and relationship that will allow the addict to understand, expose, process, and reduce shame. One of the challenges for clinicians is that the addict will not always be forthcoming with admitting, describing, and revealing the addictive behaviors that produced the shame. If addicts are not forthcoming with an admission, clinicians must be able to read the defensive structure in order to determine if the addict is in the addictive cycle.

Kaufman (1980) identified six defenses against shame. These may be markers of an addictive cycle:

1. **Rage**—When ashamed, the addict may rage out against those around him in an effort to insulate the self against exposure and pain by transferring the shame onto others. It functions to keep others away so no one will suspect or question addicts' behaviors. It also allows addicts to be enraged at others, rather than noticing their own feelings of shame. A spouse or family member may complain about the raging. Periodic couple's or family sessions may be helpful. When clinicians pick up rage, underlying shame should be a consideration.

2. **Contempt**—Contempt for others may be an attempt by addicts to bolster their feelings of low self-worth and self-contempt, which are caused by the burden of shame. In viewing others contemptuously, they no longer feel their own shame. This can be directed at a spouse, child, or another person close to the addict. It may also include groups of individuals differentiated by race, sexual orientation, or gender.

3. **Striving for power**—Addicts may attempt to compensate for a sense of feeling defective by gaining power over others. This allows them to remain in control over others in interpersonal situations and to prevent access to the inner, secret world of sex addiction and shame. This can be seen with those addicts who exploit and violate boundaries of trust that are inherent in a relationship. Examples include clergy, health-care professionals, attorneys, or supervisor/supervisee relationships.

4. **Striving for perfection**—After periods of acting out, shame follows. The addict may then become preoccupied with perfection to make up for a sense of not being worthy. Overmoralizing, religious preoccupation, or overcontrol regarding body functions, such as eating or exercise, may be a manifestation of this defense. The addict hopes to present an image to others of being perfect so no one suspects the hidden shame and out-of-control sexual behavior.

5. **The transfer of blame**—This is a frequently used strategy by addicts who are confronted with their behavior—for example, "If you would have been a better lover, then maybe I wouldn't have had to have an affair." Here, the addict transfers the shame by blaming another in an attempt to disarm the confrontation, rationalize the behavior, and avoid feeling the shame and guilt.

6. **Internal withdrawal**—Addicts may withdraw and live inside themselves in an attempt not to feel the pain of the shame that would emerge in interactions with others. They appear distant and preoccupied. Withdrawal allows them to insulate themselves from others so as not to feel responsible and ashamed.

When a clinician is confronted with a significant indicator of any of these defenses with a sex addict, relapse into the sex addiction cycle should be considered. Gentle probing such as (therapist), " Sometimes people feel ashamed about things they have done and can't see any way out of feeling bad. They try hard to hide it from others, when in fact, as difficult as it is, it is in talking about it that the release from shame happens. What experiences have you had recently that may have left you feeling ashamed or bad about yourself?"

From here, the clinician can begin to elicit more information, explore the meaning and origin of the shame and behavior, provide a framework of understanding about addiction and shame cycles, and then assist in reducing the shame.

Shame-Reduction Strategies

One of the first interventions for clinicians is to assist the addict in disrupting the addictive cycle. The following are shame-reduction strategies:

1. **Establish rapport**—Universal to all treatment, rapport is particularly important with sex addicts. They must feel safe that they will not be judged. Work to establish an understanding framework. Help them to see that they are not their behavior.

2. **Education and support**—Educate the client during sessions about shame, its role in the addiction, defenses against it, and risks and outcomes if it is not dealt with. Participation in a support group such as Sex Addicts Anonymous (Parker & Guest, 1999) allows the addict to expose shameful events in an accepting atmosphere, along with others struggling with the same problem. This allows for the reduction of shame, eliminates the double-life phenomenon, and increases responsibility and healthy guilt. These are necessary experiences for the addict to successfully recover.

3. **Define powerlessness**—Help them to understand the meaning of being powerless over their compulsive sexual behavior. This will help disrupt the faulty strategy of trying to "control" the forbidden impulses. Teach that control is part of control–release cycles that underlie shame-based compulsive behaviors (Fossum & Mason, 1986). Here, they begin to understand that control is part of the addictive cycle, not evidence of the ability to keep sexual boundaries.

4. **First step inventory**—The first step of the 12-step program for sex addicts is "We admitted we were powerless over our compulsive sexual behavior and our lives had become unmanageable." Have them write out a first step inventory of their sexual history by listing incidents of loss of control, consequences or potential consequences of those behaviors, and feelings about the incidents. Using a timeline format, the addict can experience more fully the breadth of the addiction and its consequences. A timeline exercise begins with a line drawn across a sheet of paper and marking the first experience of the addiction to the last, with all significant episodes in between, that reflect powerlessness and unmanageability. This will assist them in seeing that control hasn't worked and that they have an addiction. Although grief, sadness, and loss will emerge, shame will be reduced.

5. **Face feelings**—Facing shame means facing feelings (Fossum & Mason, 1986). Underneath the painful feeling of shame are feelings of inadequacy, unworthiness, mistrust, loneliness, sadness, and anger. Help them develop ways to cope (affect-regulation strategies) with the feelings. An increased sense of mastery will follow, and feelings of adequacy and worthiness will heighten. Simple strategies like having clients breathe into their bodies, feel the feeling,

and report the feelings will assist them in developing awareness. Dayton (2000) has outlined four steps in assisting shame-based clients to unravel feelings: feel the fullness of the emotion, label it, explore its meaning and function within the self, and choose whether or not to communicate the inner state with another person.

6. **Deal with the guilt**—As the addict begins to separate shame from guilt, it becomes time to use the guilt to guide making amends toward others. In taking responsibility, the individual develops empathy for others and gains a sense of *healthy* shame. Although evoking a sense of sadness and loss, amends making gives addicts important self-respect regarding behaviors that once left them feeling ashamed of themselves. The amends steps (Steps 8 and 9) of the 12-step program are useful here. See *A Gentle Path Through the 12-Steps* (Carnes, 1993) for further discussion on amends making.

Shame reduces its grip when exposed in an understanding context made possible by feeling the emotion of shame and other painful emotions related to the sexual addiction cycle: loneliness, sadness, and guilt. It is important that the emotions are felt *fully*, not just intellectualized. Without feeling and processing the painful emotions, the addict will seek to escape again through the addiction. Only by sharing the shame in a supportive and understanding context, such as a therapist's office and a 12-step support group, will the shame begin to lessen and provide the relief the addict needs. The sharing has the additional benefit of creating bridges of attachment to the part of the self the addict has felt contempt for or suppressed from awareness. In time, feelings related to the original childhood trauma begin to emerge.

Trauma Shame

Shame drives the addictive cycle and, at the same time, is added to by the addictive behavior. As previously discussed, reducing shame related to the addictive behavior is crucial to arresting the addiction. However, this is insufficient for long-term freedom from the addiction. Reduction of trauma-based shame is also necessary.

Shame caused by early childhood trauma through neglect, abuse, abandonment, or enmeshment becomes rooted in identity formation. Children blame themselves for failures by their caretakers. The fact that someone has failed them is assimilated as their own personal inadequacy, which is reactivated in emotionally vulnerable and dependent states. Subsequent self-appraisals regarding needs, feelings, and desires are now shame-based. Here, the self is in contempt of the self (see figure 5.1). The addiction becomes an attempt to compensate for this failure and to hide, from the self and others, the pain of this core shame.

This core shame needs to be felt and processed through, new beliefs about the self and others created, and intimacy skills developed. The following are guidelines to assist this process:

1. **Group therapy**—Group therapy allows for more complete healing of core shame than individual treatment alone. The addict hides the shame from others. A group evokes the painful feelings and memories associated with the shame. A safe and supportive environment allows for letting go of the shame and a reorganization of the perceptions that have held the shame in place. Permission to feel, to have needs, and to depend on others becomes a gateway to freedom from the shame. Expressive or experiential techniques like psychodrama (Dayton, 2000) are useful in assisting the client to feel and process feelings, rather than rationalize them. Understanding alone is not sufficient to reduce shame. It is paramount for the clinician to guard against the tendency of the client to "talk about" the shame as evidence of healing. It must be felt and reprocessed in order to reduce its presence in shaping perceptions and experiences. Shame is removed from the self, and the individual begins to feel fewer urges to act out a shameful, sexually addictive pattern.

2. **Expressive techniques**—Group therapy is not always available, so expressive techniques during individual treatment become a vehicle to assist the client in exposing the emotion of shame. Art therapy, which can also be used in group therapy, is an excellent way to expose the shame (Wilson, 2000). Figure 5.1 is an outcome of an art therapy session in which the client was asked to draw his shame. More discussion of this case will follow. Gestalt (Friedman, 1999) and EMDR (Shapiro, 1989) are other methods that can assist in helping the client expose and reduce shame and rework self-defeating beliefs.

3. **Change negative core beliefs**—Addicts with painful shame cores of identity have negative beliefs that reflect the original trauma—for example, people can't be trusted, I can only depend on myself, I am basically a bad and unlovable person, and sex is my most important need (Carnes, 1983). These beliefs impair adult functioning and contribute to dysfunctional patterns of living that create an increase in the dependency on the addiction and reinforce the core shame. Introducing new, positive beliefs following the discharge and processing of feelings allows a different view of self and others to be assimilated. If the original sources of pain are not first felt and processed, cognitive techniques designed to alter beliefs have little lasting effects. Without the addict's feeling the emotions fully, the attempt to change beliefs will amount only to the rationalization and intellectualization of the shame. The addictive cycle will eventually be leaned on again.

Shame and other painful emotions are difficult for the addict to regulate without the addictive cycle. Once the addiction is arrested, and underlying feelings and memories surface, the addict will need assistance in developing ways to regulate and respond to his internal world.

AFFECT REGULATION

There are four major areas of consideration in the development of affect regulation as a means of assisting the recovering sex addict to develop and maintain intimacy:

1. Understanding the meaning of affect relative to other internal sensory states;
2. Understanding the significance of early developmental attachment failure on affect regulation and dysregulation;
3. Understanding the role of affect dysregulation in intimacy disorder and sexual addiction; and
4. Knowing the therapeutic implications of affect regulation and the process of establishing and maintaining healthy intimacy.

The term *affect regulation* is gaining increased recognition and use. However, the word *affect* is often used interchangeably with other words, such as *emotion* and *feeling*. It is important for both the therapist and the client to differentiate between the meanings of these words, as they are so closely associated and often used in the same context. The establishment and maintenance of sexual sobriety call for knowledge and proficiency in distinguishing between these internal states. The ability to regulate affect becomes pivotal to the recovery process. Shame reduction and boundary setting, both key components of any recovery program, depend on the ability to recognize, identify, and process strong emotional experiences.

In order to understand more completely the significance of affect regulation, researchers (Batson, Shaw, & Oleson, 1992; Bradley, 2000; Goodman, 1999; Nuttall, 2000; Schwarz & Clore, 1988) have attempted to distinguish between these concepts either based on how they are formed within a particular individual or through their relative function for the individual. The importance of affect is apparent when we consider that affect is responsible for awareness of internal states, as it focuses attention on the stimulus that is provoking it. It is also affect that impels one into action in response to the awareness of the affective state. It is precisely the ability to differentiate, and respond appropriately to, internal states that enhances the ability to develop a repertoire of behaviors necessary to relate to one's environment.

Nathanson (1992) provides a clear delineation of affect in terms of how it originates within an individual and how it may be experienced in terms of its intensity. For example, affect describes innate responses to stimuli, which are instinctive. Feelings, however, describe the subjective experience of affect states. In this sense, feelings provide conscious representation and awareness of affective states. Emotion is described as the memories of subsequent experiences with particular affective states. It is the recollection of past episodes involving distinct affect that provides the intensity experienced as emotion, whether strong or weak. Nathanson (1992) summarizes the distinction between these three terms as *affect* is biology, *feeling* is psychology, and *emotion* is biography.

A practical and mutually understood categorization of these terms, like the one just presented, makes possible the recognition and description of affect and other sensory states, which may be central to the content of the therapeutic intervention. For the client, who may have been previously unaware of all but the most extreme feelings, the opportunity to develop a greater awareness of his or her internal realities and the ability to express these is increased. This can prove to be an important first step in reversing the damage done to the ability to regulate affect through the prolonged use of sexual behavior to manage feelings.

Van der Kolk and Fisler (1994) stress the significance of the ability to regulate internal states as being central to self-definition and one's attitude toward one's surroundings. Without a clearly defined sense of themselves, the newly recovering sex addicts experience difficulty in developing patterns of adaptability to situational, environmental, or event-driven stimuli. A maladaptive strategy, like sex addiction, helps addicts to discharge or escape from troublesome feelings. Although unrelated to the stimulus, it becomes the primary modality for addressing emotions. The use of addiction gives rise to a different set of problems that must be managed. It ultimately creates other troublesome affects that may then reactivate the addictive process. The solution has become the problem.

The experience of abstinence from behaviors associated with sexual addiction ("bottom-line" behaviors) renders the recovering sex addict to being overwhelmed by feelings that had previously been avoided through sexual behavior. Abstinence alone is insufficient to manage strong emotional arousal because of changes to brain chemistry, which have been reinforced by the repetitive use of sexual behavior and which create urges to engage in those behaviors long after a particular behavior has stopped. Over the course of the addiction, the addict does not succeed in developing the ability to identify, differentiate, and express emotion. The therapist, who is able to bridge the gap for the client between feeling and acting, helps the client tremendously by promoting the development of strategies to address strong affective arousal. Helping the client to understand the impact of early attachment experiences and affect regulation can enhance this process.

Affect Regulation and Attachment

Disrupted attachment in early childhood affects children's (and eventually adults') ability to regulate affect. There is a causal relationship between the attachment patterns experienced in childhood and the attachment styles of adults. The capacity to function in healthy intimate relationships is directly related to the expectations and beliefs about oneself and others. These internal working models are created during early childhood and remain relatively constant throughout life (Bowlby, 1979).

A major consideration for the therapist treating a client in the early stages of recovery from sexual addiction is examining attachment patterns. Ainsworth, Behar, Waters, and Walls (1978) identified patterns of attachment as secure or anxious. Main and Hesse (1990) later introduced another category, which they called disorganized-disoriented attachment. The relative importance of these patterns of attachment comes from the information they hold on the individual's ability to regulate strong emotion when faced with an adverse situation. In the case of anxious attachment patterns, there is an inability of the child to tolerate stressful or discomforting situations. The child either resists or avoids being comforted or soothed. Characteristics of the disorganized-disoriented attachment pattern are an inconsistent reaction to stress distinguished by confusion and an inconsistent pattern of relating to attempts to being soothed or comforted.

Linehan and Heard (1994), in their discussion of the environmental factors that they called invalidating environments, proposes a set of conditions and interactions that likely distort development and lead to maladaptive strategies to self-regulate. A summary of these factors are presented here:

- Caregivers respond erratically and inappropriately to a child's private experiences.
- Caregivers respond in extremes—that is, either overrespond or underrespond to emotional distress.
- Insensitivity, unresponsiveness, or punitive reactions occur after children's communication of thoughts, feelings, or preferences.
- Strong emphasis is placed on the control of emotional expressiveness (especially of negative emotion).
- There is trivialization of painful emotional experiences, which are also then attributed to personal flaws in the individual—in this case, the child.
- The family system is restrictive and often dismissing to the demands placed upon it by its members.
- The family system discriminates on the basis of arbitrary characteristics.
- Punishment may be used to control behavior, ranging from criticism to sexual, physical, or emotional abuse.
- Displays of extreme inhibition or disinhibition of behavior occur.

These factors are instrumental for the clinician to understand attachment failure and dysregulated affect as they contribute to the ability to accurately determine the cause of painful emotions, strongly held beliefs, or actions taken in response to either of these.

The ability to master the tasks and the ensuing emotional conflicts inherent in successive stages of development is impacted by the attachment patterns and relational styles that have been present during the progression of development. Atwool (1997), in summarizing childhood attachment irregularities, writes:

> Where a child has never experienced secure attachment, their ability to trust is severely limited. Past experience is likely to mean that they are wary of adults and may expect the worst . . . they may not have internalized any of the normal rules that govern daily existence. They are likely to rely on external guidelines but their cooperation with these is by no means guaranteed.

Over the course of development and without an internal working model developed from positive interactions with a healthy caregiver, children may resort to maladaptive coping responses, relying only on themselves for soothing and comfort. This creates a mistrust of others to meet their needs and predisposes individuals to depend solely on external action (Goodman, 1999) to cope with the ability to respond to emotional demands of the environment. Constricted emotion (Main & Hesse, 1990) and a tendency to either create or seek out experiences in their environment that are reminiscent of early invalidation contribute to the experience of futility and hopelessness relative to attempts at making meaningful connections with others. The pervasive nature of the strongly held beliefs compels these individuals to recreate previously experienced patterns of attachment. This helps to explain the destructive relational choices made throughout sex addiction.

Sex addicts have learned to either escape or avoid strong feelings through the addictive use of sexual behavior and, often, multiple addictions (Carnes, 1989). In the therapeutic setting it is possible to determine the pattern of acting out, based on the particular type of sexual addiction a person engages in. The Ten Types of Addicts, developed by Carnes (1991), is summarized here as a tool to explain the different types of sexual behavior:

1. Fantasy Sex—Sexually charged fantasies, relationships, and situations
2. Seductive Role Sex—Seduction of partners
3. Voyeuristic Sex—Visual arousal
4. Exhibitionistic Sex—Attracting attention to body or sexual body parts
5. Paying for Sex—Purchase of sexual services
6. Trading Sex—Selling or bartering sex for power
7. Intrusive Sex—Boundary violations without discovery
8. Anonymous Sex—High risk sex with unknown partners
9. Pain Exchange Sex—Being humiliated or hurt as part of sexual arousal, sadistic hurting or degrading another sexually, or both
10. Exploitive Sex—Exploitation of the vulnerable

By understanding attachment and its impact on affect, the therapist is presented with an opportunity to interpret significant events and conditions that have predictive value relative to the development of maladaptive coping strategies. The clinician is provided with valuable information regarding the client's early and subsequent attachment patterns, as well as about the way in which sexual behavior may have been used to regulate affect. This information can be derived from a number of sources, such as the client self-report, an intake/assessment instrument, a written First Step shared with the therapist, or a written sexual inventory, also shared with the therapist.

The inability to successfully moderate affective states increases vulnerability to being overwhelmed by affect, limiting the ability to respond in a coordinated, organized manner that is specific to the experience. The person experiencing affective stimuli is likely to respond in an undifferentiated manner, which includes a level of reactivity that exceeds the current circumstance. This vulnerability is further described by Gottman & Katz (1990) as

1. High sensitivity to emotional stimuli,
2. Intense response to emotional stimuli,
3. And slow return to baseline.

This is an accurate description of what is described in addiction literature as trigger events and demonstrates how compelling the use of ritualized addictive behavior is for the person experiencing such an event. In the case of the sexual addict, sex is used to manage the level of anxiety created by the affective experience.

Affect Dysregulation and Sexual Addiction

Diagnosis and assessment of sexual addiction will continue to occur long after the initial sessions have taken place. The therapist will need to have a discriminating sense as to the role of attachment in impairment of affect regulation. Several factors, when recognized, may be used to educate the client on the need to acknowledge the impact that affect regulation has on the perpetuation and maintenance of addiction. They include the following:

1. The inability to label and modulate arousal,
2. The inability to tolerate distress,
3. The inability to trust own experiences as valid interpretations of events,
4. The invalidation of one's own experiences, relying instead on external cues from the environment,
5. The over-simplification of ease related to solving life's problems, and
6. The inability to set realistic goals (Linehan & Heard, 1994).

Magai (1999) emphasized the connection between addictive and pre-addictive behaviors to help regulate affect. The use of addictive behavior allows for the distraction or the abbreviation of negative emotion. Escaping or diminishing the experience does not allow for familiarity of the situation precipitating the affective state or success at managing it. This may contribute to the development of fixed and ritualistic behaviors that consistently provide emotional relief and the release of tension.

Goodman (1999) proposes that addiction originates from impairment, in what he describes as the self-regulation system. The systems he describes consist of three primary functions:

1. *Affect regulation functions:* These include the ability to avoid becoming over-whelmed by strong affective states with the use of self-soothing, self-enlivening, and arousal-balancing skills.
2. *Self-care functions:* These involve an individual's ability to provide protection and nurturance to himself or herself. The ability to recognize high-risk or dangerous situations and to respond appropriately is a self-protective skill. The ability to recognize and articulate needs and to set priorities to meet them are a part of self-nurture.
3. *Self-governance functions:* These involve having internal beliefs, values, and standards that contribute to the experience of appropriate esteem and a cohesive and consistent sense of self.

Impairment to this system predisposes the individual to overreliance upon things external to the self to regulate the self. Bradshaw (1988) describes this phenomenon as "an outer reach for inner security." Addictive behavior provides security, as it relieves intense stress or anxiety, which become viewed as a threat to either real or imagined well-being. Addicts' reliance upon addictive behavior demonstrates a belief that they are able to exert control over the behavior and thus calm themselves. By its very nature, however, the addiction creates its own set of problems. To cope, the addict uses the addictive behavior again and creates a cycle of compulsion and despair.

A catalytic sexual event (Carnes, 1989) is associated with the development and perpetuation of sexual addiction. It becomes the unifying experience that alleviates the inner turmoil that is experienced as the inability to regulate strong affective states. The pleasure derived from engaging in sexual behavior is the additional benefit to the relief from painful experiences. The pleasure associated with the continued and escalating involvement with sexual behavior becomes the inducement to continue beyond the point that negative consequences are experienced.

Implications for Treatment

Development of treatment strategies to address sexual addiction must include skill building designed specifically to learn to identify and regulate emotion. In order to regulate emotion, the client must learn to experience and label specific affect states and to decrease the intensity of the triggering event or situation. The clinician must be able to communicate the clinical significance of this process as it relates to emotionally charged situations that reactivate symptoms of the sexual addiction or generate behaviors related to secondary disruptive behaviors.

Emotion regulation as used here means the ability to

1. Inhibit inappropriate behavior related to strong negative or positive affect,
2. Self-soothe any physiological arousal that the strong affect has induced,
3. Refocus attention, and
4. Organize oneself for coordinated action in the service of an external goal (Gottman & Katz, 1990).

There does not seem to be one therapeutic intervention that stands out significantly from others in terms of its efficacy in dealing with affect dysregulation. It has been suggested (Bradley, 2000) that most effective intervention strategies have the result of improving the ability to regulate affect. Psychodynamic, cognitive-behavioral, or experiential techniques appear to contribute to developing a client's ability to avoid being completely overwhelmed by affect. With respect to treatment of sexual addiction, research demonstrates that the most effective strategies involve a combination of individual, group, and 12-step recovery groups that are specific to sexual addiction (Swisher, 1995). The objectives for successful therapy have been described as

- Establishing a relationship of trust and empathy, which enables and facilitates the clients' ability to come to terms with their disturbing emotional issues;
- Promoting an understanding of the difference between emotion, feeling, and affect;
- Increasing awareness regarding impairments in attachment and bonding;
- Facilitating awareness regarding the relationship between disrupted bonding and the inability to develop strategies to regulate affect;
- Increasing skills helpful in the recognition, identification, and modulation of affect; and
- Increasing awareness of environmental, emotional, and situational stressors associated with dysregulated affect.

The important message is that recovery includes the development of skills that allow for increased effectiveness with regard to self-regulation. Sexual boundary development plays an important role in assisting clients to regulate affect, as well as to reduce shame.

SEXUAL BOUNDARY DEVELOPMENT

One of the key components for establishing a program of recovery from sexual addiction is the development of external, sexual boundaries. Here, a set of boundaries, when honored, keeps the addict from entering the ritual phase of the sexually addictive system. Thus, the compulsive phase of the system is less likely to be activated. Boundaries need to be clear, specific to the type of pattern, and as numerous as necessary to interrupt the system. Sharing and accountability with a therapist, a 12-step member, or both are also necessary. It is the ability to identify and maintain boundaries that promotes the awareness of self as consistent and congruent and allows the newly recovering person to set boundaries from a place of self-respect and integrity.

A mistaken belief is that abstinence is the equivalent of recovery. Clients who are not aware of the need to set appropriate boundaries may attempt to limit arousal or desire as evidence of recovery. Because of the shame and inability to regulate impulses to act out sexually, the newly recovering addict sees repressing sexuality as an attractive option. The reality, however, is that such action amounts to the use of deprivation as an attempt to exert control over the behaviors. Furthermore, although the addict may be successful in inhibiting impulses, sexual obsession and preoccupation will likely continue.

The fact that control had been previously unsuccessful during the active stage of the addiction may not be a part of the client's conscious awareness at this point in the recovery process. This strategy is largely unsuccessful because the deeper underlying issues related to the addiction are not addressed and remain unresolved. Further complicating this method of attempting sexual sobriety are the cycles of escalation and de-escalation that are a characteristic pattern of sex addiction. That is, periods of acting out sexually may be followed by periods of aversion to anything sexual, which further increases shame and the sense of hopelessness that had been alleviated previously through sexual behavior.

During periods of abstinence, and without a recovery plan that includes sexual boundaries, a false sense of security develops that may lead the client to engage in high-risk behaviors, believing that enough time has elapsed between acting-out episodes to prevent the reemergence of the addictive behaviors. This generally proves to be untrue. A lapse in abstinence occurs and eventually leads to a complete return of behaviors associated with the active addiction.

Boundary setting in recovery from sexual addiction is primarily an example of self-care and self-governance, which was described earlier. The relevance of boundary setting to good self-care and governance is found in recovering sex addicts' willingness to define themselves according to a newly developed set of values and beliefs that is internally oriented and structured.

Boundaries are described in *Promises of Grace: Recovery From Sex Addiction* (Sex Addicts Anonymous, 1992) as being: " . . . Established and set to warn us of the destructive effects of acting out and to prevent us from such destructiveness."

This example of a boundary suggests that self-care and self-governance functions are present in individuals as they engage in healthy self-protective and nurturing behaviors. It implies an internal shift away from external actions to provide internal comfort and the development of a belief system that is self-enhancing, instead of self-destructive. The importance of boundary setting as part of a program of sexual recovery is that it helps to addicts recognize high-risk situations that are connected to the use of sexual behavior as a means of regulating affect. The boundary itself is used as a cue to signal potential danger and to activate and guide appropriate action.

"Three Circles, Defining Sexual Boundaries in S.A.A." (1991) is a pamphlet that is useful in helping clients to develop and maintain sexual boundaries. It provides a context for identifying behaviors for abstinence, but also behaviors that may become part of the healthy expression of sexuality. Examples of behaviors and boundaries in the inner circle that will be abstained from are

- Voyeurism—Cruising places that were formerly frequented for acting out; owning binoculars
- Masturbation with pornography—Possessing pornographic materials; using any visual material for the purpose of sexual arousal
- Exploitive sex—Manipulation of a partner to engage in questionable behavior; coercive sexual behavior
- Solicitation—Cruising areas where prostitutes are; visiting strip clubs or peep shows
- Exhibitionism—Dressing provocatively; creating situations that allow others to view

Examples of "outer circle" behaviors, or behaviors that are not associated with the addiction, are

- Attending 12-step meetings
- Reading recovery-related material
- Keeping a journal
- Establishing open communication with a partner and other support persons
- Developing hobbies and participating in regular exercise programs, if appropriate

Behaviors included in the third, or middle, circle are those that are not or have not been a part of an addictive process, but that may be questionable. The purpose of the middle circle allows for continued revision of boundaries, which allows removal and implementation of boundaries whenever appropriate. It is the middle circle that represents the reality that recovery cannot be defined in black/white or extreme terms. It encourages the addict to respond to sexuality with integrity and appropriate control, while realizing and accepting that it is a dynamic and fluid experience.

Increased accountability is guaranteed when boundaries are part of a regular "check-in" with a therapist, 12-step recovery group, therapy group, or persons identified as part of a support network. Accountability is an important component to the recovery process. Addictive sexual patterns usually contain an absence of accountability, which allows participation in bottom-line behaviors without the threat of detection. Recovery plans that include boundaries around structure, disciplined living, and increased accountability promote the maintenance of long-term sexual sobriety and the development of intimacy-enhancing behaviors.

CASE EXAMPLE

Figure 5.1 is a depiction of shame drawn during an art therapy exercise by a 30-year-old client struggling since early childhood with an obsessive preoccupation with masturbation and fantasies of women's violence against him that were both erotic and shameful. When he entered treatment, he was masturbating 15 to 20 times per day and could only be sexual with a partner when he fantasized about violence against himself or encouraged his partner to participate in the fantasy. The drawing depicts his contempt for himself and self-loathing and the filter in which he assimilated most feelings and emotionally charged experiences.

He was unable to successfully bond with a woman and experienced break-ups as extremely painful, depressing, and riddled with a disproportionate amount of guilt and self-loathing. His preoccupation interfered with his work and he was unable to advance in his career. He was unable to soothe himself in times of distress of any type and turned exclusively to the addiction for comfort.

Family history revealed an emotionally violent, intrusive mother and a passive father. Little nurturing was available to the client, and attention was largely negative, critical, and punitive. The client witnessed open masturbation by the mother and the older sister in the home. The client, while living in the home, maintained a collection of pornography that was known to other family members. He was often shamed for the collection he kept.

Treatment focused initially on the development of sexual boundaries to reduce the compulsion and allow the client to experience feelings without the use of medication. Participation in a 12-step program and specific boundaries to reduce the likelihood of engaging in the compulsion were established. Alternative affect-regulation strategies were encouraged to help the client cope with the pain and shame of his addiction and family trauma. Group therapy was utilized to assist him in discharging painful affects from the past and to allow him to tolerate feelings in the present and stay away from using the addictive behavior to cope. His drawing was utilized in both group and individual sessions. He used the drawing to dialogue with the shame and begin to remove himself from the shame.

In time, he began to experience the shame as something that happened to him and not something that he was. As sexual sobriety became established (over 1 year of complete abstinence from masturbation), memories of childhood emotional and sexual trauma began to emerge. More affect discharge work was done to deal with the memories. Cognitive restructuring to enhance new beliefs was utilized. He also established a relationship with a woman that did not include his past fantasy material.

This client's story is an example of sexual addiction developing from a lack of adequate attachment and a way to cope with sexual and emotional trauma and the extreme loneliness that was incurred. However, as with all sexual addiction, the solution to the problem becomes its own problem. Treatment required addressing both the core shame and the shame resulting from the addiction for success to occur. Only after repeated intervention in both areas did sexual sobriety occur and the ability to form an attachment and soothe internal distress become possible.

CONCLUSIONS

Sexual addiction treatment presents clinicians with unique challenges. This disorder has multiple facets to its etiology and requires multiple interventions at critical points in the process. Facing and reducing shame; developing affect-regulation strategies to cope with feelings, impulses, and urges; and developing and maintaining sexual boundaries are key and necessary to successful treatment of sexual addiction. Intervention of both the addictive behavior and its causes is more likely to assure success than treatment of one area over the other. As a result, the ability to form successful attachments and assimilate feelings and life experiences through a filter of hope, love, and worthiness is greatly increased.

REFERENCES

Adams, K. M. (1996). Case study. *Sexual Addiction & Compulsivity: Journal of Treatment and Prevention, 3,* 273–281.

Ainsworth, M. D. S., Blehar, M. C., Waters, E., & Wall, S. (1978). *Patterns of attachment: A psychological study of the strange situation.* Hillsdale, NJ: Erlbaum.

Atwool, N. (1997). *Attachment as a context for development: Challenges and Issues.* Community and Family Services, University of Otago. [Online]. Available: http://www.otago.ac.nz/CIC/papers/Atwool.html.

Batson C. D., Shaw, L. L., & Oleson, K. C. (1992). Differentiating affect, mood, and emotion: Toward functionally based conceptual distinctions. In M. Clark (Ed.), *Review of personality & social psychology* (Vol. 13). Thousand Oaks, CA: Sage.

Bowlby, J. (1973). *Attachment and loss: Volume 2. Separation: Anxiety and anger.* New York: Basic.

Bowlby, J. (1979). *The making and breaking of affectional bonds.* New York: Routledge.

Bradley, S. J. (2000). *Affect regulation and the development of psychopathology.* New York: Guilford.

Bradshaw, J. (1998). *Healing the shame that binds you.* Deerfield Beach, FL: Health Communications.

Carnes, P. (1983). *Out of the shadows: Understanding sexual addiction.* Minneapolis, MN: CompCare.

Carnes, P. (1989). *Contrary to love: Helping the sexual addict.* Minneapolis, MN: CompCare.

Carnes, P. (1991). *Don't call it love: Recovery from sexual addiction.* Minneapolis, MN: CompCare.

Carnes, P. (1993). *A gentle path through the twelve steps.* Minneapolis, MN: CompCare.

Dayton, T. (2000). *Trauma and addiction: Ending the cycle of pain through emotional literacy.* Deerfield Beach, FL: Health Communications.

Fossum, M. A., & Mason, M. J. (1986). *Facing shame: Families in recovery.* New York: W. W. Norton.

Friedman, H. R. (1999). A gestalt approach to sexual compulsivity. *Sexual Addiction & Compulsivity: Journal of Treatment and Prevention, 6,* 63–75.

Goodman, A. (1999). *Sexual addiction: An integrated approach.* Madison, CT: International University Press.

Gottman, J. M., & Katz, L. F. (1990). Effects of marital discord on young children's peer interaction and health. *Developmental Psychology, 25,* 373-381

Kaufman, G. (1980). *Shame: The power of caring.* Cambridge, MA: Schenkman.

Linehan, M. M., & Heard, H. L. (1994). Dialectical behavior therapy: An integrative approach to the treatment of borderline personality disorder. *Journal of Psychotherapy Integration, 4,* 55–82.

Magai, C. (1999). Affect, imagery and attachment: Working models of interpersonal affect and the socialization of emotion. In J. Cassidy & P. Shavers (Eds.), *Handbook of attachment: Theory and research* (pp. 787–802). New York: Guilford.

Main, M., & Hesse, E. (1990). Parents' unresolved traumatic experiences are related to infant disorganized attachment status: Is frightened and/or frightening parental behavior the linking mechanism? In M. Greenberg, D. Cicchetti, & E. Cummings (Eds.), *Attachment in the preschool years: Theory research, and intervention* (pp. 161–182). Chicago: University of Chicago Press.

Mooney, J. (1986). *Love maps: Clinical concepts of sexual/erotic health and pathology, paraphilia and gender transposition in childhood, adolescence and maturity.* New York: Irving.

Nathanson, D. (1992). *Shame and pride: Affect sex and the birth of the self.* New York: W. W. Norton.

Nuttall, B. (2000). *Emotion, affect and feeling.* [Online]. Available: http:affectivetherapy.co.uk/news.htm.

Parker, J., & Guest, D. (1999). *Clinicians' guide to 12-step programs: How, when, and why to refer a client.* Westport, CT: Auburn House.

Sex Addicts Anonymous. (1992). *Promises of grace: Recovery from sexual addiction.* Minneapolis, MN. Unpublished manuscript.

Sex Addicts Anonymous. (1991). *Three circles: Defining sobriety in S.A.A.* Minneapolis, MN: SAA Literature.

Schwartz, M. F. (1996). Reenactments related to bonding and hypersexuality. *Sexual Addiction & Compulsivity: The Journal of Treatment & Prevention, 3,* 195–212.

Schwartz, M. F., & Masters, W. H. (1994). Integration of trauma-based, cognitive, behavioral, systemic, and addiction approaches for treatment of hypersexual pair-bonding disorder. *Sexual Addiction & Compulsivity: The Journal of Treatment and Prevention, 1,* 57–76.

Schwarz, N., & Clore, G. L. (1988). How do I feel about it? The informative function of affective states. In K. Fiedler & J. Forgas (Eds), *Affect, cognition and social behavior* (pp. 44–62). Lewiston, NY: C. J. Hogrefe.

Shapiro, F. (1989). Efficacy of the eye movement desensitization procedure in the treatment of traumatic memories. *Journal of Traumatic Stress, 2,* 199–223.

Swisher, S. (1995). Therapeutic interventions recommended for treatment of sexual addiction/compulsion. *Sexual Addiction and Compulsivity: The Journal of Treatment and Prevention, 1,* 31–39.

van der Kolk, B. A., & Fisler, R. E. (1994). Childhood abuse and neglect and loss of self-regulation. *Bulletin Menninger Clinic, 58*(2), 145–168.

Wilson, M. (2000). Creativity and shame reduction in sex addiction treatment. *Sexual Addiction and Compulsivity: Journal of Treatment and Prevention, 4,* 229–248.

Winnicott, D. (1965). *The maturational processes and the facilitating environment.* New York: International Universities Press.

CHAPTER 6

Manifestations of Damaged Development of the Human Affectional Systems and Developmentally Based Psychotherapies

MARK F. SCHWARTZ
STEPHEN SOUTHERN

Sexual compulsion is the end point of a series of developmental events that begin in early attachment difficulties with caretakers, subsequent overwhelming experiences the child is unable to assimilate, affect dysregulation, and impaired self-development and gender-related behavior, all which is then activated. This chapter will review the developmental psychopathology of sexual compulsive behavior, with suggestions for psychotherapeutic amelioration.

DEVELOPING HUMAN AFFECTIONAL SYSTEMS

The capacity for bonding with others is vital for human survival and well-being. Allan Schore (1994) emphasized the importance of the mother–child dyad in his review of the development of the brain and origin of self. He states

> The child's first relationship acts as a template and it molds the individual's capacities to enter into all emotional relationships. Development essentially represents a number of sequential mutually driven infant–caregiver processes that occur in a continuing dialectic between the maturing organism and the changing environment. It now appears that affect is what is actually transacted within the mother–infant dyad, and this highly efficient system of emotional communication is essentially nonverbal. (p. 7)

The mother's attunement to her child facilitates the experience-dependent maturation of the child's neurological structure, which directly influences the child's biochemical growth process, as well as dendritic and axonal development, in the first year of infancy. "Hard-wiring" of the brain hierarchically, from lower limbic emotional structure, through the mid-brain, and then cortical structures, occurs during this early, critical period (Maclean, 1962), so that genetic systems are either activated or inhibited by socio-emotional stimulation. Because 83% of the brain is differentiated postnatally (Dobbing & Sands, 1973), the human infant is maximally dependent upon its caretakers. If the child's need for attention, soothing, stimulation, affection, touch, discipline, validation, information, and so on goes unmet, or is met with feedback that is absent, punishing, frustrating, invalidating, or rejecting, the consequences can be structurally written into the developing personality. Children may become emotionally constricted (Main & Solomon, 1995), turning into themselves and disconnecting from others, or emotionally dysregulated, failing to learn to utilize others to soothe or comfort themselves. These adaptations, in turn, increase children's vulnerability to psychopathology. Children then actively seek familiar, consistent environmental interaction, thereby recreating and reenacting familiar early rejections and frustrations in new formats, with peers and in school (Stroufe, 1988), further cementing their original isolation. Some individuals, however, seem to be "saved" by novel experiences with a loving caretaker, teacher, friend, or therapist. These experiences prove transformative, influencing them to compensate with new cortical structures and learn relatively healthy attachments. Indeed, the purpose of psychotherapy is fundamentally to facilitate these transformations. Because, as Schore (1994) emphasized, affect—not cognition—is the means of exchange in relationships, the client will not remember events; rather, emotions will be the primary form of communication.

More than four decades ago, Harry Harlow (cf. Harlow & Harlow, 1962, 1963, 1965) began a systematic investigation of the development and differentiation of affectional systems of rhesus monkeys. Implicitly, he understood that due to the increased size of primates' cerebral cortex, in comparison to that of lower mammals, the gonadal hormones would exert less control on mating behavior. This separation of mating from the menstrual cycle allows for mediation by higher-level systems, involving more complex factors such as attractiveness, solicitousness, courtship, and mating behaviors. Behaviors that may lead to mating were labeled "proceptive" by Frank Beach (1977), as distinguished from the acceptive and conceptive phases of the affectional systems. This distinction has been useful across species for comparative psychology. Proception, then, is behavior leading up to acceptive or copulatory behavior, whereas conception denotes the later phase, involving pregnancy and parental–infant behavior.

Many acceptive and conceptive difficulties actually are proceptive in nature. In the case of a monkey with experimentally induced developmental deprivation, the animal can copulate, but approaching a mate is associated with fear and ambivalence (Schwartz & Becklin, 1975). In the male monkey, this inhibition translates behaviorally into impulsive behavior, typically expressed by attacking mates violently. The female deprived similarly will bite her own body and cower. This model of differential effects of deprivation on male and female brains also holds true for humans (Stroufe, 1988). Stroufe found that avoidant boys were more likely to bully, lie, cheat, destroy things, brag, act cruelly, disrupt class, swear, tease, threaten, argue, and throw temper tantrums, whereas girls became depressed and blamed themselves. Early deprivation in both monkeys and humans (Putnam, 1997) is associated with definable biochemical changes in the brain and body that involve regulation of adrenal calechlamine, dopamine, and serotonin, as well as the opiate system, which seems to mediate and exacerbate dysfunctional responsiveness (cf. van der Kolk, 1989).

The study of affectional systems, particularly proceptive disorders of humans, remains theoretically underdeveloped. It has only been within the last 30 years, with John Bowlby's influence upon the field of developmental psychology, that there has been an attempt to study systematically actual biographical events that predictably damage the affectional systems (Bowlby, 1969, 1973, 1980). Several generalizations can be generated from Bowlby's model of attachment:

1. If the individual has confidence that the attachment figure will be available, he or she will be less prone to chronic fear;
2. Confidence in the availability, or lack of, the attachment figure is built up slowly during the early years and these expectations persist; and
3. Expectation of accessibility and responsiveness of the attachment figure is an accurate reflection of actual experience.

These propositions, which simply implied that biographical input is related to developmental output, were so radical that Bowlby was ostracized by mainstream psychiatry. Now, however, these principles form a bedrock of developmentally based psychotherapy of the affectional systems. Proceptive bonding disorders are probabilistically related to specific early insults to the differentiating early attachment systems. Conceptual confusion has also resulted from a mislabeling of many bonding disorders as "sexual disorders."

Many cases of psychogenic impotence, desire impairment, or arousal disorders are due to disturbances in the capacity for intimacy and closeness. Thus, medical interventions such as Viagra are sometimes ill-advised. What is needed is a taxonomy of manifestations of intimacy disorders that are functions of childhood abuse, neglect, or the misattunement of caretakers. In addition, paraphiliac (meaning "besides-loves," in Latin) and other sexually compulsive disorders have proceptive, acceptive, and conceptive aspects to both their etiology and their course. For this reason, focusing on symptom change techniques in psychotherapy, such as relapse prevention, abstinence, arousal reconditioning, and social and empathy skills training, is necessary, but rarely sufficient. Successful treatment ultimately relies upon amelioration of the underlying attachment disorder and manifestations on adult intimacy.

VANDALIZED LOVE MAPS

John Money (1986) defined a love map as a "Personalized, developmental representation or template in the mind and in the brain that depicts the idealized lover and the idealized program of sexuoerotic activity with the lover as projected in imagery and ideation or actually engaged with that lover" (p. 10).

Money has pioneered the study of structural and developmental contributions to the affectional systems. Like Bowlby, he believed that love maps can become "vandalized" by a variety of biographical events occurring between the infant and the caretaker in the first 5 years of life. During this critical period of brain differentiation, the child is programmed to establish gender identity, genital sexuality, and attachment to caregivers. Events that block the differentiation and development of these systems can alter the love map. The developing love map would include proceptive events, such as the range of partner characteristics that arouses the body's response to touch or other contact with an attractive partner; the responsiveness of the genitals; and the sense of self as attractive and worthy, which obviously influences the perception of other as pursuable. Proception is influenced by a variety of emotions, such as illicitness, conquest, fear, intimidation, love, and challenge. The activation of a variety of proceptive templates from childhood is related to themes such as "saving a partner" or "getting back at someone who injured." Some theorists assert that pathology in the development of the affectional system becomes delayed, fixated, or regressed, whereas others suggest that deviant development continues, but along a different, distinct, or complex route (cf. Calverely, 1990; Fischer & Bidell, 1997). Thus, the love map of a child molester may be "fixated" and require "unblocking," or, alternatively, it may have differentiated along a distinct alternative pathway, suggesting that a new pattern of attachment needs to be "carved" or structurally developed in the brain.

Resiliency, or the capacity to rebound, can be determined within the total context of developmental influences. If children believe that they are bad, defective, or damaged and attribute (or misattribute) the source of their "badness" to their gender or genital sexuality, disorders may emerge. For example, "Mommy drinks because she doesn't like me because I'm a boy" or "Daddy molests me because I have a vagina" could contribute to gender dysphoria or sexual desire disorder (hypo- or hypersexuality). Similarly, if a parent has unresolved rage related to his or her gender or shame related to sexuality (e.g., "I hate men," "Sex is dirty"), the child can absorb the parent's affect and be similarly affected. The symptom becomes the recapitulation of the "vandalized love map" and often serves as a clue to developmental events of the child's perceptions and misperceptions of biographical experiences, which deleteriously impacted the differentiating affectional systems. When the therapist is attuned to strong emotions of grief or rage that are manifested by the adult client in psychotherapy, these emotions become the window into the developmental disturbance.

ATTACHMENT AND SELF SYSTEMS

Within the developmental model of affectional systems, critical capacities must be assimilated, or symptoms may emerge. These include affect regulation, social skills, perceived efficacy in attempting to negotiate social relationships, empathy and compassion for others, and capacity for accurate attunement regarding cues from others. These structural capacities set the stage upon which psychological drama unfolds (Greenspan, 1977), and these are the targets of developmentally based psychotherapies. Child abuse and neglect are common factors in the histories of individuals who manifest hypo- or hypersexuality. It is critical to dissect structural deficits that occur with abuse and neglect.

At the core of one's capacity to bond is self-empathy and the capacity for self-care. In the absence of alternative validating caretakers, the developmentally disturbed individual does not internalize a caring relationship with self. A child who is rejected or abandoned tends to develop negative core schemas or beliefs about the self. Accompanying modes of processing and organizing information (including affects) unfold in such a way that these beliefs become self-perpetuating. These modes ultimately organize an individual's range and type of interactions, constraining possibilities for new learning with respect to intimacy.

The self comes to exist in the context of others, within an aggregation of experiences of the self in relationship. Invariant aspects of the self and others in relationship are abstracted into what Bowlby (1969) called "internal representational models." New experiences are then absorbed into earlier representations, creating and maintaining an individual who is distinct from others.

The individual also creates self-functions, which are tools to negotiate interactions with others, manage the intensity of the experience, and balance inner and outer experiences. Self-functions navigate the balance between old and new experiences by moderating intense feelings. Availability of self-soothing and self-efficacy determines behavioral manifestations of balancing degrees of closeness and distance. When this balance is dysfunctional, rather than adaptive, intimacy disorders emerge.

One type of intimacy disorder originates when the child experiences a disorganized attachment (Main & Solomon, 1987; Stroufe, 1988). The infant becomes highly sensitized to soothing the caretaker, presumably to exert control and self-protection (Main & Solomon, 1987). The cost of surviving then is to give up the development and differentiation of an autonomous self, because sufficient safety is required to individuate. The individual then attempts to create safety and consistency in maladaptive ways (i.e., distorted survival strategies). In this intimacy dysfunction, an adult repeatedly finds individuals who need care, which creates an illusion of safety and control. These adults become an extension of their partner's identity and their boundaries become blurred to the extent that it feels as though the other is vital to the self's survival. They simultaneously experience a need to merge, like a child with a caretaker, and a need to run for fear they will be engulfed or abandoned. They also experience ambivalence related to their need to use others for self-soothing, as opposed to being independent. If sexuality has also been injured in its unfolding, through association with violence or loss of control, ambivalence more profoundly extends into the closeness/distance continuum. This ambivalence can be played out in a myriad of destructive ways, ranging from repetitive affairs to low sexual desire.

Deficits in the 1st year of life typically lead to self-cohesion difficulties, leaving the individual vulnerable to fragmentation. Epstein (1997) suggests that the result of internal self-fragmentation is the creation, metaphorically speaking, of "black holes that absorb fear and create the defensive posture of the isolated self—unable to make satisfying contact with oneself or others" (p. 5). Without basic integration, the individual experiences identity as many "selves" or feels like an imposter, due to an inherent experience of contradiction. Each of these "selves" has the capacity to produce behavior and has impulses for action. One system can be cut off from another, leading to unconscious motives for behavior. This fragmentation may explain why some individuals find young children sexually arousing (i.e., a part of the self with a developmental age of 6–10 takes executive control, but has the sexual arousal of an adult). Where there is extreme internal encapsulation, a person can act with seeming integrity (such as a member of the clergy or the principal of a school), have multiple sexual partners, molest a child, lie to others, and seem quite sincere, while not actually experiencing conflict or the implied contradiction. The mechanism of dissociation allows for the apparent anomaly in which "good people do bad things." This explanation of deviant sexual arousal patterns is consistent with repeated findings of early neglect, abuse, and few or no early friendships in the biography of sexual offenders (Marshall & Barbaree, 1989).

During the 2nd and 3rd years of life, self-constancy is established. Children develop tolerance for separation and the capacity for self-soothing. They begin to internalize the belief that they are loved and valued, and do not need constant reassurance. Children form a positive self-object (Mahler, 1995), which allows them to experience an internal schema for being cared for in the absence of the caretaker. Children raised in state institutions in Romania who have been adopted in the United States may need to be told "I love you" by their caretaker a hundred times a day, because they do not have an internal structure to retain the belief (Chigani, 1997).

By 4 years of age, the child develops self-agency, the ability to operate in the world and actively create or elicit responses from others. The child develops a lexicon for affect and forms a framework for self-efficacy and mastery. The result of the healthy development of self-cohesion, self-constancy, and self-agency is self-esteem. Positive affect becomes integrated with self-representation.

Individuals with intimacy disorders may lack a positive self-object and require others' continual mirroring to maintain their sense of self. They become highly suggestable and susceptible to influence. They chronically lack self-esteem and become human "doing," rather than human "being," because they experience themselves as being only as good as their last response. Men who have anonymous sex with multiple partners in a night may verbalize that they "feel only as good as their last trick." This is similar to individuals driven to make one business deal after another, at great cost to their family life, in order to attain more money, status, or other illusions of safety.

The love map, which organizes self-functions and facilitates relational choices, is structured by the age of 5 or 6 years. Perceptions of what is attractive in oneself and one's potential partners are organized in the care of the love map. Persons with vandalized love maps maintain a "confirming bias" by selecting interactions with others in the environment. They choose relations that fit the existing core schemata and avoid or devalue relations that might refute central beliefs and affects of the schemata. In this manner, the intimacy-disordered individual is held captive by the damaged love map until new learning can occur.

AFFECT REGULATION AND THE AFFECTIONAL SYSTEMS

Judith Herman (1992) observed that abused children develop maladaptive self-regulatory mechanisms:

> Abused children discover that they can produce release though temporary alterations in their affective state by voluntarily including autonomic crisis or extreme autonomic arousal. Purging, vomiting, compulsive sexual behavior, compulsive risk taking or exposure to drugs become vehicles with which abused children regulate their internal state. (p. 56)

The abused and neglected child experiences or anticipates abandonment, unfairness, or conflict with caretakers, which leads to powerful feelings of rage, anxiety, and helplessness. Manifestations of such frustration are dangerous, given the child's dependence upon the caretaker for survival. Protests may be actively suppressed by punishment (i.e., severe discipline, ostensibly "for the child's own good," cf. Miller, 1990) administered for "being bad." Later stressors lead to reemergence of the powerful suppressed feelings of helplessness, rage, and anxiety, which then activate a search for tension-reducing behavior.

Tension reduction affords self-soothing anesthesia from pain and restoration of affective control, increasing the likelihood of repeating the behavior.

Suppression of affect also is often accompanied by a "leakage" into somatic functions, such as eating, sexuality, or pain. The individual seems to express strong emotions by the "releases" inherent to compulsive behavior. These releases are exacerbated by increased autonomic arousal, which is chronically dysregulated by overwhelming trauma. Suppressed affect and cognition lead into consciousness during early adulthood (van der Kolk, 1989), and the individual experiences somatic memories and cognitions of early trauma experiences. In addition, symptoms of severe depression begin their onset (Putnam, 1997), as if the event is affectively remembered while the individual may cognitively remain amnesic. Such intrusions are often associated with increased compulsive behavior, which distracts and numbs the individual (i.e., a form of behavioral self-medication). It also expresses indirectly the intrusion's referent (i.e., enactment instead of remembering).

If the discrete events were so traumatic that the child could not integrate or assimilate them, the result may be post-traumatic stress disorder. This disorder is characterized by an " . . . abnormal highly sensitized and finely attuned hypopituitary axis with habituation and adaptions to chronic stress (decreased control and increased negative feedback regulation), that leaves the individual hypo or hyper responsive to a variety of stimuli" (Yehuda & McFarland, 1998, p. 168). The result is alexithymia and an inability to use emotions as negative cues for action. Inability to recognize emotions, absence of internal emotional signals, and opiate receptor changes occur in response to severe trauma (van der Kolk, 1989), causing analgesia to pain, anhedonia, internal dysphoria, confusion, and eventually sensation-seeking. These changes may lead to substance abuse as another form of attempted self-regulation.

Addictive behavior can begin as a way to cope with a myriad of dysphoric emotions and a lack of internal self-cohesion. The addictive behavior can be maintained through habituation and generalization, although the source (cause) of the emotions is long forgotten. For the sexually compulsive, acting out serves as a "release" and an expression of suppressed affect related to past injustice, which simultaneously reduces anxiety and causes the individual to become "high" from opiate release. These individuals then use the behavior as a form of self-soothing, develop a habit, and cognitively define themselves by their behavior (e.g., "I am an exhibitionist"). When individuals are numb due to overstimulation or intrusion of dysregulated affect, they become able to "feel" by experiencing a "release" or intrusion of dysregulated affect. When they feel overwhelmed by acting out, individuals can experience calming through the same mechanism of release that mediates a shift in internal state. Eventually, the individual may feel pleasure and safety only when acting out. The individual has bonded with the object of the addiction as a means of internal regulation and calming. The relationship with the object insulates this person from anticipated or real rejection from other people. For this reason, abstinence from acting out is often experienced by flooding of both affect and cognition. The ultimate goal of treatment is to reorient the addict from a state of constriction to begin utilizing others for self-comfort. This begins a process of change to rebuild the structure of the self, attain control of affect dysregulation, and allow structural evolution of the affectional systems.

REHABILITATION OF THE DEVELOPING AFFECTIONAL SYSTEMS

With greater appreciation of early bonding disorders, there is some question as to how much change is possible after the ages of 8 to 10, much less in adulthood. Numerous studies have documented that amelioration of attachment disorders becomes more and more difficult as the child approaches puberty. The child with attachment problems has trouble showing concern for others (Stroufe, 1988), remains self-centered and impulsive, does not trust others, and exhibits many behaviors that are aimed at keeping people at an emotional distance. Other symptoms include poor eye contact, withdrawal into self, aggression, indiscriminate affection, overcompeting, lack of self-awareness, constant control issues, and delayed conscience development (Fahlberg, 1991). These symptoms are characteristic of several personality disorders in the *DSM-IV* (APA, 1997) Attention deficit disorder symptoms in school, sometimes manifested as defiant and delinquent behaviors, reflect early bonding disorders in many cases (Karr-Morse & Wiley, 1997). Acting out and aggressive behaviors in males, as well as depression and self-injurious behaviors in females, represent learned survival mechanisms. Clinical syndromes and addictive behaviors must be reliquished during the course of pyschotherapy to promote intra- and interpersonal development.

Adults with histories of childhood neglect and abuse are notoriously poor reporters of such histories; many will consider their childhood "normal." They therefore blame themselves and identify with their psychiatric diagnosis. Psychiatry overemphasizes advances in psychotropic medication, which promotes this "diseased" notion of oneself. Rehabilitation initially is dependent on reexamining and contextualizing events of their lives. Because early events are encoded effectively, emergence of strong affect typically is a window into the disorder. The trauma reconstruction model focuses on "what happened," rather than on "what's wrong" with the person. Compulsive symptomatology always has biographical contributing factors and is comprehensible within the "trance logic" or childhood associational processes from respective developmental ages.

Repairing vandalized love maps in psychotherapy requires revisiting critical experiences and reactivating the affect in the safety and containment of the therapist's office, allowing for therapeutic reconstruction of core schema. This process is called "information reprocessing" through exposure therapy (Foa et al., 1991), which is demonstrably effective in the treatment of anxiety disorders. Refocusing strong affect on events in the dysfunctional family's interactions allows for expression of affect and completion of the stress response cycle (Horwitz, 1997). Trauma reconstruction has been a central feature of effective pschotherapy since Freud's pioneering work.

In trauma reconstruction therapy, the individual learns the self-functions that were never assimilated during childhood and adolescence. The developmental tasks are accomplished through role-playing and problem-solving in the "safe place" or "holding environment" (Winnicott, 1958) afforded by the therapeutic relationship. Specific skills are developed, as well as an overall sense of mastery or self-efficacy. Psychodrama and expressive therapy are extremely useful in practicing effective self-functioning; there is an active process of strengthening the self by learning how to interpret feedback and accomplish personally meaningful goals.

The most complex aspect of this rebuilding process is encouraging interactions with others who are not dysfunctional and preventing fears from sabotaging such connections. By allowing oneself to be genuinely supported by another (including the therapist), the self is "reseeded" and begins to have structures sufficient for continual growing. When fears are activated, insight and confrontation allow the individual to separate the past from the present, breaking the trauma bond. The goal of preserving loving interactions with their own children often is the initial impetus that motivates individuals to seek or maintain therapeutic experiences, even though they are terrified. In our experience, the human love map accommodates significant repair of even very severe early disruptions of attachment in some individuals when they are "ready." The challenge to psychotherapy is recognizing when the client is developmentally evolved enough to make changes and pace the therapy accordingly.

REFERENCES

Beach, F. (1977). *Distinction and interrelations between sexual receptivity, proceptivity, and attractivity.* Unpublished reprint.

Bowlby, J. (1969). *Attachment and loss: Volume 1. Attachment.* New York: Basic.

Bowlby, J. (1973). *Attachment and loss: Volume 2. Separation.* New York: Basic.

Bowlby, J. (1980). *Loss.* London: Penguin.

Calverely, R. (1990). *Self representation and self-understanding in sexually abused adolescent girls.* Unpublished doctoral dissertation, Harvard University, Cambridge, MA.

Chigani, D. (1997). *Turning point.* (January 6, 1997).

Epstein, S. (1997). Cognitive-experimental self therapy. In L. A. Pervin (Ed.), *Handbook of personality* (pp. 165–1929). New York: Guilford.

Fahlberg, S. (1991). *A child's journey through placement.* Indianapolis, IN: Perspective.

Fisher, K. W., & Bidell, T. A. (1997). Dynamic development of psychological structures in action and thought. In R. M. Lerner (Ed.) & W. Damon (Series Ed.), *Handbook of child psychology: Vol. 1. Theoretical modes of human development.* New York: Wiley.

Foa, E. B., Rothbaum, B. O., Riggs, D. S., & Murdock, T. B. (1991). Treatment of post-traumatic stress disorder in rape victims: A comparison between cognitive-behavioral procedures and counseling. *Journal of Counseling and Clinical Psychology, 59,* 715–723.

Greenspan, S. I. (1977). *Psychopathology and adaption in infancy and early childhood.* New York: International Universities Press.

Harlow, H., & Harlow, M. K. (1962). The effect of rearing conditions on behavior. *Bulletin of the Menninger Clinic, 26,* 213–224.

Harlow, H., & Harlow, M. K. (1963). The maternal affectional system of Rhesus monkeys. In H. L. Rheingold (Ed.), *Maternal behavior in mammals.* New York: Wiley.

Harlow, H., & Harlow, M. K. (1965). The affectional system. In A. M. Schrier et al. (Eds.), *Behavior of non-human primates, Volume 2.* New York: Academic.

Herman, J. (1992). *Trauma and recovery.* New York: Basic.

Horwitz, M. J. (1997). Stress response syndromes: A review of post traumatic and adjustment disorders. *Hospital and Community Psychiatry, 37,* 241–249.

Karr-Morse, R., & Wiley, M. (1997). *Ghosts from the nursery.* New York: Atlantic Monthly Press.

Maclean, P. (1962). Phylogenesis. *Journal of Nervous and Mental Disease, 27,* 135, 289–301.

Main, M., & Solomon, J. (1995). Discovery of an insecure, disorganized/disoriented attachment pattern: Procedures, findings, and implications for the classification of behavior. In M. Yogman & T. B. Brazelton (Eds.), *Affective development in infancy.* Norwood, NJ: Ablex.

Mahler, M. (1995). *Split self, split object: Understanding and treating borderline, narcissistic, and schizoid disorders.* Northvale, NJ: Jason Aronson.

Marshall, W., & Barbaree, H. (1989). Sexual violence. In *Clinical approaches to violence* (pp. 205–245). New York: Wiley.

Miller, A. (1990). *Banished knowledge.* New York: Doubleday.

Money, J. (1986). *Lovemaps: Clinical concepts of sexual/erotic health and pathology, paraphilia, and gender transposition, childhood, adolescence, and maturity.* New York: Irving.

Putnam, F. (1997). Psychobiological effects of sexual abuse. In R. Yehuolz (Ed.), *Psychobiology of post traumatic stress disorder.* New York: New York Academy of Sciences.

Schore, A. N. (1994). *Affect regulation and the origin of the self: The neurobiology of emotional development.* Hillsdale, NJ: Erlbaum.

Schwartz, M. F. (1998). *Post traumatic stress, sexual trauma, and dissociative disorders.* Unpublished manuscript.

Schwartz, M. F., & Becklin, R. (1975). Sexually evoked aggression of aggression-induced sex in the Rhesus monkey. *Cornell Journal of Social Relations, 7,* 117–131.

Schwartz, M., & Masters, W. (1984). Treatment of paraphiliacs, pedophiles, and incest families. In A. Burgess (Ed.), *Rape and sexual assault: A research handbook.* New York: Plenum.

Schwartz, M. F., & Senko, M. (1972). *The effect of an antiandrogen on the social behavior of male isolate rhesus monkeys.* Unpublished thesis, Franklin and Marshall College, Lancaster, PA.

Stroufe, L. (1988). The role of infant–caregiver attachment in development. In J. Beltske & T. Nezorsne (Eds.), *Clinical implications of attachment.* Hillsdale, NJ: Erlbaum.

van der Kolk, B. (1989). The compulsion to repeat the trauma: Reenactment, revictimization, and masochism. *Psychiatric Clinics of North America, 12,* 389–411.

Winnicott, D. W. (1958). Mind and its relation to the psyche-soma. In *Through pediatrics to psychoanalysis*. London: Hogarth.

Yehuda, R., & McFarland, A. (1998). *Psychobiology of post traumatic stress*. New York: New York Academy of Sciences.

CHAPTER 7

Clinical Boundary Issues With Sexually Addicted Clients

TIMOTHY M. TAYS
BRENDA GARRETT
RALPH H. EARLE

This chapter discusses common boundary violations committed by sexual addicts against clinicians. Case examples illustrate transgressions against clinicians, implications are considered, and practical interventions suggested with which to deal with boundary issues.

The nature of sexual addiction brings boundary issues regularly to the forefront in therapy. Clear boundaries for both clinicians and clients make sense. Clinicians' understanding of the therapeutic utility and personal security resulting from appropriate boundaries is crucial. This understanding leads to more timely and effective interventions and reasonable consequences. In this way, boundary crossing and violations can result in productive therapeutic interactions.

BOUNDARY CROSSING AND VIOLATION

A boundary is the edge of appropriate behavior in a given situation (Gutheil & Gabbard, 1993). Crossing a boundary in the therapeutic relationship occurs when clinicians step out of the usual therapeutic framework in some way, but this action neither exploits nor harms the client. Clinicians cross boundaries after prudent consideration when attempting to advance the therapeutic alliance or the therapy itself (e.g., offering a client a tissue, therapeutic self-disclosure). Clients cross boundaries when they step out of the usual therapeutic framework, but the action is not addictive acting out or manipulative (in a countertherapeutic sense).

Clinicians need to know when boundaries are crossed. For example, a client requests a different chair, resulting in his or her head being higher than the clinician's head. This raises a number of issues for clinicians, who are responsible for understanding whether these requests are attempts to unbalance the therapeutic relationship and become one-up, or to better identify with, idealize, and move toward clinicians (i.e., use clinicians as self-objects to facilitate clients' desired therapeutic change). Knowing the appropriateness of boundary crossing often requires directly asking the intentions of clients, with an ear for lies, joking, and testing limits, which would then possibly be indicative of inappropriate boundary crossing. Other times clinicians simply rely on experience, knowing the client, considering the interaction in context, and being aware of any emotional reactions that may signal an inappropriate boundary crossing or even danger. Of course, clinicians need to have done their own work in therapy, especially if sexual issues have been problematic in their lives (e.g., sexual abuse, sexual addiction). An example of appropriate boundary crossing occurred when a male clinician self-disclosed his own struggle and recovery with sexual addiction in an attempt to strengthen the alliance and identification with his male sexually addicted client. The intervention was premeditated and timely. However, the client responded with inappropriate boundary crossing. "Yeah, well, let's go out and get laid tonight," he said, then laughed and added, "Just kidding."

A boundary violation in the therapeutic relationship is exploitative or harmful. This occurs when clinicians take advantage of the transference, intimacy, dependency, idealization, rapport, empathy, and closeness felt with a confidant for self-gratification, rather than for the client's welfare (Gutheil, 1999). In the other direction, clients may attempt to use clinicians for self-gratification in a way that is countertherapeutic and abusive. Clients use clinicians to facilitate their healing, but there are boundaries to the extent clinicians may be used. Exploiting or harming clinicians is unacceptable, as well as countertherapeutic for clients. In the previous example of a client's inappropriate boundary crossing, the transgression would have been a boundary violation had the client instead said, "Yeah, I could tell you were a pervert when we first met," and laughed and added, "Just kidding." The difference between this and the last example is that the boundary crossing may have simply been inappropriate use of humor to build the alliance, spiral into shame, or defuse anxiety, whereas the boundary violation is abusive toward the clinician, in jest or not. In either example psychoeducation is a warranted intervention, followed by the clinician stating where the therapeutic boundary is set.

Clinicians working with sexually addicted clients set boundaries to prevent clients from

1. Sexually acting out if triggered by clinicians;
2. Sexually fantasizing about clinicians;
3. Using sexualized or predatory language or innuendo directed at clinicians;
4. Grooming clinicians for sexual acting out;
5. Physically touching clinicians;

6. Entering clinicians' personal space; and
7. Attempting to continue psychotherapy outside the designated time and space frame.

Clinicians must have a clear sense of appropriate, therapeutic boundaries in order to promote the therapeutic relationship. They should know where each boundary is best set and be able to state the consequences for boundary violations. The responsibility for defining, maintaining, and enforcing boundaries always belongs to clinicians, and nuances abound. It is clinicians' responsibility to model clear, healthy boundaries and enforce them in a way not done in their clients' pasts. Adequate training, supervision, and ongoing consultation are necessary to tease apart the many boundary scenarios presented while serving this population.

Once the relationship of clinician–client is established, all boundary violations are therapeutic issues. Clients will self-disclose a plethora of boundary violations from their past, but very often boundary violations will continue to occur over the months and years in counseling and even while in-session. These in-session boundary violations can be excellent in-vivo experiences for clinicians and clients to process together, to include clinician modeling of appropriate delineation and enforcement of boundaries. Boundary violation in-session can be abusive, and although it is still a therapeutic issue, no clinician should endure abuse. Some interventions are a confrontation by the individual clinician, confrontation by the individual clinician and another clinician on the treatment team, and confrontation in a process group. For chronic or more serious boundary violations, consequences can be terminating the relationship and making a referral. In any circumstance, the clinician maintains control of appropriate personal and professional boundaries.

For example, a female clinician met a sexually addicted male client for the first time. He said, "You make me feel like masturbating." The clinician set a clear boundary by stating, "You are sexually offending me. If you continue to objectify me, I will refer you to a male therapist." This boundary allowed the two to go on to work productively together.

However, clinicians do not always immediately understand boundary violations. Supervision or consultation is often necessary. For example, a young and attractive female intern was in-session with a 53-year-old male corporate executive who told her, "I'm triggered by you. My addict would have sex with you right now if you let me." The intern felt paralyzed with indecision as she anxiously awaited the end of the session. She untangled her thoughts in supervision and realized that she felt victimized. "I struggled with knowing that addiction is fueled in part by shame, so how should I deal with this without shaming him or taking on his shame? Yet I also thought it was important to share my experience and to give honest feedback, as well as affirm that he acknowledged that he had been triggered." She realized her client used the pretext of "being honest" to victimize her, using his maleness, age, and status for advantage. In their next session, the intern honestly processed this with her client, telling him she had not realized the impact of his statement in the moment, but that she had felt objectified and victimized. This proved helpful to the client, who believed that he had flattered her and had not ever hurt anyone by such behavior, including himself, because he had never seen or felt the pain of others, many of whom were female employees and likely felt as confused and victimized as the intern.

CLINICIANS' EMOTIONS

Some common emotions clinicians may experience while working with sexual addicts are disgust, frustration, anger, and fear. Working with an addicted population tends to evoke disgust, as clients disclose the lurid manifestations of their irrational, self-centered acting out. Clinicians' frustration can mount over clients' denial, minimization, and resistance, making clinicians feel therapeutically impotent. Clinicians may feel anger at clients' lack of victim empathy, overt hostility, and passive-aggressiveness displaced toward clinicians despite their best efforts to help. In addition, fear may be aroused at the dynamic that clients may consciously or subconsciously create in an effort to promote a predatory agenda. Although these are normal reactions and are likely felt by many people who have passed through clients' lives, for clinicians these emotions are signs of possible boundary violation within the therapeutic framework. Thus, clinicians' emotional reactions at boundary violations are "grist for the mill" and provide more data on clients' methods of operation of violating others' boundaries.

It is important that counselors do not "own" clients' psychopathology or take responsibility for their recovery (i.e., projective identification, or when clinicians take into themselves their clients' inner state and defenses). Clients' recovery is for clients themselves to own and is their therapeutic work to do or not to do. Clinicians' owning clients' behavior, thoughts, and emotions can enable sexual addicts to stay out of recovery.

Clinicians set a boundary at having an emotional investment in their clients. This means that clinicians have an internal boundary set at not owning their clients' emotions or recovery. This is not to say that clinicians do not care about their clients—the relationship is crucial and change builds upon it. However, clinicians do not give control of their emotional well being to clients, especially clients who are sexual addicts not yet in recovery. Feelings of professional "burnout," taking on clients' pain, and owning clients' lack of therapeutic progress should prompt clinicians to process their boundaries in supervision or consultation.

Frequently, partners of sexual addicts also have questionable boundaries, which can enable the addict. Bringing the partners of sexual addicts into treatment can prevent further enabling behavior, as well as begin to rebuild their relationship if that is what they desire. However, clinicians must be wary that their sympathy for the wronged partner does not become a boundary violation. For example, a 32-year-old professional athlete self-disclosed a string of one-night stands he had had over the course of a number of years. His wife, a 31-year-old homemaker with two children, endured the betrayals in the belief she could not survive financially or emotionally without her husband. The husband would "come clean" every few years and enter couple's counseling. Unfortunately, the wife's codependent behavior saw little improvement. The wife always claimed to forgive her husband and then sunk deeper into depression. She eventually became an inpatient when she became actively suicidal. Posthospitalization, the wife rejoined her husband and he continued his pattern of sexual acting out, followed by tearful self-disclosure. A clinician who was inappropriately emotionally invested in the wife's codependent recovery would experience extreme emotional discomfort.

The point is that sexual addicts enter and remain in recovery on their own, and partners and clinicians can at best merely facilitate this process, at worst enable the addict. Regardless, partners and clinicians cannot make the choice for the addict. Whether the relationship with the sexual addict is as significant other, clinician, or merely an acquaintance, boundaries need to be set so as not to become another victim, whether directly or indirectly. This is also true when treating the codependents of sexual addicts.

Clinicians set a boundary of professional competency. The boundary of professional competency begins with appropriate education, training, and experience and continues with willingness to consult, attend conferences, and read within the field.

Clinicians take a competent, professional stance in counseling with a deep understanding of their own issues. They respect themselves and others and do not allow clients to victimize them. This attitude, modeled to clients, can serve as an effective intervention and is a boundary.

TRANSFERENCE

When treating this population, expect to see defensive reactions by clients at having their addiction confronted, feeling accountable to another, feeling entitled, or activating a core of shame. These interpersonal reactions are surface and core issues and interpreted as such. However, transference can also develop, whether in brief or longer therapy. Transference in the analytic sense is any displacement of an affect from one object to another, specifically the displacement of affect toward the parent to the clinician (Chaplin, 1975). Clinicians often use this term too loosely to describe simple reactions of clients toward clinicians that are not technically transference. Regardless, awareness of transference and reaction issues and the boundary violations they can engender is crucial.

Many sexual addicts come from backgrounds of abuse at the hands of their parents. The deep childhood wounds that resulted in low self-worth, shame, dysphoric emotion, loneliness, and lack of self- and other intimacy are self-medicated via sexual acting out. As transference develops, clients displace these issues onto clinicians. Clients with little insight sometimes begin to view clinicians—instead of their own core issues, the addiction, or the addictive acting out—as the problem. Clients make subconscious, childlike attempts to assert themselves in ways they were unable to do with caregivers years before. This looks like petulance or anger. Clients can defensively shut off emotion or become passive as feelings of shame and hopelessness surface. Passive-aggressive behavior is common, seen as late cancellations, tardiness, incomplete homework, limited self-disclosure, and even taking clinicians' parking spaces. As clinicians recognize the manifestations of displaced affect, they verbalize and enforce boundaries, interpreting the transference and bringing the dynamic to consciousness. This enables clients to gain more control over affect, cognition, and behavior, as well as often promoting healing via catharsis. Clinicians "re-parent" by modeling safe, open communication and empathy in ways clients did not originally experience as children. Handled competently and with care, clients can begin to manifest increased appropriate emotional release and more grounded, controlled behavior with appropriate boundaries.

IN VIVO ACTING OUT

Many sexual addicts act out within clinicians' offices. This occurs in both subtle and obvious ways that may appear clear to clinicians, but perhaps not to clients. Clinicians should raise each boundary violation to clients' consciousness and verbalize boundaries and consequences for future similar transgressions.

The sexual addict is by definition out of control. This includes denial and unawareness of some of his or her behavior and the resulting consequences. Still, it is reasonable to expect clients to work hard to control not only their consciousness, but also their behavior to the point of being able to actively participate in therapy and respect therapeutic boundaries. However, some clients do not wish to be in recovery, but enter treatment under coercion (e.g., a partner threatens to leave). Others voluntarily get into recovery, but have extremely limited insight into their behavior and psychodynamics.

As a 40-year-old male homosexual delineated his sexual timeline, he suddenly laughed and commented how aroused he had become. Was this an attempt to titillate the male clinician (i.e., boundary violation)? Was it euphoric recall (i.e., inappropriate boundary crossing)? This provided a good opportunity for exploration of the client's motivation, and to provide psychoeducation on the dangers of sexual fantasy. All clients are responsible for controlling this cognitive dimension of their recovery. Boundaries and interventions for homosexual

sexual addicts are similar to those with a heterosexual population. However, awareness and training concerning the special challenges facing the homosexual population are necessary. In this case, an effective intervention was to "spit in your soup," or de-eroticize and thus spoil the memory via dissecting the event from a therapeutic viewpoint, pointing out the event's exploitive nature and dire consequences.

It is necessary to enforce boundaries even for apparently benign transgressions because of the "slippery slope" nature of addictive acting out. Enforcement may simply mean pointing out transgressions and processing the psychodynamics. However, from triggers to gross sexual acting out, clinicians need to be aware of not only clients' symptomotology, but also their own boundaries, for self-protection and to better serve clients.

Triggers

For many clients the "slippery slope" begins with triggers. Any number of idiosyncratic things can trigger clients, such as certain words, time, mood, smells, and interpersonal dynamics. Although clinicians help clients identify as many triggers as possible, a boundary is set for clients to act upon their triggers, at least in-session or toward clinicians.

A client with a fetish for women's feet in open-toed shoes presented a challenge to an intensive outpatient treatment team. The client enjoyed masturbating beneath parked vehicles in mall parking lots as feet passed nearby. Some female clinicians on his case wore open-toed shoes. Here was a clear trigger, and treatment team members needed a clear boundary regarding the trigger. Were open-toed shoes appropriate for female clinicians on the case? Ultimately, the clinical decision was not to change the existing dress code for female clinicians. The reasoning was that the client would encounter females in open-toed shoes in the "real world" and needed to learn to cope. At least in-session, he could process his thoughts and feelings and prevent his typical behavioral response (i.e., to masturbate in public). Although his open-toed shoe trigger was clear, avoiding his many other triggers was not pragmatic (e.g., attractive women, loneliness, shame, boredom).

Fantasy

Fantasy is often the beginning of clients' sexual acting-out cycle. Fantasy creates an altered state where sexual addicts can dissociate, get into their ritual, and eventually act out sexually. Therefore, clients should set a boundary against sexual fantasy that includes fantasy about clinicians.

Clinicians rely on clients' self-reports and on their own intuition and experience to know what clients are thinking. It is important for clinicians to continue to ask clients about sexual or romantic fantasies or obsessions. Most addicts will not bring up their fantasies until clinicians ask and explain the importance of fantasy to clients' addictive cycles.

Clients should not indulge in sexual fantasy in general, but particularly not about clinicians, which is a boundary violation. Fantasizing is acting out and is harmful to clients' recovery because it feeds the addiction and sets clients up to relapse. Furthermore, fantasizing about clinicians contaminates the therapeutic relationship. This sometimes manifests due to transference issues and because of the nature of the population. Fantasy can fuel the addiction and inhibit uncensored communication between clients and clinicians.

When clinicians become aware of the fantasizing, it needs processing with clients. Once clinicians and clients understand the nature of the sexual fantasizing, clinicians can give clients tools to interrupt fantasy. One tool is the "3 second rule" to thought-stop, which gives clients up to 3 seconds to recognize that they are fantasizing before they redirect their attention to healthy thoughts, or at least away from the unhealthy sexual fantasy. This can help clients maintain their boundary against fantasy, and clinicians should insist upon it. For example, the clinician might state, "Although I appreciate your openness, fantasizing about me is a boundary violation. I feel objectified by you. I want you to use the 3-second rule in regard to all sexual fantasy, with the single exception of your wife." Explore the various consequences of failure to control the fantasizing, which ultimately might include referring the client to another clinician.

Grooming

Clinicians should psychoeducate clients to the importance of curtailing all grooming behavior. Grooming behavior consists of the myriad subtle and overt manipulations that clients undertake to curry favor with potential sexual partners. Clients need to know how this behavior violates others' physical and emotional boundaries and is an important part of the addictive cycle. Clinicians should continue to identify and verbalize all grooming behavior in clients' self-reporting. Clinicians should repeatedly ask clients about their grooming behavior and expect clients to increasingly identify it for themselves.

Boundaries against grooming behavior by clients must be set and enforced. Clients might groom other clients in the waiting room or after group, office staff, and clinicians in and out of session. Front office staff needs to be aware of what grooming behavior looks like and report it to the primary clinician. Do not dismiss attempts by clients to minimize their grooming behavior. Once clients are aware of their inappropriate behavior, they should abide by the boundary or consider themselves as having "slipped" or even relapsed. Assuming that clients have at least normal intelligence, then it can also be assumed, within normal limits, that the new awareness will generalize and therefore cannot be used as an excuse for not knowing every nuance of possible boundary violations.

One example of grooming occurred when a 35-year-old female physician regularly wore revealing clothing to therapy and did not check in at the front desk, but instead went directly to her male clinician's office and coyly stated, "Am I late?" which she typically was. This pattern raised a "red flag" for the clinician, who then processed it with the client. She had been subconsciously grooming the clinician, but with awareness was able modify her behavior and even generalize it to her social and work environments.

Grooming clinicians can occur for many reasons, among them for sex, approval, perceived favoritism, or in the hope of getting away with pushing more boundaries (e.g., not have behavior confronted in group or in–session). Ideally, clinicians have done their own therapeutic work in order to not need the approval of the client, and their training has been adequate for them to feel confident in their interventions. Still, sometimes clinicians discover themselves wondering whether they were seduced, thinking they had a strong alliance with the client when in fact it was a boundary violation, and having only a vague sense of feeling manipulated to guide them. This is another reason supervision and consultations are important when working with this population. Is a client's casual comment "I like what you're wearing today" appropriate boundary crossing in an attempt to move closer to the clinician, an inappropriate boundary crossing used as time-filler to lower client anxiety while moving from the chair to the door, a boundary violation in the form of grooming behavior, or an attempt to manipulate the goodwill of the clinician? The biggest help to answering these questions is to know the client and the context and to seek consultation.

Touch

The general rule of thumb when working with this population is to have a relatively rigid boundary against touch. This includes whether clinicians initiate touch with clients, and whether clinicians allow touch initiated by clients. Boundary issues come to the forefront of consciousness when clients touch clinicians, particularly so when clients are also sexually addicted and clinicians meet their sexual inclinations. Touch can be very healing (e.g., an appropriate hug when permission is asked and it is not therapeutically counterindicated); however, it can also be quite harmful to clinicians' sense of integrity and clients' recovery. Clinicians must consider what reasons there are for the desired physical contact. Possibilities are innumerable, ranging from such benign motivation as decreasing anxiety during a socially awkward moment, to seeking reassurance from clinicians when clients should be consciously working on self-validation. Grooming can also motivate touch. Regarding hugs, questions arise: What kind of hug was it? Was it full-body or held too long or too tightly? Clinicians have different boundary thresholds regarding touch, depending on training, therapeutic orientation, and personality, but overall, it is best to avoid touch and always consider motive if it does occur. Psychoeducating clients on the many issues surrounding boundaries on touch makes sense, to include how others may feel upon being touched and clients' own recovery issues.

A 49-year-old minister referred by his church board had used church funds to compulsively access gay pornography sites on the Internet from his church office. When taking his sexual history, he also disclosed visiting adult bookstores for oral sex with other male patrons. His sense of shame was great, as well as his need for reassurance while facing the prospect of losing his church position. He sobbed in-session and stated how he needed a man to hold him in a way his father never had. His pleas for external validation were contrary to one treatment goal of promoting self-validation. Neither males nor females on the treatment team hugged him, and at the end of his intensive outpatient treatment, his ego strength had become more robust. By discharge, a hug may have been appropriate boundary crossing, but before that, touch was countertherapeutic.

COMMON CLIENT BOUNDARY VIOLATIONS

When are clients more likely to cross or violate a boundary with clinicians? This may begin as the client senses the ending of the session. Often "bombs" dropped at this time disclose sexual acting out or slips in recovery. Sexual addicts who also have Axis II features (e.g., Borderline Personality Disorder) tend to violate boundaries. As always, it is the clinician's responsibility to maintain and enforce boundaries, to include the time-frame in-session. If a pattern emerges of the client pressing the time boundary, then it is certainly a therapeutic issue. Boundary violation is most apt to occur in the transition zone "between the chair and the door" (Gutheil & Simon, 1995). This is where the therapeutic frame is most easily broken. Clinicians and clients tend to become more social when sessions end and thus more vulnerable to hugs, handshakes, superficial communication, grooming, and sexualized remarks.

Clients may attempt to become "one-up" at this point. Upon standing, the physical power differential becomes more obvious and may intimidate a smaller clinician. From this position, clients may begin to groom. Clients may attempt to decrease their sense of vulnerability by becoming physically or intellectually intimidating. However, clinicians are aware of clients' behavior, as well as of their own reactions. An intervention may be for clinicians to silently reassert personal power and boundaries, consult, and wait for the next week's session. Alternatively, clinicians may choose to wait until the therapeutic alliance is stronger to interpret clients' process in-session. This may be the first time clients are consciously aware of their intimidating behavior. A therapeutic boundary should be set, stating that intimidating behavior is within clients' control and is intolerable.

Clients may cross or violate boundaries after group, in the waiting room, in the parking lot, or even during a chance meeting in public. A 25-year-old male sex addict who also had a diagnosis of Borderline Personality Disorder followed a female clinician out to her car after group. The client was angry at a perceived slight from the clinician. The clinician firmly told him to bring the issue up with his primary clinician in their next session or to bring it back into group the following week. The client did not respect this boundary, but instead allowed himself to become emotionally escalated, stating that he felt belittled as if he were a child, and that he was told to be more assertive and that was what he was now appropriately doing. The clinician communicated the inappropriate setting of his "assertiveness" and went on to state how he was not only violating a therapeutic boundary, but he had moved beyond assertiveness to aggression. He had violated her personal boundary, and she felt angry and frightened at his angry pursuit of her. She got in her car and drove away, albeit a bit shaken.

Interactions such as this are certainly the exception when working with this population, but they can occur. The clinician however, maintained both her personal and her professional boundaries by being assertive and clear in her communication and behavior. Thus she modeled these desirable personal characteristics to the client, characteristics that kept her safe, and attempted to honor the therapeutic relationship and the frame of therapy, as well as honor what strength and healthy boundaries look like. She also documented and charted the interaction. The next week the clinician used the interaction as an in vivo example of the client's poor sense of personal boundaries, his lack of respect and empathy for others' boundaries, how he had overreacted due to activation of his core sense of shame, and how the interaction served as a microcosm, revealing how he does his life. The clinician continued to share her emotions and encourage the client to identify and share his own feelings in an attempt to foster victim empathy and perhaps a healthy guilt.

SELF-DISCLOSURE

What is the boundary when working with a sexually addicted population regarding self-disclosure by clinicians? Do we take a tabula rasa (i.e., blank tablet) stance and allow the transference to develop or use therapeutic self-disclosure in an attempt to capitalize on the alliance and model authenticity? What works best with sexual addicts? Of course, every client is different, but in today's financial climate, there is often not time to take an analytic stance, nor would that necessarily be the best stance anyway. Sometimes, a more directive and assertive stance makes the most sense. Free association is valuable, but time is limited due to funds to pay for treatment and client availability to do therapy.

There is much discussion regarding therapeutic self-disclosure, and the range runs from none at all to doing so frequently in a discrete manner and always with the best interest of clients in mind. This is a particularly touchy issue with clients who probe clinicians to find out such things as "Are you also in recovery?" "Haven't you ever acted out sexually inappropriately?" "How often do you want sex/masturbate/sexually fantasize?" This could be an attempt by clients to minimize their own addiction, a manifestation of denial, or an attempt to move toward the idealized clinician, among many possibilities. Clinicians' self-disclosure can be very helpful to clients, but it must be prudent. Rule of thumb: If there is a question as to it being beneficial to clients, then do not do it. Information about clinicians may prevent clients from exploring certain areas. For example, a clinician's revelation that she did not have sex before her marriage due to religious views could constrain clients from sharing more lurid sexual history information due to fear of being judged negatively. This limits information necessary for accurate diagnosis and conceptualization of length and severity of the addiction.

However, a self-revelatory approach could normalize certain experiences of clients, which could then degrade the shame that fuels the addictive acting out. The most prudent approach is to make decisions on a case-by-case basis. As treatment progresses, clinicians may shift their therapeutic stance. For example, from a beginning of joining and empathy and blank slate early in treatment, as clinicians get to know clients and build the alliance, it may later become more helpful to be more confrontational, directive, and self-disclosing as the alliance solidifies and clients can "hear" better.

Self-disclosure may facilitate authentic engagement in the therapeutic process in one context, but may be seductive, coercive, or destructive intrusion on a client in another. Again, having done their own work in therapy, clinicians recognize activation of their own issues in-session, as well as keep those issues to themselves when it is not in service to the client.

Clients often push boundaries in an attempt to learn more about clinicians. Again, it is important for clinicians to understand clients' motivation for pushing at these boundaries. But there are times that even clients' "healthy" motivation to move toward the idealized self-object embodied by clinicians by asking increasingly invasive questions can be uncomfortable for clinicians and countertherapeutic. Sometimes no reply at all allows clients to catch on to the inappropriateness of their questioning, but other times an assertive statement such as "You seem defensive when I refuse to give you additional information about my personal life" diffuses clients and opens up the issue of boundaries again.

A more dramatic example occurred when a client reported that although he had been sexually sober for over 18 months, he had difficulty managing his "rubber-necking" behavior, that entailed the objectification of women. He reported surveying female pedestrians and drivers while commuting between job sites. He acknowledged actively seeking professionally dressed women wearing skirts with stockings and high heels. He relayed instances of rapid lane changes,

U-turns, and even following a female driver into a residential neighborhood, hoping to observe her. In-session with his female clinician, the client grew increasingly intrusive with his personal inquiries of her, which she adroitly managed. Eventually, the client disclosed that he always noticed what she was wearing and routinely contemplated what she might wear the following week. He reported that he had remained in his car before sessions and watched her exit her car and walk from the parking lot into the office building. He stated, "I know which car is yours, where you park, and when you leave. I notice those things." The clinician challenged him to view his objectification of women on a continuum from noticing to stalking/voyeurism. In addition, she challenged him to own his grooming and increasingly predatory behavior within the context of his sexual addiction cycle. They went on to process how he violated her choice not to disclose personal information, for her own personal and professional integrity, as well as for the client's benefit.

What is the boundary for clients' self-disclosure? Is there ever a boundary on this, considering that full self-disclosure shines light on the shadows where the addiction thrives, gives clinicians the needed information to better help them, and the confession itself can be healing? Again, take this on a case-by-case basis and in context. Some possible scenarios would be client self-disclosure in order to experience euphoric recall or to titillate, shock, groom, or victimize clinicians. Clinicians should address these boundary violations and then set appropriate boundaries.

CONCLUSION

Clinicians must be aware of boundary issues when working with sexual addicts. For clinicians to do their best therapeutic work, they must identify and enforce boundaries. There are innumerable possible boundary crossings and violations that range from subtle to abusive. Therefore, seek regular supervision, consultation, or both. Consistently processing boundary issues protects both clinicians and clients and can more effectively promote clients' recovery.

REFERENCES

Chaplin, J. P. (1968, 1975). *Dictionary of psychology* (rev. ed.). New York: Dell.
Gutheil, T. G. (1999). Clinical concerns in boundary issues. *Psychiatric Times*, 16(8).
Gutheil, T. G., & Simon, R. I. (1995). Between the chair and the door: Boundary issues in the therapeutic "transition zone." *Harvard Review of Psychiatry*, 2(6), 336–340.

CHAPTER 8

The Integration of Psychotherapy and 12-Step Programs in Sexual Addiction Treatment

JAN PARKER
DIANA GUEST

Integrating psychotherapy and 12-step program membership can be both challenging and rewarding for the therapist and the client. Twelve-step programs can provide the daily support clients may need to transfer their primary coping strategy from the compulsive sexual behavior to a healthier system that will assist them to gradually develop alternative coping skills. When a client is acting out on a daily basis, he or she needs more support than weekly psychotherapy can provide.

There is some controversy among clinicians regarding the use of the term *sexual addiction* when referring to these clients.

> The rationale for conceptualizing sexual compulsivity as an addiction is the existence of a physiological component to sex and/or love addiction which is used as a primary way to alter mood and as a coping mechanism. Brain chemistry is altered when endorphins are released, creating a "high" similar to that induced by mood-altering drugs. (Parker & Guest, 1999, p. 52)

A major component of 12-step program work is requiring the member to admit his or her behavior and to make amends for it to the people involved. The application of the disease model of addiction to compulsive sexual behavior and the use of 12-step programs can assist the client in taking responsibility for the behavior, while reducing the shame associated with it. In addition, conceptualizing compulsive sexual behavior as an addiction provides a structure with which many people are already familiar. Most clients with sexually compulsive behavior have another addictive process. Most often, the recognition of sexual compulsive behavior as separate from the other addiction does not become apparent until the person is in recovery from that addiction. For example, an alcoholic who has been sober for 6 months and is still frequenting prostitutes can no longer blame it on being drunk. Therefore, it is more likely that this individual will begin to recognize the sexually acting-out behavior as a distinct process separate from his or her drinking.

Involvement in 12-step program work can often enhance and support the therapeutic process. The clinician who is successful in utilizing 12-step program membership as a therapeutic tool understands the boundaries between these two modalities, as well as the role of the therapist differentiated from that of the 12-step program sponsor and meetings. An example of the boundary between these two approaches is the degree of daily or weekly access to the support system. A client has only limited access to the therapist and must pay for the time. Twelve-step program members often tell newcomers to the program to call them as much as necessary, especially when about to act out. Meetings are free and are scheduled at least once a day, more often in larger urban areas. Consequently, the client has virtually unlimited access to the 12-step program support.

Participation in all 12-step programs includes working the 12 steps, regular attendance at a variety of meetings, the concept of sponsorship, some form of spirituality, a sense of fellowship, and an emphasis on service.

The essentials of all 12-step programs include the following:

1. Addiction is a disease.
2. Individuals with an addiction require support from other recovering, addicted members.
3. Reliance on a "power greater than self" is necessary for recovery.
4. Abstinence from the addicted behavior is the foundation of recovery.
5. Recovery is a lifelong process.
6. Helping other addicted people is essential to long-term stable abstinence from addicted behavior.
7. Acceptance of the realistic limits of being human is imperative. (Parker & Guest, 1999, p. 3)

The 12 steps are the core of the program. The basic philosophy of the program is contained in the steps, and working the steps is how members learn a new approach to life. Therapists who work with clients in such a program should learn the actual phrasing of each step, in order to follow the client's discussion about and process in working each step. The 12 steps are:

1. Step One: We admitted we were powerless over (addictive sexual behavior) (sexual compulsion)—that our lives had become unmanageable.
2. Step Two: Came to believe that a Power greater than ourselves could restore us to sanity.

3. Step Three: Made a decision to turn our will and our lives over to the care of God, as we understood God.
4. Step Four: Made a searching and fearless moral inventory of ourselves.
5. Step Five: Admitted to God, to ourselves, and to another human being the exact nature of our wrongs.
6. Step Six: Were entirely ready to have God remove all these defects of character.
7. Step Seven: Humbly asked God to remove our shortcomings.
8. Step Eight: Made a list of all persons we had harmed and became willing to make amends to them all.
9. Step Nine: Made direct amends to such people wherever possible, except when to do so would injure them or others.
10. Step Ten: Continued to take personal inventory, and when we were wrong promptly admitted it.
11. Step Eleven: Sought through prayer and meditation to improve our conscious contact with God as we understood God, praying only for knowledge of God's will for us and the power to carry that out.
12. Step Twelve: Having had a spiritual awakening as the result of these steps, we tried to carry this message to (sex addicts) (sexually compulsive people) and to practice these principles in all our affairs. (SAA, 1997, p. 6; SCA, 1995, p. 2).

In addition the steps can be put into three different categories.

Steps One through Three address the addicted person's lack of ability to control the behavior alone and his/her need to begin recovery. Each of these first three steps is viewed independently. Steps Four through Nine focus on taking responsibility for one's actions and personality characteristics, and beginning the process of change. Here the steps are paired. Steps Four, Six, and Eight are more self-reflective in nature while Five, Seven, and Nine require some form of action as a result of the self-reflection. Steps Ten through Twelve concentrate on maintaining and continuing recovery. The steps are a progressive process, with each step building on the previous steps. (Parker & Guest, 1999, p. 5.)

Another component of 12-step programs is the focus on spirituality, which helps members feel part of something larger than self. This part of 12-step program philosophy is sometimes misinterpreted as religious, rather than spiritual. In actuality, any form of spiritual belief is acceptable, even if that is a belief in the power of the group, rather than the individual.

All 12-step programs have a spiritual component. The concept is that members have not been able to control their addictive behavior on their own and so what the program calls a "power greater than self" is necessary for recovery. Most clients with an addiction have a distorted view of their power over life's events. Acceptance of the inability to control these events, while taking responsibility for one's actions, is essential for successful long-term change. Spirituality, as used in 12-step programs, teaches these concepts.

Every member decides what his/her "Higher Power" is. Many people use "God" but others use the power of the group or other concepts. This is probably the most central tenet of the entire program. Seven of the 12-steps contain some reference to a "Higher Power." At the time the original 12 steps were written the cultural context in the United States included prayer in schools, and public references to God by political and social leaders. Both of the major religions in the United States, Christianity and Judaism, supported the language and concepts used in the program.

Spirituality can often be the largest stumbling block for people entering 12-step programs, especially those who have been wounded by a religious organization or have no spiritual belief. Atheists and agnostics do exist in 12-step programs but tend to be silent about their lack of belief in "God." In larger geographical areas an officially recognized branch of AA, "We Agnostics" follows the Steps, Big Book, and Traditions of AA without the religious overtones. Regardless of one's belief in God or a Higher Power 12-step programs have a lot to offer that is very practical. It is important for the clinician to understand the function of the spiritual component of these programs. (Parker & Guest, 1999, pp. 20–21)

Attending meetings is how a person becomes involved in a 12-step program. There are three types of 12-step program meetings: sharing or discussion meetings, step-study meetings, and speaker meetings. Sharing meetings are led by a different person each week, who usually chooses a topic to discuss. Members volunteer or are called on, depending on the structure of the individual meeting. Step-study meetings focus on one of the steps each week. There are two types of step-studies: open and committed. In an open meeting there is a 12-week cycle, where each step is discussed and then the cycle is begun again. Committed step-studies are formed by a small group, and material on each step is written and shared by each member. Once the committed step-study has begun, no new people are allowed to join the group. Once the steps are completed, which may take as long as 6 months, the group usually ends. Speaker meetings are usually larger and one or two people share their "story" of addiction and recovery. This type of meeting is not as common in sexual addiction programs as in Alcoholics Anonymous, Narcotics Anonymous, or Overeaters Anonymous. Knowing the types and functions of the different meetings allows the clinician to make a more informed referral. Clients with significant difficulties with bonding may need a larger meeting at first where they can feel more anonymous. Clients with high dependency needs will usually respond better to smaller meetings, where they are individually recognized. The clinician who knows how to assist the client in finding the appropriate meeting will greatly facilitate the client's participation in a 12-step program.

It is in meetings that the client meets fellow 12-step program members in various stages of recovery, who potentially form a support system. From this support system the client chooses a sponsor who serves as a mentor and guide through the 12-step program recovery process.

> Sponsorship is a one-to-one relationship between a member with more experience and growth in the program and a newer, less experienced member. The bond between sponsor and member can be similar in significance to a therapeutic relationship. The member, especially in early recovery, relies on the sponsor for guidance, affirmation of progress, encouragement, support, and education about the program. It is in this relationship that most of the work is done. As the member establishes . . . abstinence . . . a major component becomes "working" the 12 steps. The sponsor guides the sponsoree through this process. The sponsor/member relationship requires a high level of trust, a willingness to be honest, and an ability to give and receive feedback and encouragement in order to be effective. The sponsor is available, often twenty-four hours a day, for the member to call particularly if s/he is tempted to practice whatever addiction s/he may have. (Parker & Guest, 1999, p. 19)

Twelve-step program work was never intended to be therapy. The role of the sponsor or other program members is not that of a therapist. When the client enters therapy, he or she brings a presenting problem. However, the therapist sees it in the context of the client's entire life and psychological structure. How this is conceptualized will vary according to theoretical orientation. The role of a sponsor and other 12-step program members is narrower in focus. The topic of discussion is always related in some way to the sexual addiction behavior. An example of this is the sharing of written responses to each of the 12 steps, which is more likely to be done with the sponsor than with the therapist. There is more sharing of one's own experience and advice giving than in psychotherapy. The initial goal when entering a 12-step program is abstinence from the addictive behavior. Consequently, most of the conversations between the client and other 12-step program members will center around achieving and maintaining abstinence.

The goal of the therapist working with the sexual addict is to help the client stop the acting-out behavior, learn new appropriate coping skills, and develop a healthy sense of sexuality. Twelve-step program goals are similar within the context of a spiritual approach to living. The clinician who integrates 12-step program concepts into psychotherapy must be comfortable discussing all of the 12-step program principles, including spirituality.

The process of referring a sexually addicted client to a 12-step program is complex. Factors to consider include the client's ability to identify him- or herself as having sexually compulsive behavior and to accept the addiction model, the therapist's assessment of the client's ability to be in a group with other potential acting-out partners, as well as the fact that there are more different and distinct programs focusing on sexual addiction than on any other single addictive disorder. It is important that the clinician understand the differences between these programs so that he or she can make an informed referral, understand the nuances of the various 12-step programs' structures, or both. These various programs developed independently, often without knowledge of the others. The complexity and variety of behaviors are reflected in the differences between these programs. Programs whose primary focus is sexual behavior include Sex and Love Addicts Anonymous (SLAA), Sex Addicts Anonymous (SAA), Sexaholics Anonymous (SA), and Sexual Compulsives Anonymous (SCA). These programs have subtle variations in their treatment of sexual addiction; however, the core beliefs of all of these programs include the need to define abstinence or sexual sobriety, the value of psychotherapy, and a stronger need for anonymity based on the degree of shame associated with this addiction. A period of celibacy is either required or encouraged in each program. With the exception of SLAA, each of these programs requires that potential members have a screening interview before meeting times and locations are revealed. This is to discourage visitors and ensure a heightened sense of anonymity and safety.

SEX AND LOVE ADDICTS ANONYMOUS

Founded in 1976, SLAA was the first program to address issues related to compulsive sexual and relationship behavior as an addiction. Stopping compulsive behavior related to sex and love and developing the ability to be in a healthy sexual relationship is the primary philosophy of SLAA. This program differs from the other sexual addiction programs in its focus on love addiction in addition to sexual addiction. SLAA defines love addiction as extreme dependence on one or more love objects, being preoccupied with romantic fantasies, having serial relationships, or any combination of these. Due to the focus on more covert sexual acting-out behaviors, SLAA has the largest female membership of all of the sexual addiction programs. Its philosophy includes the concept that sex and love addictions are the same basic problem. SLAA believes that a continuum exists from extreme dependence on one person to compulsive acting out, all in the service of regulating mood. Abstinence or sexual sobriety is individually defined, usually with the help of the sponsor. This always includes an individual list of "bottom line" behaviors, which trigger the addiction. Examples of these behaviors could be having sex on the first date, obsessional fantasies about a real or fictitious person, watching certain TV programs or movies, having unprotected sex, or driving into a red light district. Sexually addictive patterns are so individual that a great deal of time must be spent on determining each person's "bottom line" behaviors. SLAA is usually an inappropriate referral for a sex addict whose behavior involves victimization. SLAA is open to all sexual orientations and is one of the most accessible of the sexual addiction 12-step programs.

SEX ADDICTS ANONYMOUS

Several men who felt a need for greater anonymity founded SAA in 1977. They developed a screening process to interview potential members prior to receiving information about meeting locations. Individually determined, abstinence or "sexual sobriety" is defined as refraining from a personalized list of compulsive sexual behaviors. Consequently, a wide variety of definitions of sobriety exist, and members are encouraged to respect these differences. Due to self-defining abstinence, it is important for the client to have the capacity for insight into behavior patterns and fantasies.

SAA has developed a concept of three circles. Behaviors from which the member must clearly abstain are placed in the inner circle. Examples of these behaviors may be sex with or being a prostitute, sadomasochistic behavior, anonymous sex, or acting out with a nonconsensual victim. The outer circle lists behaviors that are definitely healthy recovery practices, both sexual and nonsexual. These may include sex with a partner in a committed relationship, enjoying affectionate touch, masturbation without pornography, finding a hobby, going to a dance class, or any other activity that replaces time spent acting out. The middle circle contains those behaviors that may lead to inner circle acting out, but are not considered breaking abstinence in and of themselves. Examples of these include cruising for a prostitute, contacting an old acting-out partner, or acting seductively in an inappropriate situation. SAA members are encouraged to identify these middle circle behaviors as indicators of potential relapse and to take action before they actually act out.

Open to diversity, SAA creates a safe environment to discuss heterosexual, homosexual, and bisexual behaviors. A small minority of the membership has a history of sexual acting-out behavior with a victim. It will be especially important with these clients that rationalizations regarding behaviors and fantasies be examined by both the sponsor and the therapist.

SEXAHOLICS ANONYMOUS

The exact start date of SA is uncertain. However, it is known that it began in California. SA has one definition of sexual sobriety and does not allow individuals to self-assess. Sobriety is defined by SA as abstaining from any sexual activity with self or anyone outside a sanctified relationship—in other words, marriage. Of all the sexual addiction 12-step programs, SA most strongly encourages a period of celibacy and even states that celibacy be considered a lifestyle choice. This group adheres to the Judeo-Christian spiritual philosophy and beliefs. Therefore, a client who has a different spiritual or religious perspective will need to adjust or may not be appropriate for this program. In addition, clients who are not married or are homosexual would best be served in another program. However, SA may be a very helpful program for clients who subscribe to the previously mentioned belief systems.

SEXUAL COMPULSIVES ANONYMOUS

Founded in 1982, SCA was begun primarily to address the issues specific to sexually addicted gay men. Although there is an increasing number of women and heterosexual men, the majority of members consists of homosexual males. In SCA sexual sobriety is individually defined by developing a personal recovery plan and is modeled after the work of Patrick Carnes. Carnes (1991) developed the concept of a sex plan that is similar to the three circles in SAA. The sex plan has three columns: abstinence, high risk, and recovery. The abstinence column consists of a list of bottom-line behaviors. If the addict intends to be healthy, he or she agrees to refrain from these behaviors. The high-risk column includes emotions, ritualized activities, and situations that make the addict vulnerable to relapse. Examples of these may be contact with a previous acting-out partner or group, cruising red light districts, or something as basic as having a fight with a partner. The recovery column includes positive activities and interactions where the member has learned to get his or her needs met in a healthy manner. Items in this column might be therapy, attending 12-step meetings, a hobby, or time with family. The sex plan is the blueprint for the addict's recovery. SCA meetings are more likely to be found in large urban areas.

> There are many similarities between the various 12-step programs addressing sexual compulsive behaviors; however, there are also some very basic differences. The most important difference between SAA and SA is the definition of abstinence. In referring a client to SA it is important that s/he hold the belief that sex outside of marriage is unacceptable. SLAA, SAA, and SCA share the view that abstinence is individually defined. When determining which of these three pograms is appropriate for a client, factors such as sexual orientation, degree of sexual acting-out behavior, presence of love addiction, and availability of meetings in your geographical area need to be considered. (Parker & Guest, 1999, pp. 55–56)

In the early stages of recovery the sex addict is attending his or her 12-step program and the partner may be going to S-Anon, or Codependents of Sex Addicts (COSA). At the beginning this can be healing for a relationship because the sex addict is admitting the behaviors and the co-addict is looking at his or her part in the relational difficulties. After that process has been established, however, there may come a time where it becomes divisive rather than healing. One of the primary issues for the co-addict in early recovery is working through the anger related to the sex addict's behavior. As the co-addict makes the transition into middle recovery, at about two years, it becomes important to let go of the anger and for both partners to consider the relational patterns that exist in the absence of the sexual acting out. At this time a referral to such programs as Recovering Couples Anonymous (RCA) or S-Anon Recovering Couples Anonymous may be helpful. RCA is a 12-step program for couples recovering from any addiction, which allows members to hear how other couples have handled similar issues. As with any 12-step program, this can instill a sense of hope. Common topics for these meetings include trust building, forgiveness, communication, boundaries, healthy sexuality, and roles in relationships. The availability of these programs will vary according to geographical location. In smaller areas clients may have to rely on Co-Dependents Anonymous (CODA) as a resource. In addition, couple's therapy with a therapist who understands the relational aspects of sexual addiction will usually be helpful.

CONCLUSION

When therapists work with a client who has a sexual addiction, it is vitally important that they be comfortable with both their own sexuality and discussing many different sexual practices. The treatment of sexual addiction is not about societal values and norms, but rather about assessing the way the client goes about getting his or her needs met. Revealing the core self in any therapeutic relationship is difficult. In addition, the sex addict's sense of self and poor self-esteem are directly linked to his or her sexuality and are deeply rooted in shame. The therapist must be able to tolerate that which the client deems intolerable. See Chapter 7 for more discussion regarding therapists' reactions to a client's disclosing of sexual details. These clients in particular have radar that is sensitive to any signs of disapproval.

Sex addicts can be among the most motivated, rewarding, and frustrating clients. They often enter therapy with presenting problems other than the sexual addiction and the therapist must be able to identify the existence of the compulsive sexual behaviors. Similar to eating disorders, much secrecy and shame surrounds these behaviors and more relapse occurs among sexually compulsive clients. Therefore, identifying sexual addiction can be a complex process. Once the sexual addiction has been confirmed by both the therapist and the client, the timing of a referral to a 12-step program needs to be carefully considered. The client must acknowledge the addiction, be able to tolerate the screening process, as well as be able to enter a room knowing he or she will be automatically identified as a sex addict. If the therapist makes a referral too early, this may sabotage the client's ability to bond into the 12-step program. In addition, as discussed in detail previously, choosing the appropriate program for each individual client is equally important.

It is important for the therapist to understand the benefits, language, and limitations of 12-step programs in order to integrate therapy into the recovery process for sexually compulsive clients. Therefore, we encourage therapists to obtain additional information about the different 12-step programs in their area, acquaint themselves with 12-step program language, and acquire education and training about sexual addiction in order to facilitate the client's therapeutic progress.

REFERENCES

Carnes, P. (1991). *Don't call it love: Recovery from sexual addiction.* New York: Bantam.

Parker, J., & Guest, D. (1999). *The clinician's guide to 12-step programs: How, when, and why to refer a client.* Westport, CT: Auburn House.

SAA. (1997, November). *Getting started in sex addicts anonymous* (11th ed.). Houston, TX: ISO of SAA.

SCA. (1995). *Sexual compulsives anonymous.* San Diego, CA: ISO of SCA.

CHAPTER 9

Recovery for Couples

MARK R. LAASER

When at least one member of a couple is sexually addicted, restoring trust and building intimacy can be very difficult. These couples must work as hard on their recovery together as a couple as they do on their individual recoveries. A number of key characteristics of these relationships can be understood and allowed to inform the work that needs to proceed. Relationships develop very much as individuals do. Margaret Mahler's developmental model can help couples understand this process. The 12 steps can be applied to couple recovery in order to facilitate the work of intimacy and trust building.

One of the great challenges to recovery from sexual addiction/compulsivity is restoring or building an intimate relationship with a committed partner. Many existing relationships are seriously impaired and often don't survive because of sexual acting out. A partner's ability to trust is obviously damaged. The psychodynamic and behavioral issues underlying sexual addiction/compulsivity contribute to serious obstacles to overcome in building intimate and committed relationships. Intimacy in a primary relationship can, however, be a vital part of recovery.

Scarce research and very little writing have been devoted to recovery for couples. Schneider and Schneider (1991) have conducted a study of some of the main issues for sexually addicted couples. Carnes (1991) has briefly addressed the characteristics and psychodynamic issues for sexual co-addicts. I (Laaser, 1992) have also briefly addressed the issue of couple recovery.

My wife and I have worked with several hundred couples, both professionally and in couple recovery programs, over the last 10 years. We have seen that not only is it possible to repair, rebuild, or newly build a committed relationship, but the level of emotional, spiritual, and physical intimacy that is attainable is miraculous indeed. In this chapter, I would like to present some of the presuppositions we believe are true of relationships in which at least one partner is a sexual addict and a 12-step program that we use and have found to be effective in the process of healing and building.

125

PRESUPPOSITIONS ABOUT SEXUAL
ADDICT/CO-ADDICT RELATIONSHIPS

Sexual Addicts and Co-Addicts Are Like Heat-Seeking Missiles

Carnes discovered, in his now classic study (1991), that in a cohort of sex addicts the percentage of those with a history of sexual abuse was 81%; with a history of physical abuse, 72%; and with a history of emotional abuse, 97% (p. 109). In a follow-up study (1991), he also found that the percentages were virtually identical for sexual co-addicts (p. 146). Therefore, in a relationship in which either partner is a sex addict, it is quite likely both partners are trauma survivors. In addition to the invasive kinds of trauma that these statistics suggest, our experience is that virtually all of these partners have significant issues of physical or emotional abandonment by one or both of their parents.

The types of relationship impairment these levels of trauma and abandonment create are myriad. Individual trauma breeds couple dysfunction. In a number of workshops for couples, I have asked participants to relate the story of their first encounter or meeting. The question is, "What attracted you to each other?" It is not surprising that sex addicts usually report attraction to physical qualities. Both addicts and co-addicts, however, also relate they are attracted to characteristics in their partner that they perceive as abilities to be emotionally nurturing. It is apparent that both addicts and co-addicts seek to repair trauma-created wounds in themselves. They are like "heat-seeking missiles," attracted to the perceived emotional warmth or nurturing abilities of their partners.

One of the challenges of recovery for couples who have experienced sexual addiction is that each partner must accept his or her own individual responsibility for the broader dysfunctional characteristics of the relationship. Each partner must be willing to engage in a healing process for his or her own individual traumas before relationship healing can begin. This often conflicts with the "identified patient" role that co-addicts may assign to a sex addict. The sex addict is the one the co-addict blames for any problems the relationship has. This may translate to "As long as he remains sober, we'll be fine." Much of the anger that these partners experience toward each other can be related to the disappointment each one feels because of unmet needs. This perception can be based on an unconscious experience of an individual's not-yet-healed trauma wounds. This dynamic, often manifested in surface issues, breeds resentment, which is really the expression of deeper wounds. Repetitive arguments about seemingly trivial content never seem to be solved and remain rather unmanageable because the real issues are not addressed.

Sex Addicts and Co-Addicts Suffer From Arrested Couple Development

Individual trauma often creates emotional, behavioral, and spiritual developmental arrest. The age at which the trauma first occurs will be reflected in arrested individual development. Sex addicts and co-addicts usually have never experienced healthy bonding with and nurturing from their parents. This impairs their ability to have successful bonding and separation in subsequent relationships during adolescent and adult life.

We have found that this developmental impairment mirrors itself in similar developmental issues as couples. Bader and Pearson (1988) have compared individual development, based on the theories of Margaret Mahler, with couple development. A child between the ages of birth and 3 years goes through several distinct stages:

Autism—Children are only aware of what they experience through their basic senses.

Enmeshment—Children are totally bonded with their primary caregiver. Their identities are totally fused with this person.

Differentiation—Children learn that they are different, separate from the caregiver, with a separate identity.

Practicing—Children learn to "leave" the caregiver, maybe just to go into another room where there is no direct experience of the caregiver.

Rapprochement—Children come back to the primary relationship, recognizing that they still need it and feel safe only in it.

Interdependence—Children learn that it is safe to come and go, that there is always a "home base," but that there also is freedom to practice away from it.

The successful completion of these developmental tasks in childhood allows for this cycle to be successfully repeated in later developmental periods. Couples, likewise, go through these stages:

Autism—The stage of being alone.

Enmeshment—The stage of being totally immersed in one another, the feeling that at last one has found the perfect partner. Adrenaline is pumping. Excitement is felt. Bells are ringing and music is playing. This may more commonly be referred to as the "honeymoon phase" or, in our culture, "falling in love."

Differentiation—The realization that we have differences and there are features of the partner we don't like. These may be minor, such as "He never puts the cap on the toothpaste," or major, such as "Our sexual appetites are quite different." These differences result in the feeling that this is not the perfect partner.

Practicing—The stage in which one or both partners experiment with finding themselves again outside the relationship. This may mean experimenting with new friends, pursuits, jobs, or interests. A sex addict may experience this stage as an excuse to find a new sexual or romantic partner. Other addictive or dysfunctional pursuits, such as working, may also be a part of practicing.

Rapprochement—The stage where partners continue to recognize and experiment with their own individual strengths; they also learn to come back to the relationship. There may be a feeling the relationship is not so bad, and partners may recognize there are elements that they need in it. Renewed romantic interest is a feature of this phase.

Mutual Interdependence—The stage in which both partners have lives outside of the relationship, but also feel committed to it. The partners need each other, but are comfortable with independent lives of their own.

Most couples are stuck in one of the earlier developmental stages, and very few reach mutual interdependence. One partner could be in one phase, while the other partner is stuck in another. This is entirely dependent on each one's individual developmental experience. There can be several different combinations of this. One common scenario is for a sex addict to be caught in the practicing stage, while the sexual co-addict is in the enmeshment stage. When this happens, long periods of estrangement, fighting, and addictive activity may be followed by a brief enmeshed, or "honeymoon," period.

Recognizing the nature of these stages allows couples to determine developmental tasks they must experiment with in order to grow and move more toward mutual interdependence. If one partner stays stuck, it points to individual developmental work that needs to be done before progress as a couple can be made.

Sexual Addict/Co-Addict Couples Suffer From Intimacy Disorder

As Carnes (1991) has described, sex addicts experience four core beliefs: (1) I am a bad and worthless person. (2) No one will love me as I am. (3) No one will take care of my needs but me. (4) Sex is my most important need. Sexual co-addicts experience the same first three beliefs, with the fourth being: Pleasing my sex addict is my most important need.

In either case, the core issue of shame impairs ability for intimate relationship. Sexual addicts and co-addicts believe: "If you knew me, you'd hate me and leave me." This belief obviously leads to a relationship in which the true self is hidden in favor of an image that is perceived to be more attractive and desirable. Intimacy disorder is an inability to reveal the true self for fear that it will be rejected.

We have found that this leads to another form of communication impairment. The sexually addicted partner often believes: "The person I'm most afraid of losing will be the person I'm the least likely to tell the truth to about myself." A co-addict of any nature conversely often believes: "If my partner loved me, he or she would tell me the truth." These two beliefs work against each other to convince both partners in a relationship that they don't really love each other. Dishonesty and blaming are the typical results.

Both partners must learn to risk revealing themselves. They must face their fear that if they tell the truth, the other partner will leave. It is a first-step issue: "I am powerless over my partner." Co-addicts must learn that lying and deceitful behavior may be a indications not of how little, but of how much, an addict loves or needs them. We believe that this risk must be practiced in small steps. Patience about total and brutal honesty is a necessary part of the process. For example, a critical issue for all sex addicts and co-addicts is if and when the total truth about past sexual behaviors will be told. Practice with telling the truth and patience with the truth-teller are a vital part of self-disclosure between partners and ultimately will lead to intimacy.

Sexual Addicts and Co-Addicts Are Both Codependents

Codependency is an overworked word, and definitions become confusing. To me, it is a consciously or unconsciously experienced fear of losing the approval and presence of others. Particularly when experienced with significant others, this fear can result in manipulative behaviors focused on maintaining the partner's presence. Developmentally, codependency can be an indication of unsuccessful enmeshment and differentiation in early childhood.

Obsequiousness, anger, caretaking, and a variety of defensive behaviors can all be manifestations of codependent controlling behavior. In sexually addicted/ co-addicted relationships, we have found that both partners are codependent. The difference is how the form of control is expressed. A sexual addict may feel that as long as his or her partner is sexually willing, approval is present. Controlling sexual initiation may be a form of codependency, one that many sexual trauma survivors learn. Sexual aggressiveness and withholding of sexual availability are one set of opposite forms that this control takes. Letting go of control and recognizing powerlessness are a first step in the challenge of recovery.

Sexual Addicts and Co-Addicts Experience Couple Shame

It follows that if two shame-based individuals create a relationship, the cumulative effect will also be shame-based. If individuals believe they are bad and worthless persons, when they become a couple they will believe they are a bad and worthless couple. They may perceive their sexual dysfunction as only one manifestation of this worthlessness. They may also believe that they are terrible friends and parents, that they manage money poorly, or that they can't get anything right. My wife and I experience, for example, a certain "house shame." We believe that we don't own or maintain a respectable house. The result is that we don't invite people over for fear of exposing our deficiencies, which serves to isolate us from social support. For shame-based couples, repetitive and unresolved arguments confirm the fact that they are bad. The next logical and resulting belief of couple shame is that the relationship is a mistake and the couple should be divorced or separated.

As Couples, Sexual Addicts and Co-Addicts Create a "Oneness"

This dynamic, I believe, is true for any couple. Two people in a committed relationship are a collective identity, a "oneness." They form an entity, whether it be called marriage, relationship, or coupleship. This became clear to us when our kids became teenagers and suddenly developed issues with their "parents." In their minds, we are a oneness.

In recovery, this oneness must be treated with the same kind of resources that an individual would use. A recovering individual needs therapy, sponsors, meetings, and lots of support. So does a couple. Recovering couples will also need therapy, sponsors who are couples, meetings of other couples, and lots of support for their coupleship.

Individual recovery may, on the other hand, become divisive to a relationship. An assumption sometimes operates in many recovery settings that as an individual becomes stronger in recovery, he or she will be able to be more independent. Although this is good, there may also not be the accompanying challenge to see how one can be independent and in relationship at the same time, that is, mutually interdependent. There will be challenges to why one is putting up with a partner's problematic behavior. One person may be challenged to "take care of yourself and get out of the relationship." Undoubtedly, there are many situations in which safety demands getting out. In other situations, however, it might be appropriate to learn how to set healthy boundaries and see if the relationship can work.

USING A 12-STEP PROCESS FOR COUPLE RECOVERY

Many 12-step fellowships, including those for sexual addiction, have spawned groups for co-addicts. Often the addiction program and its co-addiction counterpart will host open meetings together. It has not been that common, however, for these fellowships to encourage a couple approach to the 12 steps. One exception to this has been Recovering Couples Anonymous (RCA)*, which has adapted the steps in couple language. I use this adaptation to describe a 12-step process for couples.

    1. We admitted that we were powerless over our relationship and that our life together had become unmanageable.

This step assumes that both members of the relationship accept mutual responsibility for the disease in the relationship. As long as one partner is blaming the other for all of their couple problems, an honest first step is not possible. Like any first step, a couple's first step challenges both partners to let go of trying to control healing themselves.

Recounting the history of the relationship will be a part of this process. How have each other's addictions and co-addictions affected the relationship? What consequences have been experienced? What strategies have the partners tried to heal themselves that haven't worked? What are the repetitive arguments and fights? What is the nature of their collective shame?

Some sexual addict/co-addict couples will begin their relationship after each has been in individual recovery. They will not have a long history of dysfunction. The first step, however, encourages them to recognize they will repeat the mistakes of their previous relationships if they don't consider the dysfunctional characteristics each one brings from the past. Exploring psychodynamic wounds in each other will be a part of this process. This does not mean that partners are responsible for each other's wounds. It is important, however, to accept that these wounds will uncontrollably affect the relationship. One partner will trigger the other's issues. Learning to recognize and accept this will begin the process of building a healthy relationship.

    2. We came to believe that a power greater than ourselves could restore us to commitment and intimacy.

    3. We made a decision to turn the will and control of our lives together over to the care of God, as we understood God.

The deepest form of intimacy that can be experienced is spiritual intimacy. Because it is the deepest, it is the most frightening for most couples. Partners may come from totally different religious traditions or no tradition at all. Defen-

---

*For more information about RCA, contact the organization at P.O. Box 11872, St. Louis, MO, 63105; or call (314) 830–2600.

siveness about one's own traditions can be zealous because of the ultimate nature of the factors concerned. The second and third steps simply ask members of a couple to begin a process of spiritual exploration together. This will be like a journey or a quest. It is hoped that it will lead them to what they trust and ultimately find meaningful as a couple together.

Some couples will agree to traditional forms of spirituality together, such as prayer, meditation, scripture study, or church attendance. Others will look to less obviously religious approaches, such as nature walks, reading poetry, listening to music, or mutual reading. Some couples have undertaken geographic pilgrimages to spiritually significant places for them. Simply reading a 12-step meditation guide might be a start.

The third step asks that if a source of mutual belief or meaning can be found, the partners recognize that this is a source of support and strength for them. Making a commitment to each other in light of this support may be an initial expression of turning their relationship over. Many couples have found that renewing their vows or initiating commitment vows is an important part of this process.

4. We made a searching and fearless moral inventory of our relationship together as a couple.

5. We admitted to God, to ourselves, and to another couple the exact nature of our wrongs.

Individual partners should not make the mistake of confusing their individual moral inventory for a couple inventory. Individual fourth and fifth steps should be accomplished, but these steps concern the moral inventory of the relationship. A starting point for many sexual addict/co-addict couples may be an inventory of the sexual immorality their relationship has experienced. This can be difficult at points because there may be a disagreement about morality/immorality.

Couples working this step should examine how they have abused or neglected their relationship; how have they not taken time for themselves; how have they not played, communicated, or fought fairly; or how have they allowed themselves to be depleted.

Once the moral inventory has been completed, we have found it quite significant for the process of confession to include another couple. Doing so does a great deal to reduce the sense of couple shame. There will be a feeling of forgiveness or grace for the relationship.

6. We were entirely ready to have God remove all these defects of character, communication, and caring.

7. We humbly asked God to remove our shortcomings.

Defects of the character of a relationship, of commitment, and of communication can be extensive. Given the fact that communication may be a problem, it may be difficult even to define what the problems are. These two steps point to a lifetime process involving a commitment to change. Both partners must be "entirely ready" to give up patterns of interaction that they perceive have kept them alive and in the relationship.

We find it helpful to identify these issues in broad categories and ask for commitments or contracts for change. The use of a sponsoring couple or, in cases of more severe dysfunction, a therapist to help negotiate and monitor these contracts will be important. Briefly, we find the following issues to be important.

Sexuality.   Sexual dysfunction will normally be a part of sexual addict/co-addict couples. Even though sexual addicts may be quite sexually experienced, they may also be quite ignorant of normal human sexual response. Couples may contract for a process of education about sexuality. If functional sexual problems such as impotence are issues, medical evaluation, sex therapy, or both may be important. Finally, a couple may wish to contract for periods of abstinence. In the early days of recovery, abstinence may be important for the sex addict for its detoxifying quality. It may also help to reverse the core belief that sex is the most important need. A sexual co-addict must agree to this form of abstinence and accept it for the potential benefit of increased emotional and spiritual intimacy and not as another form of abandonment. A period of 90 days has been the standard recommendation as a period of abstinence. Recently, I talked to two partners who had extended this for 17 months, slowly building increased physical intimacy until they eventually experienced genital intercourse again. Doing this, they found that they had allowed themselves the time to heal from many of their emotional issues that sex had previously triggered.

Communication.   The ability to listen without being triggered into old feelings and the ability to express feelings without blaming a partner are skills that can be modeled or taught. A couple may wish to contract for therapy or communication workshops to facilitate these skills.

The ability to express anger and resentment is crucial to a communication contract. It is imperative for a couple to learn how to create a safe environment in which to share these feelings. This can be a separate agreement, sometimes called a "fighting contract," although the healthy result will not resemble anything like a fight. Some couples have regularly experienced fighting in their relationship; others never fight. In either case, partners should establish rules for safety, including scheduled times and places, for fights.

Recreation/Play.   Many sex addict/co-addict couples have forgotten how to have fun together. Others never knew in the first place. The trauma issues of one or both partners may have impaired childhood and left them without much ability to play. It is not uncommon for either partner to be totally without play experience. In these cases we have found it helpful to encourage couples to play at ages appropriate to the stage in which they feel developmentally stuck. They can use their own or other children as consultants. Contracts to make time for play help the couple to be accountable to this process.

Money.   In an informal and unscientific study, we found that whereas sex was the number one issue for sexual addict/co-addict couples, money was number two. Compulsive debt may be an issue the couple experiences. Contracts for who earns or manages the money, or both, and how it is spent should be established.

Roles.   We live in a time when the traditional roles of men and women have changed. Healthy couples will want to negotiate the roles in the relationship: Who earns money, who does the laundry, who cares for the house, and how parenting is shared are examples of this negotiation. These issues may be large or small. My wife and I had to negotiate who called the baby-sitter, because she felt that she always had to do it. I discovered that I hadn't liked calling 12-year-olds when I was 12, and I still don't.

Trust.   Sexual addict/co-addict couples may contract for behavioral changes that are necessary to build trust back into a relationship. Schneider and Schneider (1991) have described the main points that need to be addressed in such a contract (pp. 79–91). Maintenance of sobriety, letting go of control of your partner's behavior, consideration of each other's feelings, and sharing the truth about past behaviors are some of the elements of this process.

8. We made a list of all people we had harmed as a couple and became willing to make amends to them all.

9. We made direct amends except when to do so would injure them or others.

Like Steps 4 and 5, Steps 8 and 9 must not be confused with how each partner works individually on them. Partners must be encouraged to look at any people they have *collectively* harmed. The list could include their own children, other family members, and friends. For example, partners might recognize that due to their dysfunction as a couple, they have not been healthy parents. How has this damaged their children? How will they make restitution and change (amend) their behavior? This might seem to give children ammunition to criticize their parents in the future. We have found that it serves to model healthy responsibility taking and to open the lines of communication.

Doing this step collectively means that the couple has accepted the mutual nature of the couple dysfunction. This may even allow both partners to see how one partner's behavior, which has created damage, is something to be collectively sorry about.

Steps 8 and 9, like all the steps, are a matter of lifetime process. Partners should always seek to accept whom they've harmed, what has been the damage, and how they can make amends. These steps should also be the ones a couple checks out most carefully with a sponsor to prevent creating further damage to others.

10. We continued to take personal inventory and, when we were wrong, promptly admitted it.

The tenth step is obviously a continuation, for a lifetime, of the fourth and fifth. We have found that partners can do an exercise to help them practice this step with each other. It is called the "weekly inventory." Once a week, at an agreed-upon time, each partner makes two lists. The first is a list of those things he or she personally did over the past week that were *harmful* to the relationship. The second is a list of those things over the past week that his or her partner did that were *helpful* to the relationship. Each list can contain as many items as seem appropriate. The two people then exchange lists without each person's being able to comment on or add to his or her partner's list.

This basic exercise does two things. It teaches partners to accept and be responsible for their own mistakes. Second, it gives each person the opportunity to give his or her partner affirmations. The weekly inventory reverses the process of blame and helps the couple be more affirming. From this basic practice with each other, the partners will learn how to accept responsibility for their mistakes as a couple and how to affirm others.

11. We sought through our common prayer and meditation to improve our conscious contact with God as we understand God, praying only for knowledge of God's will for us and the power to carry that out.

The eleventh step continues the work of the second and third. We find that it is also important in this step for a couple to consider what is the meaning and purpose of their relationship. Is the purpose of the relationship to have children, to exist for each other's nurturing, or to contribute or be of service to the world in some large way? Often, we have seen one partner's individual sense of purpose for his or her life unfulfilled because of the relationship. My wife spent a lot of time working while I went to graduate school. She sacrificed whatever goals for herself she might have had in order to support me and our relationship financially. If we don't accept this sacrifice mutually, if I take her support toward our purpose for granted, she may feel resentment and anger.

Both members of the couple should communicate their own sense of individual purpose and their own sense of purpose for the relationship. How will the partners be supportive of each other in these individual dreams? What do the partners see as their purpose together? One exercise we find helpful is for a couple to write a couple mission statement. What do the partners seek to do as a couple? They can then share this with their sponsoring couple and seek accountability in achieving their goals.

12. Having had a spiritual awakening as the result of these steps, we tried to carry this message to other couples and to practice these principles in all aspects of our lives, our relationship, and our families.

If recovery is going well for a couple, the successful intimacy the partners are achieving will be a model to others. Their own success can be enhanced by sharing with others, not in a grandiose way, but with the humility of recognizing how hard the work has been. Building a successful committed relationship will also help each partner in relationships in other areas of life. Relationships with other family members, coworkers, and people in the wider community will be improved because of the transfer of these new skills.

SUMMARY

Building any committed relationship is hard work. For recovering couples, much practice and patience are required. Old wounds that create impairments to individuals and the relationship must be addressed. Support in the community and fellowship of other couples must be found. Recovering couples search to be accountable to contracts for change. Each individual in a couple learns how to exchange instant, perhaps addictive, gratification for the joy of ongoing intimacy. Sexual addict/co-addict recovering couples find that this intimacy and the trust it creates are things that few other couples ever know.

REFERENCES

Bader, E., & Pearson, P. T. (1988). *In quest of the mythical mate.* New York: Brunner/ Mazel.

Carnes, P. J. (1991). *Don't call it love: Recovery from sexual addiction.* New York: Bantam.

Laaser, M. (1992). *The secret sin.* Grand Rapids, MI: Zondervan.

Schneider, J. P., & Schneider, B. (1991). *Sex, lies, and forgiveness.* Center City, MN: Hazelden.

CHAPTER 10

Disclosure of Extramarital Sexual Activities by Persons With Addictive or Compulsive Sexual Disorders

Results of a Study and Implications for Therapists

JENNIFER P. SCHNEIDER
M. DEBORAH CORLEY

Despite religious and cultural precepts that forbid sexual activities outside marital relationships, such behaviors have continued in most societies and are common in the United States. Fifty years ago, Kinsey and associates found that one in two husbands (Kinsey, Pomeroy, & Martin, 1948) and one in four wives (Kinsey, Pomeroy, Martin, & Gebhard, 1953) had engaged in extramarital sex. During the peak of the "sexual revolution" 20 years later, the reported numbers of unfaithful women increased (Tavris & Sadd, 1975), and categories of affairs were defined on the basis of approval or disapproval and knowledge or lack of knowledge by the spouses about the affair (O'Neill & O'Neill, 1976; Rubin & Adams, 1986). In surveys published in the United States in the past 2 decades, more than 50% of men and women admitted they had engaged in marital infidelity at some time in their marriage (Glass & Wright, 1992; Hatcher et al., 1990; Thompson, 1983).

In attempts to understand extramarital sexual behavior, clinicians and researchers have utilized various definitions. Moultrup (1990) defines an extramarital affair as "a relationship between a person and someone other than his [sic] spouse that has an impact on the level of intimacy, emotional distance, and overall dynamic balance in the marriage" (p. 11). Pittman (1989) defines infidelity as "a breach of the trust, a betrayal of a relationship, a breaking of an agreement. . . . We might define adultery as a sexual act outside the marriage, while we might define infidelity as a sexual dishonesty within the marriage." It is not, however, entirely clear what constitutes sexual relations outside the marriage, or, for that matter, sexual relations at all. In a study reported in 1999 (Sanders & Reinisch, 1999), 59% of college students surveyed believed that oral sex does *not* constitute "having sex," and 19% believed that even penile penetration of the anus did not constitute "having sex." A more recent and burgeoning example of uncertainty about infidelity relates to cybersex, which can be defined as any form of sexual activity involving the computer. This can include viewing and downloading pornography, exchanging sexual talk online, and videostreaming, in which two persons participate in real-time sexual activities online while cameras attached to each participant's computer transmit images to the other, showing what each one is doing. Is cybersex cheating? When the cybersex user engages in real-time online sex with another person, most partners react as though skin-to-skin adultery has taken place (Schneider, 2000).

Persons who suffer from addictive sexual disorders engage in a wide variety of sexual behaviors, frequently outside of their marriage or primary relationship (Carnes, 1991). Many chemically dependent persons who are not sexually addicted also engage in extramarital sexual behaviors, sometimes because their judgment is impaired or the chemical use is disinhibiting, at other times as part of an exchange of sex for drugs. When help is finally sought, one of the questions most frequently asked by patients is whether or not to disclose the sexual behaviors to the partner. Regardless of the presence or absence of an addictive disorder, the secret existence of sexual activities involves several ethical considerations:

- The accumulation of lies about the behavior;
- The possibility of health risks to the partner; and
- The ethical dilemma of the couple's therapist, who is told by one partner about extramarital sexual behavior, but is asked not to reveal the information to the other partner.

Honesty and fidelity are implied or clearly stated in most marital contracts or agreements (Brown, 1991; Hyde, 1990; Reiss, 1980). Pittman (1989) states that dishonesty may be a greater violation of the rules than the affair (or misconduct) is and acknowledges that more marriages end as a result of maintaining the secret than do in the wake of telling. He firmly supports rigorous honesty. He speculates that the partner may be angry, but will be more angry if the affair continues and the partner finds out later.

Brown (1991) advises that in most circumstances, the unfaithful person must tell the partner if healing is to occur. When an affair remains secret, communication about other matters is gradually impaired. She does indicate that behaviors from previous relationships or the long ago past do not always have to be revealed. Brown also advises that time and support for the partner are necessary and often take longer sessions or more sessions of therapy to help the partner express her or his anger and sadness about the infidelity before actual rebuilding of the relationship can occur.

When secret extramarital sexual activities intrude on a primary committed relationship, one question inevitably surfaces: Should one disclose the infidelity to the partner? Some authors have asserted the need for honesty and disclosure (Pittman, 1989; Subotnik & Harris, 1994; Vaughan, 1989), and some even give advice about what and when to tell (Subotnik & Harris, 1994; Vaughan, 1989; Wallerstein and Blakeslee, 1989). In contrast, many clinicians hesitate to recommend full or even partial disclosure because of the client's fears that the uninvolved spouse may choose to leave the relationship. Many partners who have suspected the existence of extramarital sexual activities have in fact threatened to leave should their suspicions be confirmed; on the basis of such threats, both the involved spouse and the therapist may consider it too risky to disclose. The concern is exacerbated when there has been a long-standing pattern of infidelity, as typically exists when one partner has a compulsive sexual disorder.

INFIDELITY AS AN ELEMENT OF ADDICTION

When the extramarital sexual activity is part of an addictive pattern, the need for honesty takes on an additional dimension. An assumption of addiction-sensitive therapy is that rigorous honesty is required if one is to remain sober and in recovery. These assumptions are based on the teachings of the book *Alcoholics Anonymous* (1976), which states that those who do not recover are men and women who are "constitutionally incapable of being honest" (p. 58). The eighth of the 12 Steps of Alcoholics Anonymous (AA) relates that "We made a list of all persons we have harmed, and became willing to make amends to them all." The purpose of the eighth step is to identify the individuals who have been harmed by the addict's behavior as well as assigning responsibility for the addict's behavior. By addicts' preparing to eliminate the burden of emotions they carry, they may release guilt and other feelings that have been mismanaged through the addictive sexual behavior.

However, another assumption of the 12-step recovery model is stated in Step 9, "We made amends to such people wherever possible, except when doing so will injure them or others." Fear of hurting the partner and fear of the partner's response are common reasons for minimizing the disclosure (Carnes, 1991; Schneider & Schneider, 1990; Schneider, Corley, & Irons, 1998). This presents a dilemma for the addict, his or her partner, and the therapist. Berry and Baker (1996) advise those who have great fear about disclosure that to effectively manage the fear, the first step is to be honest about the behaviors. These authors speculate that one of the reasons AA is so effective is that it emphasizes making amends, then asking forgiveness for what one has done.

When referring to sex, however, the author of *Alcoholics Anonymous* favors nondisclosure:

> We know of situations in which the alcoholic or his wife have had love affairs. In the first flush of spiritual experience they forgave each other and drew closer together. . . . Then, under one provocation or another, the aggrieved one would unearth the old affair and angrily cast its ashes about . . . and they hurt a great deal. . . . In most cases, the alcoholic survived this ordeal without relapse, but not always. So we think that unless some good and useful purpose is to be served, past occurrences should not be discussed. (pp. 124–125)

How not to disclose to the spouse is spelled out in greater detail:

> If we are sure our wife does not know, should we tell her? Not always, we think. If she knows in a general way that we have been wild, should we tell her in detail? Undoubtedly we should admit our fault. She may insist on knowing all the particulars. She will want to know who the woman is and where she is. We feel we ought to say to her that we have no right to involve another person. We are sorry for what we have done and, God willing, it shall not be repeated. More than that we cannot do; we have no right to go further. . . . We have often found this the best course to take. (p. 81)

Sex addicts who have sought guidance about disclosure have likewise received mixed messages. On the one hand, they are repeatedly reminded that they are in a program of "rigorous honesty" and that honesty is essential for recovery. On the other hand, *Sexaholics Anonymous* (1984), a 12-step guide for recovery used by members of Sexaholics Anonymous (SA), cautions the recovering addict to be very careful about disclosure to the spouse. The book advises newcomers to the program not to discuss their sexual past with partners who do not already know of it until some time has elapsed, and even then only after first talking about it with group members. Echoing the AA *Big Book*, *Sexaholics Anonymous* cautions that some marriages might otherwise not withstand the shock. Avoiding compulsive sexual behaviors and working the steps of the program will, it is hoped, cause improvement in behavior and attitude that the partner will see and feel. "The best amends is a changed life over time" (p. 87).

Hope and Recovery (1987), a 12-step guide for sex addicts that is often considered comparable to the *Big Book* of AA, expresses the same point of view: One should wait to tell the partner until one has first discussed it with the group, prayed about it, and felt it was the right time to do so.

> Some of us found that it was helpful to have our sponsors with us when we told our partners about our addiction. And if our partners also happened to be in recovery, it was helpful to have their sponsors present too. . . . We wrote

down exactly what we wanted to say to our partners and shared it with other addicts first. (p. 97)

A study of wives of male sex addicts found that many of the wives had ceded to their husbands the power to make them happy or unhappy and to make decisions about their emotional lives (Schneider, 1988). Many wives had lived with an ongoing pattern of deception and dishonesty. For the addict to continue to withhold information about the infidelity felt to these wives like perpetuation of the old pattern, in which the husband decides what is best for the wife and what information to withhold. Nearly every woman felt it should be her decision how much to be told; most did not ask for information that they were not ready to hear. According to Schneider (p. 251), "If a relationship is to survive the crisis of disclosure of his affairs, a spirit of honesty and respect for each partner is essential. Treating one's wife with respect means letting her decide how much she needs to know and then giving her answers to the questions she asks." Based on her interviews, Schneider strongly recommended disclosure guided by the spouse's desire to know.

A STUDY OF DISCLOSURE OF EXTRAMARITAL SEXUAL ACTIVITIES

Few published studies have addressed whether disclosure is advisable and how the therapist might facilitate the process of disclosure so that it may be healing to both the couple and the individuals involved. Relationship issues resulting from addictive or compulsive sexual problems have long been an interest of ours (Corley & Alvarez, 1996; Schneider, 1991; Schneider & Schneider, 1989, 1990a, 1990b, 1990c, 1996), as have relationship problems resulting from sexual exploitation by a professional member of the couple (Irons & Schneider, 1999). Because of the compulsive nature of the behaviors, there is usually an extensive history of sexual infidelities. The emphasis on honesty in the patient's recovery process results in pressure to disclose infidelities to partners despite fears of the consequences. For that reason, such a group can be expected to be particularly informative for studying issues of disclosure.

Using an anonymous, self-administered survey, Schneider, Corley, and Irons (1998, 1999) carried out a qualitative study addressing the consequences of choice of timing, extent, and manner of disclosure of the extramarital sexual behavior to the partner. Separate surveys were constructed for addicts and partners. The survey contained closed, multiple-choice (with a 5-point, Likert-like scale), and open-ended questions. Examples of open-ended questions were those related to the meaning of disclosure to both the addict and the partner, what each individual identified as helpful or unhelpful actions or advice by the therapist, and what was the outcome of the disclosure for the couple's relationship. The survey took approximately 1–1.5 hours to complete. A convenience sample of American and Canadian psychotherapists who treat sex addicts and their partners was asked to distribute surveys to current and former clients. Additional surveys were sent to five contact persons within the sex addiction recovery community for distribution to self-identified recovering sex addicts and partners

The respondents consisted of persons and partners (or former partners) of persons who had been diagnosed by a professional as having an addictive or compulsive sexual disorder (Sexual Disorder NOS in the *DSM-IV*) and a few who were self-identified as sex addicts or partners (or former partners) of sex addicts. Originally, surveys were distributed to persons who were members of a couple. A subsequent mailing specifically targeted persons whose primary relationships had ended as a result of sexual compulsivity problems and who were now separated or divorced.

A total of 161 surveys were returned following the initial mailing, a return rate of well over 16.0% of those actually distributed. Of the total, 81 addicts and 80 partners responded. Of the partners in this group (Group A), 4 out of 78 (5%) were separated or divorced. In addition, the second mailing of 120 surveys directed to therapists working with persons who were separated or divorced yielded 36 responses (30%), consisting of 20 addicts and 16 partners (Group B).

Of the entire group, half the respondents were male, and half female; 75% were currently married or in a committed long-term relationship, whereas 25% were separated or divorced. The mean age of the respondents was 43.8 years (SD = 9.1), with a range of 26–70; the mean age of the addicts was 45, and the partners' mean age was 42.6 years. Among the addicts, 93 (91.2%) were male; among the partners, 88 (93.6%) were female. As to sexual orientation, 91.7% of the respondents identified themselves as heterosexual, and 8.3% were homosexual or bisexual.

The occupations of the respondents are summarized in table 10.1.

The licensed helping professionals included physicians, nurses, psychologists, social workers, physical therapists, and clergy. Other regulated professionals included lawyers, professors, and teachers. Most respondents were employed, and most had received higher education.

Of 100 sex addicts who specified their compulsive behaviors, 91 (91%) had engaged in sexual activities with other people outside the marriage. Many had engaged in multiple behaviors, including having affairs with opposite- or same-sex persons, having sex with prostitutes, visiting massage parlors, frequenting

TABLE 10.1. Occupations of Respondents [*n* = 155]

Licensed helping professionals	38	(24.5%)
Other regulated professionals	36	(23.2%)
Other employed (CEOs, trades, etc.)	64	(41.3%)
Nonwage earners	17	(11%)

pornographic bookstores or theaters, or engaging in sexual activities with patients or clients. Among the 9 persons whose sexual activities had not involved contact with other people, several had engaged in illegal behaviors such as voyeurism or exhibitionism. The survey did not ask specifically about sexual involvement with patients or clients in a professional setting. However, several addicts stated that their compulsive sexual behaviors did involve crossing professional boundaries. The study was done before there was widespread use of the Internet for sex, so it did not address this emerging problem.

Persons with addictive disorders often have more than one type of addiction or compulsive behavior. Only 42% of the 102 sex addicts in this study stated that they had no other addiction; 49% reported they were also recovering from addiction to alcohol, other drugs, and/or nicotine (3 persons identified nicotine as their only drug of addiction), or some combination of these; 25% identified an eating disorder; 12% were compulsive spenders; and the remainder identified other addictions and compulsions. Among the partners, 29% reported having an eating disorder and 17% were in recovery from chemical dependence (of whom 3 identified nicotine as their only addictive drug).

Among the addicts, the median time in recovery from sex addiction was 3.4 years, with a range of from less than 1 month to 16 years; 35% had less than 2 years, 33% had 2 to less than 5 years, and 32% had at least 5 years recovery. A majority of the partners had attended self-help programs based on the Al-Anon model. Nearly all (90.8%) of the respondents saw or were seeing a professional counselor or therapist; 59.2% of the entire group had seen more than one type of professional. In other words, members of this population had received both professional and peer support in their recovery process.

Relapses

Addictions are generally recognized as being chronic disorders with an ongoing propensity for relapse. In a relapsing disorder, disclosure, too, is likely to be a process or a series of events rather than a single occurrence. In the present study, 41 out of 80, or 51.2% of addicts, reported at least one significant slip or relapse, which was self-defined. Table 10.2 presents the results to this question separated out by length of time in recovery.

TABLE 10.2. Have You Had a Relapse or Significant Slip? (*n* = 80)

Time in recovery	< 2 years	2– < 5 years	5 or more years
Yes	9 31%	14 60.8%	18 64.3%
No	20	9	10
Total	29	23	28

Twice as many addicts who were in recovery for more than 2 years had a relapse than did addicts in short-term recovery. Among those with at least 5 years in recovery, 64.3% reported having had a significant slip or relapse, in many cases occurring well after the first year or two. This result confirms that sex addiction, like other addictions, is a chronic relapsing disease; a corollary is that recovering sex addicts and their partners will be faced with disclosure decisions and consequences more than once in the course of their relationship.

Information Withheld

When asked, "Are you still withholding some significant information about your past sexual behaviors from your partner?" 33 out of 79 addicts, or 41.8%, answered yes. As to withholding significant information about *current* sexual behaviors, 28 out of 78, or 35.9% responded affirmatively. Table 10.3 summarizes the responses.

Again, more of those in long-term recovery than in early recovery reported withholding significant information about both past and present behaviors, confirming that disclosure is an ongoing issue for couples.

Threats to Leave Before the Disclosure

Long before disclosure took place, many partners suspected correctly that affairs or other extramarital sex was occurring. Over half of the partners (52.8%) were suspicious enough to confront their spouses. Most (84%) of the addicts who were confronted denied any wrongdoing. Before the first disclosure, 29 out of 77 partners (37.7%) in the still-married group (Group A) threatened to leave because they had some suspicions, as did 7 of the 16 (44%) of the divorced/ separated group (Group B). Among the addicts, 44.4% of Group A and 60% of Group B recalled receiving such threats. Understandably, this might have given pause to the offending partners about the wisdom of disclosing that these activities had actually taken place. Threats to leave were common whether or not the couples eventually stayed together.

TABLE 10.3. Ongoing Withholding of Information by Addicts

Time in Recovery	< 2 years	2– < 5 years	5 or more years
yes, past behaviors	9/28 = 32.1%	8/23 = 34.8%	16/28 = 57.1%
yes, current behaviors	8/29 = 27.6%	7/22 = 31.8%	13/27 = 48.1%

Threats to Leave After Disclosure and Outcomes of the Threats

In Group A, 47 (60.2%) of the partners reported threatening to leave after hearing the disclosure. However, of the 47 marriages where threats to leave occurred after disclosure, only 11 (23.4%) of the couples actually separated. In 34 cases (72.4%) the couples stayed together throughout. Table 10.2 summarizes the data for 45 partners of Group A who responded. It is notable that of those spouses who threatened to leave, one-quarter actually did so, only temporarily.

When the partners who did not leave despite having threatened were asked for an explanation, half (36.2%) of the 45 who had threatened to leave stated that they stayed because one or both went to therapy and 12-step programs (those based on the Alcoholics Anonymous model) and were working actively on their recovery. An equal number of partners (36.2% of the 45 who threatened to leave) were unable to take effective action, changed their minds, or decided to "give him another chance."

In Group B, consisting of 16 former partners who did leave the marriage, 10, or 62.5%, threatened to leave at the time of disclosure. Compared with the 60.2% of partners from Group A who threatened to leave, there is clearly no difference. Thus, a threat to leave did not predict the eventual outcome.

How Much to Disclose Initially

When they first get into recovery, addicts wonder how much to disclose to the partners. In addition to fears that the partner will leave the relationship, female addicts in particular may fear physical or sexual violence from their partners as a response to the disclosure. Both male and female addicts may worry whether an angry spouse will use the information against them as a means of emotional blackmail or in a future battle for custody of the children.

Addicts often get conflicting advice from therapists, friends, and sponsors about this, especially when the acting out involved sexual contact with other people. Some addicts were glad they had revealed "all." Others, however, regretted having told too much:

> I feel I offered too much information. To admit I was involved with another woman was one thing, but I truly wish I had never told her who the woman was. Some people cannot handle truth and honesty as well as others. You have to know your partner and what they can handle. [10 months' recovery]
>
> I hope it wasn't just "dumping" but I felt cleaner, relieved. But I shouldn't have shared so much hurtful to her. Now it's hard for her to have so much information. The knowledge doesn't help her and seems only to cause pain as dates roll around or if we drive past a particular place. [11 months' recovery]

Partners also had mixed opinions:

> I needed total disclosure so I could have a "level playing field" to start to trust
> my spouse. If he could still lie and hide the past, how could I be sure he
> wouldn't continue to do so in the future? There are no guarantees, but dis-
> closure of secrets on both our parts at least gave us an honest place to start.
>
> I created a lot of pain for myself by asking questions and gathering in-
> formation. I have a lot of negative memories to overcome; this ranges from
> songs on the radio to dates, places, and situations; there are numerous triggers.
>
> I think it's best for the addict to work through it with a knowledgeable
> therapist, then disclose the nature of the problem and have the partner de-
> termine what level of detail they are comfortable with. For me, I didn't want
> any more detail, because it tormented me. Others feel they want to know
> everything. Not me. The bottom line I needed to know was whether he was
> exposing himself to disease and then not protecting me. The actual details of
> who, where, when were extremely distracting to me and caused me to lose
> ground. I'd make some progress, then think about one of those details and
> spiral down.

Recurrent themes expressed by partners were (1) a desire to feel empowered,
to be the one to decide how much to be told, and (2) a wish they had sought or
received more support from peers and counselors at the time of disclosure.

Staggered Disclosure

It is tempting for an unfaithful partner to attempt damage control by initially
revealing only some information, not all. A majority of addicts (58.7%) and
partners (69.7%) reported that there had been more than one major disclosure.
Several partners described the adverse effects of staggered disclosure. One woman
wrote,

> There were several major disclosures over 6 months. I was completely devas-
> tated. He continued to disclose half truths, and only increased my pain and
> made the whole situation worse. Each new disclosure was like reliving the
> initial pain all over again. I wish the truth had been disclosed all at once and
> not in bits and pieces.

A man who was sent to prison as a consequence of his sexual behavior
disclosed to his wife only some of his activities. She wrote,

> Disclosure came in parts during the first year. Some of the past was reported
> to the presentence investigator and I read it while he was in prison for 3
> months. I felt immense pain and anger. Part of that was not being told. I felt
> lied to and didn't trust any of the relationship.

Adverse Consequences of the Disclosure

When asked, "Did you experience any adverse consequences as a result of the disclosure?" the vast majority of both groups, as expected, said they had—97.3% of the addicts and 92.2% of the partners. The most common consequences for the addicts were compromise of the relationship (40.8%), followed by emotional problems and depression (25%). Among the partners, 59.4% reported emotional problems and depression, and 23.4% felt their relationship was compromised. Of course, many of these consequences can be considered secondary to the behavior, rather than to its disclosure. Other adverse consequences included damage to other relationships such as with children, parents, and friends; legal consequences such as arrests; and financial consequences such as job loss and costs of treatment.

Disclosure During Inpatient Treatment

In several cases, disclosure to unsuspecting spouses was done long-distance over the telephone. The wife of one physician who had had sexual relations with several patients reported,

> My husband phoned me from the psychiatric hospital, where he was surrounded by nurturing, caring professionals and fellow addicts. I was in our bedroom painting furniture, surrounded by our five small children. I never would have believed for a minute he would actually have sex with anyone outside the marriage. I was absolutely shocked by the seriousness and extent of his behaviors. There never would have been an easy way to disclose all this stuff, but I should have been given the same supportive environment as my husband. The spouse needs just as much guidance and support as the addict.

A dentist who had multiple affairs and other forms of sexual acting out had sex with a fellow patient during inpatient treatment for sex addiction. He phoned his wife and told her about this. He reported that it ended the marriage. "She was very angry. I wish I had told her in person, with the counselor present."

Adverse experiences were also reported by partners who received disclosures of significant sexual activities during a therapy session at the inpatient facility and were then left to process the news alone and were not provided with referrals for follow-up back home:

> After the disclosure, I should never have been allowed to return to my motel room. I truly believe God drove the car to the motel, because I didn't even see the road. I needed 24-hour attendance. Since then I have felt loneliness and the lack of counselors in our city with the expertise I saw at my husband's treatment facility. I still long for an opportunity to speak with other profes-

sionals' wives who have common backgrounds as myself. I am recovering from a traumatic experience.

Public Disclosure

A particularly egregious type of betrayal of the primary relationship occurs when a physician, psychotherapist, or clergy person becomes involved sexually with a patient, client, or other person with whom he or she has a fiduciary relationship. Such relationships are expressly forbidden by their professional associations, and in at least a dozen states they are considered felony crimes. In cases when the extramarital sexual behavior is illegal (e.g., solicitation of a prostitute, professional sexual misconduct), the disclosure and its aftermath may be played out in the public arena. The wife of an exploitative professional may be seen as an accessory to the misconduct. A 49-year-old health professional who had been married to a clergyman reported,

> Because he was charged with a sexual offense against a minor and it was announced on the local radio, each member of our family suffered humility and loss of face in public. . . . It was extremely difficult for any of us to walk down the street in our town. My husband and I were both well known in the community. When the disclosure came, many of our friends were stunned and pulled away; many have not contacted me to this day. The church as a whole avoided us. Even the friends who were "there" for us presentence fell away. Quite accidentally I discovered that they believed I had known all along about my husband's secret behaviors and had not spared their children exposure; in other words, I conspired with my husband to lure their unsuspecting children to our home. . . . I felt I had to leave the community for my sanity. I resigned my job, my husband and I separated, and I moved to another state.

Positive Outcomes of Disclosure

Both addicts and partners reported significant positive aspects of disclosure. Honesty, an end to denial, and hope for the future were recurrent themes mentioned by addicts. Partners described the main positive outcomes to disclosure as clarity, validation, and hope for the future:

> One of the most helpful things about it for me was that it confirmed my reality. My husband had repeatedly told me how crazy and jealous I was. Over time I had started believing him. Finding out I had not misread the situation helped me to begin trusting myself, that I wasn't as crazy as he said or as I had thought. It was the best and worst day of my life. I knew for once that he told the truth at the risk of great personal cost. It gave me hope that he could grow up and face life's responsibilities. It was the first time his

words of love and his actions were congruent. I felt respected, relieved, out-raged, sick. It gave me hope for our relationship.

The responses of Group B, now separated or divorced, were similar. A ca-reer woman, now divorced, wrote, "I had been in such a crazy-making state for so long. Learning it had been a 12-month affair helped me put it all in perspective. I was angry, hurt, shocked—and relieved."

How Important Is It to Disclose to Your Partner?

The survey asked addicts and partners whether they felt at the time that disclo-sure was the right thing to do, and how they feel about it now. At the time, 44 (57.9% of the addicts in Group A) felt it was definitely or probably the right thing to do, but significantly more, 73 (96.1%) felt that way at the time of the survey ($p < 0.01$). Nine (11.8%) of the addicts felt at the time that it was probably or certainly wrong, compared with only 1 (1.3%) of the addicts at the time of the survey.

In contrast, despite the pain of experiencing disclosure, a large majority of partners (81.3%) felt it was a right thing, even at the time, and this proportion increased even further with the passage of time (93%), although the difference was not statistically significant. Significantly more partners than addicts ($p < 0.01$) initially believed in the rightness of disclosure, but at the time of the survey, the difference between addicts and partners was no longer significant.

Among addicts who thought it was important to disclose, the primary rea-sons for this belief were that it was essential for one's own recovery, that the partner deserved and needed to know, that truth was needed for the couple relationship to be healthy, and that it was important because there were health and safety considerations.

Among partners who recommended disclosure, the chief reasons were that the offending partner needed honesty to begin healing and reduce the shame and guilt felt; the partner needed to know in order to assess her health risk, to be able to make informed choices about the future, and to obtain validation.

Even among those who eventually divorced, the consensus was in favor of disclosure. A woman who is now divorced stated, "Should he fully disclose? Absolutely. As soon as possible. Within couple's therapy so both partners are safe, or with two individual therapists present. Trust cannot be rebuilt until all the secrets are on the table."

When asked, "Would you recommend disclosure to other couples?" 71% of the addicts in Group A and 82.7% of the partners said definitely or probably yes. The responses for Group B were similar, despite the demise of their mar-riages: 65% of the 20 addicts and 87.5% of the 16 partners said definitely or probably yes.

Several partners felt strongly that in cases where the offending spouse is already in treatment or in counseling and is advised to disclose, consideration should be given to providing the partner with support to handle the disclosure.

Study Conclusions: The Threat and the Reality of Disclosure

Disclosure of an affair or other extramarital sexual activity is often delayed because of fears of the partner's reaction, specifically, the fear that the partner will leave the relationship. Although the partners in this study often described their reactions to the disclosure in terms of despair, devastation, and hopelessness, and although most initially considered ending the relationship, most chose to stay and to work it through.

Threats to leave the relationship, a common expression of anger, are a frequent initial reaction by the partner to disclosure of extramarital sexual behavior: 60.3% of spouses stated they had threatened or considered leaving, and 51.3% of addicts reported that they knew of such threats or feelings by the betrayed partner. However, only one quarter of partners actually followed through on their threats with separation. An interesting finding was there was no difference in the percentage of partners who threatened to leave among those who ultimately stayed (60.3%), compared with those who eventually did separate or divorce (62.5%). Thus, threatening to leave after receiving a disclosure is very common and is not a predictor of the eventual end of the marriage.

Initially, adverse consequences were inevitable. Addicts whose partners had threatened to leave "if I find out you had an affair" were fearful of the loss of the relationship. Many addicts reported feeling shame and loss of self-esteem at the time of disclosure. Both members of the couple reported significant emotional consequences. Many partners were angry, as reflected in their threats to exit the marriage. However, most of those who threatened did not actually leave, either because one or both partners went into counseling or other treatment, or because the consequences of leaving appeared to outweigh those of remaining in the relationship.

Most of the partners (81.3%) felt right from the time of the initial disclosure that the disclosure had been a good thing. A smaller majority of the addicts (57.9%) felt this way at the time of disclosure, but many more (96.1%) came around to this point of view after the passage of time. The majority of both groups (71% of addicts and 82.7% of partners) recommended disclosure to other couples. Addicts favored disclosure because it represented hope for the future, an end to denial, and a chance to come clean and put an end to secret keeping. Partners recommended receiving the disclosure because it provided validation for their perceptions and suspicions, which had frequently been discounted by the addict, because it provided hope for the future, and because it often led to a shift in focus from the addict's needs to their own. Both groups believed that honesty is an important healing characteristic, for each partner, as well as for the couple relationship.

Because the study subjects were not a random sample of sex addicts and partners, it was not possible to assess the statistical probability that a couple will separate or divorce following disclosure of the sexual acting out. However, the value of the particular study population selected is that the betrayal and lying involved were generally more egregious and longer-lasting and involved more offenses than relationships in which disclosure of only one or two affairs was the issue. If such couples can work through the issues of restoring trust, forgiveness, and getting the marriage back on track, then other couples for whom addiction and recurrent betrayal are not present might be expected to recover with less difficulty. The experiences of the couples reported here can provide valuable information for therapists who counsel all couples about disclosure.

One factor that is both a strength and a limitation of this study is that the couples were sampled at varying times in the course of recovery from the betrayal and disclosure—from a few weeks to many years. Many of these couples were still in the process of working through the consequences of the betrayal. The study therefore provided a cross-section of the recovery process at a particular time. Only a longitudinal study would reveal how many of the couples who were separated at the time of the study will ultimately reconcile, and how many of the couples who were together will eventually separate.

DISCUSSION AND IMPLICATIONS FOR THERAPISTS

Disclosure is an important and recurrent theme in couple recovery from sexual addiction. Long after the initial major disclosure has taken place, both addicts and partners can describe in detail exactly what happened and how they felt about it. The way the disclosure was handled can have long-lasting effects on the couple's relationship and can have a major positive or adverse impact on the partner's ability to forgive or rebuild trust. Implications for therapists are discussed in the following sections.

The Therapist and Concealed Infidelity

The therapist who knows of a concealed affair or other sexual acting out faces an ethical dilemma about its revelation. Glass and Wright (1992, p. 327) believe "it is inappropriate to conduct conjoint marital therapy when there is a secret alliance between one spouse and an extramarital partner that is being supported by another secret alliance between the involved spouse and the therapist." However, they are willing to see the couple without addressing the affair if it is first terminated.

Brown (1991, p. 56) writes, "I believe that the integrity of the therapeutic process with couples depends on open and honest communication. Nowhere is this truer than with affairs. The therapist cannot be effective while colluding with one spouse to hide the truth from the other." She does list a few exceptions in which maintaining the secret with the client is the wiser choice: When there is the potential for physical violence or for destructive litigation in divorce courts, or if the unfaithful client is remaining in the marriage to care for a permanently incapacitated spouse. Brown's position is clear (p. 68):

> Sometimes the Infidel refuses to tell the Spouse. In that case marital therapy cannot continue. Once you know about the affair, nothing else can be done until the affair is out in the open. . . . If you are tempted to see [each of] them individually, consider the impact on the therapeutic relationship when the Spouse finds later that you knew about the affair all along. Refer each of them to separate therapists.

In her book *After the Affair* (2000), Spring disagrees and reminds the reader that it is not always better to confess or to conceal if the goal is to rebuild the relationship. She goes on to clarify that there are disadvantages of telling. She outlines four situations in which it may turn out badly if the partner's spirit to work on the relationship will be crushed or if telling will create an obsessional focus on the affair or keep both partners from examining the problem that caused it. She also includes advice not to tell if the partner fears physical harm or someone is staying only to provide support to a disabled partner. In her recent presentation at the annual conference of the American Association of Marriage and Family Therapists, she indicates that she no longer demands that the unfaithful partner tell; instead she works with the unfaithful partner to deal with the consequences of not telling and what got the couple into the situation in the first place.

Clearly, determining what intervention is appropriate is a difficult decision for the therapist. It is further complicated if the primary reason the client seeks care is for the addiction or if the couple has come to address relationship problems. If the addict is continuing to act out, then the first clinical action must be toward sobriety. How disclosure enhances the efforts to increase motivation toward sobriety has to be weighed in a case-by-case situation. Often, the most powerful reason for an addict to disclose is because his or her sobriety depends on it. However, if the sexual acting out or affair has ended, getting the marital relationship on stronger ground can be enhanced by disclosure if the partner is also working on his or her recovery program. Unfortunately, that is not always the case, so working with the partner to understand his or her own counterproductive behaviors is a helpful first step prior to the disclosure.

Although we agree that a structured disclosure is the favored action to help the recovery process for both partners, as well as and to rebuild the relationship, often the addict is so new to the process of being honest that to "demand" a disclosure early in therapy results in the addict dropping out of therapy and continuing to act out due to high levels of anxiety. My (MDC) clinical experience supports giving the addict time to ask other addicts about their experience with disclosure (usually painful, but healing), while "coaching" him or her to look at the value of an authentic, respectful disclosure through a structured process. It is critical to discuss the risk that disclosure brings of increased pain and being under more scrutiny for a period and to help the addict prepare for the likely negative reactions of the partner.

In counseling addicts, it is important to remember that secrecy and lies are part of the disease of addiction and to remind the addict of the risk he takes to his sobriety by keeping the secret. A wise therapist will take into consideration the context of the couple's relationship and the individual strength of each partner to sustain the impact of the information. Rather than collude with the addict, take a proactive approach to deal with increasing the addict's motivation to change if he or she is still acting out. If the addict is no longer acting out, then help the partners start to rebuild the relationship by rebuilding their friendship. When friendship is discussed, honesty is almost always used to describe a best friend. Use the value of honesty that they *both* share as the reason for disclosure. This makes the decision for the disclosure the couple's, rather than the therapist's.

To Conceal or Reveal a Secret?

Therapists often see clients only after the initial disclosure. If, however, disclosure is to be a part of the therapy process, the reasons for disclosure should be discussed. Recognition of each partner's motivation can influence the timing, nature, and extent of disclosure. Some legitimate reasons for immediate disclosure are

- The partner suspects and is asking questions.
- The partner is at risk for a sexually transmitted disease and needs testing and protection.
- The information is about to be revealed to the spouse by another person or agency, and the addict recognizes that it would be much better for him or her to tell the spouse directly.
- The relationship is being adversely affected by the secret.
- The addict's recovery is being adversely affected by his or her dishonesty.

On the other hand, disclosure might best be deferred if

- The addict is disclosing out of anger, in order to hurt the partner.
- The addict is disclosing out of exhibitionism—for example, "All these women want me."

- The addict feels like "dumping" all the details of the sexual activities in order to assuage his or her guilt
- The partner is particularly vulnerable at the time—physically or emotionally fragile—and might be harmed by the disclosure.

Safety

Schneider and Schneider (1990c) surveyed several husbands of recovering female sex addicts and learned that it was common for these men who had learned of their wives' affairs to fantasize harming the wife or the affair partner, and some reported destroying furniture and other objects in anger. Before a therapist recommends disclosure to any client, an assessment of the risk of domestic violence needs to be carried out. Another safety issue is that of the risk of acquiring sexually transmitted diseases (STDs): If the straying partner has had unprotected extramarital sex and has exposed the spouse to disease, then disclosure should not be delayed. Because an increased risk of disease is so common among sexually compulsive persons, more therapists are now insisting on disclosure of extramarital sexual behaviors to the partner (Brown, 1991; Schneider, Corley, & Irons, 1988).

Disclosure as a Process

Disclosure is usually a process, rather than a one-time event (Schneider et al., 1998). Much of the time, the sexually compulsive person does not tell all at first, then comes back to reveal more. In particular, sexually exploitative professionals often initially minimize their misconduct, not only to licensing boards and assessment teams but also to their spouse. When a wife who has publicly supported her husband because she believed in his innocence eventually learns that he continued to lie to her about the allegations after they were made public, her public humiliation and sense of betrayal are compounded, and the healing is that much more difficult.

Even when the sexually compulsive person intends to give a full disclosure, it often happens that some material is omitted, only to come up later. One reason is that addicts, who typically participate in at least three categories of sexually compulsive behaviors and often more, may simply have forgotten some of their past behaviors. This is particularly true because addictive behaviors are often carried out in what addicts describe as a "trance" or "the bubble" and may not be recalled clearly in the person's more rational state. Another reason is that addicts may not initially realize that some behaviors constituted betrayal or infidelity and need to be revealed. Later in recovery, as they become more honest, they may recognize that these activities need to be disclosed. Finally, a slip or relapse to some extramarital sexual acting out will result in the necessity for additional disclosure.

Early disclosure and a willingness to answer the partner's questions honestly and fully provide the information requested are factors that will make it more likely that the relationship will survive the crisis. A therapist can help facilitate this process. When a partner receives a subsequent disclosure after believing he or she has been told of everything initially, the impact can be devastating, setting the process of rebuilding trust back for months. The therapist can partly forestall this by explaining to the clients that disclosure is not a one-time event, and that it is likely that additional disclosures will be necessary in the future.

How Much Information to Disclose to the Partner Initially

In a desire for relief and an end to denial, some addicts reveal everything to the spouse, who may be taken by surprise. Other people disclose in anger. The therapist can assist in monitoring the intent of the disclosure: Moving toward greater intimacy is a positive intent; to obtain ammunition to punish, control, or manipulate the partner is a poor intent.

Although disclosure is the gateway to recovery for the individual and the relationship, it also brings shame to the addict, pain to the partner, and fears about loss of the relationship. Consequently, addicts tend to avoid complete disclosure and to report, in retrospect, the negative consequences of the disclosure and their wish that they had disclosed less. This is particularly true for addicts in early recovery (whose partners, of course, are generally also in early recovery).

The therapist working with addicts needs to recognize that characterologic defenses such as narcissism and dependency influence the willingness of addicts to disclose. Narcissistic addicts may withhold information out of pride, out of a desire to appear healthier than they really are. Dependent addicts may minimize their disclosure out of fear of losing their relationship, and may tell their partner only what they believe he or she wants to hear or knows already. Addicts who withhold information do so in multiple dimensions; they do not limit their withholding just to the partner. By recognizing and confronting the client's characterologic defenses, therapists may avoid the pitfall of believing that the addict has not withheld information from *them*.

Partners, in contrast, often begin by demanding complete disclosure, which is for them a way to make sense of the past; to validate their suspicions and the reality they had experienced, which had often been denied by the addict; to have a sense of control of the situation, to assess their risk of having been exposed to sexually transmitted diseases; and to evaluate the commitment of their partner to the future of the relationship.

Spouses who believe they have received full disclosure are often significantly set back in the process of forgiveness and rebuilding trust if subsequent events prove that only partial disclosure has occurred. In our study, deliberately staggered disclosures—initially revealing only the most benign behaviors, or only those behaviors that the spouse already suspects—are very damaging to the couple's efforts to rebuild the relationship. On the other hand, the betrayed partner often wishes to know "everything," in the false believe that increased knowledge will provide increased control over the addict's behavior. In reality, however, details about the nature of the sexual activities, the number of times and places, and so on, may be replayed over and over again in the partner's head and may interfere with recovery. We have found that what is most helpful for the restoration of the relationship is for addicts initially to disclose at least the broad outlines of *all* their significant compulsive sexual activities, rather than holding back some damaging material. However, because early on the partner tends to want "all the details," we recommend that the partner discuss with a counselor or therapist what details are really important to know and what the likely effect will be on the partner. One effective tool is to ask the partner to write a list of every question to which he or she wants a detailed answer and to elicit a promise from the addict to reply fully at some particular time in the future, say 1 or 3 months. The therapist then puts the list away and retrieves it at the later session. By that time, it is hoped, the couple will have made some progress and the partner's need to know "everything" will have abated.

In later recovery, partners recognize that knowledge is not necessarily power—that no matter how much information they have, they are still unable to control the addict. Instead, they develop guidelines for themselves about what information they want (typically, more general information such as risk of STDs, commitment to recovery and the relationship) and what they did not want (details of sexual activities, locations, numbers, etc.). It can be very helpful for them to have a therapist encourage them to consider carefully what information they seek rather than to ask for "everything."

Threats and Outcomes

As shown in the study, although threats to leave the relationship are a common response by partners to the disclosure of sexual acting out, these threats are not usually carried out. The study was not designed to assess what fraction of all partners who threaten to leave ultimately do so. Nonetheless, considering the egregious and recurrent nature of the sexual acting out by many of the addicts, it is striking that 76% of the partners who had threatened to leave did not carry through their threats. This finding should enable therapists to reassure their clients that threats to leave, although likely, are not usually followed by action.

Threats to leave, which occurred in a majority of relationships, did not ultimately prevent significant slips or relapses, which also eventually occurred in a majority of the relationships. Threats are not an effective way to control and direct the addict's behavior. Threats do not prevent relapse. Threats appear to be not only ineffectual, but even counterproductive, because they can serve to deter disclosure and thereby delay the honesty that is necessary for the addict's individual recovery, the partner's sense of validation and empowerment, and the open communication that is essential in the relationship for rebuilding trust.

Threats may also box in the partner, who may feel compelled to follow through on them, even if he or she now feels differently. Some partners of sex addicts have reported a fear that if they do not follow through on threats, then anything they say in the future will not be taken seriously. One women described her dilemma:

> He knows and I know that if he relapses I will walk. Therefore he knows he must hide the truth should it occur or risk losing me. I know he may lie and I might not find out the truth.

One way out of this double bind is to recognize that (1) threats about divorce are not an effective way to prevent relapse, and that (2) even the most sincere stance about divorce may change if a relapse or slip does occur. Although it is desirable for the partner to have a clear set of guidelines about which behaviors are unacceptable to her or him, the partner also needs to recognize that every situation is unique and that there may be other options than leaving the relationship.

Co-addicts need to understand that threats in themselves do not have much power; the honesty of communication and the commitment to individual recovery is what has power. The most effective way to prevent and reduce the severity and number of relapses is for the addict to do his or her own recovery work, not to be reactive to the partner's threats.

How Much Information to Disclose to Partner About Ongoing Struggles

Even when not dealing with actual relapses involving other people, a frequent issue for recovering sex addicts is deciding how much information to disclose to partners about ongoing struggles and addictive thinking and behaviors—and for partners to decide how much they want to be told. The survey results show a wide variety of solutions to this problem. Some couples share a great deal; others work their individual recovery programs and share only generalities about the addict's progress or setbacks. The counselor can help couples understand that each couple needs to work out its own solutions, and this is best done though open discussion and negotiation between each partner. Often couples learn by trial and error which approach works best for them.

Honesty and the Book Alcoholics Anonymous

Though stressing the importance of rigorous honesty in working a recovery program, the AA *Big Book* places itself squarely on the side of nondisclosure of the addict's sexual past. The recommendation of the *Big Book* (pp. 81, 124–125) is not to disclose to the spouse more than he or she already knows and to use as a justification that it is wrong to compromise another person, because to disclose to the partner is to risk relapse and the end of the marriage. It is likely that the inconsistency between the emphasis on honesty in all other matters and advice not to disclose about sex resulted from the author's own personal history. Bill Wilson, the founder of AA, appears to have switched addictions, from alcohol to sex, and remained in his second addiction until his death. According to Nan Robertson (1998), author of *Getting Better: Inside Alcoholics Anonymous*, "Particularly during his sober decades in AA in the forties, fifties, and sixties, Bill Wilson was a compulsive womanizer. His flirtations and his adulterous behavior filled him with guilt, but he continued to stray off the reservation. His last and most serious love affair . . . began when he was in his sixties. She was important to him until the end of his life, and was remembered in a financial agreement with AA" (p. 36). Helen W., his last mistress, received 1.5% of the royalties of the book *Alcoholics Anonymous*. As for Lois, Bill's wife, "She never mentioned his philandering. . . . She wouldn't share such a thing. It would have offended her sense of dignity, of the rightness, the appropriateness, of things," wrote Robertson (p. 40).

When these facts are taken into account, the recommendations in the Big Book concerning disclosure of sexual infidelity can best be understood in their historical context—as a reflection of the denial process inherent in an active addictive sexual disorder, rather than as a reasoned recommendation of a group of recovering people.

Role of 12-Step Participation in Coping With a Partner's Sex Addiction

It goes without saying that therapists are a major positive influence in the recovery of couples dealing with extramarital sexual activities. When the members of a couple are also a sex addict and his or her partner, involvement by *both* partners in a 12-step program is a tool that is often not sufficiently stressed for the partner. Some reasons why partners choose not to get involved in recovery work are

- If the addict is in recovery prior to getting into the relationship, the spouse may believe that the problem is under control and does not require his or her attention or involvement. Disclosures about behaviors that preceded the relationship may be perceived as having no relevance to the current relationship.

If a slip or relapse is then disclosed, the partner may be shocked or unprepared.

- If the addict is in early recovery, the partner may not yet realize that "addiction is a family disease" and that it might be helpful for his or her own healing to become involved with a 12-step program.
- Some partners may deal with the problem by using denial. Denial may take the form of simply not talking about the problem, of assuming that it is not a significant part of the addict's life, or explaining away the addiction in some reassuring way (e.g., it is part of another problem—drug dependency—which is being dealt with).

Partners who are not actively involved with a 12-step program may experience isolation and a lack of support. Should a disclosure take place under these circumstances, the partner may experience difficulty rebuilding trust in the addict, even after years of 12-step work by the addict.

In a survey of 88 couples recovering from sex addiction, Schneider & Schneider (1996) found that it took an average of 2 years for partners to rebuild trust in the addict after disclosure. In addition to the benefits previously listed of attending 12-step meetings, the couples in the earlier survey reported that an important element of forgiveness and rebuilding trust was for the partner to work on her or his own recovery. This led to less blaming and shaming, willingness to take some responsibilities for the difficulties in the relationship, ability to speak the same (12-step) language, and a greater understanding of addiction as a family disease.

Other significant benefits for the partner of working a 12-step program are an improvement in self-esteem, support for getting out of the victim role ("as children we were victims—as adults we were volunteers"), and the empowerment of the partner. The partner becomes able to make a real choice about staying in the relationship or leaving. In counseling a couple in the aftermath of disclosure, therapists should encourage partners of sex addicts to become involved with a 12-step support group, in particular S-Anon or COSA, if they are available, or else Al-Anon or another 12-step program. Twelve-step attendance is a very beneficial adjunct to therapy, and one that is available long after therapy is terminated.

REFERENCES

Alcoholics Anonymous. (1976). New York: Alcoholics Anonymous World Services, Inc.

Anonymous. (1987). *Hope and recovery: A twelve-step guide for healing from compulsive sexual behavior*. Center City, MN: Hazelden Educational Materials.

Berry, C. R., & Baker, M. W. (1996). *Who's to blame: Escape the victim trap and gain personal power in your relationships*. Colorado Springs, CO: Pinon.

Brown, E. M. (1991). *Patterns of infidelity and their treatment.* New York: Brunner-Mazel.

Carnes, P. J. (1991). *Don't call it love: Recovery from sexual addiction.* New York: Bantam Doubleday Dell.

Corley, M. D., & Alvarez, M. (1996). Including children and families in the treatment of individuals with compulsive and addictive disorders. *Sexual Addiction and Compulsivity, 3*(2), 69–83.

Glass, S. P., & Wright, T. L. (1992). Justifications for extramarital relationships: The association between attitudes, behaviors, and gender. *Journal of Sex Research, 29*(3), 361–387.

Hatcher, R. A., Stewart, F., Trussell, J., Kowl, D., Guest, F., Stewart, G. H., & Cates, W. (1990). *Contraceptive technology.* New York: Irvington.

Hyde, J. S. (1990). *Understanding human sexuality* (4th ed.). New York: McGraw Hill.

Irons, R., & Schneider, J. (1999). *The wounded healer: Addiction-sensitive approach to the sexual exploitative professional.* Northvale, NJ: Jason Aronson.

Kinsey, A. C., Pomeroy, W. B., & Martin, C. E. (1948). *Sexual behavior in the human male.* Philadelphia: Saunders.

Kinsey, A. C., Pomeroy, W. B., Martin, C. E., & Gebhard, P. H. (1953). *Sexual behavior in the human female.* Philadelphia: Saunders.

Moultrup, D. J. (1990). *Husbands, wives & lovers: The emotional system of the extramarital affair.* New York: Guilford.

O'Neill G., & O'Neill, N. (1972). *Open marriage: A new life style for couples.* New York: M. Evans.

Pittman, F. (1989). *Private lies: Infidelity and the betrayal of intimacy.* New York: W. W. Norton.

Reiss, I. L. (1980). *Family systems in America* (3rd ed.). New York: Holt, Rinehart, & Winston.

Robertson, N. (1988). *Getting better: Inside alcoholics anonymous.* New York: William Morrow.

Rubin, A. M., & Adams, J. R. (1986). Outcomes of sexually open marriages. *Journal of Sex Research, 22*, 311–319.

Sanders, S. A., & Reinisch, J. M. (1999). Would you say you "had sex" if . . . ? *Journal of the American Medical Association, 281*, 275–277.

Schneider, J. (1991). Women sex addicts and their spouses: Recovery issues. *American Journal of Preventive Psychiatry & Neurology, 3*, 1–5.

Schneider, J. (2000). A duality study of cybersex participants: Gender differences, recovery issues, and implications for therapists. *Sexual Addiction and Compulsivity, 7*(4), 249–278.

Schneider, J. P. (1988). *Back from betrayal: Recovering from his affairs.* New York: Ballantine.

Schneider, J. P., Corley, M. D., & Irons, R. R. (1998). Surviving disclosure of infidelity: Results of an international survey of 164 recovering sex addicts and partners. *Sexual Addiction and Compulsivity, 5*, 189–217.

Schneider, J. P., & Schneider, B. H. (1989). Rebuilding the marriage during recovery from compulsive sexual behavior. *Family Relations, 38*, 288–294.

Schneider, J. P., & Schneider, B. H. (1990a). Marital satisfaction during recovery from self-identified sexual addiction among bisexual men and their wives. *Journal of Sex and Marital Therapy, 16*, 16–21.

Schneider, J. P., & Schneider, B. H. (1990b). Sexual problems in married couples recovering from sexual addiction and coaddiction. *American Journal of Preventive Psychiatry & Neurology, 2*, 16–21

Schneider, J. P., & Schneider, B. H. (1990c). *Sex, lies, and forgiveness: Couples speaking on healing from sexual addiction.* Center City, MN: Hazelden Educational Materials.

Schneider, J. P., & Schneider, B. H. (1996). Couple recovery from sexual addiction/coaddiction: Results of a survey of 88 marriages. *Sexual Addiction & Compulsivity, 3*, 111–126.

Sexaholics Anonymous. (1984). *Sexaholics Anonymous.* Simi Valley, CA: Sexaholics Anonymous.

Spring, A. (1997). *After the affair: Healing the pain and rebuilding trust when a partner has been unfaithful.* New York: Harper Perennial.

Spring, A. (2000). After the affair: Helping couples rebuild trust and earn forgiveness. AAMFT 58th Annual Conference. Denver, CO.

Subotnik, R., & Harris, G. (1994). *Surviving infidelity: Making decisions, recovering from the pain.* Holbrook, MA: Adams.

Tavris, C., & Sadd, S. (1975). *The* Redbook *report on female sexuality.* New York: Dell.

Thompson, A. P. (1983). Extramarital sex: A review of the research literature. *Journal of Sex Research, 19*(1), 1–22.

Vaughan, P. (1989) *The monogamy myth: A new understanding of affairs and how to survive them.* New York: New Market.

Wallerstein, J. S., & Blakeslee, S. (1989). *Second chances.* New York: Ticknor & Fields.

CHAPTER 11

Art Therapy

Treating the Invisible Sex Addict

MARIE WILSON

This chapter will examine the benefits of art therapy as a treatment modality for sex addicts. Sex addiction is often a hidden disease; the artwork of sex addicts offers a tangible representation of the disorder, with the potential to instruct both client and clinician. Art can function as a conduit for the healing of childhood trauma, providing safety and containment through the use of metaphor and personal symbolism, while facilitating direct expression of emotions and experiences through the use of images rather than words. Creativity gives adult clients permission to play without serious regression, thereby nurturing the child within and providing an opportunity to accomplish as adults what they could not do as children. Perhaps most important, art creates a place where the sex addict can become visible, actively confronting the secrecy of the addictive system. There is great power in the imagery of sex addicts. In addicts' committing these images to paper, they become real to all who see them.

ART AS THERAPY

There has been a long association between creative expression and healing. Artistic expression, regardless of what form it takes, is a normal and even necessary behavior of human beings. Art can be viewed as an inherent universal trait of the human species. The motivation and need for self-expression are reflected in all cultures and encompass all of human history (Dissanayake, 1992).

Artistic expression fulfills both emotional and psychological needs. The arts, accustomed to speaking the language of the soul, have more immediate access to emotional conflicts and psychological pain (McNiff, 1986). Artists by nature stay in touch with their inner process first by exploring, then expressing themselves in some creative form. Artists have the ability to go deeply within themselves in order to reach others through their artistic creations. They know from personal experience that the source of their creativity is seldom clear or articulate at a conscious or even verbal level. Moon (1994) describes the artistic process as "meta verbal" or beyond words, suggesting that the images that artists create come from someplace deep within them.

A treatment approach that involves the use of creative modalities such as art therapy is well suited for work with individuals in treatment for sex addiction. Art therapy combines the inherent healing capacities of the creative process with the informed use of psychological principles in the service of compassion, thereby integrating the essentials of creativity and healing. As with any clinical approach, art therapists work from a variety of philosophical perspectives and counseling theories. An integrative approach that combines both a person-oriented and a process-oriented approach seems most effective when working with addicted individuals.

Person-oriented art therapy is defined as art therapy that has an introspective focus and concentrates on examination of personal symbols and associations. This is also called psychodynamic art therapy. The art therapist encourages the client to produce free, expressive artwork. The therapist then uses the imagery to help the client discuss and reflect on the meaning of the picture, bringing repressed conflictual thoughts, fantasies, and feelings to the surface and allowing for insight and understanding. Each art product is unique to the creator, and the only way to interpret the meanings behind the work is with the creator present and involved. Process-oriented art therapy looks at how the person creates the art and examines his or her interaction with art materials and the art process. In a group setting, the art therapist monitors interaction between peers and the therapist. Each person has his or her own style of interaction, and the art process can foster communication and social contact (Ault, 1986).

Generally, art therapy is based on three basic assumptions. First, *every picture tells a story*. Our artistic expressions make a statement about the person who creates them. Every picture is a self-portrait that emphasizes that person's unique style of perceiving, conceptualizing, and expressing themselves. Second, *artistic expression is language*. Artistic expression can be a substitute for words, or artistic expression can go beyond words, when words are not enough. When emotion is strong and intense (and therefore frightening), art therapy can offer a focus and a container for the feelings and provides a structure that creates a safe environment for exploration of strong emotions. Third, *the artistic process reflects life*. A person's style and approach to working with art materials are good indicators of how he or she deals with people and activities outside the session (Ault, 1986). The selection of materials, the pressure applied, the individual's overall relationship to the artistic process, and the sequence of the images expressed are all relevant to the person's style and offer valuable insight. In an art therapy session much happens. The untrained eye may simply observe art being made. For the art therapist, however, every subtlety of the artistic process is noticed, evaluated and appreciated.

Sherbun (1990) believes that "traditional verbal approaches can allow a client to intellectualize and to avoid addressing issues, situations, and memories on a closer level. . . . Cognitive approaches do not always effectively tap into the emotional, experiential core of a client's issues" (p. 82). Many individuals with addictive illnesses avoid experience of their emotions and are overwhelmed by feelings that begin to surface in early treatment. Clinicians recognize the difficulty of providing the emotional safety necessary for exploratory work while confronting clients about their maladaptive patterns and self-destructive choices. The creative forum allows for both emotional safety and containment through the use of metaphor and personal symbolism, while facilitating direct expression of emotions and experiences through the use of images rather than words.

Creative methods like art therapy confront passivity, placing the person in the here and now. The creative forum allows the individual to try out new creative solutions to life's problems that were previously dealt with through abuse of chemicals or compulsive behaviors. Creativity strives to liberate the client from rigid, maladaptive behaviors and increases spontaneity and problem solving. Spontaneity allows the individual to develop new and more adequate responses. The creative forum allows the individual to try out new creative solutions to life's problems. This laboratory for human behavior provides opportunity for exploration and experimentation with new ways of being, feeling, and responding. Clients can see themselves through the eyes of their images, allowing for greater emotional clarity and objectivity.

ART THERAPY WITH SEX ADDICTS

Risking Visibility

Art therapy provides a tangible representation of the disease of sexual addiction, with the potential to educate both the client and the clinician. Art is a way to make the invisible visible. Many sex addicts live invisible lives, carrying out their sexual activity in secrecy. Brockway (1997) noted that sex addicts, especially those who have been sexually abused, have learned unconsciously to become invisible. Once the pattern of isolation is established, the evolution of social and sexual interactive skills becomes increasingly difficult. Being invisible feeds the secrecy of their addiction, making recovery more difficult. Art creates a place where the sex addict can become visible. Visibility is very threatening to the addictive system, and art therapy provides clients with the aesthetic distance necessary for integration of such a threatening experience.

Fred was a 32-year-old, married father of three. He was referred into treatment by his private therapist whom he had seen for only a short while. Fred was diagnosed with both alcohol and cocaine dependence and sexual addiction. Fred was a self-described "peeping tom" who was arrested when caught hiding in a ladies bathroom with a mirror that he had used to peep up underneath bathroom stalls in order to watch women as they used the bathroom. This arrest, however, was only the tip of the iceberg. In truth, Fred had been peeping and engaging in voyeuristic and intrusive sex since he was a teenager. After the arrest, in a desperate attempt to stop his sexual behaviors, Fred had attempted suicide and this incident precipitated his admission to residential treatment.

In figure 11.1, Fred drew himself peeping into the window of a house. He used broad-tipped markers to create a scene at night, making strong, deliberate marks over and over to cover all of the paper. He drew himself with his back to the viewer, wearing a hat to further conceal his identity. He described the picture as "dark and secretive, just like my addiction." In order to help Fred gain more information about this behavior, the group asked him to talk about what events preceded this scene and how he was feeling emotionally as he stood there. Fred said that probably he had just had a fight with his wife and would feel the urge to peep. He said he was aware of feeling "very sad, lonely, empty." This description was very similiar to the way Fred described his feelings as a child in a previous art therapy group. He was raised the middle child in a very large and emotionally disengaged family and had little memory of any parental guidance or nurturance. Fred had described considerable emotional neglect and said that, as a child, he was "always on the outside looking in." Group members pointed out how the warmth coming from the windows and the door were such a con-

FIGURE 11.1

trast to the darkness outside where he was standing and that indeed he had portrayed himself on the outside looking in, recreating a scenario similar to his childhood. Voyeurism is the ability to be intrusive without discovery. Fred had learned to become invisible, like the voyeur, in his childhood and in his addiction he recreated that pattern. This is often the case because many times sex addicts will recreate in adulthood the very scenarios that were visited upon them as children. Frequently, the elements of abuse and neglect that remain powerful emotional connectors to their childhood reveal themselves in the artwork. Through his picture, Fred was able to make a connection between his experience in childhood and his compulsive sexual behavior. In addition, Fred acknowledged how an argument with his wife generated feelings of rejection similar to those he experienced in childhood and that his urge to peep was his way to soothe himself by watching others. Recognition of the impact of childhood abuse and neglect on their lives helps sex addicts create a basis of understanding of their sexual disorder. This realization assists in decreasing some of their shame in the recognition that they, too, were victims of some type of abuse at one time.

A few weeks later, in another group, Fred drew figure 11.2 which depicted him in his house alone, preparing to drink alcohol and snort lines of cocaine while masturbating to pornography. He drew himself from the front and in the nude. The wall of the house appears to be made out of glass. He is on the inside looking out this time. This picture suggests Fred's movement from the darkness

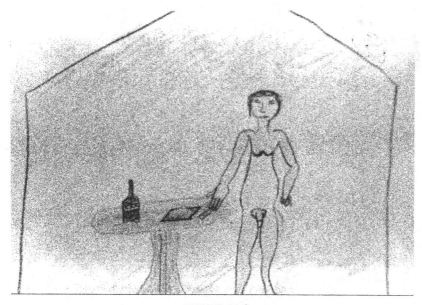

FIGURE 11.2

and secrecy of his first picture into the light of day. He is ready to risk greater exposure by facing us. His depiction of himself is realistic and not intended to be provocative. He has provided the viewer with a glass wall, suggesting that he no longer has anything to hide. He is no longer invisible. This picture supported the treatment team's positive prognosis for Fred's ongoing recovery.

Risking Perfectionism

Many sex addicts grew up in dysfunctional families of origin. There is consider-able documentation with regard to these dynamics in sex addiction literature. Carnes (1998) reports that many addicts tended to come from families where there were addictions of all kinds and described their families as rigid, disen-gaged, and emotionally distant. Failure to bond was a norm in these families. So, in part, their addiction stemmed from their search for nurturing without the risk of intimacy or trust. Earle and Crow (1989) add, "So often reared in chaotic homes by parents they could not please and whose behavior they could rarely predict, sex addicts have grave difficulty negotiating the demands of daily living" (p. 100). Many other authors have addressed similar issues with regard to the significance of early life experiences for the sex addict (Fossum & Mason, 1986; Hastings, 1994; Hunter, 1990; Kasl, 1989; Schaef, 1989).

When a parent is absent from the home either physically or emotionally, due to addiction or to his or her priorities being outside the home and not with the role of parenting, children may be left unattended and be expected to raise themselves. In such an environment, few children have the luxury of play and may need to take on the role of parenting younger siblings or of being overly responsible. In either case, if children do not play, they miss out on crucial developmental steps. Robinson (1989) observed that children who grow up in addicted homes need to be taught to play, "It is through play that the free child emerges and kids learn to deal with their feelings" (p. 145). Claudia Black (cited in Robinson, 1989) noted that through interactive play, children of addicted parents learn to work out mutual problems and learn flexibility and negotiation skills. Growing up in an addicted home is serious business and surviving in it takes every bit of energy that a child has. None can be wasted on something so "trivial or frivolous as play" (Robinson, 1989, p. 144).

Children who grow up in this type of environment may themselves, as ado-lescence approaches, turn to the use of chemicals as a form of play. Others may begin their sexual acting out as a way to feel in control or to medicate feelings. Under the influence of mood-altering substances or behaviors, they no longer have to think about the problems associated with home life and can be irrespon-sible and reckless. Children who grew up in parentified roles can shake off the limitations of this role and join peers in activities that, at least in the onset, appear to be great fun. Initially, they may take great satisfaction in acting out in a way they were never able to do as children.

The creative forum gives permission for adult addicts to play in healthy, structured ways, challenging their need for perfectionism and control. Clients can explore and create without fear of reprisal. They are allowed to make mistakes and take risks. The simple act of building up and tearing down may be an activity never experienced by a client who was fearful that his every move was either under the scrutiny of critical parents or never tried because mistakes are not allowed (Rubin, 1984). Creativity gives adult sex addicts permission to play without serious regression or significant loss of control, thereby nurturing the child within and providing an opportunity to accomplish as adults what they could not do as children.

Risking Vulnerability

The images rendered by sex addicts can be provocative for both the clinician and the client. Sex addicts seem to be particularly visually inclined and highly sensitive to the imagery that they produce in the art therapy session. This sensitivity enables great vitality and richness of expression; however, there is also a greater risk of images triggering addictive reactions. Triggering reactions to the imagery can create an opportunity for instruction about the disease, provided that the behavioral cues are noticed and confronted. A particular incident comes to mind to illustrate this. A young man drew a picture of his foot fetish (figure 11.3). After completing his picture and prior to the group discussion, he asked to be excused to use the bathroom. When the client was gone for awhile, the group became suspicious and upon returning to the art room, he was questioned about his prolonged absence. Unable to make eye contact, he confessed that his drawing had triggered his disease and he had left the room in search of women who might be outside without shoes on (the weather was warm), hoping to find stimulation in seeing their bare feet. Upon finding two young women sunning themselves, he hid undetected, watching them (voyeurism) for several minutes before returning to the session. In doing this, the client had violated a behavioral contract set in place several days earlier by the staff. This information resulted in a group discussion of the power of triggering experiences and examined ways to deal with the impulse, rather than to react. The client acknowledged that if he had allowed himself to become vulnerable enough to risk sharing with the group what he was feeling, rather than acting, the resulting behavior might not have occurred. With sex addicts, in particular, the images may trigger shameful feelings about their disease, and because addicts lack adequate skills to react any differently, this creates an urgency to escape into the compulsivity of the disease in order not to feel the feelings. The simple act of asking for help is a painful admission of their vulnerability.

FIGURE 11.3

The client's picture speaks further to the pain, confusion, and entrapment of his disease. A fetish is described as an object or body part whose real or fantasized presence is psychologically necessary for sexual gratification. In addition to the striped sock in the picture, the penis is held erect by a dark shape resembling a shoe. This client was able to achieve an erection only when engaged sexually with his fetish, such as sucking a woman's toes while masturbating or having a woman use her feet to masturbate him. The client acknowledged that he experienced shame and embarrassment in witnessing the rawness of his imagery.

Therapists working with the sex-addicted population must be aware of personal reactions and biases with regard to treating this disorder. This is particularly so for art therapists because the artwork is sexually graphic and can sometimes be disturbing in nature, forcing the art therapist to react carefully. Piccirillo (1995) encountered this in her work with the disturbing imagery produced by many AIDS patients and cautions, "The content of some art pieces can be very provocative, even raw, and requires finely tuned responses by the therapist. An honest inventory of our deepest beliefs . . . will spell out the subliminal influence we will have on discussions as they occur during groups, individual treatment, and as they manifest in the artwork" (p. 64). Piccirillo's words of caution are well advised. Many times, sex-addicted clients will ask permission to portray graphic or provocative material, concerned, perhaps, that they will be judged or criticized. It takes considerable courage and risk for them to reveal their secrets.

The images allow for little escape from the stark reality of their addiction. Many times clients view fully, perhaps for the first time, how their addiction has victimized both themselves and others. The images actively confront the secrecy of the disease. Schaef (1989) believes that there is more shame around sexual addiction than around any other addiction, partly due to the fact that there is less cultural judgment against chemical addiction these days. She also adds that sexual addiction is so hidden and so well integrated into our society that it has historically remained untreated.

Risking Exposure

Art is instrumental in the working through of trauma experiences. Carnes (1998) addresses the role of child abuse in the early experiences of most sex addicts. In a study of more that 1,000 sex addicts, the impact of childhood abuse was significant. Addicts reported physical abuse (72%), sexual abuse (81%), and emotional abuse (97%). Emotional abuse was a significant factor in addicts who abused children themselves. Carnes notes that it is clear that trauma and addiction are inextricably connected for the sex addict. Children who are abused very early in life lack the developmental ability to articulate their experiences with words and, consequently, as adults, have difficulty describing their experiences verbally. Lacking adequate verbal skills for describing their abuse, many clients are able to depict their experience in images. In addition, trauma experiences and memories seem to be encoded in intense, specific visual images. Expression and exploration of these experiences and memories flow very naturally through visual art media (Peterson, 1997). Van der Kolk, McFarlane, and Weisaeth (1986) address these points with these words:

> Prone to action, and deficient in words, these patients can often express their internal states more articulately in physical movements or in pictures than in words. Utilizing drawings and psychodrama may help them develop a language that is essential for effective communication and for the symbolic transformation that can occur in psychotherapy. (p. 195)

Art functions as a safe container for extremely intense feelings, such as rage, despair, terror, and pain. It provides both safety and distance from the content of the experience through use of metaphor and symbolism, yet also allows opportunity for full expression of traumatic experiences. Art making can be an open channel to expression of trauma, even when the client is dissociated from the full meaning of the experience and feelings about the images produced. Abstract symbolic art expression can provide an opportunity for the clients to express the intensity of their experiences fully without exposing specific content to themselves or others. Art making can provide a way to reconnect from a dissociated state or to clarify or partialize in order to cope with overwhelming memories. Art is a way to "tell" without telling, to bypass past threats of injury or reprisal for telling (Peterson, 1997). Head (cited in Moore, 1983) asserts, "A patient who has passively experienced a traumatic event can begin to master it in the artwork, because he is now taking the active role."

Other Benefits

Art therapists working in addiction treatment over the years have recognized the importance of adapting art therapy guidelines to the specific treatment needs of the program and utilizing literature and concepts already familiar to clients. Allen (1985) commented on the need for art therapists to integrate art therapy into the overall treatment approach of the facility and conducted highly structured groups while working on an alcoholism unit. Both Julliard (1994) and Feen-Calligan (1995) designed art therapy sessions around concepts embraced by Alcoholics Anonymous and the 12 steps, especially issues related to powerlessness, spirituality, and higher power. Moore (1983) addressed the uniqueness of the art product as tangible documentation and used it to assist in the recognition and reduction of distortions such as denial, a defense mechanism that is actively confronted in verbal groups during addiction treatment. She asserts that images confront well-practiced verbal defenses, and that contradictions are more easily identified. There is often truth in images when addicts are adept at manipulation with words. Head (cited in Moore, 1983) viewed the art experience as a less frightening release of affect because creativity involves nonconflicted ego functions.

Bagan (cited in Earle & Earle, 1995) uses art extensively in combination with sand play therapy in her treatment of the sex addict, the co-addict, and the children of sex addicts. She believes that techniques like art therapy and sand play therapy draw on the right side of the brain and bypass left brain controls and defenses. She further examines how verbal therapies alone may not adequately access, release, or integrate denied or repressed thoughts or feelings. She cites the book *Pictures of a Childhood* by Alice Miller (1986). In the book Miller describes her own personal journey of self discovery and how her own painful childhood memories were released and explored through her artwork. Through two analyses, Miller reports that she managed to keep the truth about her childhood hidden from herself, and only when she began to use art materials did she give the "silent child of long ago the right to her own language and her own story" (Earle & Earle, 1995, p. 204).

ART THERAPY EXERCISES FOR SEX ADDICTS

The data related here comes from a composite of clinical work at a treatment facility in the Southwest. This is a residential facility specializing in the treatment of a variety of addictions, including sex addiction. The duration of the stay is 5 weeks. The art therapy group was psycho-educational, as well as experiential, and was structured around certain topics or assignments. Art therapy met once a week for 1.5 hours and a maximum of 10 clients were assigned to the group. Clients were both male and female, heterosexual and homosexual, educated, and of various ethnic backgrounds. Clients had considerable choice with regard to artistic medium, and personal interpretation of the topic was encouraged. Clients in group for the first time and unfamiliar with art materials were given a basic orientation, demonstration, or both. As the art process unfolded, assistance was available with regard to technique and application.

All art materials used were of good quality and strong and durable, in order to stand up to the aggression often expressed by the clients. When art materials collapse or cannot hold up to aggressive stroke marks, this creates considerable frustration for clients and conveys the subtle message that it is not okay to express strong emotion in this place, because if they do, there will be destruction. Given that many sex addicts come from environments where they were not able to express themselves fully and where strong emotions of any kind were not allowed, any experience that mirrors this may only reinforce their belief that feelings are destructive and should be kept hidden. Here is a review of assignments typically given:

1. The Ten Types of Sex Addicts: Based on the 10 types of sex addicts (Carnes, 1991), draw the type you most identify with. This exercise is instrumental in helping the addict identify patterns of abuse, thereby decreasing denial and increasing awareness of the disease. Step 1 issues, from the 12 steps of Sex Addicts Anonymous, are examined related to unmanageability and addicts' powerlessness over their sexual addiction. The images drawn help concretize the experience, and the group discussion provides an opportunity for identification. One male client depicted his exhibitionism and sexual intrusiveness by drawing figure 11.4. The picture includes the words "watch me, watch me," "I want to jack off in front of you," "look at me, look at me" repeated many times in the picture. This client had a history of exposing himself while sitting in a parked car and also frequented crowded shopping malls where he would brush up against women without being discovered. The client said that the words in his painting represented his obsessive thoughts about his desire to be watched while exposing himself. He added that this picture expressed his desire to be loved, validated, and "touched" by others through his sexual behaviors. The images are barely contained within the edges of the paper and demand to be seen. The provocative language and shock appeal of the piece offers a visual representation of the client's attention-seeking behaviors and clearly are boundary violations in their attempt to force the viewer to look at sexually explicit images. An exhibitionist gains sexual arousal from the reaction of the viewer, pushing cultural norms and violating social conventions. The intrusive sex ad-

FIGURE 11.4

dict violates the personal boundaries of others by making inappropriate sexual remarks or touching with no accountability for his or her actions.

2. Sexual Fantasy Versus Reality: Draw a picture that compares your ultimate sexual fantasy with the actual reality of the experience. This helps sex addicts recognize the illusion behind the perfect sexual encounter and contrasts the illusion with the reality of the experience. The illusion fuels the compulsion to continue with the sexual fantasy until the addict "gets it right" or perfect. Often the desire is to create that same rush of excitement of the first encounter, much as the drug addict hopes to find a high just like the first. An example was a picture drawn by a male client, who with some amount of humor, contrasts his fantasy—which involves a beautiful/professional woman with a "nice bod" and a BMW convertible in an exotic location entitled "Exciting"—with the reality, which depicts an unattractive woman described as "not beautiful or professional" and "not nice bod," a Chevy Cavalier in a "Boring" scene. In rendering the picture, the client spent most of the group time working on the fantasy part, giving attention to detail and adding color. This is contrasted with the reality part, which is drawn only in outline and lacks detail and color. This represents an excellent example of the power of the fantasy for this client and his lack of investment in the reality.

3. Abuse Inventory: Clients are asked to assess their experience of child-

hood abuse, based on the Abuse Inventory from *The Betrayal Bond* (Carnes, 1997, pp. 94–97), then portray the aspects of the abuse that they have carried into adulthood.

This inventory provides reflection on issues of emotional abuse (such as neglect, excessive punishments, verbal threats, and emotional enmeshment), physical abuse (such as beatings or deprivation), and sexual abuse. Many abuse victims either minimize their abuse or deny the long-term implications. This exercise helps clients recognize the connection between the abuse and the behaviors that resulted and validates that the abuse really occurred. Patterns of behaviors that were established in childhood in the form of survival roles frequently become the self-defeating behaviors that form the foundations of their sexual addiction. An example would be a picture (figure 11.5) drawn by one client who depicted his childhood abuse on a large piece of paper with markers. He drew himself as an adult on one side of the picture, tearful and reaching out to other people in the picture who run away from him. This picture demonstrated how the client pleaded for validation from those around him and how his emotional neediness pushed people away. This client was abandoned at age 3 by his mother and raised by a violent, alcoholic father whose sadistic punishments included beating his son with a tree branch on his genitals. Although the client was drawn as an adult, his arms appear fragile and childlike. The client acknowledged that the arms looked like those of a 3-year-old child, which was

FIGURE 11.5

the age when both the abandonment and abuse began. His picture captured the sadness of a child longing for love and connection.

4. Addiction Interaction Disorder: Clients are asked to read a handout and assess the different types of addictions they have in addition to their sex addiction, such as drugs, alcohol, gambling, high risk, spending, food, and codependency. This is rated and based on the criteria of addiction set forth by the American Society of Addictive Medicine and the National Council on Alcoholism and Drug Dependence and involves behaviors such as loss of control, preoccupation, efforts to stop, escalation, continuation despite adverse consequences, losses, and so on. After a brief discussion, clients were asked to portray in a picture the interaction between their addictions. This provides clients with additional information about the interplay and connection between their sex addiction and other compulsive behaviors. Figure 11.6 depicts one client's frustration in trying to control his addiction to alcohol, love, work, drugs and sex.

These art exercises represent only a small percentage of the assignments appropriate for artwork. Any issue that is worked on verbally or behaviorally with a client can also be addressed in artwork. The 12 steps of Sex Addicts Anonymous is a good place to begin with specific recommendations around issues of powerlessness, unmanageability, higher power, moral inventory, amends, humility, and gratitude. In addition, artwork can be used to address family issues, grief and loss, and relapse prevention, to name only a few. A favorite exer-

FIGURE 11.6

cise for clients near discharge is to have them draw a 6- to 8-frame cartoon strip that documents their first 2 weeks out of treatment. It is important to look for evidence of commitment to ongoing recovery, such as 12-step meetings; sponsorship; avoidance of people, places, and things; and therapy. When these are not evident, it provides a powerful tool for confronting hidden, residual aspects of denial as discharge approaches.

In the art therapy group for sex addicts, after the art making is complete, a lively discussion usually follows. Clients are usually eager for group feedback and enjoy learning from one another's work, making connections to their own experiences and bringing clarity to their feelings. Generally, groups end with a heightened, almost palpable feeling of connection and comradery. Client artwork is bound by the same convictions of confidentiality and respect given to documentation in the clinical setting. Artwork is kept confidential and only shared with primary treatment staff. Each group begins with a vow of confidentiality by the group members who pledge that they will reveal neither the contents of the session nor the details of the artwork to anyone. This helps set the tone for serious work and provides clients with the safety with which to explore very personal issues. Rigorous honesty is the expectation for each session. Artwork can offer a bridge from residential treatment to aftercare, and clients are encouraged to take their work with them and share it with their primary therapists upon their return home. The artwork offers a concrete documentation of their experience in treatment and can function as a transitional object from the caregiving of the residential clinical staff to aftercare and self-care.

CHARACTERISTICS OF ARTWORK

Although no specific research was conducted, a careful review of the pictures notes the frequent occurrence of particular characteristics in the artwork of sex addicts.

1. Sexual or erotic content:

Because clients were given specific directives to depict sexual behavior, the presence of sexual or erotic images was expected. However, often further emphasis was given to these images through size, proportion to other items on page and color.

2. Paraphernalia related to sex:

Items such as pornography (videos and magazines), telephones (phone sex), and computers (cybersex) frequently appeared, in addition to establishments selling sex, such as sex clubs, nude shows, places of prostitution, and so on.

3. Images that depict constraint or entrapment:

Items such as boxes, chains, jails, or bars on windows. These may be indicative of being controlled or imprisoned by addiction.

4. In artwork by men, women are frequently depicted as sexual objects:

An example would be a female body depicted without a head or with just sexual parts drawn. This objectification of women creates an environment of anonymous sex for pleasure without risk of intimacy.

5. Themes of loneliness:

Loneliness is the most pervasive feeling expressed in the artwork, as evidenced by pictures that contain either no human figures or only one figure. In addition, depiction of empty rooms and disconnected, isolated objects were common. This may speak to the isolation brought on by the disease and the loneliness experienced by the addict.

6. Themes depicting dichotomy:

Depictions of opposites such as good and bad, light and dark, devil and angel, or addiction and recovery are examples of dichotomous themes. These may well represent the psychological and emotional splits brought about by the addictive system or the "all or nothing" thinking of many addicts.

With regard to these characteristics, a review of art therapy literature related to chemical dependency supports similiar findings. For instance, Dickman, Dunn, and Wolf (1996) researched the use of images as predictors of relapse in chemically dependent adults. Their findings showed that 86% of their clients who relapsed included images of psychoactive substances or paraphernalia of use in their artwork, and 74% drew the substance proportionally larger that the rest of the items on the page. Moore (1983) cites the research of Gantt and Howie, who noted the depiction of actual drug experience and drug paraphernalia in the artwork of drug users, and Albert-Puleo and Osha, in research of 150 alcoholic men, found themes of isolation and prejudice toward women. Images of constraint and entrapment and also themes of both loneliness and dichotomy were frequently noted in artwork produced by chemically dependent clients (Wilson, 1997). This list of characteristics offers only a beginning hypothesis for clinicians; more rigorous and systematic investigation needs to take place.

CONCLUSION

Art therapy offers both client and clinician valuable insight into the experience of sex addiction in a manner that words simply cannot convey. Although many clients enter the art therapy room with some hesitation and may not easily submit to the emotional risk required of them there, most leave with a renewed curiosity about themselves and others. After the initial hesitation, there is little resistance to the art-making process in future groups. The experience is the proof.

Because images bypass many of the well-practiced defenses of the addict, art therapy can access deeply held feelings and memories and open up issues that have been hidden or obstructed by denial and repression for many years.

Art therapy offers the unique combination of both safety and containment through the use of metaphor and personal symbolism, while facilitating more direct expression of emotions and experiences through the use of images rather than words. Although a single work of art may offer valuable insight, a series of works offers a broader representation of the issues applicable to assessment and treatment. Clinicians should be reminded that it takes considerable courage and risk for sex addicts to reveal themselves in the artwork. Clinicians working with the sex addicted population, who are not trained in the use of art therapy, are cautioned to enter slowly into this process, using art assignments judiciously. Artwork should be done during scheduled sessions and with the clinician present and involved. Sending clients home to complete assignments that may trigger emotional responses could be unintentionally setting clients up for difficulty. In risking the art-making process, the sex addict has taken one more step on the road toward recovery.

Addendum

Educational, professional, and ethical standards for art therapists are regulated by the American Art Therapy Association. The Art Therapy Credentials Board grants postgraduate registration (ATR) after reviewing documentation of completion of graduate education and postgraduate supervised experience. The registered art therapist who successfully completes the written examination administered by the Board is qualified as board certified (ATR-BC), a credential requiring maintenance through continuing education credits. Further information is available by contacting: The American Art Therapy Association, Inc., 1202 Allanson Road, Mundelein, IL 60060; (847)949-6064; e-mail: arttherapy@ntr.net; Website: http://www.arttherapy.org.

REFERENCES

Parts of this chapter appeared in The Journal of Sexual Addiction and Compulsivity, 1998, 5(4), and The Journal of the Americna Art Therapy Association, 1999, 15(1).

Allen, P. (1985). Integrating art therapy into an alcoholism treatment program. American Journal of Art Therapy, 24, 10–12.

Ault, R. (Writer), & Kempner, J. (Producer). (1986). Art therapy: A healing vision (Film). Menninger Video Productions, Topeka, Kansas.

Brockway, S. (1997). Living on the 13th floor: The invisible sex addict. Sexual Addiction & Compulsivity, 4(4), 371–376.

Carnes, P. (1991). Don't call it love: Recovery from sexual addiction. New York: Bantam.

Carnes, P. (1997). The betrayal bond: Breaking free of exploitive relationships. Deerfield Beach, FL: Health Communications.

Carnes, P. (1998). The obsessive shadow: Profiles in sexual addiction. *Professional Counselor, 13*(1), 15–17, 40–41.

Dickman, S., Dunn, J., & Wolf, A. (1996). The use of art therapy as a predictor of relapse in chemical dependency treatment. *Journal of the American Art Therapy Association, 13*(4), 232–237.

Dissanayake, E. (1992). Art for life's sake. *Journal of the American Art Therapy Association, 9*(4), 169–175.

Earle, R., & Crow, G. (1989). *Lonely all the time: Recognizing, understanding and overcoming sex addiction for addicts and co-dependents.* New York: Simon and Schuster.

Earle, R., & Earle, M. (1995). *Sex addiction: Case studies and management.* New York: Brunner/Mazel.

Feen-Calligan, H. (1995). The use of art therapy in treatment programs to promote spiritual recovery from addiction. *Art Therapy: Journal of the American Art Therapy Association, 12*(1), 46–50.

Fossum, M., & Mason, M. (1986). *Facing shame: Families in recovery.* New York: W. W. Norton.

Hastings, A. (1994). *From generation to generation: Understanding sexual attraction to children.* Tiburon, CA: Printed Voice.

Hunter, M. (1990). *Abused boys: The neglected victims of sexual abuse.* New York: Fawcett Columbine.

Julliard, K. (1994). Increasing chemically dependent patients' belief in step one through expressive therapy. *American Journal of Art Therapy, 33,* 110–119.

Kasl, C. (1989). *Women, sex, and addiction: A search for love and power.* New York: Ticknor and Field.

McNiff, S. (1986). *Educating the creative arts therapist.* Springfield, IL: Charles Thomas.

Miller, A. (1986). Pictures of a childhood: Sixty-six watercolours and an essay. New York: Farrar, Straus and Giroux.

Moon, B. (1994). *Introduction to art therapy.* Springfield, IL: Charles Thomas.

Moore, R. (1983). Art therapy with substance abusers: A review of the literature. *The Arts in Psychotherapy, 10,* 251–260.

Peterson, J. (1997, January). *Art and trauma recovery.* Presentation at the American Society of Group Psychotherapy and Psychodrama Annual Conference, New York, NY.

Piccirillo, E. (1995). Taking inventory in the age of aids. *Art Therapy: Journal of the American Art Therapy Association, 12*(1), 62–66.

Robinson, B. (1989). *Working with children of alcoholics: The practitioner's handbook.* MA: Lexington.

Rubin, J. (1984). *The art of art therapy.* New York: Brunner Mazel.

Schaef, A, (1989). *Escape from intimacy: Untangling the love addictions: Sex, romance, relationships.* San Francisco: Harper and Row.

Sherbun, J. (1990). Self-parenting: Treating ACOA's using action methods. In R. Fuhlrodt (Ed.), *Psychodrama: Its application of ACOA and substance abuse treatment.* Sherburn, NJ: Thomas Perrin.

van der Kolk, B. A., McFarlane, A. C., & Weisaeth, L. (1986). *Traumatic stress: The effects of overwhelming experience on mind, body and society.* New York: Guilford.

Wilson, M. (1997, October). *The art of addiction: Creativity as an antidote to shame.* Presentation at the Arizona Counselors Association Annual Conference, Arizona State University.

Wilson, M. (1999). Art therapy with the invisible sex addict. *Art therapy: The Journal of the American Art Therapy Association, 16*(1), 7–16.

Wilson, M. (2000). Creativity and shame reduction in sex addiction treatment. *Sexual Addiction & Compulsivity, 7*(4), 229–248.

Wilson, M. (in press). *Art therapy in addictions treatment: Creativity and shame reduction. The handbook of art therapy*, C. Malchiodi, Ed. New York: Brunner-Mazel

CHAPTER 12

The Value of Group Psychotherapy for Sexual Addicts

ALYSON NERENBERG

Therapists treating sexual addicts have long advocated the use of group psychotherapy as a treatment modality in both inpatient and outpatient settings (Carnes, 1991; Goodman, 1998; Turner, 1990). In fact, group psychotherapy is the most commonly used treatment modality in many residential inpatient treatment programs for sexual compulsivity. Although the use of group psychotherapy is prevalent in treatment for this population, very little research has examined the value of utilizing psychotherapy groups for sex addicts. This chapter attempts to examine what about the group therapy experience helps clients recover. It also discusses some of the benefits of group psychotherapy with sex addicts and some of the obstacles to overcome when facilitating these groups. Furthermore, it describes each of the therapeutic factors, first depicted by Irvin Yalom (1975, 1985; Yalom & Yalom, 1990), and provides clinical examples to illustrate how the therapeutic factors impact sex addicts in groups. Finally, it describes the results of a survey in which 40 sex addicts who had completed group therapy rated which therapeutic factors they found the most valuable. Also included are some practical recommendations for therapists who are interested in facilitating group psychotherapy with sexual addicts.

Many residential treatment facilities utilize group psychotherapy as their primary modality for treating sexually addicted individuals. In addition, most therapists who treat sexual addicts on an outpatient basis recommend that their patients attend group therapy in addition to 12-step meetings (Carnes, 1991; Goodman, 1998; Protter, 1993; Travin, 1995; Turner, 1990). Although many therapists are facilitating groups with sex addicts, very little has been written about the value of group psychotherapy with this population. This chapter is intended to fill in some of the gaps in the literature by describing both the benefits of group psychotherapy with sex addicts and some of the obstacles to overcome when facilitating these groups. It examines the question "What is it about the group therapy experience that helps sexual addicts get better?"

In writing this chapter, the author took into account information from various sources, including Irvin Yalom's (1975, 1985; Yalom & Yalom, 1990) extensive writings describing therapeutic factors, the current research available on both group dynamics and sexual addictions, her own experiences facilitating group psychotherapy with sex addicts in a residential setting, and, most important, the feedback from members in the groups.

YALOM'S THERAPEUTIC FACTORS

When confronted with the question "How does group therapy help patients?" Irvin Yalom might contend that change results from the interplay of various human experiences, which he categorizes as 11 therapeutic factors. These therapeutic factors are the essential things that make patients get better (Bernard & MacKenzie, 1994) and include instillation of hope, universality, imparting of information, altruism, the corrective recapitulation of the primary family group, development of socializing techniques, imitative behavior, interpersonal learning, group cohesiveness, catharsis, and the existential factors. The following briefly describes each of the therapeutic factors and provides clinical illustrations of how these apply when therapists facilitate group psychotherapy with sex addicts.

Instillation of Hope

According to Yalom, the "instillation of hope" refers to a patient's faith that treatment can and will be effective. Bloch, Reibstein, Crouch, Holroyd, and Themen (1979) described the instillation of hope as the clients' sense of optimism that they have the potential for therapeutic progress. Yalom (1985) proposed that this factor would be highly valued in the early stages of group. Burton (1982) also predicted that the instillation of hope would be most prevalent early on in a group's development.

When therapists facilitate groups with sex addicts, it is essential to provide hope immediately. In my clinical experiences of facilitating groups in a residential treatment program for sex addicts, I have found that patients enter treatment feeling extremely hopeless. Generally, patients enter treatment after they have hit "rock bottom." Their lives have become unmanageable and their circumstances have spiraled out of control. Often when patients first begin treatment, they have suffered traumatic consequences such as losing their jobs, their marriages, or their health. They have often suffered legal consequences or public humiliation. Many patients have tried to stop their sexually compulsive behaviors on their own and have been unsuccessful. They enter the group therapy experience with much fear and apprehension.

As a group therapist, one can use many interventions to increase the level of hope for the patient, even as early as the first session. One example of this occurs during the introduction process. All members are asked to introduce themselves, state their bottom-line behaviors (sexually compulsive behaviors that they agree to no longer participate in), how long they have been in treatment, and what they have gained from the treatment experience thus far. The act of identifying behaviors that members are abstaining from and stating the progress that has already been made is an important way of accentuating the positive. This is often a different way of thinking for sex addicts, who are often quick to be self-critical. For new group members, this process provides a great deal of hope. They recognize the similarities between their behaviors and others' and see that other members are making progress. When new members introduce themselves, they are asked to disclose their bottom-line behaviors and their goals for treatment. The process of setting goals for oneself is another valuable way of gaining hope for the group therapy experience.

An additional way that the group therapist can develop hope for patients is by sharing letters of gratitude from graduates of the program. In my treatment program, I often receive correspondence from alumni who wish to share their successes with the group of newly recovering addicts. The advice, support, and encouragement from alumni can serve as powerful catalysts for the instillation of hope. On some occasions after patients have graduated and completed their first year of recovery, we encourage them to come back and speak to the group to provide hope and serve as a role model for recovery.

Universality

Universality refers to the realization that an individual is not alone in his or her addiction and that others have experienced similar problems (Yalom, 1975). Universality operates when a group member believes that other members have similar problems and feelings. This experience tends to reduce a member's sense of uniqueness and reinforces the fact that each person is not alone with his or her problems (Bloch & Crouch, 1985). Clients consistently rate universality as the most highly valued therapeutic factor (Butler & Fuhriman, 1983; Lieberman, 1983).

Universality is one of the most helpful of all the therapeutic factors, particularly in facilitating a group with sex addicts. Sex addicts are often alienated from others and experience a great deal of loneliness. They also experience a tremendous amount of shame. Carnes (1991) described three reasons for the shame inherent to addiction. First, there is shame because other people seem able to set appropriate limits on their sexual behavior. Addicts feel less worthy than others and wish they were normal. Second, sex addicts believe that no others exist like themselves. They believe that their behaviors make them unique. Third, sex addicts feel shame caused by their family messages, which often convey that having sexual feelings makes a person "bad." Furthermore, because most sex addicts were physically, sexually, and emotionally abused, the amount of shame and self-hatred is compounded.

For sex addicts, the group therapy experience completely contradicts their internal messages. Often, the shame and self-loathing a sex addict initially experiences with the group makes that person afraid to connect with others. One man stated, "I never wanted to get close to anyone because I always thought I was bad, dirty, and not worthy of anything." For him and other sex addicts, the experience of meeting others who have lived through both abuse and the pain of sexual addiction was extremely valuable. The group provides a safe place to practice trusting others. As group therapists, we have the job and responsibility of actively helping members recognize similarities between themselves and other members. This can be done by encouraging patients to identify similarities in their life histories and in their addictive behaviors. One member stated his observation after entering the group, "For the first time in my life, I met a group of people just like me. I felt like I came home."

IMPARTING INFORMATION

The third therapeutic factor, imparting information, refers to the didactic instructions given by the therapist, along with advice and suggestions for dealing with life's problems given by both the therapist and other group members. Often, it is the group therapist's job to engage in the "teacher role" by educating patients about the importance of 12-step support groups, the addiction cycle, identification of healthy relationships, and relapse-prevention strategies.

Twelve-step programs have utilized didactic methods for years (Bloch et al., 1979). They teach slogans, principles, and strategies in an effective way that members can readily understand because the information is coming from peers. However, in group psychotherapy several problems can occur when the group leader takes on the educator role. First, because many addicts have a history of adversarial relationships with authority figures, they are more likely to accept information from their peers than from a group therapist. Second, in my experience, it is very common for sex addicts to be passive and expect group leaders to arrive at solutions for their problems. It can inhibit the patient's recovery if a therapist assumes a problem-solving role. In addition, because sex addicts were often victimized in childhood, it is common for them to reenact the helpless victim role in group. They act dependent on the leader for advice and guidance. It is very important for group therapists to avoid falling into this trap. At times, it is essential for the leader to take a passive role and encourage members to create their own solutions by giving each other advice, suggestions, and personal opinions about how to deal with problems. This tends to empower members by allowing them to acknowledge their own strengths and competencies. Generally, a group therapist should be more active in the educator role when many new members are in the group. As time goes by and the group members get healthier, it is important to encourage them to take on a more active role.

Altruism

Altruism, the fourth therapeutic factor, refers to taking the opportunity to help another person and feel useful. Being helpful to others increases self-esteem and challenges one's own demoralized position (Kobak, Rock, & Greist, 1995).

Sex addicts often feel weak, stupid, and incompetent. They believe they have nothing to give to others. Helping other group members can challenge this sense of worthlessness. The following clinical example illustrates the power of altruism. Nate, the son of two Holocaust survivors, felt very fearful about graduating from our program. He was very comfortable in the martyr role and came up to the group leader before a session and began sharing his feelings of despair. He stated that he was worried that he would relapse and let his whole family down. Not only did he question his ability to recover, but he felt he was unworthy of recovery. He was very tearful and did not want to attend the group. With some reluctance, Nate entered the room and sat down in his seat, with his shoulders slumped and his eyes focused on the floor. As the group began, another member, Joe, revealed an extremely painful and humiliating experience. Although Nate was in his own pain, he was able to look up and make eye contact with Joe. Nate was able to support and comfort Joe by showing compassion and telling him that the experience was not his fault. As Nate consoled Joe, his own posture improved and he began to gain more confidence about his own ability to recover.

It is important for the group facilitator to acknowledge openly the process of altruism in helping members recognize the selfless behavior that they are capable of providing and to empower them to be aware of their ability to give to others. Being able to provide support for other members contributes to individuals experiencing a sense of competence and strength. This helps sex addicts overcome some of their sense of inferiority and allows them to feel positively about their strengths.

Corrective Recapitulation of the Primary Family Group

The fifth therapeutic factor, corrective recapitulation of the primary family group, refers to members experiencing transference relationships growing out of their primary family experiences.

Because the group resembles a family in many ways, members may interact with leaders and other members as they may have interacted with parents and siblings (Yalom, 1975). Therefore, the group experience provides members with the opportunity to relearn and clarify distortions and gain opportunities to have their needs met.

An example of this therapeutic factor occurred with a very talented artist, Anne, who entered treatment to stop her pattern of abusive relationships with emotionally distant men. She shared with the group how she rarely had her needs met in childhood and seldom received attention for her positive accomplishments. She shared her disappointment about how her parents never hung any of her paintings in their home. She took a risk and asked group members if they would allow her to hang her drawings on the refrigerator that was near the group room. Members allowed her to display her artwork, and she received praise for asking for something she desperately needed.

Another example of the corrective recapitulation of the primary family group occurred when a group member came up to me before group and asked a question. I was very busy at the time and responded rather curtly by stating, "I'm only one person. There is only so much I can do at one time." When we went into group, he shared how hurt he was by my impatient tone of voice. He stated that I was just like his verbally abusive mother. I allowed him to share his feelings and then apologized for my shortness. Because this was an extremely different reaction than he was accustomed to receiving in his family of origin, he stated that he was surprised there was no retaliation for his expression of anger and hurt. My acknowledging that I was wrong modeled accountability and the importance of taking responsibility for behaviors. He stated that this one event was the turning point in his treatment.

Sex addicts often come from chaotic, addicted family systems that are crisis-oriented and process-poor. Members try to correct this by adhering to order and structure (Turner, 1990). However, we try not to be too rigid. My cotherapist and I often feel we are doing a balancing act between flexibility and structure. In contrast to members' families of origin, group therapy models a family in which conflicts can be processed without members feeling rejected or abused. A male/female cotherapy team based on mutual respect is ideal.

DEVELOPMENT OF SOCIALIZING SKILLS

Social learning is the development of basic interpersonal skills. Our goal in working with addicts is to help the addict turn to people, instead of addictive behaviors, in times of need. This is extremely difficult for sex addicts, who often do not trust others. When their primary caretakers have failed them and they have been violated emotionally, physically, and sexually, why should they trust others? As a group therapist, I convey my understanding of how difficult it is for them to trust others. I feel honored when they let me into their world. I also stress that I am looking for progress, not perfection.

An example of the development of socialization skills occurred with Brad, a gay man, who entered treatment to stop his behaviors of anonymous sex and compulsive cybersex. When Brad began the program, he engaged in many seductive behaviors. In the group he was given feedback from other members that they felt uncomfortable when he stared at them for too long and when he leaned in too closely when having a conversation. At first Brad was insulted by this feedback, but he eventually learned how to set boundaries. When he discovered that his peers valued him for being more than just a sexual object, he began to genuinely relate to others.

Imitative Behaviors

According to Yalom (1975), the therapeutic factor of imitative behavior refers to patients modeling aspects of other group members and the therapist. Members frequently take on the characteristics of group members who are higher functioning.

Group members often serve as role models for other members through self-disclosure and honesty. When members first hear other members disclose their own abusive history or the trauma they have caused another person, the newer members often do not know how to respond and look to the therapists for their reaction. At this point, the group therapists serve as role models to demonstrate how to listen and respond to a member who is obviously struggling in pain (Isley, 1992). When the therapists listen attentively and provide the member with direct eye contact and sympathetic expressions, they promote a positive attitude and an understanding of the importance of what the client is saying. Through modeling the therapist, other members learn how to help each other feel both supported and understood. As the group proceeds, members are able to learn vicariously and are eventually able to process traumatic issues without the help of the facilitator. Throughout the group experience, members are encouraged to practice vigorous honesty and self-disclosure. When one member shares his or her secrets, it encourages others to take risks also.

Interpersonal Learning

Interpersonal learning refers to the group allowing patients the opportunity to improve their interpersonal relationships through learning about how they are seen by other people. The group serves as a social microcosm, "a miniature representation of each person's social universe where they have the opportunity to receive feedback from others and experiment with new ways of relating" (Yalom, 1975, p. 41).

For example, Joey had problems handling his anger. He had engaged in exhibitionistic behaviors and had beaten his wife on two occasions. As a child, he had been severely beaten and had a great deal of difficulty showing empathy for others. Sure enough, in group he became angry when he received negative feedback and verbally attacked the person who gave him the feedback. This behavior was observed by the group, and it helped him to identify the feelings that any perceived criticism evoked in him. In group he practiced identifying feelings before they escalated to rage. He also learned that rage was what precipitated his exhibitionism. For sex addicts, one of the most healing aspects of group therapy is having multiple sources of feedback. This is unique for people who have always viewed their possibilities alone.

Group Cohesiveness

Group cohesion refers to the attraction sense of belonging that members feel toward the group (Day, 1981). Bernard and MacKenzie (1994) expanded this definition by describing cohesiveness as the element that causes members to connect with the group and take seriously the events that occur in it. They explain that cohesiveness is what adds magic to group therapy and what makes the group really matter to its members.

Establishing cohesion is extremely important for the effective facilitation of sex addict groups. Yalom (1975) suggested that therapists can promote group cohesion by effective preparation of members, optimal group composition, and the setting of healthy group boundaries and norms. When these suggestions are followed and a cohesive group results, many positive consequences may emerge. First, group members try harder to influence others, are more willing to listen and accept others, and experience more security and relief from tension in the group. Second, in a cohesive group, members participate more readily and self-disclose more frequently than in a noncohesive group (Yalom, 1975). An example of group cohesion is the passionate effort that one member, Jeffrey, made to convince another to give up his self-destructive behaviors. As he challenged his peer to give up his arrogance, there were tears in Jeffrey's eyes and both love and concern in his voice.

Another example of group cohesion occurs each time there is a graduation, and a member completes treatment. In these instances there is an intense reaction from the group. Often this is because each person contributes to making the group a special, safe haven for healing. Each individual brings unique characteristics and skills to the group, and the loss of even one member alters the makeup of the community. This causes members to feel sadness and, at times, grief. Sex addicts generally have suffered many losses in their lives. They have often lost parents and partners, as well as jobs and friends. Because they were acting out sexually in the past, they stayed numb and never allowed themselves to feel the pain that loss inevitably causes. When there is a graduation in a cohesive group, members often reconnect with a profound sadness that they never allowed themselves to feel while acting out. Thus, the loss of a valued group member reactivates previous losses, and the group provides a safe place to address past grief. Although this is painful for sex addicts, it is crucial for them to begin to mourn their losses. It is also extremely powerful to point out to sex addicts, who have spent years of avoiding intimacy, what a blessing it is to have bonded with another person.

A successful termination is extremely important for sex addicts, who have often experienced relationships that were not formally or appropriately terminated. Because sex addicts have been hurt so badly in childhood, they tend to refrain from personally investing themselves in their adult relationships. Often, they protect themselves from emotional investment by being only superficially involved in their relationships. Consequently, it is easier for them to walk away from a relationship than to honor it with a meaningful ending. In some instances, group members try to avoid having a graduation ceremony and ask to just quietly leave treatment without acknowledging their successes. The group therapists should encourage sex addicts to attend the closure exercise and, as a result, experience a healthy ending for perhaps the first time in their lives. Thus, the group experience offers an opportunity for sex addicts to confront the fears of termination and accomplish a sense of closure. A graduation ceremony, where each member states his hopes and concerns for the graduate and what he has gained from getting to know the other members, forces the sex addict to have an ending with dignity.

Catharsis

Catharsis can be defined simply as the open expression of affect (Yalom, 1975). Experiencing and expressing strong feelings is extremely important for many sex addicts, who have often repressed their emotions. Most sex addicts fear that if they express their true emotions, they will experience alienation from others. In actuality, members of the group generally learn that emotional experiences can promote feelings of connection with others and not a sense of isolation.

A powerful example of catharsis that occurred in one of my groups involved a 31-year-old man named Jonathan. Jonathan entered treatment after discovering that he was HIV-positive. He had been involved in anonymous sex with hundreds of older men. Each of his partners was between 10 and 20 years older than himself. Jonathan recognized, on an intellectual level, that he was searching for a father figure. While in treatment, he decided to inform his father about his HIV status and to reveal that he desperately needed his father to come in for a family therapy session. Just before his group therapy, he telephoned his father and asked for what he needed. The father responded calmly that he would not be able to attend family therapy because he had a church function that weekend. He said that he would see his son some other time. Jonathan hung up the phone and described the conversation to me. He described how he wanted to go to bed and pull the covers over his head. I looked empathetically at his expressionless face and stated, "that is what you used to do. Isolating will not make you feel better. Let's get the support of your group to help you through this." As we walked into the group room together, Jonathan recounted his phone conversation to the members. He ended his description by stating, "I feel numb."

Group members responded with empathy, compassion, and anger at Jonathan's father. One member expressed, "I am so angry at your dad I could scream." Another member chimed in, "Me, too. I want to scream. How could your dad not realize how wonderful you are?" At this point, a third member suggested, "Let's do it. Let's have a group scream." As the group bonded together to support and care for Jonathan, I was touched by the level of empathy, concern, and emotion they were expressing. I decided to honor their idea and permitted the whole group to scream on the count of three. We screamed for the tragedy of AIDS, for the disappointment of fathers, and for the pain of a child who just wanted to be loved. After the group finished screaming, Jonathan began to sob. He accessed the feelings of sadness and disappointment that he had been hiding from for many years. His gut-level sobbing allowed him to ventilate the sorrow he had carried with him and allowed members to identify with their own pain. They supported him, affirmed him, and expressed their deep respect and love. Although the "group scream" is not an orthodox therapeutic technique and I had never utilized it previously, I followed the group process and encouraged this group member, who had difficulty accessing his feelings, that it was acceptable to experience his emotions and release his deep reservoir of pain.

An important point to keep in mind when evaluating the intensity of members' emotional expression is that it is highly individual (Yalom, 1975). An expression that may not seem significant to the leader may be a terrific stride for the member. It is much easier for some members to express their feelings than for others. It is important for the group leader to view catharsis in terms of each individual's potential and not to compare this with the degree of catharsis that other members display. For example, for some sex addicts who have denied their feelings for many years, the act of simply identifying how they feel is monumental.

Existential Factors

These five statements identified by Yalom depict important existential issues that help patients contend with the pain and ambiguity of their lives:

1. Recognizing that life is at times unfair and unjust.
2. Recognizing that ultimately there is no escape from some of life's pain and from death.

3. Recognizing that no matter how close I get to other people, I must still face life alone.
4. Facing the basic issues of my life and death, and thus living my life more honestly and being less caught up on trivialities.
5. Learning that I must take ultimate responsibility for the way I live my life, no matter how much guidance and support I get from others.

Several of the existential factors addressed by Yalom concern responsibility and isolation and are issues with which sex addicts struggle, despite a desire to feel a sense of empowerment and form connections with others. In her work with survivors of childhood abuse, Judith Herman (1992, p. 133) stated that a survivor "must be the author and arbiter of her own recovery." A therapist may offer advice, support, assistance, affection, and care, but not a cure. A group leader should not claim to have all of the answers, but should guide the members to search for the answers within themselves. We can lead them in the right direction, by teaching the tools for recovery, but whether patients choose to use them is ultimately their existential choice. Twelve-step programs support this philosophy by promoting the existential belief that individuals are ultimately responsible for their lives, not by stressing how much support is available from others (Wheeler, O'Malley, Waldo, Murphey, & Blank, 1992). There has been evidence that these existential factors have special significance for victims of undesirable life events (Silver & Wortman, 1980). Therefore, one might assume that sex addicts, who have often suffered from physical, sexual, or emotional abuse (Carnes, 1991), might especially value the existential factors as operative in their treatment.

TABLE 12.1. Sex Addicts Who Have Completed Residential Treatment Rate: *How Helpful They Felt Each of the Therapeutic Factors Was for Them in the Group Therapy Experience*

Therapeutic Factors	Average Value
Instillation of Hope	3.5
Universality	3.6
Imparting Information	3.2
Altruism	2.8
Corrective Recapitulation of the Primary Family Group	3.0
Development of Socializing Techniques	3.2
Imitative Behavior	3.4
Interpersonal Learning	3.5
Group Cohesiveness	3.7
Catharsis	3.7
Existential Factors	3.0

N = 40
Note: Average values based on Likert + scale of 0 = not at all helpful to 4 = extremely helpful.

In group, members often try to make meaning out of both their addictions and their traumatic histories. Members speak freely about the unjust pain and suffering they experienced as well as about the impact of their sexually compulsive behaviors on others. It is essential for group members to come to terms with the roles they played as both victim and victimizer. One member, Judy, stated it clearly on her last day of group, "I now realize that I was not responsible for the abuse I received as a child. I had no control over that. What I do have control over are the choices I make as an adult."

THERAPEUTIC FACTORS MOST VALUED BY PATIENTS

Forty patients who had completed the Residential Program at KeyStone Center's Extended Care Unit—The Center for Healing from Sexual Compulsivity and Trauma were given questionnaires to identify what they believed were the most beneficial aspects of their group therapy experience. These questionnaires were given to them on their last day of treatment, and they were asked to rate on a Likert scale the amount they valued each therapeutic factor. These patients' treatment experience ranged from 1 to 6 months between September 1998 and May 1999.

One interesting finding was that all 11 of the therapeutic factors were rated as very helpful by patients. Although this research was done with a relatively small sample, it highlights the fact that sex addicts find group therapy to be helpful in their recovery process. Specifically, the therapeutic factors that were most highly valued by patients were catharsis, cohesion, interpersonal learning, and universality. Catharsis and cohesion were both consistently ranked the highest. The statement "Revealing embarrassing things about myself and still being accepted by others" was endorsed as the single most healing aspect of group therapy. This finding suggested that acceptance and a sense of belonging, the very aspect of intimacy that addicts fear, is also what they crave. Interestingly, altruism was the least valued therapeutic factor. This suggests that group members often do not recognize how valuable it is for their own healing process to help others.

It is hoped that further research will be conducted to explore the value of group psychotherapy in the treatment of sex addicts. At this point, group psychotherapy in a residential setting appears to be a highly effective treatment modality for sex addicts. It reduces the shame and denial, limits isolation, and increases socialization skills and the development of empathy. These aspects of group psychotherapy foster the development of intimacy and help sex addicts develop the skills they need to meet their emotional needs in healthier ways.

RECOMMENDATIONS FOR THERAPISTS WHO ARE INTERESTED IN FACILITATING GROUP PSYCHOTHERAPY FOR SEXUAL ADDICTS

There are many different considerations to take into account when deciding to facilitate a group for sex addicts. First, what type of setting is available for the group? Is it going to be an outpatient group that meets weekly or part of an already established inpatient facility? Another question is that of treatment duration. It is important for a therapist to take into account what model he or she is going to follow and what type of group is best for the individual needs of the clients.

Short-Term Versus Long-Term Model?

Is the group going to follow a short-term, time-limited model or is the group aspiring to follow a long-term, time-unlimited model? There are advantages and disadvantages with both types of groups.

One of the advantages of short-term group therapy is that when members recognize that their time together is limited, they experience more of an urgency to share and cohesion develops much more quickly. Second, a group that focuses on members' painful experiences of trauma and harm done to others is stressful and often overwhelming. A time limit could provide a structure within which the regressive nature of the treatment could be contained (Herman & Schatzow, 1984). Third, the short-term nature of the group could keep the focus on the common experiences of sexual addiction and thereby serve to set boundaries. Finally, a brief group encounter provides members with a unique opportunity for sex addicts to succeed and "graduate" from a concrete experience in their recovery process. This serves to help create a sense of mastery and accomplishment in regard to their continual struggle with past feelings of victimization. Brief psychotherapy is also a cost-effective method for sexual addicts to begin their journey toward trusting others. I would recommend a short-term group to last for at least eight to ten 90-minute sessions. The main disadvantage of facilitating a short-term group is that a limited amount of intrapsychic change can occur in just several months. This would not be the ideal approach for sexually compulsive clients who also have personality disorders and would need much more intense, long-term group psychotherapy. However, many sex addicts have commitment issues and may initially only be able to tolerate a time-limited focus on painful issues.

Some of the advantages of long-term time-unlimited psychotherapy groups include diminishing a sense of alienation and isolation and establishing trust over time. Unlike in 12-step support groups, therapists are available to direct the process and monitor each patient's progress. Accountability is monitored, and sex addicts have an opportunity to develop healthy long-term relationships with each other. The main disadvantage to this type of group is that it may be overwhelming for a sex addict who has never had a long-term relationship and may provide him with an opportunity to drop out and once again experience a failure. However, the paced nature of group therapy, along with the expertise of the therapists, may allow for the processing of these overwhelming feelings and the possibility of significant growth in the area of staying connected in relationships while tolerating the anxiety around this.

Leadership Dimensions

It is crucial that the therapists' technique reflects an attempt to promote an atmosphere of safety and mutual support (Bernard & MacKenzie, 1994). In order to accomplish this goal, therapists will find it valuable if they are able to connect emotionally with members, as sex addicts feel that no one can relate to their feelings. In work with sexually compulsive clients, it is important not to view each group member as "the other," who is totally different from oneself because of his or her experience. Therefore, therapists who internally differentiate themselves too much from the group may be compromised in their effectiveness with this patient population. However, the therapist who overly identifies with group members is similarly not ready to do this type of work.

When a therapist overly identifies with members, he or she often experiences an unbearable feeling of helplessness and becomes enmeshed in the patients' sense of despair. As a defense against these feelings, the therapist may try to assume the role of a rescuer and take on more of an advocacy role for the patients (Herman, 1992). By so doing, the therapist implies that the group members are helpless and that it is necessary for the therapist to take care of them. This ultimately disempowers the patients. I also strongly advocate for the use of a cotherapy team. The benefits of having two therapists to support each other are tremendous. Ideally, two therapists can model a healthy interpersonal relationship, in which leaders are free to model agreeing and disagreeing with each other and with the group. Also, members are safe to express anger at one leader and still feel supported by the other.

Leadership Style

When therapists facilitate groups with sex addicts, it is important to adopt a more active style than is commonly recommended in analytic group therapy. An active leadership style is necessary when working with a group of traumatized sex addicts, in order to keep the group safe enough to contain the pain and suffering experienced in these sessions. It is necessary for the therapist to be encouraging and reassuring to group members, as well as be direct and confrontative when necessary.

One approach that can be very effective in leadership is that of use of the self (of the therapist). An authentic presence, combined with genuine "here-and-now" feedback that incorporates an emotional response on the therapist's part, can have a powerful impact. Clearly, it models genuineness and the capacity to state who one is in a given moment. Second, it fosters interpersonal connections in an immediate way. These factors are likely to have been weak in the kind of families of origin we often see in this population, where there was no permission to speak the truth about one's experience in the here and now.

Implementing "Check-ins" and "Closing Rituals"

Having each client participate in a check-in during the opening of group is a practical tool that provides a warm-up for the group process and valuable information about where the client is in terms of his or her recovery process. For instance, a check-in could be structured along the lines of a report on abstinence from bottom lines the past week; what the client's physical, emotional, and spiritual state is; followed by a report on that person's utilization of a 12-step support network (how many meetings, sponsor contact and use of phone, step work, etc.).

The value of this check-in cannot be understated. The client is held accountable to his group to provide information about his or her recovery or relapse and to share his or her progress with developing and utilizing a 12-step support network. It gives the client practice in identifying and sharing where he or she is physically, emotionally, and spiritually in the here and now.

It is also valuable to incorporate a closing ritual in order to provide closure for each session. Closure is extremely important, as most sex addicts have not had successful endings to any relationships. Members should be given the option of incorporating a poem or chant into their closing ritual. In my groups, members have chosen to recite the Serenity Prayer. These closing rituals make our endings special and provide closure until the next session.

CONCLUSION

Clearly, group psychotherapy is a powerful tool for the healing of sex addicts. These are just some suggestions that therapists can add to their repertoire of therapeutic techniques. It is hoped that in the future, more therapists will endeavor to facilitate group psychotherapy with this population.

REFERENCES

Bernard, H. S., & MacKenzie, K. R. (1994). *Basics of group psychotherapy.* New York: Guilford.

Bloch, S., & Crouch, E. (1985). *Therapeutic factors in group psychotherapy.* Oxford: Oxford University Press.

Bloch, S., Reibstein, J., Crouch, E., Holroyd, P., & Themen, J. (1979). A method for the study of therapeutic factors in group psychotherapy. *British Journal of Psychiatry, 134,* 257–263.

Burton, R. L. (1982). Group process demystified. In J. W. Pfeiffer & L. D. Goodstein (Eds.), *The 1982 annual for facilitators, trainers, and consultants* (pp. 190–197). San Diego, CA: University Associates.

Butler, T., & Fuhriman, A. (1983). Curative factors in group therapy: A review of recent research literature. *Small Group Behavior, 14,* 131–142.

Carnes, P. J. (1991). *Don't call it love: Recovery from sexual addiction.* New York: Bantam Doubleday Dell.

Day, M. (1981). Process in classical psychodynamic groups. *International Journal of Group Psychotherapy, 31,* 153–174.

Goodman, A. (1998). *Sexual addiction: An integrated approach.* New York: International Universities Press.

Herman, J. L. (1992). *Trauma and recovery.* New York: Basic.

Herman, J. L., & Schatzow, E. (1984). Time-limited group therapy for women with a history of incest. *International Journal of Group Psychotherapy, 34*(4), 290–295.

Isley, P. J. (1992). A time limited group therapy model for men sexually abused as children. *Group. 16*(4), 233–246.

Kobak, K. A., Rock, A. L., & Greist, J. H. (1995). Group behavior therapy for obsessive-compulsive disorder. *Journal for Specialists in Group Work, 20*(1), 26–32.

Lieberman, M. (1983). Comparative analysis of change mechanisms in groups. In R. R. Dies & K. R. MacKenzie (Eds.), *Advances in group psychotherapy: Integrating research and practice* (pp. 191–208). New York: International Universities Press.

Protter, B. (1993). *Sexual perversion: Integrative treatment approaches for the clinician.* New York: Plenum.

Silver, R. L., & Wortman, C. B. (1980). Coping with undesirable life events. In J. Garber & M. E. P. Seligman (Eds.), *Human helplessness. Theory and applications* (pp. 279–340). New York: Academic.

Travin, S. (1995). Compulsive sexual behaviors. *Psychiatric Clinics of North America, 18,* 155–169.

Turner, M. (1990). Long-term outpatient group psychotherapy as a modality for treating sexual addiction. *American Journal of Preventive Psychiatry and Neurology, 2*(3), 23–26.

Wheeler, I., O'Malley, K., Waldo, M., Murphey, J., & Blank, C. (1992). Participants' perception of therapeutic factors in groups for incest survivors. *Group Work, 17*(2), 89–95.

Yalom, I. D. (1975). *The theory and practice of group psychotherapy.* New York: Basic.

Yalom, I. D. (1985). *The theory and practice of group psychotherapy* (3rd ed.). New York: Basic

Yalom, V. J., & Yalom, I. (1990). Brief interactive group psychotherapy. *Psychiatric Annals, 20*(7), 362–367

CHAPTER 13

Psychopharmacologic Intervention in Addictive Sexual Behavior

JOHN R. SEALY

As the treatment of sexual addiction is explored, therapists seek guidelines on the use and appropriateness of psychotropic medications. This chapter is based on a retrospective consideration of over 300 cases of sexual behavior disorders in a 28-day inpatient setting, using the sexual addiction model of treatment. The categories, criteria, and rationale used for prescribing psychotropic medications are outlined, and case examples are presented. The focus of this chapter is confined to nonviolent sexual acting-out and hence does not include antiandrogenic (e.g., medroxyprogesterone, or Depo-Provera, and cyproterone acetate) medication. The medical treatment of the many somatic complaints presented by sex addicts, including sexually transmitted diseases, is also beyond the scope of this chapter.

THEORY

Many theories have been proposed to explain the wide variety of sexual behavior disorders. Money (1980, 1986) pioneered, making distinctions between normophilic, hypophilic, hyperphilic, and paraphilic behaviors, leaving to the therapist the dilemma of deciding what were "normal" infant, childhood, and adult sexual behaviors. Carnes (1983, 1989, 1990, 1991), Diamond (1983), Schneider (1988), and Kasl (1989) present the concept of sexual addiction with specific shame-based behavior cycles of acting out and acting in and utilize a 12-

Special thanks to Bill Reeve, PharmD; Rob Weiss, LCSW; Michael Alvarez, MFCC; and Sharon O'Hara, primary therapist.

step model as a primary treatment. Coleman (1987, 1990) challenges the addiction model as an oversimplification that prevents appropriate medical treatment and discounts other biopsychosocial factors. He describes "compulsive sexual behavior" as a symptom of an underlying obsessive-compulsive disorder. Hollander (1993) suggests that impulse control disorder may be a more appropriate classification. Kafka (1989) proposes the model of a drive dysregulation syndrome associated with a primary mood disorder that may be responsive to antidepressant medication.

REVIEW OF LITERATURE

Studying the psychiatric literature for guidelines to medications for addictive sexual behavior presents two problems: the literature is limited to case studies, and terminology is often inconsistent, outdated, and poorly defined. Fedoroff (1993), for example, still speaks of "deviant sexual interests" when describing serotoninergic drug treatment. Sexual addiction is referenced in the following titles: "Successful Antidepressant Treatment of Nonparaphilic Sexual Addictions and Paraphilias in Men" (Kafka, 1991); "Fluoxetine Treatment of Nonparaphilic Sexual Addictions and Paraphilias in Men" (Kafka & Prentky, 1992a); "A Comparative Study of Nonparaphilic Sexual Addictions and Paraphilias in Men" (Kafka & Prentky, 1992b).

Several authors describe specific medications for specific paraphilias: fluoxetine (Prozac) for voyeurism (Emmanuel, Lydiard, & Ballenger, 1991) and exhibitionism (Bianchi, 1990); buspirone (Buspar) for transvestic fetishism (Fedoroff, 1988); lithium for autoerotic asphyxia (Cesnik & Coleman, 1989) and obsessional gender dysphoria (Coleman & Cesnik, 1990); and clomipramine (Anafranil) for exhibitionism (Wawrose & Sisto, 1992).

Other authors address paraphilias as a category: Kafka and Coleman (1991) describe the convergence of mood, impulse, and compulsive behaviors in paraphilias and serotonin. Fedoroff and Fedoroff (1992) use buspirone (Buspar) for paraphilic sexual behavior. Gottesman and Schubert (1993) use low-dose medroxyprogesterone acetate (Provera) to manage paraphilias. Lorefice (1991) treats a fetish with fluoxetine (Prozac); and Perilstein and colleagues (1991) describe three cases of paraphilias responsive to fluoxetine. Abel and associates (1992) provide a comprehensive overview of treatment of paraphiliacs, focusing on sexual offenders. They claim that increasing pharmacologic data with SSRI medications "could lead to a new formulation of our understanding of what a paraphilia is in relationship to other psychiatric disorders."

Some authors focus on specific behaviors, whereas others speak to general categories; therefore, it is difficult to discern what medications or families of medications are helpful for what disorders. As Hollander and Wong (1995) state,

"Sexual obsessions and compulsions have long eluded definitive classification and categorization as far as symptomatology, conceptual aspects and treatment."

TERMINOLOGY AND THE *DSM-IV*

DSM-IV diagnostic criteria were used in our treatment milieu whenever possible to promote clearer communication between referring professionals, treatment teams, medical consultants, and third-party payers. It is the purpose of the *DSM-IV* to be "a helpful guide to clinical practice . . . useful for clinicians by striving for brevity of criteria sets, clarity of language and explicit statements of the constructs embodied in the diagnostic criteria. An additional goal [is] to facilitate research and improve communication among clinicians and researchers . . . improving collection of clinical information" (APA, 1994, p. xv).

The *DSM-IV* defines nine paraphilias: Exhibitionism, Fetishism, Frotteurism, Pedophilia, Sexual Masochism, Sexual Sadism, Transvestic Fetishism, Voyeurism, and Paraphilia Nor Otherwise Specified (see table 13.1). It adds that Exhibitionism, Pedophilia, and Voyeurism make up the majority of sex offenders and are the most common presenting problems to clinics treating paraphilias. Money (1986) defined almost 50 paraphilias, and there are no doubt hundreds more. The DSM-IV describes paraphilias as

> intense recurrent sexually arousing fantasies and sexual urges . . . with variable intensity . . . frequent, unprotected sex may result in infection with or transmission of a sexually transmitted disease . . . may cause clinically significant distress or impairment in social, occupational, or other important areas of functioning . . . may lead to arrest or incarceration. . . . Social and sexual relationships may suffer. . . . They may selectively view, read, purchase, or collect photographs, films, and textual depictions that focus on their preferred type of paraphiliac stimulus. . . . Others report extreme guilt, shame, and depression at having to engage in an unusual sexual activity that is socially unacceptable or that they regard as immoral. There is often impairment in the capacity for reciprocal, affectionate sexual activity and Sexual Dysfunctions may be present. . . . The behaviors may increase in response to psychosocial stressors, in relation to other mental disorders, or with increased opportunity to engage in the Paraphilia. (APA, 1994, pp. 522–523)

However, although these statements refer to sexually addictive characteristics, the *DSM-IV* never mentions sexual addiction or refers to the compulsive or impulsive features. The *DSM-IV* also fails to mention the vast array of other sexually addictive behaviors, which must be lumped under the unhelpful diagnosis of Sexual Disorder Not Otherwise Specified. This deficiency has promoted

TABLE 13.1. Nine Paraphilias Defined in *DSM-IV*

Pedophilia
> Recurrent, intense sexually arousing fantasies, sexual urges, or behavior involving sexual activity with a prepubescent child or children (generally, age 13 years or younger).

Exhibitionism
> Recurrent, intense sexually arousing fantasies, sexual urges, or behavior involving the exposure of one's genitalia to an unsuspecting stranger.

Voyeurism
> Recurrent, intense sexually arousing fantasies, sexual urges, or behavior involving the act of observing an unsuspecting person who is naked, in the process of disrobing, or engaging in sexual activity.

Sadism
> Recurrent, intense sexually arousing fantasies, sexual urges, or behaviors involving acts (real, not simulated), in which the psychological or physical suffering (including humiliation) of the victim is sexually exciting to the person.

Masochism
> Recurrent, intense sexually arousing fantasies, sexual urges, or behaviors involving the act (real, not simulated) of being humiliated, beaten, bound, or otherwise made to suffer.

Transvestic Fetishism
> In a heterosexual male, recurrent, intense sexually arousing fantasies, sexual urges, or behavior involving cross-dressing.

Fetishism
> Recurrent, intense sexually arousing fantasies, sexual urges, or behaviors involving the use of nonliving objects (e.g., female undergarments.)

Frotteurism
> Recurrent, intense sexually arousing fantasies, sexual urges, or behaviors involving touching and rubbing against a nonconsenting person.

Paraphilia, Not Otherwise Specified
> Paraphilias that do not meet criteria for any other category. Examples include, but are not limited to telephone scatologia (obscene phone calls), necrophilia (corpses), partialism (exclusive focus on part of the body), zoophilia (animals), coprophilia (feces), klismaphilia (enemas), and urophilia (urine).

Source: DSM-IV (APA, 1994).

the term *nonparaphilic sexual behavior*, which is conventional, normative sexual behavior taken to the extreme. Coleman's (1992) five subtypes of nonparaphilic behavior and their characteristics help organize this enormous spectrum: Compulsive Cruising and Multiple Partners, Compulsive Fixation on an Unattainable Partner, Compulsive Autoeroticism, Compulsive Multiple Love Relationships, and Compulsive Sexuality in a Relationship (see table 13.2). Nevertheless, despite the *DSM-IV*'s limitations, it is the accepted standard and therefore the best tool for promoting accurate communication among clinicians focusing on sexual behavior.

TABLE 13.2. Types of Nonparaphilic Compulsive Sexual Behavior

Compulsive Cruising and Multiple Partners
   Constantly searching or "scanning" the environment for a potential partner.
   Relentless search to find, conquer, and satisfy the demand for a sexual outlet.
   Insatiable demand for multiple partners as part of a strategy for management of
       anxiety and maintenance of self-esteem.
   Cruising is ritualistic and trance-inducing.
   Partners are "things to be used."
   Comorbidity with narcissistic, schizoid, and self-defeating personality disorders.
Compulsive Fixation on an Unattainable Partner
   Compulsive fixation on unattainable partner despite lack of a reciprocal response.
   Fantasies are elaborated upon without the intrusion of reality.
   The fantasy is fueled by the potential and fantasized reciprocation of love.
   The love object is idealized and fictionalized.
   Comorbidity with narcissistic, schizoid, and borderline personality disorders.
Compulsive Autoeroticism
   Obsessive and compulsive drive toward sexual self-stimulation of the genitalia.
   Cessation of masturbation is caused by exhaustion, injury, or extreme social
       pressure rather than sexual satisfaction.
   Loneliness is felt keenly after an orgasm.
   Masturbating 5–15 times a day is common.
   Physical injury is common.
   Interference in occupational, social, interpersonal, and intimacy functioning.
   Comorbidity with avoidant and schizoid personality disorders.
Compulsive Multiple Love Relationships
   Obsession and compulsion toward finding the intense feeling of a new
       relationship.
   Lack of capacity to freely choose multiple love relationships.
   Fantasy and role-playing are essential in relationships; reality is intrusive.
   Highly skilled romance artists.
   Comorbidity with narcissistic and dependent personality disorders.
Compulsive Sexuality in a Relationship
   Compulsive expressions of sexuality in a relationship.
   Demanding sexual expression through manipulation, coercion, or violence.
   Absence of expression of sexuality results in anxiety, depression, and anger.
   Unending needs for sex, expressions of love attention, and signs of affection that
       temporarily relieve anxiety.
   Relationships are characterized by intense possessiveness, jealousy, and anger.
   Comorbidity with narcissistic and dependent personality disorders.

Source: Coleman, 1992.

DEFINITION OF SEXUAL ADDICTION

Sexual addiction can include any of the paraphilic and nonparaphilic behaviors described previously, but the type or intensity of sexual acting out does not diagnose sexual addiction itself. Carnes (1991) identifies an anatomy of sex addiction, which is outlined in table 13.3. Coleman (1992) states, "Compulsive sexuality can be a coping mechanism similar to alcohol and drug abuse."

TABLE 13.3. Anatomy of Sex Addiction

---

1. A pattern of out-of-control behavior.
2. Severe consequences due to sexual behavior.
3. Inability to stop despite adverse consequences.
4. Persistent pursuit of self-destructive or high-risk behavior.
5. Ongoing desire or effort to limit sexual behavior.
6. Sexual obsession and fantasy as a primary coping strategy.
7. Increasing amounts of sexual experience because the current level of activity is no longer sufficient.
8. Severe mood changes around sexual activity.
9. Inordinate amounts of time spent in obtaining sex, being sexual, or recovering from sexual experience.
10. Neglect of important social, occupational, or recreational activities because of sexual behavior.

Source: Carnes, 1991, pp. 11–12.

A sexual addict finds himself locked in a cycle of compelling fantasies and increasing sexual urges to avoid emotional pain and anxiety triggered by highly individualized psychosocial stressors and intense needs. The tension builds, leading to impulsively acting out the sexual urges with increasingly risky behaviors that can last from several hours to days. Because these behaviors often are antithetical to the addict's own ethics, principles, and goals and create severe consequences, these individuals are filled with shame that promotes secrecy, social isolation, depression, and spiritual and emotional bankruptcy. They may use other addictive behaviors to maintain an illusion of control, but remain in denial about being trapped in an out-of-control cycle.

TREATMENT MILIEU

All patients in our treatment milieu were voluntary, presenting with a wide range of nonviolent, sexual acting-out paraphilic and nonparaphilic behaviors. Some sex offenders were included. The amount of emotional pain (shame, humiliation, remorse, guilt, loneliness, anger, suicidal ideation, fear, anxiety) was not presumed to be any greater in the professional who was being ostracized by his entire town for multiple extramarital sexual affairs, exhibitionism, and pending legal consequences than in the patient who was masturbating alone four or five times per day. All patients, without exception, were required to sign a 12-week Celibacy Contract with the following conditions: no masturbation, no seductive behavior, no pornographic material, no sexual contact with another person, and instruction to report all sexual fantasizing to appropriate staff. Hence the milieu directly confronts the use of sexual behavior as a coping mechanism. Patients often describe feeling as if they are in "withdrawal."

Sex addicts participated in intensive treatment (usually 28 days), which included cognitive therapy, challenging core self-beliefs, 12-step workbooks, and attending Sex Addicts Anonymous and Sex and Love Addicts Anonymous, as well as groups focusing on addictions, men's and women's issues, grief and loss, healthy sexuality, healthy options for being nurtured, managing anxiety, identifying shame-based thinking and behavior, spirituality, and relapse prevention tools. Art therapy, psychodrama, supervised recreation, and fitness were other modalities. Family week was held during the final week; all those hurt by the sex addict's behavior were invited, including spouses, parents, and friends, to promote honesty and recovery for all those in pain.

EVALUATION FOR MEDICATION

Although full histories of sexual acting-out behavior were collected, use of medications was not based on the type (paraphilic or nonparaphilic) or consequences of sexual behavior. Because sexual addiction does not disqualify one from having other psychiatric disorders, it was essential that prior to being prescribed medication each patient received a full psychiatric evaluation; a Sexual Dependency Inventory; appropriate psychological testing; referring therapist and treatment team observations and impressions regarding mood, affect, and OCD behavior; medical history and physical exams; blood laboratory values; and EKG results. Testing for HIV infection with the patient's permission is always indicated, even if recently performed. (See table 13.4.) The level of denial this patient population holds carries over into health issues, thus putting spouses or partners at risk of becoming infected. Sex addicts will often take health risks that others would never consider because of the intensity of the addictive process. It should not be assumed that sex addicts are knowledgeable in this area, as they frequently know very little about healthy sexuality.

When clinicians become aware that sexual acting-out behavior does not necessarily represent sexual addiction, patients with schizophrenia, dementia, or other severe cognitive impairment, or patients actively abusing alcohol or other substances, with no prior rehabilitation treatment or in serious withdrawal, are transferred to another unit or facility.

THREE MAJOR CATEGORIES OF MEDICATION RESPONSE

Because success has been reported for treatment that uses several different types of medication, it was suspected that different responses might be due to sub-

TABLE 13.4. Need for Medication Is Based on

Psychiatric Evaluation
    Detailed questioning that seeks symptoms of
        depression/vegetative dysfunction
        suicidal ideation
        mania, hypomania
        other compulsions and obsessions
        dissociation
        anxiety
        panic
    Past treatment history
    Substance abuse history
    Family history, especially
        emotional abuse
        physical abuse
        sexual abuse
    Past medical history, including
        allergies
        history of head trauma, seizures
        medications
    Mental status, especially
        memory
        intellectual functioning
        abstract thinking
        mood and affect
        perceptual processes—hallucinations, illusions
        thought processes—thought disorders, loose associations
        insight and judgment
    Sexual Dependency Inventory
        to promote full disclosure of sexually addictive behavior
    Psychological testing, when indicated:
        MMPI-II, MCMI III, Bender Gestalt, BSI, Rorschach, TAT, Dissociative
           Experience Scale
    Observation and impressions
        of referring therapist, treatment team, nursing, primary therapist, group
           therapists, recreational therapists, dietitian, art therapist, chemical
           dependency therapist
    Personality
        Axis II
    Medical History
        and physical examination, laboratory results, EKG
    HIV Status

types of sexual addiction or other closely associated psychiatric disorders, or both. Indeed, three major distinct categories emerged in terms of psychotropic medication intervention and treatment response: Sexual Addiction with Three Subtypes, Sexual Addiction with Major Mood Disorder, and Sexual Addiction with Obsessive-Compulsive Disorder (see table 13.5).

TABLE 13.5. Categories of Medication Responses

Category	Psychotropic Medications
Sexual addiction with three subtypes	None
Sexual addiction with major mood disorder	Antidepressants Lithium
Sexual addiction with obsessive-compulsive disorder	SSRI antidepressants, high doses

Sexual Addiction with Three Subtypes

The Sexual Addiction with Three Subtypes group included highly impulsive individuals with poor boundaries, in denial over their degree of being out of control, isolated emotionally, and highly avoidant of any anxiety or other uncomfortable feeling state. Psychotropic medications were not indicated, as there was minimal to no response to them in our milieu. This is in accord with Hollander and Wong (1995), who, although they separate sexual addictions from paraphilias and sexual obsessions, report, "The sexually addictive or impulsive patients had a mixed response, with some patients actually having greater difficulty inhibiting their sexual impulses on high dose SRIs." (See table 13.6.)

Our patients responded instead to a highly structured treatment with support from peers and staff, clear boundaries, cognitive restructuring, task orientation, and working the first through fourth steps in the 12-step Sex Addicts Anonymous and Sex and Love Addicts Anonymous programs. Three subtypes were identified.

The first subtype included patients who were recovering from alcohol or substance abuse, or both, and had been through a prior drug rehabilitation program. Many had relapsed related to recent sexual acting-out behavior and

TABLE 13.6. Treatment of Sexual Obsessions and Impulsions with Serotoninergic Agents (*N* = 15)

Agent	N	Dose (mg/d)
Fluvoxamine	1	200–300
Clomipramine	4	200–400
Fluoxetine	10	60–80

Disorder	Group Response
Sexual obsessions	Improved
Paraphilias	Partial response
Sexual addictions	Unchanged/worse

Source: Hollander & Wong, 1995.

admitted that the sexual and drug addictions promoted each other. This group frequently complained of depressive symptoms early in treatment, including dysphoria, anxiety, agitation, insomnia, poor concentration, and poor short-term memory. However, remission of symptoms typically occurred by the 3rd and 4th week without psychotropic intervention. The resolution of severe depressive symptoms in early recovering alcoholics without use of medications is frequently observed in addiction programs (Brown et al., 1995; Raskin & Miller, 1993).

The second subtype included patients who rotated among several other severe addictive behaviors, including eating disorders, compulsive exercise, codependency (attempting to control peers and staff), caffeine and nicotine abuse, excessive gambling, and overspending. They tended to focus on how well they were "recovering" in one addiction, ignoring how out of control they were in another. Other than a nicotine transdermal patch to help in withdrawal from cigarettes, these addicts needed strong boundaries and anxiety management skills, not medication.

The third subtype included entrenched personality disorders—particularly Dependent, Narcissistic, and Antisocial—which became clearer in the second half of the treatment. Interestingly, what were thought to be Schizoid, Borderline, Histrionic, and Avoidant personality disorders tended to abate during the treatment course. Again, no psychotropic medications were indicated.

Clinical Case Example.   Robert was a 29-year-old high-powered, successful stockbroker who was involved in multiple relationships. He frequently used prostitutes and cocaine. He was used to gaining power through money, an attractive appearance, and intelligence; yet he complained of lacking intimacy in his life and having no true friends. He was taking ever more dangerous risks in his sexual acting out, which led to his seeking treatment. Once he was in withdrawal from sexual and cocaine addiction in the treatment milieu, he complained of feeling very depressed, with fleeting suicidal ideation, insomnia, loneliness, despair, and intense anxiety. He was obsessive about wanting to maintain his physical attractiveness through exercise. His core beliefs about his shame were challenged, whereas strict boundaries were maintained. As he experienced more pain, he finally reached out to peers in desperation, making his first real connection. He slowly became more self-disclosing, increasing his sincerity and honesty depite his narcissistic wounds. Depression complaints abated. He used the structure of the 12-step programs Cocaine Anonymous, Sex Addicts Anonymous, and Sex and Love Addicts Anonymous to design a structured discharge plan to maintain sobriety. After discharge, he entered long-term individual psychotherapy to work through his past emotional abuse.

Sexual Addiction With Major Depression

The second major category included patients with no major substance abuse history, but clear clinical symptoms of major depression, including nontransient dysphoria, extreme fatigue, severe insomnia, social isolation, poor concentration, poor short-term memory, suicidal ideation, high irritability, hopelessness, helplessness, and profound low self-esteem. These patients responded to SSRI (selective serotonin reuptake inhibitor) antidepressant medications, most commonly fluoxetine (Prozac) 20 mg q.d. If side effects of nausea, diarrhea, nervousness, or insomnia were too severe, sertraline (Zoloft) 50–100 mg q.d. was often effective. Failure to respond to one SSRI antidepressant does not necessarily mean failure with another SSRI antidepressant. Severe insomnia secondary to the fluoxetine or sertraline was managed with trazodone 25–50 mg q.h.s. A few patients were taking paroxetine (Paxil) 20–30 mg q.d. on admission and continued on that medication unless they were responding poorly; they were then changed to fluoxetine (Prozac). The tricyclic antidepressants were also very effective when the SSRI side effects were intolerable or insomnia was severe (e.g., desipramine 150 mg q.d., imipramine 150 mg q.d., or amitriptyline 100–150 mg q.d.). (See tables 13.7 and 13.8). The tricyclic antidepressants were also preferred by some because they are inexpensive compared to the SSRIs.

Monoamine oxidase inhibitor (MAOI) antidepressants or combination therapies would have been used if success had not been achieved with the previous regimen (see table 13.9). In general, the MAOIs appear to be indicated in patients with atypical depression or who are unresponsive to other antidepressive therapy. They are rarely a drug of first choice. The most serious reactions to these medications involve changes in blood pressure; hypertensive crises have sometimes been fatal. Patients are to avoid foods high in tyramine.

Venlafaxine (Effexor), fluvoxamine (Luvox), and nefazodone (Serzone) were not yet available. Clomipramine was considered too sedating for most patients.

Although all antidepressants, but particularly the SSRI antidepressants, can affect sexual functioning, and although all of our patients were on celibacy contracts, they were informed of possible sexual side effects, including decreased libido and difficulty in achieving orgasm or orgasmic enjoyment for men and women. Also, in men, ejaculatory delay and decrease or absence in the sensation of the organ can be present. This information helped sex addicts work with their physicians to treat the dysfunction, rather than assume that they themselves were "defective," when they ended celibacy and began to practice healthier sexual behavior.

A very few patients displayed intermittent hypomanic behavior, including expansive mood, flight of ideas, pressured speech, and sleeping short hours. There was a mixed response to lithium carbonate within therapeutic range. In-

TABLE 13.7. Major Side Effects of Commonly Used Antidepressant Medications Within Normal Dose Range

	Anti-cholinergic Effect	Sedation	Blood Pressure Changes	Amine Uptake Blocking Activity	
				Norepinephrine	Serotonin
Amitriptyline	++++	++++	++++	++	++++
Amoxapine	+++	+++	++	+++	++
Bupropion	0	+	+	0/+	0/+
Citalopram	0	+	0	0/+	+++++
Clomipramine	+++	+++	++	++	+++++
Desipramine	+	+	++	++++	++
Doxepin	++	+++	++	+	++
Fluoxetine	0	+	0	0/+	+++++
Imipramine	++	++	++++	++*	++++
Isocarboxazid	0	+	0	MAOI	
Luvoxamine	0/+	0/+	0	0	+++++
Maprotiline	+	++	+	+++	0/+
Nefazodone	0	++	0	−	+++
Nortriptyline	+	+	++	++	+++
Paroxetine	0	+	0	0/+	+++++
Phenelzine	0	++	++++	MAOI	
Protriptyline	++++	+	++	++++	++
Sertraline	0	+	0	0/+	+++++
Tranylcypromine	0	+	++++	MAOI	
Trazodone	0	+++	+	0	+++
Trimipramine	++++	++	++	+	+
Venlafaxine	0	+	0	+++	+++

* Via desipramine, the major metabolite.
0 = none; + = slight; ++ = moderate; +++ = high; ++++ = very high; +++++ = highest; MAOI = monoamine oxidase inhibitor.

terestingly, two patients with episodes of explosive anger followed by much re-morse responded very well to low doses of lithium carbonate 300 mg b.i.d.

Grandiosity was considered a manic symptom only if it was unrelenting, as it was a common symptom among sex addicts in early recovery.

Clinical Case Example. Cliff was a 34-year-old divorced male who lived alone. He struggled with severe fatigue and insomnia and as a result avoided social functions and had no real friends. He would lie in bed, often through the night, masturbating while on phone sex lines or watching pornography, ultimately resenting anyone or anything that interrupted his ritualistic behavior. His declining work attendance and performance, staggering phone bills, and increasing depression with suicidal ideation led his boss to initiate psychiatric help. Upon admission to the inpatient sexual addiction unit, he was placed on fluoxetine (Prozac), initially 20 mg and later

TABLE 13.8. Common Antidepressants

Generic Name	Manufacturer Name	Half-Life (hours)	Dose Range(mg/day)
Amitriptyline	Elavil Endep Entrafon[a] Limbitrol[b] Triavil	31–46	50–300
Amoxapine	Asendin	8[c]	50–600
Bupropion	Wellbutrin	8–24	200–450
Citalopram	Celexa	35	20–60
Clomipramine	Anafranil	19–37	25–250
Desipramine	Norpramin Pertofrane	12–24	25–300
Doxepin	Adapin Sinequan	8–24	25–300
Fluoxetine	Prozac	2–9(days)	20–80
Fluvoxamine	Luvox	15.6 hours	100–250
Imipramine	Janimine Presamine SK-Pramine Tofranil	11–25	30–300
Maprotiline	Ludiomil	21–25	50–225
Nefazodone	Serzone	11–24	300–600
Nortriptyline	Aventyl Pamelor	18–44	30–100
Paroxetine	Paxil	10–24	10–60
Protriptyline	Vivactil	67–89	15–60
Sertraline	Zoloft	1–4[d]	50–200
Trazodone	Desyrel	4–9	150–600
Trimipramine	Surmontil	7–30	50–300
Venlafaxine	Effexor	5–11[d]	75–375

[a] In combination with antipsychotic drug.
[b] In combination with antianxiety drug.
[c] 30 hours for major metabolite 8-hydroxyamoxapine.
[d] Parent compound plus active metabolite.

TABLE 13.9. Monoamine Oxidase Inhibitor Antidepressants

Generic Name	Manufacturer Name
Isocarboxazid	Janimine Presamine SK-Pramine
Pargyline	Eutonyl
Phenelzine	Nardil
Tranylcypromine	Parnate

40 mg per day. Within 6 to 8 days, he began to show fuller affect and became more verbal. Sleep, appetite, and mood improved. Using the structure of the 12-step groups Sex Addicts Anonymous and Sex and Love Addicts Anonymous and our treatment milieu, he was slowly able to overcome his intense shame and fear that others would reject him. The 12-step program, in essence, became his new family, which was a crucial part of his ongoing recovery program after discharge, as was continuing on his antidepressant medication regimen.

Sexual Addiction With Obsessive-Compulsive Disorder

The third major category included patients who suffered more typical obsessive-compulsive disorder (OCD) symptomatology, including intense and ongoing anxiety. However, their obsessions, rather than being morally repugnant to them, tended to be ego-syntonic, but nevertheless so repetitive and intrusive that the patient had severe difficulty focusing on assigned tasks. Obsessions focused on a recent lover, wife, work obligations, or paying bills, with intense urges to make impulsive phone calls, open one's laptop computer, or check papers. It was clinically clear that despite all their efforts to cooperate, the client's obsessing could not be controlled and the compulsions were not pleasure-producing but truly anxiety-reducing.

Reassurance, of course, only aggravated the situation. When they felt more trusting, these patients disclosed, with much shame, more compulsive behavior, such as compulsively counting the tiles on the ceiling or books on a shelf, rushing home from work to check that all appliances were off or doors and windows were locked, or following detailed rituals regarding everyday functions, having to repeat the entire process without a mistake. Being secretive, perfectionistic, and procrastinating, they initially felt overwhelmed within our milieu.

SSRI antidepressant medications in high doses are an essential part of the treatment for OCD. Fluoxetine (Prozac) 60–80 mg q.d. or sertraline (Zoloft) 150–200 mg q.d. was used exclusively in our program (see table 13.10). Clomipramine (Anafranil) was poorly tolerated at high doses, due to severe sedation. Psychotropic medication may need to be taken 8 weeks or longer to reduce OCD symptoms; hence, patients need to be prepared for the long run. Furthermore, relapse almost always occurs upon discontinuation of an SSRI (Greist, 1995).

Ultimately, patients also responded to the highly structured milieu and its specific tasks and the 12-step program, which is essentially behavior therapy. Based upon present evidence, a combination of pharmacotherapy and behavior therapy provides the most effective treatment for most OCD patients (Greist, 1995).

Clinical Case Example.   Michael was a 37-year-old married furniture store owner in a small town. He struggled with ongoing anxiety created by re-

TABLE 13.10. SRI Doses of OCD

Medication	Initial Dose	Dose (mg) Usual Daily Dose	Maximum Recommended Daily Dose
Citalopram (Celexa)*	20	20–60	60
Clomipramine (Anafranil)	25	25–250	250
Fluoxetine (Prozac)	20	20–80	80
Fluvoxamine (Luvox)	50	100–250	300
Paroxetine (Paxil)*	20	10–60	60
Sertraline (Zoloft)	50	50–200	200

* Under active investigation for OCD

petitive thoughts of being unclean and required rituals of bathing and washing bedding and underwear. This proved to be a particular burden for his wife, who tried to follow his instructions. When attending an out-of-town business convention, he had dinner with a woman he had just met and became obsessed with being in love with her, although there had been no further intimacy. Upon returning home, he secretly wrote her and called her daily for reassurance of her interest and to express his intense love and need of her. His wife discovered the "affair" and threatened divorce if he did not get help. He entered our program, stating that his goal was to choose with which woman he would remain. His anxiety and obsessing were intense. Fluoxetine (Prozac) was initiated and increased to 80 mg q.d. With his permission, very clear boundaries were established regarding phone calls and correspondence. The behavior tasks outlined in the Sexaholics Anonymous 12-step program were very appealing to him, and he embraced them somewhat compulsively, but with a significant reduction in anxiety and desire to continue in recovery with his wife. Both agreed to marital therapy after discharge. He also made the commitment to drive some distance to attend weekly SA meetings.

ASSOCIATED DISORDERS

The three categories described previously are not exclusive; patients can belong to all three or any combination. Because sexually addictive people have an exceptionally high incidence of having been abused as children (97% emotional abuse, including emotional neglect; 81% sexual abuse; and 72% physical abuse) (Carnes, 1991), other psychiatric disorders are commonly present. These include post-traumatic stress disorder–delayed, a wide spectrum of dissociative identity disorders, and severe eating disorders. Psychotropic medications are rarely indicated for these disorders, but the disorders must be addressed for their impact on medication response.

Generalized anxiety disorder is uncommon, but may respond slowly to buspirone (Buspar) 10 mg t.i.d. Undiagnosed adult attention deficit disorder may also be present.

DISCUSSION

This paper represents a preliminary response to the demand for clearer psychotropic medication guidelines in treating sexual addiction. It is a retrospective clinical review of treatment of more than 300 sex addicts in a 28-day primary sexual addiction inpatient unit. Medications, of course, are only part of a total treatment plan. Indeed, there is a great demand for documentation of the most efficacious and cost-effective modalities in the total treatment of this disorder. As research in alcoholism has justified specific treatments as effective, formal double-blind outcome research is needed for sexual addiction. Legitimacy of the disorder, as well as its treatment, remains unappreciated by the majority of those who hold the purse strings of medical care. Roadblocks to research include lack of universal terminology, few sources of large samples, limited interest by education centers, and minimal funding. Nevertheless, sexual addiction has a profound ripple effect in our society, as it creates pain and shame wherever it exists. Efforts must continue to educate and promote understanding of this treatable disorder.

Sexual addiction rarely exists alone, but is associated with other addictions and psychiatric disorders. Hence, when it is studied, its anatomy and dynamics are observed by the wide spectrum of behaviors through which it manifests itself. Use of the *DSM-IV* terminology, despite its limitations, provides a common ground for communication among clinicians. Sexual addiction has a unique combination of both compulsive and impulsive features, as do other disorders, including pathological gambling, body dysmorphic disorder, compulsive overspending, kleptomania, and binge-eating disorders. Research may be aided by consideration of a new classification of Bipulsive Disorders to gain common understanding.

Prescribing medication is always individualized for a particular patient. The three categories described in this paper (based on clinical experience), two for which psychotropic medication is recommended and one for which it is discouraged, should assist prescribing physicians in making appropriate choices for their patients.

CONCLUSION

Sexual addiction most commonly presents with other associated addictive behaviors, including alcohol, substance, food, nicotine, or caffeine abuse; gambling; compulsive overspending; kleptomania; personality disorders; and psychiatric disorders. Psychotropic medication clearly helps this patient population become more accessible to addressing its sexual and other addictive behaviors. Although open-trial case reports hold promise for SSRI antidepressant treatment of addictive sexual behavior, the reported benefit may actually be an associated psychiatric disorder response. Until formal double-blind outcome research studies are conducted, there is no convincing evidence that there is a "silver bullet," or specific medication interventions, for addictive sexual behavior. Meanwhile, cognitive restructuring with individual and group behavior therapy, including 12-step programs, and psychotherapists with addiction training are providing patients with skills to manage this painful, destructive disorder (Lennon, 1994).

REFERENCES

Abel, G. C., Osborn, C. A., Anthony, D., & Gardos, P.(1992). Current treatments of paraphiliacs. *Annual Review of Sex Research, 3,* 255–290.

American Psychiatric Association. (1994). *Diagnostic and statistical manual of mental disorders* (4th ed.). Washington, DC: APA.

Bianchi, M. D. (1990). Fluoxetine treatment of exhibitionism (letter). *American Journal of Psychiatry, 147,* 1089–1090.

Brown, S. A., Inaba, R. K., Gillin, J. C., Schuckit, M. A., Stewart, M. A., & Irwin, M. R. (1995). Alcoholism and affective disorder: Clinical course of depressive symptoms. *American Journal of Psychiatry, 152,* 45–52.

Carnes, P. (1983). *Out of the shadows: Understanding sexual addiction.* Minneapolis, MN: CompCare.

Carnes, P. (1989). *Contrary to love: Helping the sexual addict.* Minneapolis, MN: CompCare.

Carnes, P. (1990). Sexual addiction: Progress, criticism, challenges. *American Journal of Preventive Psychiatry and Neurology, 2*(3), 1–8.

Carnes, P. (1991). *Don't call it love.* New York: Bantam.

Cesnik, J. A., & Coleman, E. (1989). Use of lithium carbonate in the treatment of autoerotic asphyxia. *American Journal of Psychotherapy, 43,* 277–286.

Coleman, E., & Cesnik, J. (1990). Skoptic syndrome: The treatment of an obsessional gender dysphoria with lithium carbonate and psychotherapy. *American Journal of Psychotherapy, 44,* 204–217.

Coleman, E. (1987). Sexual compulsivity: Definition, etiology, and treatment considerations. In E. Coleman (Ed.), *Chemical dependency and intimacy dysfunction.* New York: Haworth.

Coleman, E. (1990). The obsessive-compulsive model for describing compulsive sexual behavior. *American Journal of Preventive Psychiatry and Neurology, 2*(3), 9–14.

Coleman, E. (1992). Is your patient suffering from compulsive sexual behavior? *Psychiatric Annals, 22,* 320–325.

Diamond, J. (1983). *Looking for love in all the wrong places.* New York: Putnam.

Emmanuel, N. P., Lydiard, R. B., & Ballenger, J. C. (1991). Fluoxetine treatment of voyeurism. *American Journal of Psychiatry, 148,* 950.

Fedoroff, J. P. (1988). Buspirone in the treatment of transvestic fetishism. *Journal of Clinical Psychiatry, 48,* 408–409.

Fedoroff, J. P. (1993). Serotonergic drug treatment of deviant sexual interests. *Annals of Sex Research, 6,* 105–121.

Fedoroff, J. P., & Fedoroff, I. C. (1992). Buspirone and paraphilic sexual behavior. *Journal of Offender Rehabilitation, 18,* 89–108.

Gottesman, H. G., & Schubert, D. S. (1993). Low-dose oral medroxyprogesterone acetate in the management of the paraphilias. *Journal of Clinical Psychiatry, 54,* 182–188.

Hollander, E. (Ed.). (1993). *Obsessive-compulsive-related disorders.* Washington, DC: American Psychiatric Press.

Hollander, E., & Wong, C. M. (1995). Body dysmorphic disorder, pathological gambling, and sexual compulsions. *Journal of Clinical Psychiatry, 56* (suppl. 4), 7–12.

Kafka, M. P. (1989). Preliminary observations on a relationship between paraphilias and major affective disorders. Paper presented at the eighth annual Research and Data Conference of the Association for the Behavioral Treatment of Sex Abusers, Seattle, Washington, October 5–8.

Kafka, M. P. (1991). Successful antidepressant treatment of nonparaphilic sexual addictions and paraphilias in men. *Journal of Clinical Psychiatry, 52,* 60–65.

Kafka, M., & Coleman, E. (1991). Serotonin and paraphilias: The convergence of mood, impulse and compulsive disorders (letter). *Journal of Clinical Psychopharmacology, 11,* 223–224.

Kafka, M. P., & Prentky, R. (1992a). Fluoxetine treatment of nonparaphilic sexual addictions and paraphilias in men. *Journal of Clinical Psychiatry, 53,* 351–358.

Kafka, M. P., & Prentky, R. (1992b). A comparative study of nonparaphilic sexual addictions and paraphilias in men. *Journal of Clinical Psychiatry, 53,* 345–350.

Kasl, C. (1989). *Women, sex, and addiction.* New York: Ticknor & Fields.

Lennon, W. (1994). An integrated treatment program for paraphiliacs, including a 12-step approach. *Sexual Addiction and Compulsivity, 1,* 227–241.

Lorefice, L. S. (1991). Fluoxetine treatment of a fetish (letter). *Journal of Clinical Psychiatry, 52,* 436–437.

Money, J. (1980). *Love and love sickness: The science of sex, gender difference, and pair-bonding.* Baltimore, MD: Johns Hopkins University Press.

Money, J. (1986). *Lovemaps: Clinical concepts of sexual/erotic health and pathology, paraphilia, and gender transpositions in childhood, adolescence, and maturity.* New York: Irvington.

Perilstein, R. D., Lipper, S., & Friedman, L. J. (1991). Three cases of paraphilias responsive to fluoxetine treatment. *Journal of Clinical Psychiatry, 52,* 169–170.

Raskin, V. D., & Miller, N. (1993). The epidemiology of the comorbidity of psychiatric and addictive disorders: A critical review. *Journal of Addictive Diseases, 12*(3), 45–57.

Schneider, J. (1988). *Back from betrayal: Recovering from his affairs.* New York: Ballantine.

Wawrose, F. E., & Sisto, T. M. (1992). Clomipramine and a case of exhibitionism. *American Journal of Psychiatry, 149,* 843.

CHAPTER 14

Dual and Triple Diagnoses

Addictions, Mental Illness, and HIV Infection Guidelines for Outpatient Therapists

JOHN R. SEALY

Therapists face the ongoing challenge of being alert to the presence of other significant diagnoses in addition to the patient's presenting complaint. For example, it is common for several addictions to exist concurrently, even though the patient is focusing on only one. Irons and Schneider state that addictive disorders tend to coexist, the presence of sexual compulsivity is a comorbid marker for chemical dependency, and addictive sexual disorders are frequently found during assessment for chemical dependence. Schneider and Schneider (1991), in an anonymous survey of recovering sex addicts, found that 39% were also recovering from chemical dependence, 32% had an eating disorder, 13% described themselves as compulsive spenders, and 5% were compulsive gamblers. Carnes (1991) had slightly higher percentages in his survey and included compulsive working at 28%. Washton (1989) reported that 50% of cocaine addicts in an outpatient setting were engaging in compulsive sex. Gordon, Fargason, and Kramer (1995) reported from their chemical dependency treatment program that over 4 years approximately 33% of patients were also sexually compulsive. There are varied interactions between substance abuse and compulsive behaviors (see table 14.1), but what is becoming clear is that sustained recovery in one addiction is only as successful as the least treated co-addiction. In other words, addicts often tend to become caught between several addictive behaviors that ultimately lead to relapse in one addiction because others remain untreated.

The therapeutic goal of continuing addiction recovery is not only treating concurrent addictions, but also treating comorbid mental illness (referred to as dual diagnosis). Regier et al. (1990), using the Epidemiologic Catchment Area (ECA) survey, found that 55% of people with schizophrenia in treatment and

TABLE 14.1. Dynamics of Multiple Addictions

Mode	Dynamic	Example
Switching	Suspending compulsive behavior dependence, but initiating new behavior and dependence.	Alcoholic who becomes sober switches to sex addiction as new "be all" of life.
Alternating	Rhythmic pattern of moving from one addiction to another.	Alternating use of eating and sexual acting out.
Masking	One addiction serves as a "mask" or excuse for another.	Alcoholic who sees sexual acting out as a problem of too much drinking.
Fusing	More than one addiction must be present to work.	Compulsive masturbator who hyperventilates tobacco smoke.
Ritualizing	One addiction is part of the ritualizing for another.	Chemically dependent person who cruises to pick up people in bars.
Intensifying	Mutual existence of addictive behavior increases intensity of experience.	Cocaine addict who is also a sex addict and pathological gambler who goes to Las Vegas for a multiple binge.
Numbing	Shame about one addiction is ameliorated by the numbing of another, and at times vice versa.	Sex addict who feels shame about his or her behavior drinks to anesthetize the pain.
Disinhibiting	One addiction serves to lower inhibitions for other addictive behavior.	Marijuana use as a way to seduce and be seduced.

From *The Assessment of Multiple Addictions* by P. Carnes (1994).

62% of people with affective illness had a lifetime diagnosis of substance disorder. Numerous studies have reported similar results (Drake, Osher, & Wallace, 1989; Pepper, Kirshner, & Ryglewicz, 1981; Schwartz & Goldfinger, 1981; Safer, 1987; see table 14.2). Minkoff (1989) outlines the principles of dual diagnosis: When a mental illness and substance disorder coexist, both diagnoses should be considered *primary*, and simultaneous primary treatment for both disorders is required. Mental illness or substance abuse is considered "secondary" only if it resolves when the other comorbid disorder is at baseline. Both major mental illness and substance dependence are examples of primary, chronic, biological mental illnesses that fit into this model of treatment.

The third major treatment concern that also must be addressed (in addition to addiction and mental illness) is a life-threatening medical illness. AIDS or HIV infection is a frequent result of high-risk sexual behavior with associated impaired judgment and impaired immune system secondary to alcohol or other substance abuse. The American Society of Addiction Medicine (Pohl et al., 1998), in its *Guidelines for HIV Infection and AIDS in Addiction Treatment* (1998), states, "Physicians should be alert to sexual addictive/compulsive behavior. One of the most profound consequences of out-of-control sexual behavior is becoming in-

TABLE 14.2. Diagnostic Criteria for Substance Dependence

A maladaptive pattern of substance use, leading to clinically significant impairment or distress, as manifested by three (or more) of the following, occurring at any time in the same 12-month period:

1. Tolerance, as defined by either of the following:
   a. There is a need for markedly increased amounts of the substance to achieve intoxication or desired effect.
   b. There is a markedly diminished effect with continued use of the same amount of the substance.
2. Withdrawal, as manifested by either of the following:
   a. The characteristic withdrawal syndrome for the substance occurs.
   b. The same (or a closely related) substance is taken to relieve or avoid withdrawal symptoms.
3. The substance is often taken in larger amounts or over a longer period than was intended.
4. There is a persistent desire or unsuccessful effort to cut down or control substance use.
5. A great deal of time is spent in activities necessary to obtain the substance, use the substance, or recover from its effects.
6. Important social, occupational, or recreational activities are given up or reduced because of substance use.
7. The substance use is continued despite knowledge of having a persistent or recurrent physical or psychological problem that is likely to have been caused or exacerbated by the substance.

From *Diagnostic and Statistical Manual of Mental Disorders*, 4th ed. (Washington, DC: American Psychiatric Association, 1994), p. 181

fected or infecting others with HIV" (p. 3). People with chronic and serious mental illness may be at increased risk of contracting HIV. Seven to twenty percent of admissions to private and public mental health facilities are reported to test positive for HIV antibodies (Knox, Davis, & Friedrich, 1995; Sacks, Dermatis, Looser-Ott, Burton, & Perry, 1992).

Therefore, clinical depression, post-traumatic stress disorder, or both may also be comorbid diagnoses leading to the term *Triple Diagnosis*. Cuestas-Thompson (1997) stated that "Quadruple Diagnosis" is common in gay men in substance-abuse treatment who also suffer from AIDS or HIV infection, depression, and sexual compulsivity. Cuestas-Thompson points out the higher incidence of substance abuse disorder in the gay population, including injectable drugs of heroin and cocaine, as well as alcohol, crystal methamphetamine, and "poppers" (amyl and butyl nitrite), which all increase risk of HIV transmission through direct transfer or impaired judgment and decision making.

Because addictions (substance and behavioral), mental illness, and life-threatening medical illness are all interactive, a major therapeutic task is to facilitate an integrated approach to the assessment, treatment planning, and monitoring progress of these dual, triple, and multiple diagnoses. Health delivery systems increasingly insist on outpatient management; thus the burden of treatment is left in the hands of the outpatient therapist. Although it is beyond the scope of this article to outline specific treatments for each of these diagnoses, it is the intent of this article to provide the outpatient therapist with general guidelines to promote ongoing recovery in all relevant patient pathology, as well as effective use of limited therapeutic time.

Therapists can be more effective in making dual and triple diagnoses when they are aware of reasons why diagnoses are often overlooked (see table 14.3). Common reasons include denial by the patient or the failure to see the crucial connection between behaviors or diseases. It is easy for a therapist to join the denial of the patient because another focus is seen as paramount. Treatment systems for substance abuse and mental health are organized separately and do not coordinate services, which often leads to patients being bounced back and forth. Treatment professionals are usually not trained in both mental health and substance abuse. In addition, families of the patient and the therapist may experience "burnout" and may not wish to see another problem. Health delivery systems often want rapid diagnosis and short-term treatment.

The recommended approach is, first, to be vigilant for all three diagnostic categories throughout the treatment course; second, to set up or support treatment plans when they are diagnosed; and third, to monitor progress.

DIAGNOSTIC VIGILANCE

There is no substitute for clinical judgment, and it always prevails over psychological testing or laboratory findings. However, structured screening questions or tests can prove very helpful in alerting the therapist and patient to a potentially serious and contributing diagnosis. When suspicious of sexual addiction

TABLE 14.3. Why Dual, Triple, and Multiple Diagnoses Are Not Made

1. There is denial, secrecy, or lack of insight into the danger of untreated diagnoses on the part of patient.
2. Therapists join the denial of the patient.
3. Alcohol and drug abuse treatment systems and mental health systems are organized separately, both locally and federally, and neither tends to be concerned with the behavioral addictions.
4. Patients are excluded from treatment because of comorbidity, as they bounce back and forth between systems of care and feel like "misfits."
5. Treatment professionals often feel overwhelmed or are ignorant because they are trained in mental health or substance abuse, but not both.
6. Families and therapists experience "burnout" and do not wish to undertake another "problem."
7. Health delivery systems tend to encourage rapid diagnosis and short-term treatment.

TABLE 14.4. Helpful Questions to Assess Whether Drug Use Is Linked to a Pattern of Compulsive Sexual Behavior

1. What percentage of your drug/alcohol use episodes involve sexual behavior or fantasies of any kind?
2. Does your drug/alcohol use involve any of the following: encounters with prostitutes, compulsive intercourse or masturbation, frequenting "peep" shows, pornography online, switching gender of sexual partner, voyeurism, sadomasochistic sex, unusual or violent sexual acts or fantasies of any kind, or sexual behavior outside of your own ethics and principles?
3. Were any of the above a problem prior to your involvement with drugs? If so, has the problem intensified along with your drug use?
4. During times when you have stopped using drugs, did you continue the above sexual behaviors? If so, did they always lead you back to drugs?
5. During times when you refrained from the above sexual behaviors, did you continue using drugs? If so, did it always lead you back to acting out sexually?

Adapted from *Cocaine Abuse and Compulsive Sexuality* by A. Washton (1989).

in treating drug and alcohol abuse, Washton (1989) has helpful questions (see table 14.4). Sexual addiction must be diagnosed by the adverse consequences it brings to a person's life, not merely by the type of behavior, its object, its frequency, or its social acceptability (Goodman, 1993).

The possibility of serious psychiatric illness hidden behind addictive behavior will usually require a psychiatric consultation. Major Depression is a most common comorbid diagnosis, yet depressive symptoms are also common in withdrawal from substance abuse. Therefore, the general rule is to treat the addiction first and wait at least 2 to 6 drug-free weeks to more clearly determine whether the depression is primary or secondary (Daley, Moss, & Campbell, 1993). Indicators that depression is primary ideally include a history of depression during abstinence, mood symptoms that surpass those appropriate to objective reality, persistent low energy distinct from sadness, suicidal ideation, inability to participate in therapy due to mood, and objective symptoms as measured by a screening test. The Beck Depression Inventory is a simple screening test taken by the patient that can be given repeatedly. Scores above 30 should initiate a psychiatric consultation.

Manic episode bipolar disorder is suspected by positive family history, persistent lack of sleep with increase in energy and no fatigue, flight of ideas, pressured speech or talkativeness that patient describes as unusual and "not like me," and an expansive or explosive mood. It must be distinguished from anxiety and chronic attention deficit hyperactivity disorder (ADHD), as these disorders can be treated after addiction recovery has been addressed. However, if there are post-traumatic stress disorder symptoms with positive trauma history (dissociation, obsessive-compulsive disorder symptoms, or panic attacks) that do not allow the patient to participate in addiction treatment, they must be addressed.

Helpful formal screening tests include the Dissociative Experience Scale (DES), the Minnesota Multiphasic Personality Inventory (MMPI-II), and the Millon Clinical Multiaxial Inventory (MCMI-III). These will also help identify subtle psychotic disorders.

In treating sexual addiction, psychiatric illness, or both, screening tests for substance abuse can supplement your observations from the four simple CAGE questions (table 14.5) to the comprehensive Addiction Severity Index (ASI) available from the National Institute on Drug Abuse (McLellan et al., 1985). Antidepressant medications are ineffective with active substance abuse; therefore, lack of response may indicate continuing substance abuse.

Minkoff (1991) clarifies that in dual diagnosis, substance abuse (expanded in this article to include behavioral addictions) and mental illness coexist, each requiring specific and intensive treatment. His four phases of recovery can be adapted to triple diagnosis as well (see table 14.6). Minkoff points out that patients more commonly stabilize one illness first. Engagement in treatment for the other diseases may not take place until much later. For example, it is not unusual for patients in full recovery from substance abuse not to seek help with sexual addiction for many years. Minkoff stresses an important principle: "There is no one type of treatment program or intervention for dual diagnosis. The proper treatment interventions for each individual depends on the phase of recovery, as well as the level of acuity, severity, disability, and motivation for treatment associated with each primary disease." This principle can be equally applied to triple diagnosis where HIV infection is the third primary disease. Most outpatient therapists will find themselves treating a single disease in phases 3 and 4. It is hoped that the therapist will be more alert to the possibility of previously unidentified multiple diagnoses when relapse is frequent.

Men are now reporting difficulty maintaining a commitment to safer sex over the long haul, and a sizable number of gay men who became sexually active well after the onset of the AIDS epidemic was first described in 1981 have seroconverted, despite a barrage of educational messages (Ball, 1996). Approximately 3 years ago, "barebacking" and "doing it raw" or "skin-to-skin" debuted

TABLE 14.5. Cage Test[1, 2]

- Have you tried to CUT down?
- Do you get ANNOYED or ANGRY when confronted?
- Do you feel GUILTY after having "excessed?"
- Do you use first thing in the morning as an EYE OPENER to get going?
1. Addiction must have three behaviors: compulsive patterns of use, loss of control over use, continued use despite adverse consequences.
2. Positive answers to any two of the above four questions indicates a high probability of addiction. The questions can be adapted to any addictive behavior.

From *The Cage Questionnaire: Validation of a New Alcoholism Screening Instrument* by D. Mayfield, G. Mcloud, and P. Hall (1974).

TABLE 14.6. Stages of Recovery for Dual/Triple Diagnosis

1. Acute Stabilization
   Stabilization of acute psychosis or mood disorder, stabilization of life-threatening opportunistic infections secondary to HIV infection, or any combination of these; detoxification
2. Engagement in Active Treatment
   Initial engagement in a treatment process, as by taking medication to control mental illness, by beginning triple medication therapy for HIV, or by participating in treatment groups or 12-step programs to control substance abuse, or any combinations of these
3. Relapse Prevention to Maintain Prolonged Stabilization
   Ongoing participation in psychiatric, counseling, or addiction treatment with a focus on learning techniques for safe sex and prevention of relapse
4. Rehabilitation and Recovery
   Once stability of all illnesses is more secure, to begin to develop new skills for managing one's life to replace the deficits that result from all three disease categories

Adapted from *An Integrated Treatment Model for Dual Diagnosis of Psychosis and Addiction* by K. Minkoff (1989).

in the gay community, all referring to having anal intercourse without protection. The feeling that latex negatively affects one's sex life has led men to be drawn to "raw sex." Health concerns that drive men back to condoms include sexually transmitted diseases (STDs) such as herpes, hepatitis, gonorrhea, and anal warts. For those already HIV positive, STDs can significantly impair the immune system, accelerating the progression of disease (Scarce, 1999). Early identification of HIV infection and appropriate medical treatment of HIV disease are critical to the survival of the HIV-infected patient. Earlier treatment in the course of HIV infection may provide a greater opportunity of supporting a still relatively intact immune system (Pohl et al., 1998). Therefore, HIV testing should be supported for any at-risk patient (see table 14.7). It is helpful to explain to patients that there is no test for AIDS; rather, testing looks for the presence of the HIV antibody. A positive HIV test then leads to a CD4 cell count (a measure of the number of cells that fight HIV) and viral-load (a measure of the amount of HIV RNA in the blood). Viral-load is measured in terms of number of single viral cells or "copies" per milliliter of blood plasma. Viral-load measurements reflect what the virus is doing in the body in the present. CD4 counts, on the other hand, measure how the virus already has affected the immune system. Therefore, CD4 counts tell where the train is going, and a viral-load indicates how *fast* the train is going, so to speak. Anonymous testing (available through local health departments or gay agencies) may be preferable for a patient in addiction treatment, because it ensures that HIV antibody test results will not be revealed to insurance companies or employers without patient permission. Providing counseling before and after testing is most important for the patient to process the emotional impact and design strategies. Fears that positive

TABLE 14.7. History Suggesting Increased Risk of HIV Infection
and Need for HIV Antibody Testing

Known sexual addict who acts out with others
Substance abuse associated with sexual acting out
Having a sexual partner, needle-sharing partner, or both who is known to be HIV positive
Having multiple sexual partners and less than 100% safe sex
Sharing needles, syringes, or both
Having a history of another STD, especially syphilis or chancroid
Having a history of hepatitis B, hepatitis C, or both
Having a history of rape or sexual abuse, or having spent time incarcerated
For men, having had sex with men (especially, anal sex)
For women, having a history of cervical dysplasia or cervical cancer
Sex workers
Persons occupationally exposed
Having a predisposing medical conditions (e.g., hemophilia, transfusion)

---

test results might so destabilize the patient that chemical use might resume, or indulgence in harmful behaviors and suicide risk might escalate, appear to be unfounded (Cleary et al., 1991). A common mistake is to celebrate with too much enthusiasm a seronegative test result. This may promote feelings of invulnerability, increase feelings of guilt, and discourage clients from expressing less positive feelings (Ball, 1996).

TREATMENT PLANS

Although this article focuses on general guidelines, it must be emphasized that each client/patient needs an individualized long-term treatment plan addressing all diagnoses, including medication, emotional, physical, psychosocial, and spiritual concerns. Recovery plans typically involve some combination of professional treatment, participation in self-help programs, and self-management strategies (Daley, Moss, & Campbell, 1993). There are a variety of therapeutic approaches (Beck & Wright, 1992), including addiction counseling, cognitive-behavioral psychotherapy, rational emotive therapy, relapse prevention, and supportive-expressive psychotherapy. Therapists must be aware that all the diagnoses discussed in this article easily lead to social isolation and severe loneliness. Emotional connection to others must be aggressively promoted, using avenues such as support groups, 12-step programs, or both. Treating addictions is more than treating the use of substances or behavior; that is, abstinence by itself is not recovery. Weiss (1997) emphasizes that fused drug use and sexual activity must both be addressed in treatment, requiring a reintroduction of human relatedness into sexual interactions to reestablish ties to intimacy and healthy sexuality. Recovery goes through stages that include behavioral, cognitive, affective, and object attachment (for discussions of stages of recovery from alcoholism, see Brown, 1985; Miller, Gorski, & Miller, 1982; Zimberg, 1985).

The psychotherapist can support HIV infection treatment by understanding the stages of HIV disease and possible interventions (see table 14.8). A wide

TABLE 14.8. Stages of HIV Diseases and Possible Interventions

Worried "At-Risk"	Evaluate risk behaviors and recommend anonymous antibody testing (see below). Diagnose and treat underlying psychopathology, including substance use. Guide toward culturally or socially appropriate support and psychoeducational groups for those at high risk in order to develop safer behaviors. Expert counseling for related issues.
Antibody Testing	Educate client as to risk factors, course realities of HIV disease, and treatment options, including postexposure prophylaxis if feasible. Guide toward support and psychoeducational groups to prevent primary infection or, if infected, transmission to others. Expert counseling for related issues (e.g., "coming out").
Newly Diagnosed as Seropositive	Assess and intervene in possible shock, anxious, or depressive reactions, including suicidal thoughts. Refer to culturally or socially appropriate support and psychoeducational groups. Liaison with primary care physician about medication decisions and address issues that affect adherence to treatment regimens if anti-HIV medication is initiated.
Healthy Survivors	Address issues of multiple loss, survivor's guilt, and adjustment to labels of "chronically ill" and "functional disabled," as applicable. Refer to psychoeducational, behavioral medicine, and psychotherapeutic groups to maximize patient's ability to manage medical symptoms emotionally and behaviorally.
Deteriorating Medical Illness	According to the severity of illness, address issues surrounding completion of life, including viatication of life insurance; wills; funeral arrangements; disposal of possessions; quality of life values; palliative care, including pain management; preparatory grief; and beliefs about death, suicide, and euthanasia. Help patient consolidate understanding of issues relating to biological family versus family of choice (e.g., spouse or partner) and determine who will help in severe illness. Encourage the patient's consolidation of this legally. Facilitate family communication about values relating to severe illness and death, including disposal of body and distribution of possessions. Refer patient and family promptly to therapeutic, social work, and legal advice community groups ready to deal with these issues.
The Moribund	Work with patient and family in dealing with preparatory grief and reactive mood disorders. Facilitate family communication and provide referrals as with the medically deteriorating.
The Lazarus Group	Address paradoxical depressive and dysphoric reactions (including suicidality) through medical treatment. Again, refer to groups dealing with this specific issue. Address deep existential questions within a psychotherapeutic setting.

From *Significance of Community Psychiatry to HIV Disease* by R. Whitaker (1999).

range of patients will present, from those who are the worried or demoralized gay HIV-negative, to those HIV-positive patients who are approaching death. Within that spectrum are those about to be tested; the newly diagnosed HIV-positive; those deteriorating; those who expected to die, but with new medications are regaining health; and those who have received no benefit from the newer regimens. Each of these patients has his own highly personal issues, which challenge the psychotherapist to use all of his or her therapeutic skills. Furthermore, being aware of the three current categories of HIV infection medications, their specific names, and how they are taken can help clarify the patient's confusion (see table 14.9). It is also important to know long-term goals of HIV management, so there can be a meaningful dialogue with both the treating HIV physician and the patient (table 14.10).

Harm reduction is an approach that has been developed to reduce the risk of acquiring HIV in substance abusers; this is now also useful in working with those who are already infected or ill with HIV disease. Harm reduction is multidisciplinary and always includes a long-term commitment to caring for the individual, whether or not he or she is using or adhering to medical plans, or both. Substance abusers are recognized as a community that contains multiple subcultures, whose members are mobilized to act as peer educators and are integrated into the multidisciplinary team. Decision making is nonhierarchical, and users of services are included in planning and evaluating services and outcomes. Harm reduction is user-friendly, in that it reaches out and engages at-risk communities to determine need and provide interventions. It expects that trust is difficult because patients often have long histories of being abused and discriminated against (Zevin, 1997). For some, the harm reduction model puts HIV/AIDS prevention over prevention of drug abuse because it presents a greater threat to the drug user, to public health, and to the national economy. Although many AIDS service organizations and providers exclude active drug users, Springer (1991), in support of the harm reduction model, believes this exclusion is unnecessary, contraindicated, discriminatory, and unethical. Springer believes that the only intervention that cannot be done with intoxicated people is psychotherapy, and that drug abusers can benefit from concrete services that include education, assistance with strategy development, risk-reduction interventions, and support. Family involvement in treatment can provide support, corroborate information, and help family members address specific recovery needs of their own. Family treatment should include not only referral to 12-step programs, but

TABLE 14.9.

1. NNRTI = Nonnucleoside reverse transcriptase inhibitor
2. NARTI = Nucleoside analogue reverse transcriptase inhibitor
3. NtARTI = Nucleotide analogue reverse transcriptase inhibitor

From *Pl Perspective*, 26 (December 1998), San Francisco, California, pp. 12–13.

TABLE 14.10. Basic Principles of Long-Term HIV Management

1. Hit Hard, Hit Early
   Use the most potent regimen possible for a given patient, usually a three-drug combination. "Never give the virus an even break. Keep drug levels up and HIV reproduction down" (Workman, 1999).
2. The First Shot Is the Best Shot
   HIV has a high replication rate AND a high mutation rate; hence, first-line treatment is of paramount importance.
3. Use Drugs in Different Classes
   Combining drugs of different classes delivers a one–two punch by attacking the virus at different stages in its life cycle. Three current classes;
   NRTIs: Nucleoside reverse transcriptase inhibitors
   NNRTIs: Nonnucleoside reverse transcriptase inhibitors
   PIs: Protease inhibitors
4. Preserve Future Treatment Options if Possible
   If initial therapy fails, salvage therapy should offer unused classes of drugs. "Keep options, don't throw them away. Let resistance develop and you've wasted an option" (Workman, 1999).
5. Simplify Regimens
   Make dosing as simple as one to three times per day, if possible.
6. Monitor Viral-Load and CD4 Count Regularly
   This is the best way to evaluate effectiveness of treatment.
7. Continue Prophylaxis Against Opportunistic Infections
   Opportunistic infections must be guarded against with other medications. These are based on the patient's lowest-ever CD4 count.
8. Address Diet, Exercise, Lifestyle, and Stress Reduction
   Emphasize the importance of general wellness.

From *HIV Frontline* (Summer 1998), pp. 2–6.

also family education and family therapy. It should be remembered that families have often experienced a tremendous toll and should not immediately be labeled "dysfunctional." The therapist should look for strengths in the family and ways to relieve the burden, especially for children, who are usually ignored during the active disease process and often continue to be excluded in the treatment processes (Daley et al., 1993; Shernoff, 1991). Regular review of professional and therapeutic guidelines can keep the therapist effective and reduce risk of professional burnout (see tables 14.11 and 14.12).

Psychotropic medications can, of course, be of enormous benefit in treating major depression, anxiety, bipolar disorders, and psychotic disorders. Referral to a psychiatrist for possible medication should be made when any mental illness is suspected. Psychopharmacological interventions can provide valuable treatment of the psychiatric and behavioral symptoms seen in clients with HIV-related cognitive impairment (Zwillich, 1998). The treatment of depression is quite feasible in HIV-infected patients, even if it is sometimes complicated. Psychopharmacologic drugs have been effective treatments for clinical depression in HIV disease, regardless of initial level of immune deficiency or number or

TABLE 14.11. Therapeutic Guidelines

1. Create a neutral, shame-free environment that encourages the patient to talk about anything, even noncompliance or nonadherence.
2. Remember that engaging a patient to recognize a problem is usually a stepwise and time-consuming process (Sciacca, 1991).
3. Let patients know you may disagree with their choices but you understand their pain, respect their choices, and respect their right to continue their behavior if it works for them (Minkoff, 1991).
4. Educate less about consequences but teach how substances work. Introduce other options for nurturing, managing anxiety and anger, and developing integrity with a lifestyle congruent with personal values.
5. Do not verbally attack. Use well-constructed confrontations where the confronter does not "lose" if the patient continues his or her behavior.
6. Remember that peer influence can be powerful.
7. Build a therapeutic alliance with the patient and family that will prevail despite slips and relapses.
8. Teach patient how to self-challenge cognitive distortions. Focus on thinking accurately, not positively.
9. Assist patient in setting goals, and make assignments session to session. Both should be written and specific.

type of HIV medications used concurrently (Whitaker, 1999)—for example, sertraline (Zoloft) and fluoxetine (Prozac) (Ferrando, Goldman, & Charness, 1997), or fluoxetine with dextroamphetamine (Dexedrine) (Rabkin, Wagner, & Rabkin, 1994). Nevertheless, medication intervention alone is unlikely to be as effective as the inclusion of counseling, education, cognitive strategies, appropriate psychotherapy, and social support to address stress, alienation, isolation, or poor adherence to treatment regimens (Singh et al., 1996). Indeed, these principles apply to the recovering addict as well.

Psychopharmacological intervention with addictive behavior is not routine. Although some sexual addicts benefit from the decreased libido and higher or-

TABLE 14.12. Professional Guidelines

1. Be knowledgeable, but not directive outside of your professional licensure or expertise.
2. Remember that each patient is different, and therefore treatment plans and progress vary.
3. Acknowledge your powerlessness, not helplessness.
4. With the patient's written permission, promote communication among the treatment team, which includes physicians, other therapists, the patient's partner, and family. You are often the only professional in a central position to coordinate care. Many treatment team members often feel alone in the battle and will welcome your efforts.
5. Establish a hierarchy of diagnoses. Treat the most dangerous diagnosis first. Treat the most dangerous addiction first.

gasmic threshold side effects of selective seratonin reuptake inhibitor (SSRI) antidepressants, other addicts merely act out longer to reach orgasm on the same drug. There is no "silver bullet" medication for sexual compulsive behavior (Sealy, 1995). Opiate and alcohol abstinence can be supported with naltrexone, but it is not uniformly helpful and it must *not* be prescribed within 10 days of last opioid use. Antabuse is an aid in the management of selected chronic alcoholic patients who *want* to remain in a state of enforced sobriety so that supportive and psychotherapeutic treatment may be applied to its best advantage.

MONITORING PROGRESS

Monitoring treatment for two, three, or multiple diagnoses (which may include co-addictions) can feel overwhelming and therefore requires an organized approach. Monitoring can be divided into those regimens that the patient controls and those that the therapist needs to assess regularly.

Patient Monitoring

It is helpful to begin each session with a "check-in questionnaire" that the patient expects to answer (table 14.13). These questions are not intended to shame, but to quickly review adherence to regimens and to identify problem areas (including potential relapse) that can be addressed during the session. Most patients want to be honest and will answer direct questions; however, they may also

TABLE 14.13. Patient Check-in Form (Individual) Dual/Triple Diagnoses

1. State name and nature of all addictive behaviors.
2. State amount of time sober from these behaviors.
3. Describe the closest you have been to acting out since last check-in.
4. Name one significant person who has been harmed by your behavior and how that person was harmed (betrayal of trust, given a disease, frightened, etc.).
5. State a lie you have told since last check-in or a secret you are keeping from anyone, including me, your therapist.
6. Name one step you have taken to further your recovery since last check-in.
7. State nature and status of any assignments or homework.
8. State locations and dates of attendance of 12-step meetings since last check-in.
9. Name a person you called for support.
10. Describe your mood over the past week, including any suicidal thoughts.
11. State any changes in your medication regimen and any missed doses.
12. Describe side effects, benefits, or changes in general functioning.
13. Describe some fun you have had in the past week.

From *Psychopharmacologic Intervention in Addictive Sexual Behavior* by J. Sealy (1995), and *Special Populations: Treatment Concerns for Gay Male Sexual Addicts* by R. Weiss (1997).

TABLE 14.14. Guidelines for Patients

---

1. Connect with your heart to a higher power, self, peers, therapists.
2. Have weekly written plan for attendance at 12-step and support meetings.
3. Make daily phone calls to people in recovery.
4. Ask for help, and help only when asked.
5. Tell the truth and tell it faster.
6. Use affirmations to counter shame and inaccurate beliefs about self.
7. Identify and *feel* your feelings. Express your feelings daily by talking, doing art, writing in a journal.
8. Identify shame-based behavior and shame-based thinking.
9. Solve nonsexual problems nonsexually. Solve nondrug problems without drugs.
10. Trust the process.
11. Get a sponsor and talk to him or her weekly.

---

withhold information when not asked directly. Patients generally like being asked routinely about their recovery, as it gives a sense of accomplishment and builds much-wanted integrity. Attendance at 12-step meetings may be supported by a signature of the secretary of that meeting (see table 14.14).

Adherence to medication regimens for mental illness, HIV infection, or both is crucial for benefits to be realized. Adherence can be very difficult for some patients because of the many pills, critical timing, and ease of forgetting. Adherence is not to be confused with noncompliance, the latter referring to an active decision not to take medication. Supporting adherence is a primary commitment of all those on the treatment team, and it involves much more than simply telling patients what they should do. Patients must be educated regarding why they need to begin treatment. If patients don't understand why medicines are important and must be taken consistently, it is unlikely they will adhere. Patients will understand that they can attain a high degree of adherence by your pointing out other things that they do routinely every day, such as eating and sleeping. Help the patient anticipate side effects and how to manage them. Ask about missed doses without eliciting shame and examine difficulties with problem solving (Workman, 1999). HIV has a rapid viral replication of approximately 6 hours, meaning that drug-resistant strains occur rapidly unless replication is suppressed to very low levels—that is, low viral-load (Pohl et al., 1998). Regular CD4/viral-load counts are essential; seeing a viral-load drop in just a few weeks provides an incredible boost to adherence.

Therapist Monitoring

The therapist must also monitor the patient's mood for excessive anxiety, clinical depression or mania, or psychotic symptoms. The Beck Depression Inventory and Hamilton Anxiety Scale can be given frequently to show changes from baseline and assist in determining suicidal risk.

Cognitive functioning, as well as impairment of movement and other physical disabilities should be observed routinely by the therapist and referred for rapid evaluation if present. Adult attention deficit disorder may be suspected and referral may be indicated for further evaluation. There is no definitive test for attention deficit disorder, but the history must include academic difficulties in childhood.

Recovery of cognitive function can be seen in recovering alcoholics, but the pattern varies. For example, verbal learning and memory tend to recover relatively quickly, often within the first month of sobriety. However, abstraction and problem-solving functions require more time, and some studies indicate continuing impairment after years of recovery. Most significant, resuming drinking (even at relatively low levels) is generally associated with less recovery, especially in patients with a family history of alcoholism (Nixon & Phillips, 1999). No clear picture of cognitive recovery in alcoholics can be established at this time; hence, the psychotherapist may find behavior-oriented treatment approaches more effective than insight-oriented therapies in many recovering alcoholics.

HIV-related cognitive impairment is complicated because symptoms may vary only minimally across the many conditions that cause it. Some aspects of cognitive impairment are treatable if addressed quickly; others are untreatable and rapidly progressive. Assessment and treatment may be complicated because more than one disorder may be present. The response is fourfold (see table 14.15). The psychotherapist need not understand the intricacies of the diagnostic tools, but by regular monitoring of negative cognitive changes, he or she can alert the HIV specialist to evaluate the patient quickly for treatable causes. Hence, it is important that the psychotherapist obtain releases from clients/patients early in the therapeutic relationship.

The most common cause of cognitive impairment is direct infection of the brain by HIV itself. This is divided into mild cognitive/motor impairment and moderate-to-severe impairment or HIV-associated dementia. Mild impairment does not necessarily lead to severe. Mild impairment may manifest itself as some slowness in thinking, memory problems, and decreased problem-solving ability, but it does not interfere with the ability to live independently or to interact

---

TABLE 14.15. Response to Cognitive Impairment in HIV Infection

1. Accurate diagnosis
2. Coordination of treatment and education
3. Aggressive treatment of the acute causes of cognitive impairment (for example, opportunistic conditions and delirium)
4. Management through psychotherapy and psychopharmacology of impairment that is not otherwise treatable

meaningfully with others. Traditional psychotherapeutic approaches are help-ful, including adaptation and compensation skills, stress reduction, exercise, goal-setting, and capitalizing on strengths to promote sense of control and competence.

On the other hand, management of HIV-associated dementia addresses three main areas: physical and cognitive changes, safety concerns, and emotional and personality changes. The key principle of intervention is to provide external support to the client/patient in order to preserve the highest level of function-ing possible. This is achieved by working with the patient and his or her caregivers to develop and maintain a structured environment that includes the use of rou-tine physical cues and safety devices. Psychotherapy can no longer be reflective or psychodynamic. The therapist needs to take a pragmatic and direct approach, giving suggestions and at times advice. The focus is on day-to-day living, and sessions may often include the partner/caregiver. Redirecting or distracting cli-ents/patients from dangerous or inappropriate behavior is likely to be more effective than directly confronting them (Zeifert, Leary, & Boccellari, 1995).

Cognitive impairment can also be caused by HIV-related opportunistic con-ditions. The four most common are toxoplasmosis (caused by a parasite), crypto-coccal meningitis (a fungal infection), progressive multifocal leukoencephalopathy (a viral infection), and lymphoma (a cancer in the lymphatic system that invades the brain).

Transient, short-lived cognitive impairment or delirium is the most fre-quently encountered organic brain syndrome. Lipowski (1985) describes delirium as a disorder of cognition, which includes global cognitive impairment with con-current disorders of memory, thinking, orientation, and perception, and distur-bances of the sleep–wake cycle. The characteristic course is marked by rapid onset, relatively brief duration, and fluctuations in the severity of the distur-bance. There is an impaired ability to process, retain, retrieve, and apply infor-mation about the environment, body, and self. The patient's level of awareness is reduced. Thinking, perceiving, and remembering are impaired. To accurately assess delirium, mental status examinations must be conducted, often several times per day. Neurology exams, laboratory and radiological testing, and neu-ropsychological testing are also used by health practitioners familiar with HIV disease. Factors predisposing to delirium in HIV infection include addiction to alcohol or drugs, brain damage, and chronic illness. Facilitating factors are emo-tional stress, sleep deprivation, and sensory deprivation during intensive care unit admission. Organic factors can be the most frequent causes of delirium; these include hypoxia (low oxygen to the brain), secondary to *Pneumocystis carinii* pneumonia and acute respiratory distress, infections as mentioned previously, septicemias (infections of the blood), and use of drugs, including opiates, antibi-otics, and chemotherapeutic agents.

Dementia is an organic mental disorder characterized by a loss of intellec-tual abilities that is severe enough to interfere with the individual's social or occupational functioning, or both. Patients are often unaware of the subtle onset of progressive central nervous system (CNS) disease. Dementia may be regarded as a global disorder of cognition, in the sense that several cognitive functions are impaired concurrently. These include memory, judgment, and abstract thinking, which are decreased in function relative to the individual's premorbid level of performance. Apraxia, agnosia, anomia, and constructural difficulty are frequently accompanied by clumsiness and poor concentration. Personality changes include alteration of the characteristic personality or accentuation of personality traits. Loss of cortical inhibitions may lead to promiscuity, assaultive behavior, or lack of awareness of social amenities. For example, individuals who were not previously known to use foul language may begin to sprinkle their conversation with obscenities or may be unaware that they are not adequately clothed or have exposed breasts or genitalia (Cohen & Alfonso, 1994).

AIDS dementia complex (ADC) and progressive multifocal leukoencephalopathy (PML) are devastating neurologic complications of HIV. They both lead to dementia, but have different courses. ADC is a degenerative condition whose most common symptoms are loss of physical coordination and significant cognitive impairment. Onset is insidious, and a first sign may be generalized slowing of movement, speech, and thinking. An unsteady gait and poor balance may be observed. PML causes deterioration of physical and mental function, but tends to progress far more rapidly than ADC. Symptoms include loss of muscle control, beginning with weakness; early blurred vision, ending in blindness; early problems with articulation or finding the right word; or early forgetfulness and confusion with diminishing mental alertness. It is often the outpatient therapist who detects these early changes in time for appropriate intervention (*HIV Frontline*, 1998, p. 4).

CONCLUSION

Therapists, particularly outpatient therapists who treat behavioral addictions (sexual addiction, pathological gambling, eating disorders), along with those who treat substance abuse and mental illness and those who counsel HIV-infected patients, need to be alert to the possibility of one other (Dual Diagnosis) or two or multiple other (Triple Diagnosis) primary diagnoses. Failure to treat the unidentified diagnosis or diagnoses increases the risk of treatment failure or relapse in the identified diagnosis. For example, often a patient infected with HIV may also be clinically depressed, a sexual addict, and a substance abuser. It can be seen that the success of HIV treatment is highly vulnerable to the extent that the other primary problems are addressed. Vigilance should therefore be maintained to ensure that the treatment plan is comprehensive, that patients are referred for evaluation/treatment outside one's expertise, and that there is ongoing coordination of all involved clinicians.

Once Dual Diagnosis or Triple Diagnosis has been made, ongoing monitoring of progress becomes complex and therefore must be organized in an efficient and concise manner to allow time-limited therapy sessions to focus on the crucial issues. Patients will have improved outcomes when all primary diagnoses are identified, addressed, and monitored over the long course.

REFERENCES

American Psychiatric Association. (1994). *Diagnostic and statistical manual of mental disorders* (4th ed.). Washington, DC: Author.

Ball, S. (1996). Serostatus and counseling. *Focus: A Guide to AIDS Research and Counseling, 11*, 1–4.

Beck, A. T., & Wright, F. (1992). *Cognitive therapy for cocaine abuse.* Unpublished manuscript.

Brown, S. (1985). *Treating the alcoholic: A developmental model of recovery.* New York: Wiley.

Carnes, P. (1991). *Don't call it love: Recovery from sexual addiction* (p. 35). New York: Bantam.

Cleary, P. D., Vandevanter, N., Rogers, T. F., Singer, E., Shipton-Levy, R., Steinlen, M., Stuart, A., Avorn, J., & Pindyzk, J. (1991). Behavior changes after notification of HIV infection. *American Journal of Public Health, 81*, 1586–1590.

Cohen, M. A. A., & Alfonso, C. A. (1994, May/June). Psychiatric manifestations of the HIV epidemic. *The AIDS Reader*, 97–105.

Cuestas-Thompson, E. (1997). Treating quadruple diagnosis in gay men: HIV, sexual compulsivity, substance use disorder, and major depression—Exploring underlying issues. *Sexual Addiction & Compulsivity, 4*, 301–321.

Daley, D., Moss, H., & Campbell, F. (1993). *Dual disorders: Counseling clients with chemical dependency and mental illness.* Center City, MN: Hazelden.

Drake, R. E., Osher, F. C., & Wallace, M. A. (1989). *Alcohol use and abuse in schizophrenia: A prospective community study.*

Ferrando, S. J., Goldman, J. D., & Charness, W. E. (1997). Selective serotonin reuptake inhibitor treatment of depression in symptomatic HIV infection and AIDS: Improvements in affective and somatic symptoms. *General Hospital Psychiatry, 19*(2), 89–97.

Goodman, A. (1993). Diagnosis and treatment of sexual addiction. *Journal of Sex & Marital Therapy, 19*(3), 225–250.

Gordon, L. J., Fargason, P. J., & Kramer, J. J. (1995). Sexual behaviors of chemically dependent physicians and nonphysicians in comparison to sexually compulsive chemically dependent physicians and nonphysicians. *Sexual Addiction & Compulsivity, 2*, 233–255.

HIV Frontline. (1998, Summer). Focus on: AIDS dementia complex and progressive multifocal leukoencephalopathy, *33*, 4.

HIV Frontline. (1998, Summer). Long-term treatment strategies for HIV disease, *33*, 2–6.

Knox, M. D., Davis, M., & Friedrich, M. A. (1995, February). The HIV mental health spectrum. *AIDS Patient Care, 9*, 20–27.

Lipowski, Z. J. (1985). Delirium (acute confusional states). In J. A. M. Fredericks (Ed.), *Handbook of clinical neurology. Neurobehavioral disorders*, Vol. 2 (p. 46). New York: Elsevier.

Mayfield, D., Mcloud, G., & Hall, P. (1974). The CAGE Questionnaire: Validation of a new alcoholism screening instrument. *American Journal of Psychiatry, 131*, 1221–1123.

McLellan, A. T., Luborsky, L., Zacciola, J., Griffith, J., Evans, F., Barr, H. L., & O'Brien, C. A. (1985). New data from the addiction severity index reliability validity in three centers. *Journal of Nervous and Mental Disease, 173*, 412–423.

Miller, M., Gorski, T., & Miller, D. (1982). *Learning to live again: Guidelines for recovery from alcoholism.* Independence, MO: Independence Press.

Minkoff, K. (1989). An integrated treatment model for dual diagnosis of psychosis and addiction. *Hospital and Community Psychiatry, 40*, 1031–1036.

Minkoff, K. (1991). Program components of a comprehensive integrated care system for serious mentally ill patients with substance disorders. In K. Minkoff & R. E. Drake (Eds.), *Dual diagnosis of major mental illness and substance disorder* (pp. 13–28). San Francisco: Jossey-Bass.

Nixon, S. J., & Phillips, J. A. (1999). Neurocognitive deficits and recovery in chronic alcohol abuse. *CNS Spectrums, 4*, 95–102.

Pepper, B., Kirshner, M. C., & Ryglewicz, H. (1981). The young adult chronic patient: Overview of a population. *Hospital and Community Psychiatry, 32*, 463–469.

Pohl, M. P., Chaffee, B., Gourevitch, M., Haning, W., Hueseman, L., O'Brien, K., Siegel, L., & Ziegler, P. (1998). Guidelines for HIV infection and AIDS in the addiction treatment. *American Society of Addictive Medicine*, 3rd Rev., p. 3.

Rabkin, J. G., Wagner, G., & Rabkin, R. (1994). Effects of sertraline on mood and immune status in patients with major depression and HIV illness: An open trial. *Journal of Clinical Psychiatry, 55*(10), 433–439.

Regier, D., Farmer, M. E., Rae, D. S., Locke, B. Z., Keith, S. J., Judd, L. L., & Goodwin, F. K. (1990). Comorbidity of mental disorders with alcohol and other drug abuse: Results from the epidemiologic Catchment Area (ECA) study. *Journal of the American Medical Association, 264*(19), 2511–2518.

Sacks, M., Dermatis, H., Looser-Ott, S., Burton, W., & Perry, S. (1992). Undetected HIV infection among acutely ill psychiatric inpatients. *American Journal of Psychiatry, 149*, 544–545.

Safer, D. J. (1987). Substance abuse by young adult chronic patients. *Hospital and Community Psychiatry, 38*, 511–514.

Scarce, M. (1999, February). A ride on the wild side. *POZ*, 52–71.

Schneider, J. P., & Schneider, B. H. (1991). *Sex, lies, and forgiveness: Couples speak on healing from sex addiction* (p. 17). Center City, MN: Hazelden.

Schwartz, S. R., & Goldfinger, S. M. (1981). The new chronic patient: Clinical characteristics of an emerging subgroup. *Hospital and Community Psychiatry, 32*, 467–474.

Sciacca, K. (1991). An integrated treatment approach for severely mentally ill individuals with substance disorder. In K. Minkoff & R. E. Drake (Eds.), Dual diagnosis of major mental illness and substance disorder (pp. 69–84). San Francisco: Jossey-Bass.

Sealy, J. (1995). Psychopharmacologic intervention in addictive sexual behavior. *Sexual Addiction & Compulsivity, 2*, 257–276.

Shernoff, M. (Ed.) (1991). *Counseling chemically dependent people* (pp. 147-149). Binghamton, NY: Haworth.

Singh, N., Squier, C., Sivek, C., Wagener, M., Hong Nguyen, M., & Yu, V. L. (1996). Determinants of compliance with antiretroviral therapy in patients with human immunodeficiency virus: Prospective assessment with implications for enhancing compliance. *AIDS Care, 8*(3), 261-269.

Springer, E. (1991). Effective AIDS prevention with active drug users: The Harm Reduction Model. In M. Shernoff (Ed.), Counseling chemically dependent people with HIV illness (pp. 141-157). New York Harrington Park Press.

Washton, A. (1989, December). Cocaine abuse and compulsive sexuality. *Medical Aspects of Human Sexuality*, 32-39.

Weiss, R. (1997). Special populations: Treatment concerns for gay male sexual addicts. *Sexual Addiction & Compulsivity, 4*, 323-334.

Whitaker, R. (1999, January). Significance of community psychiatry to HIV disease. *Psychiatric Times*, 62-63.

Workman, C. (1999). The process of supporting adherence. *FOCUS, 14*(2), 1-4.

Zeifert, P., Leary, M., & Boccellari, A. C. (1995). AIDS and the impact of conitive impairment. San Francisco: AIDS Health Project, University of California San Francisco.

Zevin, B. (1997, May/June). Harm reduction and HIV treatment. *HIV Frontline, 28*, 3-4.

Zimberg, S. (1985). Principles of alcoholism psychotherapy. In S. Zimberg, J. Wallace, & S. Blume (Eds.), *Practical approaches to alcoholism psychotherapy* (2nd Ed.). New York: Plenum.

Zwillich, T. (1998, June). Mental illness and HIV for a viscious circle. *Clinical Psychiatry News*, 8-9.

Special Populations

CHAPTER 15

Sex on the Superhighway

Understanding and Treating Cybersex Addiction

DAVID L. DELMONICO

INTRODUCTION

Robert sat in his attorney's office wondering how things had gotten so out of control. It was only six months ago that he discovered pornography online and now he was being charged with possession of child pornography. He was at a loss for words when his wife asked why this happened. What could he tell his own children about the fantasy life that he developed online? Robert remembers discovering the illicit pornography and then his life becomes a blur as his addiction spirals out of control and into a world he never thought he would enter. The next thing he remembers is being arrested at his home and his computer being taken away as if it were a weapon from a crime scene. As his attorney entered the room, Robert realizes how much worse things could have become if he had continued to progress in his cybersex addiction.

Robert's case is unique in some respects, but the feeling of being out of control in his use of cybersex is an increasingly typical story for clinicians. Not all cybersex addicts are pedophiles, heterosexual, male, or from a certain race, socioeconomic status, or background. Cybersex is nondiscriminating when the cycle begins to destroy the life of an individual or a family. This chapter examines the phenomenon of cybersex and those individuals who are directly affected by its use. Assessment and treatment issues are presented, followed by a brief discussion of what we know about cybersex and what the future may hold.

CYBERSEX AS AN ADDICTION

Robert is one of thousands of individuals who struggle with their cybersex addiction. It is estimated that 90 million people have access to the Internet and between 9 and 15 million access it each day (*Computerworld*, 1998). The Internet has truly become the microcosm of the world. With all 50 states and over 120 countries connected, nowhere is the human race more represented. Along with the tremendous communication and information benefits that the Internet affords, it also inherits the pitfalls of human behavior. Largely unregulated, the Internet is a virtual place that allows for the interaction of two individuals just looking for companionship or two criminals planning their next illegal act. The Internet is not inherently a negative medium, but rather a place that emulates many aspects of our society, including the negative ones.

The lack of regulation and level of interconnectivity do not create cybersex addicts. However, certain characteristics of the Internet may foster addictive behavior in its development and growth. In order for a behavior to be considered addictive, Schneider (1994) suggested three necessary components: (a) loss of ability to freely choose whether to stop or continue a behavior; (b) continuation of a behavior despite adverse consequences such as loss of health, job, marriage, or freedom; and (c) obsession with the activity. These three components are easily identified in cases such as Katherine's:

> Katherine couldn't explain to her partner why their relationship had dissolved. She cared for her partner a great deal, but over the past year she became obsessed with finding the "perfect" partner online. She talked to hundreds of potential partners online and even met some in her local area, hoping to find the one who would fulfill all of her intimate sexual desires. Although she never met face-to-face with Martha, Katherine decided she was the ideal partner and left her current partner to relocate across the country. After meeting Martha, Katherine discovered that things were not the way she had imagined. Now, a thousand miles from home, she had no job, money, or friends to support her. Sensing Katherine's deep depression, her mother finally paid for an airline ticket so she could come home and begin to rebuild her life.

Katherine's case illustrates how obsession and the "trance-like" state of mind lead to behaviors that often result in significant consequences. Many times, individuals report that their behavior becomes so obsessive and ritualized that they feel they have an inability to control their choices and behaviors.

CATEGORIZATION OF CYBERSEX USERS

Although Schneider's three characteristics help us to understand addiction in general, what is it about the Internet that is so luring to individuals? Carnes, Delmonico, and Griffin (2001) outline five basic groups of individuals who access cybersex on the Internet: appropriate recreational users, inappropriate recreational users, discovery group, predisposed group, and lifelong sexually compulsive group. Figure 15.1 illustrates how these groups may fit together. The following paragraphs briefly describe each of these groups.

Appropriate recreational users are those who access cybersex on the Internet and do not experience any obsession, compulsion, or consequence as a result of their cybersex use. In fact, some individuals report that they use cybersex as an enhancement to their current relationship (e.g., learn new sexual techniques or positions, etc.). Some use the Internet as an avenue to remain healthy as they recover from an addiction, sexual or otherwise (Putnam & Maheu, 2000). Others simply use cybersex as a form of entertainment and do not experience any

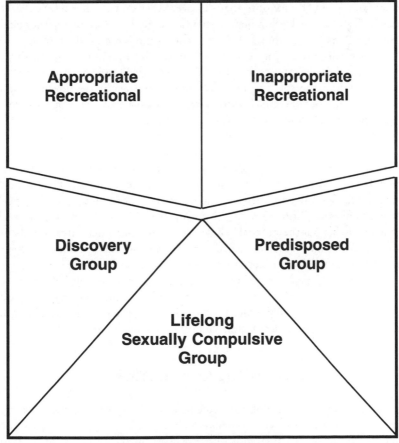

FIGURE 15.1. Cybersex User Categories

difficulties as a result of its use. As Barak and King (2000) wrote, the Internet clearly has two faces, one that can be enhancing and one that leads away from health. Others discuss the importance of the Internet for helping disenfranchised groups connect and form intimate, personal relationships, an option that was not otherwise so publicly available (Burke, 2000; Tikkanen & Ross, 2000).

Inappropriate recreational users access cybersex on the Internet and are also not obsessed or compulsive with its use. However, these individuals will often use material inappropriately with others, such as telling or showing sexually explicit materials to unsuspecting individuals. They may use sexually explicit backgrounds on their computer screens or screensavers and often use the material they find online to ignore or cross sexual boundaries with others, sometimes in an attempt to be humorous.

The discovery group includes those who have never had any problems with sexual fantasy or behavior until they discovered sex on the Internet. Sex on the Internet fostered the development of their addictive behavior, which they might not have otherwise developed. Although this group is rare, it does exist.

The predisposed group consists of those who have had some history of problematic sexual fantasies, but for the most part have kept their urges and behaviors under control. The Internet serves to foster the development of an already existing out-of-control sexual fantasy or urge that may not have developed into behavior until the introduction of the cybersex.

Finally, the lifelong sexually compulsive group is composed of those who have dealt with sexual addiction in other forms throughout their lives, and the Internet simply becomes one additional way of acting out their inappropriate sexual behaviors. This group often has well established patterns of problematic sexual urges, fantasies, and behaviors and a history of ritualized, sexually problematic behaviors. Individuals in this group may see the Internet as an additional way to act out their sexual behavior that enhances their already addictive pattern. Others may see it as a "safer" way of acting out their problematic sexual behaviors because it may reduce their direct contact with others.

A basic understanding of these five main groups will be helpful in the assessment and treatment of cybersex addicts. Identification of a client's group will help the clinician fully understand the scope of the problem, level of difficulty in treatment, historical factors, and possible treatment methods.

COMPONENTS OF THE CYBERHEX

In addition to understanding the categorization of a cybersex user, it is also imperative that the clinician have an understanding of what psychological components permit or promote addictive processes on the Internet, or do both. Various authors have hypothesized ways to explain and understand these components. The Triple A Engine (Cooper, Putnam, Planchon, & Boies, 1999) suggests that there are three basic components: Accessibility, Anonymity, and Affordability. Others suggest more facets such as convenience, escape, and social acceptability (Griffiths, 2000). This article focuses on the six components proposed by Carnes, Delmonico, and Griffin (2001), known as the "Cyberhex of the Internet" (figure 15.2).

The Cyberhex of the Internet proposes six basic components that contribute to the powerful lure of the Internet and that may be different from those in other forms of media. These six forces are Intoxicating, Isolating, Integral, Inexpensive, Imposing, and Interactive. Although many of these individual components may be present in other forms of media, the fact that they all exist in one medium makes use of the Internet a powerful and attractive method of sexually acting out. These six components are discussed as follows:

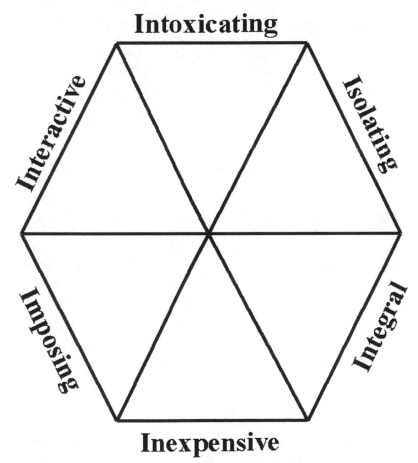

FIGURE 15.2. Cyberhex of the Internet

Intoxicating.   Some may believe that comparing the Internet to a drug is absurd. However, individuals who use the Internet for cybersex often report feeling euphoria while both preparing for and engaging in cybersex. It is this component that lures individuals back to cybersex after they have sworn off such behavior. Cybersex addicts know that the Internet is one way of getting a "quick fix" that allows for immediate gratification.

Isolating.   The Internet allows for the aforementioned intoxication to occur quickly and privately. Previous methods of obtaining pornography involved (at a minimum) a trip to an adult bookstore or the corner market. Now, those same images can be obtained with the click of a mouse button and appear on the screen with absolutely no contact with the outside world. This isolation is perhaps one of the most dangerous characteristics of the Internet for addicts.

Integral.   The Internet is an integral part of most people's lives. Whether it is used for checking the weather, shopping, or e-mail, the Internet is available publicly in a variety of settings (e.g., public libraries, coffee houses, college campuses) and simply seems to be a way of life. The integration allows convenience, but also makes avoidance of the Internet difficult.

Inexpensive.   The cost of using the Internet is relatively inexpensive, around $20-$50 per month for unlimited access. Most individuals can justify that expense, given the vast amount of information and uses of the Internet. Hardcore pornography magazines can run up to $30 each, whereas the Internet can give access to endless amounts of sexual content much more cheaply.

Imposing.   Although related to the Internet being integral, *imposing* suggests that the Internet is not simply just available and used on an everyday basis, but it is nearly impossible to avoid. Even if a cybersex addict decided that he or she would never use the Internet again, the imposing nature of the Internet would make that boundary nearly impossible for most. Although we may have some internal locus of control over using the Internet, it is also fair to say that many aspects of the Internet are external to our locus of control, and society imposes its use in our lives. In addition, the vastness of the Internet gives us the ability to have an infinite number of choices. Whereas choice may be good in some circumstances, having too much choice is not always healthy because our culture is based on "having it all," and on the Internet we can never "have it all," but cybersex addicts continue to obsess and pursue.

Interactive.   As opposed to other forms of media, the Internet is also interactive. Although we may talk to the television or a magazine, it does not respond. The Internet relies on our interactions to guide it to the next screen. Whatever we say to do, it does. The Internet often prompts us for information, which allows for the interaction to feel more "real" than other forms of media. This closer approximation to reality can be fuel for the fantasy life of a cybersex addict.

These six components illustrate the aspects of the Internet that make it so alluring to individuals. Pair these components with a person's predisposition for addiction, and you have a recipe for cybersex addiction. The "Cyberhex" model is named thus not only because it has six sides, but also because of the altered state of mind that individuals report they enter while engaging in cybersex. Whereas any one of these six components can be powerful enough to entice addicts toward the Internet, it is often a combination of these six that draws the cybersex addict back into the ritual of sexually acting out on the Internet.

BASIC FORMS OF CYBERSEX

Two general categories of cybersex are the asynchronous exchange of sexual content, and the synchronous exchange of sexual content.

Asynchronous. Asynchronous refers to the exchange of sexual information (e.g., pornography, stories, movies, etc.) through Internet methods that do not require both or all parties to be online at identical times. For example, e-mail is asynchronous because one can send an e-mail to a colleague who may retrieve it several days later. Asynchronous forms of cybersex discussed further on include e-mail, newsgroups/discussion groups, and CD-ROM/software.

The most common form of cybersex that uses asynchronous methods is the exchange of pornography. It is important to remember that in the digital world of the Internet, pornography includes not only digitized photographs, but also text-based stories, animated graphics, video clips, and audio sounds. Individuals may also use asynchronous exchanges to assist in arranging live, offline sex with partners who are met online.

One way to exchange pornographic pictures and text is through the use of e-mail and discussion/newsgroups. These forums allow participants to post and read e-mail on a specific topical area. Participants use their e-mail to post stories, ideas, photographs, or software related to the topic of the group. These messages are then stored for other group participants to read or retrieve. You may be familiar with the story of a University of Michigan student who posted a fantasy of abducting and raping a fellow student. This message was posted on a newsgroup that was dedicated to sexual stories. Examples of other sexual-related newsgroups are presented in figure 15.3. Although thousands of newsgroups exists, figure 15.3 represents some of the many sex-related groups. The "erotica" newsgroups accommodate the highest volume of traffic of all newsgroups, so much so, that they are often excluded from Internet statistics because of their extremely high use. Forum participants may also meet others in these forums who share similar

sex.anal
sex.bestiality
sex.bondage
sex.breast
sex.enemas
sex.erotica.marketplace
sex.exhibitionism
sex.magazines
sex.masturbation
sex.movies
sex.stories
sex.voyeurism
sex.strip-clubs
sex.fetish.diapers
sex pictures
sex.pictures.male
sex.pictures.female
binaries.pictures.erotica
binaries.pictures.erotica.bestiality
binaries.pictures.erotica.children
binaries.pictures.erotica.teen
binaries.pictures.erotica.pedophilia
binaries.sounds.erotica

FIGURE 15.3. Sample of USENET Newsgroups for Discussion and Picture Exchange.

sexual fantasies or behaviors. These forums can then be a place to meet others for the private exchange of pornography via e-mail, or to meet others for offline, real-life sex.

An additional category of cybersex does not take place online at all. The invention of more sophisticated multimedia systems allows individuals to play X-rated movies, engage in sexual games, or view the latest issues of erotica magazines, all from the comfort of their own keyboard (Chase, 1994; Maxwell, 1996). Compact Disc—Read Only Memory (CD-ROM) technology has provided a way for companies to release various software titles with sound and video clips. These multimedia productions may also include erotic information. Maxwell (1996) estimated that erotica CD-ROMs account for 20% of all CD-ROM business. Sales of erotic CD-ROMs in 1994 were reported to be $260 million. Others report that the CD-ROM market has turned XXX-rated cyberspace into a $1 billion-plus business (Tharp, 1994). Consider the case of Sean.

Sean had his computer set up in the basement of his home. He would often spend hours at a time at the computer. His wife did not think much of his time spent at the computer, because he often worked from home and she assumed he was working. Sean also visited computer trade shows nearly every weekend. Although he often spent hundreds of dollars, he reported to his wife that he was required to continually upgrade his computer to have the necessary technology for work. It was 2 years into their marriage when Sean's wife discovered the closet in the basement near the computer that was packed with nearly $5,000 worth of pornographic CD-ROMs.

Whereas CD-ROM technologies do not require individuals to go online to engage in computer-based sexual behavior, it is considered cybersex because it requires the technology of the computer, and many of those same factors previously listed in the Cyberhex also apply to the CD-ROM technology.

Synchronous.   Synchronous refers to the exchange of sexual information (e.g., conversation, audiovisual, etc.) through Internet methods that require both or all parties to be online at identical times. For example, chat rooms require that participants be logged in at the same time in order to engage in "real-time" virtual conversations. If one party of the conversation logs off the Internet, the "live" interaction with that individual is lost.

Real-time chatting is the computerized version of the citizens band (CB) radio. There are a variety of channels, each with varying numbers of people discussing a specific topic area. There are several differences between the Internet chat and the CB radio, however. At any one time there are typically about 3,000–6,000 channels available to join. In addition, Federal Communications Law limited the types of communication that could take place over the airwaves; however, these laws do not necessarily apply to international cyberspace. There are many positive applications of Internet Relay Chat. Figure 15.4 displays actual channel names and their topics from the Internet Relay Chat (IRC) system. It seems that to find a "safe" channel for talking to others may be more difficult than one would think. It is possible that the sex addict may use the IRC to discuss recovery issues with other addicts, but the channel names themselves may serve as triggers for some. The IRC is only one of many ways to engage in online chatting, but the end result is often the same . . . cybersex is widespread and accessible in most of the public chatting areas.

After a review the list of channels in figure 15.4, it is not difficult to understand how one may engage in sexual conversation with others online. Advanced technology has also provided ways to exchange images and files online during a live conversation. In addition, there are also "virtual locations" where you may engage in online chatting with others. For example, you may start in the dining area and talk with someone over virtual coffee, and later you are invited to the "virtual bedroom," where cybersex may be pursued and expected.

Furthermore, advanced technology now allows for the exchange of voice and video images over the computer lines. By simply providing your credit card number, you can take advantage of live video cameras that capture and transmit

- There are 7940 users and 10490 invisible on 89 servers
- There are 231 operator(s) online
- There are 6832 channels formed

#LouisianaSex	M/22 from Louisiana seeks fem for discrete sex!!
#playroom	truth or dare.......anything goes.....+18 pls
#608_Fuck	M seeking hot Female
#virginsexchat	
#SubFemWanted	Dom Male ISO R/L sub females in Cherry Hill, NJ/Phila, PA area
#kinkymoms	if you want this room gots it
#TeenSexPix	2 fserves here! Send Ops teen pose or action
#BIGCLITS	
#GirlsWhoFuck	
#ohio3some	bi maile – looking for n.e. ohio couple for threesome
#younggirlfuck	
#deepthroats	oral girls suck ... throaters swallow
#preteensexpics	Little Girls – They're not just for breakfast anymore
#daddaughtersex	
#boysex&pics	
#boy&teensexpics	IRC's Only Boy & Teen Boy FTP Trading Channel !
#fuckmywife	this is the it...u might find the right wife to fuck!

FIGURE 15.4. Sample Channel Names and Descriptions From Internet Relay Chat

images of males or females engaged in sexual acts. These live video sites also take requests for specific sexual behaviors that appeal to any individual's personal fantasy. These virtual video booths are steadily growing in number and allow for a cybersex addict to have near complete control over the "object" at the other end of the phone line, even though the "object" happens to be a human being.

CYBERSEX AVAILABILITY

Those who disagree that pornography is widespread on the Internet argue that only those seeking sexually explicit material will find it. However, this argument is not necessarily true, given that many individuals utilize the Internet for a variety of purposes, including research. For example, one can only imagine the results of an Internet search when the keywords *cybersex and addiction* are entered, as was done for this article. Many of the hits were contrary to promoting recovery from cybersex addiction. In addition, many users have individual home pages, on which they are free to place nearly any depiction, including sexual photographs or stories. These personal pages may be a surprise to individuals searching for nonsexual information. For example, should you search for the term *photography*, you may find a great number of resources on the Internet; however, you may also find a nude photo of "Jack" on his personal home page where he has listed "photography" as a hobby. Even though one might not be searching for sexual terms, there is no guarantee that one will not be exposed to pornography online.

CYBERSEX ASSESSMENT AND TREATMENT ISSUES

The assessment of sexual addiction is a difficult clinical issue, given the few available valid and reliable instruments to assist the clinician. Hence, the assessment of cybersex addiction is even more difficult because it involves specific types of sexual behaviors. In order to assist in the screening of potential problems with cybersex, Delmonico (1999) developed the Internet Sex Screening Test (ISST). The ISST is a 25-item screening test designed to ask basic questions about typical behaviors that are reported as problematic by cybersex addicts. Figure 15.5 displays the questions used on the ISST. Although little data is available on the ISST, it has been administered to over 900 self-identified cybersexually concerned individuals. Initial results indicated that the cutoff score where a clinician should begin to be concerned about a client's online behavior is 13. Individuals who score over 19 are thought to be the most significantly impaired group as a result of their online sexual behavior. It is suggested that the ISST be used as one clinical tool to assist in the identification of problematic online sexual behavior and should serve as a guide to conduct a more in-depth interview for those individuals who endorsed any of the items. Each endorsed item could be discussed with the client to gather more information to allow for a clinical opinion regarding the level of cybersex activity and potential addictive behavior patterns.

Whereas frequency is one indicator of potential cybersex addiction, it is important to consider the intensity and duration of behaviors. Also, although behaviors are the easiest to measure, it is important to consider thoughts, feelings, and fantasies, as well as motivations that may accompany behaviors. Clinicians should address all aspects of sexual acting out on the Internet and not too narrowly focused on specific frequencies or behaviors. For example, if an individual begins engaging in cybersex because of marital discord, it would be important to address the marital issues, not just the cybersex use, in treatment.

Understanding personal characteristics of the cybersex addict therapists can assist in identifying and assessing individuals. Cooper, Scherer, Boies, and Gordon (1999) refined the methodology of collecting data via the Internet specifically for this purpose. One helpful finding in the assessment process was that those who reported significant consequences in their lives as a result of cybersex used the Internet for sexual purposes 11 or more hours per week.

In addition to the ISST, the clinical assessment process should involve interview questions that would help identify the category of cybersex user (as was outlined earlier in this article) and the primary reasons for the attraction to the

Internet Sex Screening Test

Directions: Read each statement. If the statement is True or Mostly True, place a "T" in the blank space to the left of the question number. If the statement if False or Mostly False, place an "F" in the blank space to the left of the question number.

___1. I have some sexual sites bookmarked.

___ 2. I spend more than 5 hours per week using my computer for sexual pursuits.

___ 3. I have joined sexual sites to gain access to online sexual material.

___ 4. I have purchased sexual products online.

___ 5. I have searched for sexual material through an Internet search tool.

___ 6. I have spent more money for online sexual material than I planned.

___ 7. Internet sex has sometimes interfered with certain aspects of life.

___ 8. I have participated in sexually related chats.

___ 9. I have a sexualized username or nickname that I use on the Internet.

___10. I have masturbated while on the Internet.

___11. I have accessed sexual sites from other computers besides one in my home.

___12. No one knows I use my computer for sexual purposes.

___13. I have tried to hide what is on my computer or monitor so others cannot see it.

___14. I have stayed up after midnight to access sexual material online.

___15. I use the Internet to experiment with different apects of sexuality (e.g., bondage, homosexuality, anal sex, etc.).

___16. I have my own website, which contains some sexual material.

___17. I have made promises to myself to stop using the Internet for sexual purposes.

___18. I sometimes use cybersex as a reward for accomplishing something (e.g., finishing a project, stressful day, etc.).

___19. When I am unable to access sexual information online, I feel anxious, angry, or disappointed.

___20. I have increased the risks I take online (give out name and phone number, meet people offline, etc.).

___21. I have punished myself when I use the Internet for sexual purposes (e.g., time-out from computer, cancel Internet subscription, etc.).

___22. I have met face-to-face with someone I met online for romantic purposes.

___23. I use sexual humor and innuendo with others while online.

___24. I have run across illegal sexual material while on the Internet.

___25. I believe I am an Internet sex addict.

Total "T"rue statements _____

Total "F"alse statements _____

Total = __25__

FIGURE 15.5. The Internet Sex Screening Test (ISST)

Internet, based on the Cyberhex model. Assessing these two areas will assist therapists in the formulation of a treatment plan that considers the history, types of use, and motivation to use the Internet for sexual activity. The Cyberhex can also help in assessment and treatment. Once the most salient Cyberhex characteristics are discerned, treatment strategies can be applied to diffuse those particular characteristics. For example, if *isolation* is determined to be an important part of keeping the addictive cycle active, treatment may involve exploring why the isolation is reinforcing to the client, and treatment may focus on developing specific behaviors to counteract the feelings and behaviors that contribute to the isolation. Whereas this form of assessment is not formalized, it may take place over several sessions by the therapist asking specific questions around each of the six areas in the "Cyberhex."

PROMOTING CHANGE IN THE CYBERSEX ADDICT

Watzlawick, Weakland, and Fisch (1988) introduced the concepts of *first* and *second order change*. Carnes, Delmonico, and Griffin (2001) suggested that these concepts can be directly applied to the treatment of cybersex addiction. This article expands that notion and discusses various aspects of first and second order changes that may be helpful in the treatment of cybersex addicts.

First order changes are concrete actions taken to quickly stop a problem and to address or avoid certain consequences. These changes can be referred to as the crisis management of cybersex treatment. Second order changes are the actions taken to produce long-term effects at a deeper level of change.

First Order Changes

When treating cybersex addiction, therapists can employ several immediate types of crisis intervention strategies. These are used to help get the addict's mind clear enough to generate and implement a long-term recovery plan. These types of changes include:

Reduce Access—These concrete steps may be to move the computer to a different location in the house, install cyber-screening software, pack up the computer, position the computer monitor so that others can see what is on the screen, self-limit the time online and time of day online, disclose to one trustworthy person the nature of your problem, change Internet service providers to a family-oriented provider, or any combination of these.

Raising Awareness—Assign tasks that will help raise a client's awareness that he or she may have a problem with sexually compulsive behaviors on the Internet.

For example, provide tasks that help break through denial (e.g., taking the ISST), make cybersex a primary therapy issue, engage in support groups for sexual addiction, obtain a sponsor (or another individual to maintain accountability), conduct a sexual/cybersexual history, examine the cycle of cybersex use, make a list of consequences as a result of the client's cybersex behaviors, or any combination of these.

Second Order Changes

After therapists spend some time diffusing the crisis and raising awareness, second order changes may begin. The following are examples of tasks involved in this level of therapy:

Attack the Appeal—Remember to use the Cyberhex model of understanding the attraction to cybersex, and plan interventions to short-circuit the cycle that has been ritualized around cybersex use.

Psychiatric Evaluation—In some cases, psychiatric evaluation may be necessary in order to address collateral issues such as depression, anxiety, other addictions, or obsessive/compulsive behaviors. Medications may be helpful in reducing the obsession with cybersex and assist clients to progress further and more rapidly in their recovery.

Include the Family—The family often is overlooked as a component of treatment; however, in treatment for sexual addiction, family was found to be one of the critical elements in predicting successful recovery. Schneider (2000) addressed some of the complex issues involved in the treatment of cybersex within the family, but left no doubt that cybersex is a familial problem that must be addressed in that context. The family is an essential unit of recovery and should be addressed in cybersex addiction treatment. Difficult treatment issues, such as disclosure to partners, children, and other family members, must be considered and addressed in the therapeutic setting.

Address Collateral Issues—A number of critical issues, if not addressed, will keep the cybersex addict attracted to using the Internet for sex. These issues include unresolved grief/loss, stress management, shame/guilt, anger management, childhood trauma issues, victim empathy, and so forth. Although cybersex may be the primary focus in therapy sessions, these collateral issues must be addressed to move a client forward in his or her second order recovery.

Healthy Sexuality—One issue that is often overlooked in sex treatment approaches is the examination of what constitutes healthy sexuality. Although this definition may vary from individual to individual, it is important to address this in treatment so that the client has a comprehensive understanding of his or her goals in recovery.

Spirituality–An essential part of exploring one's sexuality is the incorporation of spirituality as a topic area. Although this may include issues of how one's religion influences an individual's sexual practices, it is broader than this and addresses issues of how one's sense of spirituality or a "higher power" or both may be beneficial during long-term recovery.

Avoiding the topics of healthy sexuality and the role of spirituality in sexuality will leave the client with unresolved issues that may return to trigger the addiction cycle in the future.

There are a variety of ways to be creative in the treatment of cybersex addicts. Many therapists take already existing treatment techniques and adapt them for use with cybersex addicts. Although, the previous paragraphs suggest many of the issues that may need to be addressed in the assessment and treatment process, the specific techniques are left to individual therapists to determine with their clients. Many theoretical approaches lend themselves to work with cybersex addicts. The process of how one works on the aforementioned treatment issues is one of preference for both the client and therapist. As with all treatment techniques and approaches, the involvement of the client in a collaborative atmosphere is often most predictive of being helpful in getting a client to institute change in his or her life.

DISCUSSION

This chapter is not aimed at criticizing the Internet, nor is it geared toward promoting censorship of the Internet; to construe it as such would be to miss the point. However, no one can deny that sexually explicit media and relationships are easily accessible via the Internet. The Internet provides a vast amount of information and a highly technological way to communicate with others. I surely do not dispute the benefits of the Internet. Provided here are examples of how sexual use of the Internet by some individuals may be unhealthy and may cause significant life problems. The list of sexual uses of computers in this article is not comprehensive because each day brings new ideas or discoveries in this area. This chapter was intended to raise the consciousness of clinicians, researchers, and the recovering community about potentially dangerous territory for individuals who may be predisposed to addictive behaviors, especially sexual addiction.

This chapter explained the various categories of cybersex users, the many forms of cybersex that are available, and hypotheses on why the Internet is such a powerful lure for cybersex addicts. Future researchers may benefit the field by continuing to gather data about who cybersex users are and how they use the Internet as part of their addiction. More valid and reliable instrumentation must be developed to help in the comprehensive assessment and treatment of cybersex addicts. Most important, this field cannot be ignored as a viable area of research that will affect millions of individuals today and into the future.

REFERENCES

Barak, A., & King, S. (2000). Editorial: The two faces of the internet: Introduction to the special issue on the Internet and sexuality. *Cyberpsychology & Behavior, 3*(4), 517–520

Burke, S. (2000). In search of lesbian community in an electronic world. *Cyberpsychology & Behavior, 3*(4), 591–604

Carnes, P. J., Delmonico, D. L., & Griffin, E. J. (2001). *In the shadows of the Net: Breaking free of compulsive online sexual behavior.* Center City, MN: Hazelden.

Chase, R. (1994). Sex on CD-Rom. *CD-ROM Today,* 47–55

Computerworld. (1998). *Commerce by numbers: Internet population.* (Online). Available at: http://www.computerworld.com/home/Emmerce.nsf/All/pop

Cooper, A., Putnam, D. E., Planchon, L. A., & Boies, S. C. (1999). Online sexual compulsivity: Getting tangled in the Net. *Sexual Addiction and Compulsivity: Journal of Treatment and Prevention, 6*(2), 79–104.

Cooper, A., Scherer, C., Boies, S., & Gordon, B. (1999). Sexuality on the Internet: From sexual exploration to pathological expression. *Professional Psychology: Research and Practice, 30*(2) 154–164.

Delmonico, D. L. (1999). *Internet sex screening test.* (Online). Available at http://www.sexhelp.com/internet_screening_test.cfm).

Griffiths, M. (2000). Excessive Internet use: Implications for sexual behavior. *Cyberpsychology & Behavior, 3*(4), 537–552

Maxwell, K. (1996). *A sexual odyssey: From forbidden fruit to cybersex.* NewYork: Plenum.

Putnam, D., & Maheu, M. (2000). Online sexual addiction and compulsivity: Integrating Web resources and behavioral telehealth in treatment. *Sexual Addiction & Compulsivity, 7*(1-2), 91–112.

Schneider, J. P. (2000). Effects of cyber sex on the family: Results of a survey. *Sexual Addiction & Compulsivity, 7*(1–2) 31–58.

Schneider, J. P. (1994). Sex addiction: Controversy within mainstream addiction medicine, diagnosis based on the *DSM-III-R* and physician case histories. *Sexual Addiction and Compulsivity: Journal of Treatment and Prevention, 1*(1), 19–44.

Tharp, P. (1994, November 3). As computer porn mushrooms, welcome to cybersleaze. *New York Post.*

Tikkanen, R., & Ross, M. (2000). Looking for sexual compatibility: Experiences among Swedish men in visiting Internet gay chat rooms. *Cyberpsychology & Behavior, 3*(4), 605–616.

Watzlawick, P., Weakland, J. H., & Fisch, R. (1988). *Change: Principles of problematic formation and problem resolution.* New York: Norton.

CHAPTER 16

Females

The Forgotten Sexual Addicts

MARNIE C. FERREE

Sexual addiction in women has received little clinical attention. Few women identify themselves as being in recovery from this disease. Females, however, comprise a significant population of sexual addicts. Due to Internet involvement, their numbers are predicted to increase. Practitioners in the field can expect to encounter more females in need of sexual recovery. This chapter explores sex addiction in women, including how its presentation differs from typical male addiction. Women's unique treatment issues are discussed, with an emphasis on the particular challenges of a male-dominated recovery environment. Specific recommendations are provided to aid clinicians who work with this special population.

INTRODUCTION

I can't believe I've found another woman who really understands what I'm going through! For years I've thought I was the only one. I've been so ashamed. I was too afraid to tell the truth, even to my counselor. Nobody talks about this sexual stuff going on with women. —Kay

Unique challenges and specific obstacles exist for females who struggle with sexual addiction. Erroneously, the problem often is still viewed primarily as a male disease. Insufficient attention has been directed toward women who are sexually addicted. Although some clinical literature has addressed women's compulsive sexual behavior (Kasl, 1989; Ross, 1996; Ross, 2000; Schneider & Schneider, 1991), more research and discussion are needed. Few women have sought help for sexual addiction, as compared to the number of males who receive treatment. Even fewer recovering women speak openly about their experience. Be-

255

cause of the veil of silence, females may be the forgotten population of those who are sexually addicted.

SHAME AND CULTURAL CONFLICT
SURROUND FEMALE SEX ADDICTION

Several reasons account for this lack of recognition of females' sexual compulsivity. It simply may not occur to the average person that women's sexual problems would be anything other than inhibited desire, which is stereotypically attributed to females. Women with headaches who want to avoid sexual activity are a cultural joke.

Perhaps the most important reason women's struggles are underestimated is the overwhelming shame experienced by sexually addicted women. In general, most addictionists agree that sexual addiction recovery is where alcoholism recovery was 30 to 40 years ago. Many today would extend respect to someone who admitted being a recovering alcoholic. However, the shame surrounding sexual addiction is still enormous. And for women who have the disease, the stigma is especially profound. "My shame is greater than your shame!" one female addict challenges her male colleagues, and her view is probably accurate. Just as it was initially believed that women didn't contend with alcoholism, many today discount the problem of sexual addiction among women. A fear of being all alone in battling sex addiction keeps many women silent about their problem. However, research may eventually show that females struggle with sexual addiction at nearly the same rate as do males.

Compounding the shame is a persisting cultural double standard, which maintains that males who are "oversexed" are "just being men," whereas females with the same problems are "whores" or "sluts." Within religious circles, the judgment reserved for female "sinners" is usually more harsh than that applied to males. In fact, when a husband has trouble controlling his sexual impulses, a finger is often pointed at his wife, who is encouraged to "be more sexual with him to keep him at home." When a woman acts out sexually herself, it is unheard of for her husband to be implicated in her problem (Schneider & Schneider, 1991). Females seem to be held to a higher standard on both fronts. This image of women as being exempt from sexual deviances (and the accompanying judgment for those who do succumb) also prevents many women from admitting their problem and seeking help.

On the other end of the spectrum, women face an opposing cultural message that is equally strong: Females are applauded for being sexually provocative and available. Sexuality is marketed as an important part of the package, in products ranging from soaps to automobiles. Enhancing "sex appeal" is a multi-billion dollar industry. Then women are condemned by the same cultural mores if they become out of control sexually. This power struggle staged through sexuality is a key factor for many women who are sexually addicted. By being seductive and sexually aggressive, women are able to wield power and control (Ross, 1996).

FEMALE SEXUAL ADDICTION

Over the past 3 years I have treated approximately 130 female sexual addicts, both through individual outpatient psychotherapy and through 4½ day clinical intensives. My perspective on female sex addiction is based on my clinical observations, my review of the scarce literature on female addiction, my conversations with scores of women from the recovering community, and my own experience.

I offer two composite case studies as broad representations of different presentations of sexual addiction in women. Names and other pertinent information have been altered to protect the clients' identities.

Clinical Case Example #1: Martha

Martha, age 31, is a single mother of two elementary school-aged children. She is a secretary in a small, rural town approximately 50 miles from a much larger, midwestern city. She has been divorced several years from a man who sporadically abused alcohol and became mean when drunk. Her ex-husband had an extensive pornography collection, which Martha also enjoyed. She suspected him of having affairs.

Martha entered treatment after an intervention coordinated by her sister, who was concerned about Martha's neglect of her children. As a recovering alcoholic, the sister recognized that Martha's out-of-control sexual behavior was similar to her own pattern with drinking. Though initially resistant about attending a clinical intensive for female sex addicts, Martha finally agreed. Most of her motivation to seek help was due to her recent fright when a sexual encounter with a man she had just met had turned toward violence.

Martha described an escalating use of Internet pornography after becoming familiar with computers through her work. She resumed a masturbation habit that had been inactive since her teens. She enjoyed flirting in computer chat rooms and developed several online relationships, which included cybersex. Eventually, she met in person the men she connected with online. She began spending weekends in the nearby large city, either with cybersex partners or others she met in bars or clubs.

"I love the feeling I get when men want me," Martha said. "Several guys will usually hit on me, and I can pick the one I want. Men do it all the time; why can't I?"

Martha's family of origin history included a rural, middle-class up-bringing. She was the middle of five children. Her father raged, was ver-bally abusive, and occasionally was mildly physically abusive. Her mother was a hard worker, but she seemed overwhelmed by her large family and shut down emotionally. When Martha was 14, she had too much to drink at a party and was date raped by an older friend of her brother's. She described this experience as "humiliating" and "infuriating," adding, "I decided I'd never be taken advantage of by a man again." She was plagued by recurring nightmares of the rape, and she described frequent bouts of anxiety and hypersensitivity.

Martha presented for the intensive workshop dressed in tight jeans and a midriff top. She looked angry and older than her years. During treatment, Martha was at first wary of the other women. She also flirted with a male therapist and had to be confronted about her attire.

Diagnostic Impressions:

Axis I: Sexual Disorder NOS; possible PTSD

Axis II: Further information/observations needed, but some his-trionic traits in evidence

Clinical Case Example #2: Kay

Kay is a professional woman with an advanced degree. Age 45, she lives in a large southern city. She has been married 23 years to Bill, a pastor in a conservative Christian denomination. He is successfully climbing the lad-der of his denomination's hierarchy and is busy with his church obliga-tions. Their marriage has been distant and unexciting for years, as they have each pursued their separate careers. They have not been sexually inti-mate in over 2 years. Bill is easy-going and conflict-avoidant. He keeps his emotions carefully guarded. The bulk of parenting their three teenagers falls mainly to Kay, and she feels unimportant and lonely.

This couple sought counseling initially for their 16-year-old son, who was acting out in a variety of ways, including the use of Internet pornogra-phy. It quickly became obvious that the most serious problem lay with the parents' relationship, not with the teen. In an individual session, Kay said she had been depressed for many years and was taking an antidepressant prescribed by her gynecologist. She denied any further problems, includ-ing any sexual or romantic involvement outside her marriage.

Therapy was unproductive for several sessions, until a crisis exploded the equilibrium. One of Bill's pastoral associates was in a distant subur-ban restaurant and observed Kay having lunch with a male companion. It was obvious the two were romantically involved. The associate followed them until they turned into an out-of-the-way motel. The encounter confirmed the rumors that occasionally surfaced about Kay, and the junior staff member felt it his obligation to inform Bill.

After initially denying that the affair had gone any further than emotional attachment, Kay finally confessed to sexual involvement. Eventually, she disclosed several other affairs, mostly with men who were co-workers or good friends. All the relationships had been long-term and intense. Although wracked with guilt, Kay found that she was unable to end her involvements. Each affair stopped only because the men grew tired of Kay's dependence, found another partner who was less high-maintenance, or moved away. With each separation, Kay thought she would die. She would vow never to enter another affair.

Kay's family of origin remarkably resembled her nuclear family. She was the oldest of two children in an emotionally disengaged home. Her father was a pastor; her mother was killed in a car wreck when Kay was 10. The family spiritualized the loss with comments like, "It's God's will," and "She's in a better place." They never discussed their grief. Kay assumed most of the caregiving for her little brother and was totally responsible for managing the household by her early teens.

Kay's father was a kind, gregarious man, but his pastoral responsibilities kept him away from home most evenings. As a young child Kay had found his pornography collection. The pictures were confusing and embarrassing, but as she grew older she enjoyed the explicit novels. When she was 13, a young man who had just finished his seminary degree came to her church as the youth pastor. He took a special interest in Kay and spent a great deal of time with her. Before long, the relationship progressed to kissing, then fondling. When she was 15, he had intercourse with her. Kay felt terribly guilty about the sexual activity, but she was too ashamed to tell anyone. She was certain she loved the youth pastor; she believed he loved her. She was heartbroken when he married and moved away. Until she entered therapy, Kay had never framed the relationship as sexually abusive.

Bill was more embarrassed than angry by Kay's affairs. He was afraid his ministry would be in jeopardy if the infidelity became public knowledge. He told the therapist to "do whatever is necessary to fix Kay's problem." He refused individual or couple's counseling. Bill wanted the matter put behind them as quickly and quietly as possible.

Diagnostic Impressions:

    Axis I: Sexual Disorder NOS; depression, recurrent

    Axis II: Dependent traits

PRESENTATION AND CONSEQUENCES
OF FEMALE ADDICTION

As these two cases demonstrate, the presentation of sexual addiction in women can take many forms, just as it can in men. Women are involved in fantasy and compulsive masturbation; use pornography; engage in Internet sexual activity in a variety of forms; have multiple sexual partners; participate in phone sex; engage in sex with people they have just met; trade sex for money, drugs, "love," or favors; have affairs; and become entangled in intense, enmeshed, dependent relationships. Women are also frequently exhibitionists, though they seem exempt from the stigma associated with men who expose themselves. Just as with men, women's acting out may be heterosexual, homosexual, with animals, or with objects. (For the purposes of this chapter, the term *sex addict* is used to refer to all presentations of female addiction, including the "love" or "relationship" addict.)

Perhaps because younger female addicts have been raised in a visually saturated culture, they seem to use pornography more than their older peers. The Triple A Engine of the Internet—accessibility, affordability, and anonymity—is drawing women, as well as men, into its dark side. Female Internet activity, though, is generally more relational. Women are usually drawn to chat rooms, rather than merely viewing pornography (Cooper, Delmonico, & Burg, 2000). Martha's case is a good example. For many women the pull and power of a relationship is stronger than the merely sexual pull. In fact, it is not unusual for a female addict to report apathy or even dislike about the sexual activity itself, including orgasm.

Thus a "relationship" addiction may be present without pornography use or compulsive masturbation. Like Kay, women are apt to have multiple affairs or a pattern of serial or even simultaneous relationships. Females also may exhibit addiction to "only" one partner, including a spouse. The same autoerotic arousal response may exist within a single relationship. These "love" or "relationship addict" presentations are the ones most often overlooked by the woman herself and by clinicians. Denial is easily maintained when fidelity is kept within a particular relationship. However, the components of addiction (compulsion, obsession, and continuation despite adverse consequences) can still be present.

A fine line exists, in fact, between sexual addiction and co-sex addiction in women. The behaviors are often similar or even identical. A helpful distinction is the reason behind the behavior. According to one explanation, the sexual addict is driven by the "good feeling of the connection—the thrill of the chase and conquest, the sense of power over the other person, or the sexual high." The co-addict is out "to influence another person—to win them over, manipulate them, or keep them in the relationship" (Schneider & Schneider, 1991). Kasl concludes that "the essential difference between the two paths is that the potential addict denies her neediness and seeks power, while the potential codependent denies her anger and searches for security" (Kasl, 1989). Female sex addicts often will act out with other sex addicts and will rotate between the roles of addict and co-addict within that relationship.

Clinicians must be aware of compounding factors among sexually addicted women. Several Axis I and Axis II disorders may be present. For example, sexual activity may be a part of a woman's chemical abuse or dependency. In other words, she may have a problem with compulsive sex only when she is impaired by chemical use. Depression or dysthymia are often presenting problems. Female addicts often suffer from post-traumatic stress disorder as a result of their trauma experiences. Sexual acting out may be one component of bipolar disorder. In terms of Axis II conditions, the connection between borderline personality disorder (or traits) and sexual acting out is clear (Rickards & Laaser, 1999). (See Chapter 15 for further discussion regarding borderline women and sex addiction.) Less well known may be the correlation between dependent personality disorder or traits and sexual behavior. In this case, a woman may be compulsively sexual as a way of pleasing or keeping a partner.

The consequences of sex addiction for females parallel those experienced by men: reputation and job losses, negative impact on a relationship or family, financial problems; sexually transmitted diseases, loss of self-esteem, or depression. Women, though, experience some unique consequences from their sexual behavior. The most obvious is unwanted pregnancy, which has long-term ramifications whether the woman chooses abortion, adoption, or to parent the child. A woman's health, and any STD in particular, has a direct impact on a fetus. A more subtle consequence of female sex addiction is the impact on her family and children. Because women are still typically the primary nurturers in the family, the children are especially affected when the mother is physically or emotionally absent because of an addiction.

ROOTS OF ADDICTION

For both males and females who are sexually addicted, the core dynamics of the disease and its root causes are the same. The vast majority of sex addicts consists of survivors of some kind of childhood abuse. In one study, 81% were sexually abused; 72% were physically abused; and 97% were emotionally abused (Carnes, 1991). Sexual abuse, in particular, seems significantly to impact a woman's sexual behavior. A full explanation of this phenomenon is beyond the scope of this article, but has been outlined by Finkelhor and others (Finkelhor & Browne, 1985). In general, sexual abuse survivors appear more prone to sexual difficulties at both ends of the behavior spectrum: sexual compulsivity and sexual anorexia.

A diagnosis of sexual anorexia can be easy to miss. This woman may fail to report any problems in the sexual area, because she herself may not recognize the energy she expends in avoiding sex. Clinicians should thoroughly probe a client's sexual attitudes and behavior, with specific attention on compulsive avoidance in clients who report no sexual activity. Watch also for a binge/purge cycle of sexual behavior. A woman may act out for a period of time, and then "act in"—that is, shut down sexually and avoid all activity as a way of self-correcting her behavior.

Although the correlation between invasive abuse and later addictive behavior is well known, another more common childhood experience of those who are sexually addicted has received little attention: the trauma of abandonment. Without exception, sexual addicts are abandonment survivors (Laaser, 1996.) Through divorce, death, parental absence due to some other cause, or merely from the lack of appropriate nurturing, sex addicts have been abandoned. This abandonment, in fact, may be viewed as the energy that fuels the addiction (Laaser, 1996). It is the desperate search for connection that is behind sexually compulsive behavior. Females who are hungry for a father's love may try to obtain validation through sex or relationships. Women who are deprived of early female nurturing may act out sexually with other females, even if they consider themselves primarily heterosexual. On the other hand, females who have experienced covert incest or enmeshment with their mothers may use sexually compulsive behavior as a way of establishing autonomy (Adams, 1991). Establishing an independent identity, as well as achieving a sense of personal power, is a driving force behind some females' sexual behavior. Whether the wound is abandonment or enmeshment, the sexual and relational effects can be profound. For women, who seem to be more relationally wired, the relationship trauma must be a key clinical focus. Laaser states definitively: "Unresolved trauma equals risk for relapse" (Laaser, 1996).

SPECIAL TREATMENT ISSUES FOR SEXUALLY ADDICTED WOMEN

Although the process of recovery for female sex addicts parallels that of their male colleagues, there are some special treatment considerations.

Abstinence

An initial period of total sexual abstinence, including from masturbation and sexual activity within a relationship, is critical. Women, too, need a time of no sexual activity to reduce tolerance and reprogram the neurological pathways altered by addiction. Generally, a time-out of at least 45 to 90 days is necessary. Many women like Kay will believe this step is unnecessary, because they are sexually anorexic in their primary relationship. However, an intentional, agreed-on abstinence within the coupleship is vastly different than merely avoiding sex.

A total relationship fast is also needed by the single female addict. This treatment intervention is usually vehemently resisted by the client and often overlooked by the clinician. However, this step is necessary to change the addict's core belief that "sex or a relationship is my most important need." Female addicts must discover their identity and worth apart from a relationship. Six months to a year of abstinence from all romantic relationships, including casual dating, is best.

Male Dominated Recovery Groups

Finding a supportive community of healthy women is crucial for a female's recovery. This objective presents some significant challenges. First, most female addicts are resistant to developing relationships with women.

"Women are the enemy!" one female addict declared. "They're the competition. I don't want to relate to other women. I have no idea *how* to relate to other women."

Practicing intimacy and relationship skills with other women is important for a woman's recovery. Same-sex friendships provide heterosexual women with an opportunity to define themselves as individuals, apart from their sexuality or romantic involvements (Parker and Guest, 1999). Finding other recovering women, though, is often challenging. Because fewer women seek help, 12-step sex addiction groups are predominantly male. It is not unusual for a woman to be the only female in attendance at a recovery meeting. Because of her typical pull toward relationships, it is especially difficult for a woman to stay emotionally present and out of her disease at male-dominated meetings. After a period of solid sobriety, attending mixed meetings is very helpful, because it helps the female addict see her male counterparts as simply other recovering people who struggle in similar ways. In the early stages of recovery, though, a non–professionally led mixed meeting may be a dangerous place for the female addict. Some sex addiction fellowships, such as Sex and Love Addicts Anonymous (SLAA), traditionally have more female participants than others. The well-informed clinician will become familiar with the offerings in his or her area. For those female addicts who are married to sex addicts, which is a common scenario, it is best for the partners to attend separate 12-step meetings.

An option for female sex addicts is to attend Alcoholics Anonymous meetings, where there are more women. However, the female addict must be carefully assessed and coached before she is sent to AA. Is she able to maintain proper boundaries to avoid hooking up with a potential partner? Can she not engage in her rituals? Is there a recovering woman who can go with her for accountability? For her own safety and sobriety, the female addict should identify herself only as a recovering person, without specifying sexual addiction. A 12-step group for food addiction is another good option, because most of the attendees are female. It often is an appropriate choice, because many women sex addicts have food issues, as well.

Finding a female sponsor is as difficult as finding safe meetings. Many women must resort to a long-distance phone or e-mail relationship. Online recovery meetings can help women connect, as can attending recovery conferences.

Another obstacle to women's recovery from sexual addiction is the absence of clinical and self-help literature concerning women's addiction. As of this writing, only two books specifically about female sex addicts are in print. Most examples in the clinical literature are about males' experience. More research and writing geared toward female addicts are clearly needed.

Healing from Trauma

The traditional treatment approach for sexual addiction is an initial focus on sobriety before addressing trauma issues. Most clinicians recommend a lengthy period of sobriety, perhaps 1 to 2 years, before tackling significant family of origin issues (Carnes, 1991). This modality is logical, in that it gives the addict a solid foundation of sobriety and practice at using healthy coping skills, which include finding support from a safe community. The probability of relapse in response to the pain of trauma work, then, is minimized.

Although this approach is ideal, female addicts often fail to achieve and maintain sobriety until they have received relief from their trauma wounds. Again, because of the relational nature of most women's acting out, they are particularly susceptible to the trauma bonds resulting from their experiences. The subset of relationship addicts, especially, seems to be at high risk until they have gained insight and a measure of healing from their wounds of abuse and abandonment. The "trauma egg" exercise outlined by Carnes is a highly useful tool for identifying such trauma and connecting it to the client's acting-out behaviors (Carnes, 1997). Other techniques include standard cognitive therapy to challenge a woman's false core beliefs that resulted from her trauma and Gestalt techniques such as empty chair work to confront a perpetrator or abandoning parent.

Fantasies will also provide a window into an addict's trauma (Laaser, 1996). In exploring the client's most common fantasies, look for themes such as setting (romantic? frightening?), characters (men? women? multiple people?), and the general nature of the activity (sexual? violating? nonsexual connecting?). These repetitive threads can be indicators of a woman's woundedness and thus identifiers of areas where healing is necessary. Interpreting fantasy is not difficult. A thorough client history, of course, is necessary. No matter what the fantasy may be—even if it is debasing or bizarre—there is always some connection to the client's trauma. In some way the fantasy serves as a metaphor for the trauma: a reenactment of earlier experiences. In some cases the connection is obvious because it parallels the traumatic events. In others, the fantasy may represent a different outcome for the trauma or different roles. The key question is to determine what the client really needs when she is engaged in her fantasy. Does she need to be nurtured? Protected? Rescued? To be in control? Help the client identify healthy ways to meet the foundational need that underlies the fantasy.

Usually, the most powerful antidote for trauma is healthy community. Connecting with recovering women for support and fellowship is crucial for trauma resolution. A key principle here is outlined by Laaser: "When we are wounded in relationship, we must heal in relationship. Healthy fellowship equals freedom from lust" (Laaser, 1996).

Rituals and Boundaries

Special attention must be given to female addicts' rituals that precede their acting out. For many women, these rituals of attire, makeup, eye contact, movement, and interaction are so subtle they may be overlooked.

"I thought flirting and being touchy-feely was just part of my personality," Kay observed. "I never realized those kinds of things or going out for coffee with men were part of my rituals."

For other women, rituals are most evident regarding their computer use. For Martha, simply connecting to the Internet is a clear first step toward acting out. Most female addicts need help to detail their rituals.

Specific triggers for acting out must also be identified. Again, there are as many triggers as there are female addicts and their own brands of compulsive behavior. The "HALT" principle of not becoming too hungry, angry, lonely, or tired is rarely sufficient for the maintenance of sobriety. A woman must be aware of her own vulnerabilities to specific people, settings, environment, activities, and emotions.

Female addicts need clear boundaries around their rituals and triggers. For some women, these would involve altering nearly every aspect of their lives, from modifying their clothing, to avoiding bars and music clubs, to installing a filtered Internet service provider. Emotional triggers can be especially potent for women. Certain music, scents, movies, or other ethereal reminders may evoke powerful "euphoric recall." When it comes to establishing boundaries, the 12-step slogan "being willing to go to any lengths" is necessary. Accountability must be established with other women around the addict's boundaries and rituals.

Couple and Family Issues

There are unique effects on a marriage when the female spouse is the addict partner. Male sexual co-addicts face particular challenges. If the shame of being a female sex addict is great, the shame of being a male sexual co-addict is surely greater. Men whose wives are addicted to sex have even less public understanding or fewer role models in recovery. Most 12-step co-sex addict groups are all female. (Attending Al-Anon is a good option for the man who is uncomfortable being in the gender minority at meetings.) It seems extraordinarily difficult for males to face their co-addiction and address their own issues, as Bill's case illustrates. When the male co-addict is willing to participate in couples' counseling, he seems less able than most female co-addicts to get beyond anger and blame. At the other end of the spectrum, some male co-addicts choose to remain in denial about the problem. The concept of addiction as a family disease is usually flatly rejected. Husbands of female sex addicts are more likely to divorce their spouses than are wives of men who are sexually addicted (Schneider & Schneider, 1991).

The female sex addict must be encouraged to pursue her own recovery, regardless of her husband's choices. The relationship addict will be especially vulnerable to relapse if her husband does not choose to enter recovery. She must be vigilant about her own path and coached about the healthy choices she can make about her marriage. If her partner is willing, 12-step groups for recovering couples are significantly helpful.

As Martha's story illustrates, the female addict must be confronted about the special consequences her addiction has had on her children. Family therapy is vital in helping children cope with the impact of an addicted mother.

Spirituality

Recovering female addicts face unique spiritual challenges. In many faith traditions, the Higher Power or "God of my understanding" is viewed as a male figure. For women who have been wounded in a variety of ways by their relationships with males, it is difficult to trust and surrender to a male god. Maleness is associated with objectification, sexuality, and often pain. It is hard to picture healing within a male framework.

Sexually addicted women are also spiritually wounded because of their deep shame. Steps 2 and 3 of the 12 steps ("Came to believe that a power greater than ourselves could restore us to sanity," and "Made a decision to turn our lives over to the care of God as we understood God") may pose special difficulty. Counseling with a spiritual adviser is often helpful. Again, the gender issue may pose a problem, because most members of the clergy are male. For women who are accustomed to sexualizing any relationship with a male, it is a challenge to remain present and appropriate. Female addicts may be better served by a female spiritual mentor, who can model a variety of roles such as mother and female friend, as well as offer spiritual guidance.

SPECIFIC RECOMMENDATIONS FOR CLINICIANS

Therapeutic Relationship Is Key

Because of the extreme shame felt by female sex addicts, establishing the therapeutic relationship is unusually important. Emotional safety is key. The clinician should go slowly and earn the right to confront. Work on shame reduction first to encourage honesty. Vulnerable disclosure, especially with a group, is helpful to counteract shame. Techniques such as writing a letter of forgiveness to oneself can be powerful. Making amends as part of a 12-step program helps lift the drape of shame.

Therapeutic self-disclosure can be enormously beneficial in reducing a client's fear. If the clinician is personally in recovery from sexual addiction, sharing appropriate parts of one's own story can build identification and trust, which will make the client more comfortable about disclosing. For those clients who have strong religious beliefs, suggest they talk with a pastor or other spiritual adviser about concepts like grace, forgiveness, and redemption. The standard, more confrontational approach, characterized by mandates such as requiring attendance at a 12-step group before proceeding with therapy, will usually do more harm than good. Most female addicts must experience safety and acceptance within the counseling relationship before they will consider going to a group. Allow them that time.

Be a Savvy Diagnostician

Because few females identify sexual addiction as the presenting problem, the clinician must be skilled at discerning the real issue. Use female language and examples about acting out. Instead of asking, "Do you engage in anonymous sex?" inquire "Are you ever sexual with someone you've just met?" Women will not identify with "cruising," but they will understand "bar hopping" and "flirting" (Ross, 2000). Watch for patterns of relationship or love addiction. A helpful tool is to ask for a timeline of all relationships and sexual activity, from the client's earliest memory until the present. The Women's Sexual Addiction Screening Test, developed by Shannon O'Hara and Patrick Carnes, is another helpful aid (1994).

Rather than argue about the "sexual addiction" label, which is particularly difficult for females to accept, take a pragmatic approach. If a woman's sexual or relationship behavior is impacting her life negatively, encourage her to address the problem. Do make a clinical judgment for your own purposes in designing a treatment plan, but proceed with caution when discussing a diagnosis with the client. The chemical addiction concepts of "abuse" and "dependence" can be useful in explaining how sexual behavior can also be plotted along a continuum ranging from "at-risk," to "in-trouble," to "full-blown addiction." To hook a woman into the process of recovery is the first goal. Labeling her a sex addict usually has the opposite affect.

Be Ethical and Appropriate

Treating female addicts is especially challenging for the male clinician. Transference and countertransference issues may be unusually strong. Male clinicians must be aware that sexually addicted females may be provocative and seductive, even with their therapists. These women may believe that sexuality is the only "currency" they can offer to get what they want or need. Therefore, the male therapist must be scrupulously careful about therapeutic touch. Clear communication can help alleviate any misperceived intentions. For example, when the therapist wants to be supportive or affirming, he might say, "I care about you as a person of worth. My concern for you has nothing to do with anything romantic or sexual." For most female addicts, that kind of healthy regard is a foreign concept. The prudent therapist will maintain rigorous boundaries and will immediately challenge any inappropriate client behavior. Documenting such instances is critical for the therapist's protection. Staffing the case with colleagues or superiors will provide objective feedback and accountability. Refer to Chapter 7 for more discussion regarding clinical boundary issues.

It is especially critical that male clinicians be aware of their own woundedness and issues around sexuality. Without awareness of sexual vulnerabilities and healing when needed, the therapist is at high risk for offending against a female sexually addicted client by accepting her sexual advances. Ideally, it is best to gender match the therapist to a sexually addicted client, especially for the female addict who is just beginning recovery.

In terms of countertransference, it is not unusual for a clinician to miss a female's sex addiction because of the professional's own issues. Both male and female therapists may be susceptible to this problem for a variety of reasons. The counselor may match a client's behavior to the therapist's own unspoken desires about a sexual relationship and thus miss the problems caused by her acting out. Or a clinician who has unresolved abandonment issues may focus on the client's choice of "unavailable partners" and miss the true addictive relationship pattern. Ethical treatment requires that the professional is free from any personal issues that would impair the therapeutic relationship.

CONCLUSION

Females who are seeking recovery from sexual addiction are faced with overwhelming shame, unique obstacles, and few resources. They need clinicians who can identify their disease and meet their distinct needs for healing. There is a critical void of clinical literature and research into women's experience of sexual addiction. More successfully recovering women are needed to serve as role models. However, with the properly tailored treatment approach, female sex addicts can also step "out of the shadows" into the light of recovery. Well-trained, sensitive, and effective clinicians can serve as important beacons to point the way.

REFERENCES

Adams, K. (1991). *Silently seduced: When parents make their children partners: Understanding covert incest.* Deerfield Beach, FL: Health Communications.

Carnes, P. J. (1991). *Don't call it love: Recovery from sexual addiction.* New York: Bantam.

Carnes, P. J. (1997). *The betrayal bond: Breaking free of exploitative relationships.* Minneapolis, MN: Hazelden.

Cooper, A., Delmonico, D., & Burg, R. (2000). Cybersex users, abusers, and compulsives: New findings and implications. *Sexual Addiction and Compulsivity, 7,* 5–29.

Finkelhor, D., & Browne, A. (1985). The traumatic impact of child sexual abuse: A conceptualization. *American Journal of Orthopsychiatry, 55,* 530–541.

Kasl, C. (1989). *Women, sex, and addiction: A search for love and power.* New York: Ticknor & Fields.

Laaser, M. R. (1996). *Faithful and true workbook: Sexual integrity in a fallen world.* Nashville: Lifeway.

O'Hara, S., & Carnes, P. (1994). Women's sexual addiction screening test.

Parker, J., & Guest, D. (1999). *The clinicians' guide to 12-step programs.* Westport, CT: Auburn House.

Ross, C. J. (1996). A qualitative study of sexually addicted women. *Sexual Addiction and Compulsivity, 3*(1), 43–53.

Ross, C. J. (2000). Power veiled by seduction: Sexual addiction in women. Presentation at the National Council on Sexual Addiction and Compulsivity, Atlanta.

Schneider, J., & Schneider, B. (1991). Women sex addicts and their husbands: Problems and recovery issues. *American Journal of Preventive Psychiatry & Neurology, 3*(1), 1–5.

Schneider, J., & Schneider, B. (1999). *Sex, lies, and forgiveness: Couples speaking out on healing from sex addiction.* Tucson, AZ: Recovery Resources.

CHAPTER **17**

Sexual Acting Out in Borderline Women

Impulsive Self-Destructiveness or Sexual Addiction/Compulsivity?

SHANNAE RICKARDS
MARK R. LAASER

Many therapists who treat sexual addiction/compulsivity are often frustrated by difficult patients who do not generally respond well to traditional treatment. These patients are often labeled "rageful," "rebellious," "noncompliant," and even "dangerous." This may be particularly so with female patients being treated for sexual addiction/compulsivity. Therapists working with other addictions and dually diagnosed populations may be equally as frustrated with female patients who present with dysfunctional sexual behavior that is not understood and is not being addressed. In both populations the presence of borderline personality disorder may not have been adequately recognized or diagnosed. In this chapter we outline our emerging theoretical ideas about the relationship between borderline personality disorder and sexual addiction/compulsivity in women. We believe that differential diagnostic features delineate three populations: sexually addictive/compulsives, sexually addictive/compulsive borderlines, and borderlines who may act out sexually, but who are not sexually addictive/compulsive. Failure to recognize these differences can lead to ineffective and frustrating treatment strategies for both the therapist and the patient.

DIAGNOSIS

One of the hallmarks of borderline personality disorder is an unstable pattern of behavior and style of living. Individuals diagnosed with this disorder engage in a variety of self-destructive behaviors, such as substance abuse, eating disor-

TABLE 17.1. *DSM–IV* Diagnostic Criteria for Borderline Personality Disorder

A pervasive pattern of instability of interpersonal relationships, self-image, and affects, and marked impulsivity beginning by early adulthood and present in a variety of contexts, as indicated by five (or more) of the following:

1. Frantic efforts to avoid real or imagined abandonment
2. A pattern of unstable and intense interpersonal relationships, characterized by alternating between extremes of idealization and devaluation
3. Identity disturbance: markedly and persistently unstable self-image or sense of self
4. Impulsivity in at least two areas that are potentially self-damaging (e.g., spending, sex, substance abuse, reckless driving, binge eating)
5. Recurrent suicidal behavior, gestures, or threats, or self-multilating behavior
6. Affective instability due to a marked reactivity of mood (e.g., intense episodic dysphoria, irritability, or anxiety, usually lasting a few hours and only rarely more than a few days)
7. Chronic feelings of emptiness.
8. Inappropriate, intense anger or difficulty controlling anger (e.g., frequent displays of temper, constant anger, recurrent physical fights)
9. Transient, stress-related paranoid ideation or severe dissociative symptoms

Notes: DSM-IV = Diagnostic and Statistical Manual of Mental Disorders (4th ed., American Psychiatric Association, 1994).

ders, sexual promiscuity, self-mutilation, and other highly dangerous and risky behaviors (see table 17.1).

Whereas the comorbidity of borderline personality disorder and other addictions and mental disorders has been elucidated elsewhere (e.g., Koepp, Schildbach, Schmager, & Rohmer, 1993; Kroll, 1993; Sansone, Fine, & Nunn, 1994), the research on the coexistence of borderline personality disorder and sexual addiction/compulsivity is relatively nonexistent. In fact, the research on borderline personality disorder and sexual behavior (addictive/compulsive or not) has been investigated only by Hurlbert, Apt, and White (1992). This study showed that borderline women, compared to nonborderline women, had higher levels of sexual assertiveness and sexual esteem and greater erotophilic attitudes and sexual preoccupation, but greater sexual depression and dissatisfaction. As such, it seems evident that some individuals diagnosed with borderline personality disorder may exhibit dysfunctional sexual behavior; whether it is addictive/ compulsive remains unclear.

The diagnosis of sexual addiction/compulsivity, though not recognized by the *Diagnostic and Statistical Manual of Mental Disorders* (*DSM-IV*; American Psychiatric Association, 1994) has generally been defined by Carnes (1998) to include the presence of three or more of the criteria listed in table 17.2. Although much research has been conducted on sexual addiction/compulsivity and borderline personality disorder, there is always a need for further research and refinement.

TABLE 17.2. Diagnostic Criteria for Sexual Addiction/Compulsivity

1. Recurrent failure (pattern) to resist sexual impulses to engage in specific sexual behavior
2. Frequent engaging in those behaviors to a greater extent or over a longer period of time than intended
3. Persistent desire or unsuccessful efforts to stop, reduce, or control those behaviors
4. Inordinate amount of time spent in obtaining sex, being sexual, or recovering from sexual experiences
5. Preoccupation with the behavior or preparatory activities
6. Frequent engaging in the behavior when expected to fulfill occupational, academic, domestic, or social obligations
7. Continuation of the behavior despite knowledge of having a persistent or recurrent social, financial, psychological, or physical problem that is caused or exacerbated by the behavior
8. Need to increase the intensity, frequency, number, or risk of behaviors to achieve the desired effect, or diminished effect with continued behaviors at the same level of intensity, frequency, number, or risk
9. Giving up or limiting social, occupational, or recreational activities because of the behavior
10. Distress, anxiety, restlessness, or irritability if unable to engage in the behavior

Note: From Carnes (1998).

ETIOLOGY

To begin to understand how these two populations may overlap, etiological considerations are important. Borderline personality disorder has been etiologically tied to ego defects and primitive defense mechanisms that are rooted in object-relational pathology (Kernberg, 1985); a failure in separation-individuation, specifically during the rapprochement phase (Masterson, 1976); and a combination of a biological vulnerability to emotional dysregulation and an invalidating environment (Linehan, 1993). More recently, however, researchers have discovered a strong correlation between borderline personality disorder and a history of childhood trauma. For example, Herman, Perry, and van der Kolk (1989) reported that individuals diagnosed with borderline personality disorder often present with significant histories of physical and sexual abuse. Likewise, Westen, Ludolph, Misle, Ruffins, and Block (1990) discovered that adolescent girls with borderline personality disorder are more likely than adolescent girls without such a diagnosis to have a history of physical and sexual abuse, and that this history affects character structure and cognitive functioning. Moreover, Zanarini, Gunderson, Marino, Schwartz, and Frankenburg (1989) noted that the development of borderline personality disorder is strongly associated with a history of abuse (particularly sexual and verbal abuse) and long-term exposure to a disturbed caretaker. In sum, it is clear that borderline personality disorder has a powerful relationship with a history of childhood abuse.

Although less frequently researched, a significant relationship has been shown to exist between sexual abuse and sexual addiction/compulsivity as well. In his landmark study, Carnes (1991) found that 82% of the sexually addictive/ compulsives in his sample had been sexually abused in childhood. Other authors have discovered a similar relationship between childhood sexual trauma and subsequent sexual addiction/compulsivity in adulthood (e.g., Anderson & Coleman, 1991; Tedesco & Bola, 1997). Although the research has clearly documented a solid association between childhood sexual abuse and subsequent borderline personality disorder and sexual addiction/compulsivity, no one has ever explored the correlation between these disorders or their co-occurrence.

DIFFERENTIAL DIAGNOSIS

When therapists investigate diagnostic issues within these populations, it is imperative to recognize both the similarities and the differences among the three groups of sexually addictive/compulsives, sexually addictive/compulsive borderlines, and nonsexually addictive/compulsive borderlines who sexually act out (see figure 17.1). It is clear that all three groups generally present with a signifi-

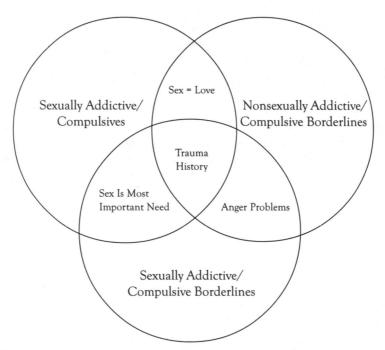

FIGURE 17.1. Sexually Addictive/Compulsives, Nonsexually Addictive/Compulsive Borderlines, and Sexually Addictive/Compulsive Borderlines

cant trauma history. This traumatic background (often sexual in nature) often lays the groundwork for dysfunctional sexual behavior in adulthood. All three groups seek trauma resolution through their sexual behaviors. The sexually addictive/compulsives and the sexually addictive/compulsive borderlines share the core belief that sex is their most important need, and they act out in a variety of sexually addictive/compulsive behaviors. The sexually addictive/compulsives and the nonsexually addictive/compulsive borderlines share the core belief that sex is equal to love, and they act out in compulsively dependent relationships. Recurrent anger problems overlap between the sexually addictive/compulsive borderlines and the nonsexually addictive/compulsive borderlines who sexually act out. For these two groups, sexual behavior can be an expression of rage.

Many of the features that characterize borderline personality disorder coincide with the symptoms and dynamics of sexual addiction/compulsivity. For example, both individuals with borderline personality disorder and those with sexual addiction/compulsivity tend to have problems with intimacy and relationships and often turn to sexual acting out to fill internal loneliness. For instance, Schwartz and Masters (1994) contended that sexually addictive/compulsives experience a "hole in the middle of the gut" (p. 65) that represents their loneliness and that they use sex to fill. Many borderline individuals note a similar chronic sense of emptiness, for which they use self-destructive means to sate. Both disorders present with poor affect regulation and impulsive or compulsive behavior to contain or modulate emotion. Furthermore, both types of patients often present with one or more comorbid disorders. For example, because of the likely history of childhood abuse, both sexual addiction/compulsivity and borderline personality disorder may co-occur with post-traumatic stress disorder (PTSD). Likewise, affective disorders or anxiety disorders may be present as well. Many sexually addictive/compulsives and borderline patients suffer from cross-addictions as well, often using drugs and alcohol to self-medicate the shame associated with their sexual acting out.

Several primary sexual issues overlap with these populations, which deserve special mention (see table 17.3). These clinical profiles are largely based on our extensive work with borderline patients, both with and without sexual addiction/compulsivity. Although we believe these profiles fit most of these populations, we recognize that our conclusions are preliminary, and we await further research and discussion.

As stated earlier, because of the nature of addiction, sexually addictive/compulsives and sexually addictive/compulsive borderlines view sex as their most important need. As such, these women fit the diagnostic criteria for sexual addiction/compulsivity. On the other hand, nonsexually addictive/compulsive borderline patients who sexually act out may use sex as one of many self-destructive or maladaptive coping strategies to alleviate intense or uncomfortable feelings. Moreover, their sexual behavior does not fit the diagnostic criteria for sexual addiction/compulsivity. Similarly, nonsexually addictive/compulsive borderlines

TABLE 17.3. Clinical Profiles of Sexually Addictive/Compulsive Borderlines, Sexually Addictive/Compulsives, and Nonsexually Addictive/Compulsive Borderlines

Sexually Addictive/ CompulsiveBorderlines	Sexually Addictive/Compulsives	Nonsexually Addictive/ Compulsive Borderlines
Sex is most important need.	Sex is most important need.	Sex is one of many things used to self-soothe.
Fit criteria for sexual addiction/compulsivity.	Fit criteria for sexual addiction/compulsivity.	Do not fit criteria for sexual addiction/compulsivity.
Sexual behavior occurs outside of relationships.	Sexual behavior occurs outside of relationships.	Sex is usually relational.
Focus on sexual obsessions and sex as a priority.	Focus on sexual obsessions and sex as a priority.	Lack sexual obsession and sex as a priority.
Sexual behavior is usually planned.	Sexual behavior is usually planned.	Sexual behavior is usually impulsive.
Sexual behavior is often a compulsive re-enactment of trauma with role reversal.	Sexual behavior is often a compulsive re-enactment of trauma.	Sexual behavior is often a compulsive re-enactment of trauma, but without a compulsive pattern.
Sex is associated with anger, power, and revenge.	Sex is used to get love (sex = love).	Sex is used to get love (sex = love).

will often present with numerous addictions, such as drug and alcohol dependence, eating disorders, compulsive shopping, and so on, whereas the sexually addictive/compulsive borderlines, although often exhibiting many other disorders and addictions as well, will usually present with sexual addiction/compulsivity at the forefront of their problems.

The sexually addictive/compulsive borderlines will use their sexual behavior both within and outside of relationships, often engaging in anonymous and one-night stand encounters that have a sense of strategic planning. For example, a sexually addictive/compulsive borderline woman may see an intriguing man while out with her husband or boyfriend and methodically plan out her seduction and plan to "conquer" this other man. On the other hand, the nonsexually addictive/compulsive borderline who is sexually acting out usually restricts her sexual misbehavior to impulsive, brief, and illusory affairs that have no previous agenda.

Sexually addictive/compulsives and sexually addictive/compulsive borderlines possess a strong sexual obsessional focus with sex as a primary priority. For example, one sexually addictive/compulsive borderline patient in our study would obsess about sex and being sexual to the point that she could not stay emotionally or cognitively present in group or individual therapy. The nonsexually addictive/compulsive borderline does not have this sexual obsession and priority.

The reexperiencing of a traumatic experience may release endogenous opioids that provide temporary relief (van der Kolk, 1988), it may give an individual a sense of mastery (albeit briefly) when feeling helpless or out of control (van der Kolk, 1989), or it may facilitate an attachment response when an individual feels alone and abandoned (Carnes, 1997). When sexually acting out, the sexually addictive/compulsive borderline displays a compulsive pattern of trauma reenactment with a role reversal. She generally feels tremendously helpless and powerless over her traumatic experience, and in an attempt to master or gain control over the experience she adopts the role of the aggressor. Conversely, the nonsexually addictive/compulsive borderline will sexually act out as a reenactment of her trauma; however, the behavior does not have a compulsive pattern; neither does it have the role reversal. The reasons for the different responses to trauma reenactment by sexually addictive/compulsive borderlines and nonsexually addictive/compulsive borderlines remain unclear. It may be that the sexually addictive/compulsive borderline endured a unique form of abuse not experienced by the nonsexually addictive/compulsive borderline and in adulthood uses her sexuality to try to master this experience. We did notice in our population that the sexual abuse endured by our sexually addictive/compulsive borderlines was more subtle, and that there often was the presence of a sadistic, yet seductive, father figure who was abusive and enmeshing at the same time.

The sexually addictive/compulsive borderline also will use sex as a means to get revenge or retaliation for a perceived slight or abandonment. The sexual behavior is often associated with rage, vengeance, and power, whereas the nonsexually addictive/compulsive borderline is often just looking for love and acceptance in her transient indiscretions. This dynamic is closely tied to the borderline's trauma history. For instance, Schwartz and Masters (1994) noted that sexually addictive/compulsive individuals experience "passive rage" against their abusers when acting in their sexual disorder. We contend that unlike traditional sexually addictive/compulsives, sexually addictive/compulsive borderlines experience *active* rage against their abuser in the form of spiteful sexual behavior. Not only are they reenacting their previous trauma, but they are now trying to overcome their trauma by identifying with their perpetrator. The sexually addictive/compulsive borderline is a classic example of the abused child grown up and identifying with the aggressor.

Prior (1996) argued that traumatized children internalize an "abuser-victim dyadic working model" (p. 92) through which they base all their future interactions. As such, the working model used by the sexually addictive/compulsive borderline may fluctuate from active victim to perpetrator rapidly and even within the same relational exchange. This may also be noted in the idealization–devaluation dynamic frequently seen in borderline patients. This dynamic may prove to be dangerous for the treating therapist if the sexually addictive/compulsive borderline patient tries to seduce the therapist and is met with rejection. When feeling rejected, the patient may attack the therpist's credibility and may use legal recourse in an effort to regain internal self-cohesion and a sense of esteem and value.

CASE EXAMPLES

The following examples are clinical samples of a sexually addictive/compulsive borderline woman and a nonsexually addictive/compulsive borderline woman who sexually acts out. The two examples have a similar presentation and etiology, but there are discrete and definite differences in their sexual behavior.

The Sexually Addictive/Compulsive Borderline

Elle is a 30-year-old divorced woman who presented with a lengthy history of sexually compulsive behaviors. Her psychosocial history revealed an intact family unit, with parents married for 35 years. Elle has an older brother and a younger sister. She reported a distant relationship with her father, with a noticeable increase in the emotional and physical distance at the onset of puberty, and an overly enmeshed relationship with her mother. She reported a vague history of sexual molestation (fondling and kissing) by her paternal grandfather at a young age. In addition, sexual boundaries in the family were quite blurred. There was no physical or sexual privacy, her parents often paraded around naked, and there was frequent sex play between siblings and cousins. Physical violence and emotional abuse were frequently perpetrated by both parents.

Elle reported that her first "consensual" sexual experience was at age 17 with her high school history teacher, a pattern that she repeated with numerous teachers and other authority figures, most of whom were married. Dating relationships were often with men who became emotionally and at times physically and sexually abusive. Elle stated that feelings of dependence and fears of abandonment prevented her from leaving these destructive relationships. At 24 years old, she married a graduate school classmate; however, the relationship lasted only 3 years, resulting in one child, who resides with the father.

After the divorce, to support herself, Elle became a dancer at a gentlemen's club. She found that the attention she received from the men in the audience gave her a sense of exhilaration and power. At this time Elle engaged in numerous, transient sexual encounters with both men and women. Her pattern with women began with staged encounters for male customers and gradually led to independent sexual encounters with female friends. Elle is currently dating a 50-year-old married customer, who is paying for her treatment.

Elle also reported feelings of emptiness and depression, with a history of numerous suicide attempts (usually after the breakup of a relationship). She also reported a history of violent rages during which she acts out against herself or others. For example, when her boyfriend has to return home to his wife, Elle goes to a bar, picks up a man, and has violent and vengeful sex.

This case illustrates the clinical features articulated in table 17.3. Elle displays a strong sense of power, rage, and revenge when engaged in her sexually dysfunctional behavior. She fits the definition of sexual addiction/compulsivity, has passing sexual encounters outside of relationships, and reverses the trauma re-enactment in a compulsive attempt to assimilate her sexual abuse.

The Sexually Acting-Out Borderline

Amy is a 26-year-old single woman who entered treatment for chemical dependence, bulimia nervosa, and symptoms of depression. Amy was raised by both parents, who are successful professionals. She has a younger sister with whom she has a distant relationship. She reported feeling very close to her father and being "daddy's little girl" growing up; however, she claimed that her mother was controlling, unavailable, and jealous of her relationship with her father. Amy reported sexual molestation by an older cousin at age 7, and a date rape at age 19, during her first year of college. She also stated that her father is a raging alcoholic, but is someone to whom she feels a great deal of closeness. There was periodic physical violence when her father was drunk, and at these times her mother would physically leave the children alone with him. One of Amy's responsibilities as a child was to placate her father when he would get drunk.

Amy began drinking at age 14 and using illicit drugs at age 18, when she began college. Her drug use escalated over the years. She reported a 10-year history of bulimia, a sporadic history of wrist-cutting, and four episodes of overdosing on sleeping pills.

Amy lost her virginity in an alcoholic blackout to a high school boyfriend at age 17. Since that time she has had several unremarkable sexual experiences. She has had few long-term relationships, most of which she sabotaged, leading the men to angrily end the affairs. To earn extra money in college, a roommate suggested that Amy accompany her as a stripper in a local club. Amy reluctantly agreed; however, she needed to drink and use drugs excessively to perform. Currently, Amy is dating several different men, with an increasing pattern of heated arguments and physical fighting.

Amy also reported a lifelong history of depressive symptoms, chronic feelings of emptiness and boredom, and no sense of identity. In addition, she had made several treatment attempts to work on her eating disorder and chemical dependence, with minimal recovery.

Amy is a good example of the nonsexually addictive/compulsive borderline who sexually acts out. Initially, we considered diagnosing her with sexual addiction/compulsivity; however, she does not clearly meet the criteria. Her sexual behavior is not planned; rather, it is impulsive and often triggered by alcohol. She does not have sex as a primary need; rather, she uses food, drugs, alcohol, and self-mutilation in addition to sex to regulate her emotions. Her sexual behavior also lacks an obsessional quality and is primarily used to get love and attention, rather than to gain power and seek revenge.

Treatment of the Sexually Addictive/Compulsive Borderline

Treating a woman with sexual addiction/compulsivity and borderline personality disorder can be a lengthy and arduous task. Initially, it is important to establish a strong therpeutic alliance, consistent boundaries, and a flexible stance. Treatment prioritization and planning are other critical issues that must be considered when addressing this population.

At the onset of treatment it is imperative to address the sexual addiction/compulsivity and other self-destructive behaviors first. Because borderline patients often present with many maladaptive and sometimes harmful behaviors, eliminating them is necessary to proceed with treatment. If these issues are not addressed at the outset, the sexually addictive/compulsive borderline patient will continue to avoid her underlying issues in treatment as her dysfunctional sexual behavior escalates.

Twelve-step programs can be of great help when working on ceasing addictive/compulsive behaviors. Moreover, specialized treatment for sexual addiction/compulsivity needs to occur as delineated by authorities in the field (e.g., Carnes, 1991; Laaser, 1996). Borderline patients have unique difficulties with interpersonal boundaries. As part of the patients' initial sexual addiction/compulsivity treatment, special attention needs to be given to educating them about healthy relationships and appropriate sexual behaviors. If this behavior is not addressed, the borderline patients will continue to use their sexual behavior to avoid looking at their underlying issues. For example, one of the patients in our study who was scheduled for a psychosocial history offered to perform oral sex on the therapist as a way of deflecting the focus away from her own issues. In this instance the therapist needed to be very careful and persistent in delineating healthy boundaries between therapist and patient.

Borderlines who understand inappropriate sexual behaviors and are willing to change will need to manage these behaviors using the standard tools of support groups and accountability, in association with the cognitive re-education that must take place. We believe that when 3 to 6 months of abstinence from inappropriate sexual behaviors has been achieved, the underlying traumatic issues can be more easily addressed.

Once the sexual addiction/compulsivity and other self-medicating behaviors are removed, an increase in affective symptoms will usually emerge. This is particularly true with the traumatized borderline, who has been using the addictive/compulsive behavior to keep intrusive traumatic memories at bay. It is critical at this time to educate these individuals about trauma and the features of PTSD, because this is when the intrusive phase of PTSD most frequently begins.

Because most borderlines are notorious for their inability to modulate their emotions and contain their intense affect, teaching them appropriate ways to regulate their emotions is crucial. This strategy is especially important when borderlines are being flooded by affect storms related to their trauma history. Linehan (1993) created a cognitive-behavioral treatment model to treat individuals with borderline personality disorder. A component of her treatment protocol is the use of skills training sessions to teach emotion regulation, distress tolerance, interpersonal effectiveness, and mindfulness. Once the borderline patient has internalized these adaptive and positive coping skills, it is then time to address the underlying trauma issues that have been feeding the sexual addiction/compulsivity and other destructive behaviors.

The subsequent trauma work should proceed according to the already-established and accepted guidelines for this work (e.g., Briere, 1996; Carnes, 1997; Courtois, 1988; McCann & Pearlman, 1990; Meichenbaum, 1994; van der Kolk, 1987). It must be reiterated at this time that treating the underlying traumatic material with a sexually addictive/compulsive borderline may trigger intense affective and behavioral flashbacks that may push the patient into compulsive sexual reenactment of the corresponding trauma. As an aspect of this reenactment, the borderline patient may attempt to deflect the underlying traumatic material by trying to seduce the therapist. It is crucial for the therapist to be mindful of the sexual addiction/compulsivity and of the potential for relapse when working with members of this population on their sexual abuse issues. It is important to recognize the fear of confronting these issues and how the sexually addictive/compulsive borderline may revert back to maladaptive sexual behavior in a desperate attempt to avoid addressing painful memories. If this does occur, postpone exploration of the traumatic material until the maladaptive sexual behavior is addressed and adaptive coping skills are in place.

Because there are well-known difficulties in treating borderline patients, we have created a set of proposed treatment guidelines that may prove helpful when treating the sexually addictive/compulsive borderline (see table 17.4).

TABLE 17.4. Practical Suggestions for Treating Sexually
Addictive/Compulsive Borderline

---

1. To avoid splitting behavior, work as a treatment team, with regular and consistent communication among all team members.
2. To minimize staff splitting and triangulation, ensure that all members of the treatment team are teaching and modeling the same set of healthy boundaries to the patient.
3. To avoid possible eroticized transferences, gender match the therapist and the patient.
4. If gender matching is not possible, conduct therapy only when another staff member is present (preferably, a staff member of the same gender as the patient).
5. Seek consultation or supervision if an eroticized transference develops.
6. Address sexual acting-out behavior as soon as it emerges in the therapeutic setting.
7. Never agree to meet the patient at a location other than a traditional treatment setting.
8. Clearly document all contacts with the patient, including all phone calls and other important interactions.
9. Carefully document the reasoning behind all treatment interventions and recomendations.
10. Keep self-disclosure with the patient to a minimum, if at all.

CLINICAL CONCERNS

Therapists should be aware that the borderline patient, sexually addictive/compulsive or not, may consciously or unconsciously plan to be sexual with people in power, including therapists. We have known patients, for example, who boasted to friends and other members of the clinical staff that they had been sexual with their therapist before therapy had even been initiated.

More discussion needs to take place on how borderlines use sex to be powerful. A therapist who maintains appropriate boundaries and rejects sexual advances may be at risk for expressions of rage. A therapist who becomes sexual with a borderline and then terminates treatment or the sexual relationship can be assured of criminal or civil charges. Without even considering sexual addiction/compulsivity, Simon (1992) noted that sexual misconduct is one of the most frequent lawsuits brought by borderline patients against their therapists. Although many borderline patients may be at risk for therapeutic inappropriateness, the issue of the patient's seductiveness and own dysfunctional sexual behavior has not been examined. This aspect of the patient's pathology still does not make sexual misconduct by the therapist acceptable.

SUMMARY

It is evident that the sexual behavior of borderline women is a topic that is in great need of further discussion and research. We have reviewed the presentation, etiology, differential diagnosis issues, and treatment for the sexually addictive/compulsive borderline and the sexually acting-out borderline. We hope that this will begin a discourse on the subject that will inspire others to conduct empirical research and improve treatment strategies for these difficult populations.

REFERENCES

American Psychiatric Association. (1994). *Diagnostic and statistical manual of mental disorders* (4th ed.). Washington, DC: Author.

Anderson, N., & Coleman, E. (1991). Childhood abuse and family sexual attitudes in sexually compulsive males: A comparison of three clinical groups. *American Journal of Preventive Psychiatry and Neurology, 3*, 8–15.

Briere, J. (1996). *Therapy for adults molested as children* (2nd ed.). New York: Springer.

Carnes, P. J. (1991). *Don't call it love: Recovery from sexual addiction.* New York: Bantam.

Carnes, P. J. (1997). *The betrayal bond.* Deerfield Beach, FL: Health Communications.

Carnes, P. J. (1998). The presidential diagnosis. *Sexual Addiction and Compulsivity, 5*, 153–158.

Courtois, C. A. (1988). *Healing the incest wound: Adult survivors in therapy.* New York: W.W. Norton.

Herman, J. L., Perry, C., & van der Kolk, B. A. (1989). Childhood trauma in borderline personality disorder. *American Journal of Psychiatry, 146*, 490–495.

Hurlbert, D .F., Apt. C., & White, L. C. (1992). An empirical examination into the sexuality of women with borderline personality disorder. *Journal of Sex and Marital Therapy, 18*, 231–242.

Kernberg, O. (1985). *Borderline conditions and pathological narcissism.* Northvale, NJ: Jason Aronson.

Koepp, W., Schildbach, S., Schmager, C., & Rohmer, R. (1993). Borderline diagnosis and substance abuse in female patients with eating disorders. *International Journal of Eating Disorders, 14*, 107–110.

Kroll, J. (1993). *PTSD/borderlines in therapy: Finding the balance.* New York: W. W. Norton.

Laaser, M. (1996). *Faithful and true.* Grand Rapids, MI: Zondervan.

Linehan, M. M. (1993). *Skills training manual for treating borderline personality disorder.* New York: Guilford.

Masterson, J. F. (1976). *Psychotherapy of the borderline adult: A developmental approach.* New York: Brunner/Mazel.

McCann, I. L., & Pearlman, L. A. (1990). *Psychological trauma and the adult survivor: Theory, therapy, and transformation.* New York: Brunner/Mazel.

Meichenbaum, D. (1994). *A clinical handbook/practical therapist manual: For assessing and treating adults with post-traumatic stress disorder* (PTSD). Waterloo, Ontario, Canada: Institute Press.

Prior, S. (1996). *Object relations in severe trauma: Psychotherapy of the sexually abused child.* Northvale, NJ: Jason Aronson.

Sansone, R. A., Fine, M. A., & Nunn, J. L. (1994). A comparison of borderline personality symptomatology and self-destructive behavior in women with eating, substance abuse, and both eating and substance abuse disorders. *Journal of Personality Disorders, 8*, 219–228.

Schwartz, M. F., & Masters, W. H. (1994). Integration of trauma-based, cognitive, behavioral, systemic and addiction approaches for treatment of hypersexual pair-bonding disorder. *Sexual Addiction and Compulsivity, 1*, 57–76.

Simon, R. I. (1992). *Clinical psychiatry and the law* (2nd ed.). Washington, DC: American Psychiatric Press.

Tedesco, A., & Bola, J. R. (1997). A pilot study of the relationship between childhood sexual abuse and compulsive sexual behaviors in adults. *Sexual Addiction and Compulsivity, 4*, 147–157.

van der Kolk, B. A. (1987). *Psychological trauma*. Washington, DC: American Psychiatric Press.

van der Kolk, B. A. (1988). The trauma spectrum: The interaction of biological and social events in the genesis of the trauma response. *Journal of Traumatic Stress, 1*, 273–290.

van der Kolk, B. A. (1989). Compulsion to repeat the trauma: Reenactment, revictimization, and masochism. *Psychiatric Clinics of North America, 12*, 389–412.

Westen, D., Ludolph, P., Misle, B., Ruffins, S., & Block, J. (1990). Physical and sexual abuse in adolescent girls with borderline personality disorder. *American Journal of Orthopsychiatry, 60*, 55–66.

Zanarini, M.C., Gunderson, J. G., Marino, M.F., Schwartz, E. O., & Frankenburg, F. R. (1989). Childhood experiences of borderline patients. *Comprehensive Psychiatry, 30*, 18–25.

CHAPTER 18

Pastors and Sexual Addiction

MARK R. LAASER
KENNETH M. ADAMS

This chapter outlines dynamics and treatment issues relevant to sexually addicted pastors. Underlying trauma, personality disorders, identity issues, and primary and secondary victims are addressed. Assessment and accountability components are a necessary part of the treatment and reentry program for this population. Sexually addicted pastors unconsciously choose their vocation to cover up childhood trauma and sexual issues. Values clarification is discussed as a necessary part of the treatment process. Shattered trust and faith in the community are part of the painful consequences of sexually addicted pastors. Therapists and other helping professionals should not try to help this population if their own countertransference issues are not addressed.

"Bob" is a successful pastor in a large Protestant denomination. He is married and has three children. His wife and he met at their denominational college. Each one came from families strong in the tradition of their faith. Since college days Bob has struggled with pornography and masturbation. He has wanted to stop, but cannot. He hoped that by getting married, his "lust" would be taken away. Over the year of his ministry, Bob has frequently used his free time to visit a variety of video stores. Lately, he has also become fascinated with the idea of going to a massage parlor. In the first three churches at which he served, Bob became very emotionally involved with several women. In his current congregation, he established a similar relationship with the organist, a married member of his church, which became sexual. Bob is depressed and is having great difficulty performing his pastoral duties. He does not know whom to talk to. His wife is questioning what is going on.

"Leo" is a priest at a small congregation in a rural area of the Midwest. Since adolescence, he has struggled with questions of his sexual identity. From a large Catholic family, Leo was the son who was always expected to be a priest. Although he dated some in high school, he never really got interested in girls. He was exposed to *Playgirl* magazine during this time and found that he was excited sexually by the pictures in it. Leo has tried to deny this fascination. In seminary, Leo became first emotionally and then sexually involved with one of his classmates. The two of them began, secretly, to experiment with homosexual bars and gathering points in their large city. Leo has hoped that his vow of celibacy would be the answer to his sexual struggles. In the isolation of his ministry, however, he finds that he is frequently drawn into the city on his day off. While there, more and more, he has been searching out those places that he frequented in seminary. Lately, he has had a series of brief and anonymous homosexual encounters. Leo rationalizes that he is at least not violating his celibacy. The loneliness of his feelings, however, threatens to overwhelm him.

Both of these brief cases illustrate pastors who are sexual addicts. As men, both Bob and Leo struggle with sexuality. As pastors, they also struggle with unique vocational issues. Inevitably, these two areas of their lives affect each other. Little has been written specifically about pastors and sexual addictions (Laaser, 1991, 1996). Some attention has been given to pastors who sexually offend (Friberg & Laaser, 1998). In this article, we describe unique qualities of pastoral sexual addicts and suggest some treatment strategies that are specific to these issues.

VOCATION AND PASTORAL SEX ADDICTION

The word *vocation*, from the same Latin root as *voice*, means "to be called." In most theological traditions, pastors feel called by God into ministry. The spiritual and emotional maturity it takes to feel totally and honestly called is a very exceptional thing. Pastors who are sex addicts have answered a call to ministry without this level of maturity. They may choose the role of pastor because of some of the following factors.

Family

Like all sex addicts, it is likely that pastoral sex addicts have come from a background of abuse. The incidence of all forms of abuse in a population of pastors is consistent with the findings for all sex addicts (Carnes, 1991). Carnes found that 81% of sex addicts are sexual trauma survivors, 74% are survivors of physical trauma, and 97% are survivors of emotional trauma. Following are some implications of this abuse in four traditional categories.

Emotional.   Pastoral sex addicts say they feel inferior. They have a difficult time distinguishing between *guilt* (making a mistake) and *shame* (being a mistake). This is consistent with all sex addicts, but a pastor theologizes this and believes that he or she is not worthy of God's grace. Pastoral sex addicts are able to preach and teach about grace, but do not accept it for themselves.

Pastoral sex addicts have been the vicitims of covert incest (Adams, 1991).

They have learned how to care for others and not for themselves. They may assume that their worth is derived from how well they care for others. This constitutes a form of "pastoral codependency." These pastors judge their worth on the basis of external approval and outward signs of success. This may result in a "righteous" workaholism and consequent burnout. Their sexual addiction represents role reversal from the overly erotic atmosphere of the covert incest experience. When assuming the pastoral role, they gain a sense of power and control that they lost in the experience of covert incest.

All pastoral sex addicts are the victims of emotional abandonment. They have a definite need for nurturing and very little idea of how to find it. Their sexual activity represents an attempt to fill legitimate needs through illegitimate or shameful means.

The consequences to their relationships are profound, and many find that although they have many social acquaintances, they have no intimate friendships. This leaves them alone and isolated, with resulting depression. Many of these pastors suffer from chronic depression, but would not be likely to recognize it and seek help for it. Psychometric testing may reveal this low level of depression, which can be masked in a one-to-one interview.

Physical. This form of abuse may influence the nature and form of addicted sexual activity. One pastor, for example, became involved with sadomasochistic activity, going to bars where this was practiced on his day off. More often, physical abuse may lead to a repressed anger that can be covered with an overt pacifism. Many addicted pastors are angry and express it passively, for example, using sarcasm and humor to put others down.

Other pastors have been physically abandoned of healthy touch and nurture or left alone as children. As with all sex addicts, this may lead to an excessive craving for touch (which is sexualized) and a pattern of being alone. The pastoral role facilitates this pattern. The alone time can be spiritually interpreted as being reflective or meditative.

Sexual. Invasive sexual abuse is an obvious factor in the formation of sexual addiction. Like physical abuse, the nature of the abuse, the age at which it was perpetrated, and the gender and relationship of the perpetrator to the victim will influence the sexual expression of addicted activity in later life (see chapters 2 and 3 in Friberg & Laaser, 1998). We need more careful consideration of how the dynamics of "trauma bonding" (Schwartz & Master, 1994) or the repetition of trauma gets acted out within the context of the pastoral role. We feel that trauma bonds can lead to what has been called the *victim-to-victimizer cycle*. Blanchard (1991), for example, has demonstrated how similar pastoral sexual involvement with parishioners is to biological incest. The role of pastor as parental and trusted figure provides a dangerous trasference of most parishioners even in situations that externally may seem like mutual sexual consent.

Spiritual.   A sexually addicted pastor may be the victim of rigid spiritual formation, in which he or she feels inferior in the sight of God, or the victim of the abandonment of spiritual modeling (Laaser, 1996). When these pastors are also the victims of other forms of abuse at the hands of someone who is a spiritual authority in their lives, the result may be a feeling of spiritual inferiority and an impaired ability to trust. They may overmoralize issues and project a public image of being angrily opposed to pornography, prostitution, homosexuality, or abortion. This is a form of reaction formation, being angry at behaviors they are ashamed of themselves.

Their "double life" of sexual pursuits may be followed by phobic, avoidant, or sexually anorexic reactions (Carnes, 1997). They may then project their angry reaction onto congregants during sermons or counseling sessions. Many pastors who have committed sexual misconduct have appeared angry to those around them.

Whatever these pastors' intellectual theology may be, they may be arrested in a rather adolescent, black-and-white theology emotionally, particularly when it comes to their self-perception.[1] They may be able to proclaim a mature theology to others and not believe it themselves.

We have talked to many pastors who believe that they can compensate, or balance, their sexual sins with good deeds. Others believe that they will be punished for their sexual sins for a proscribed period of time. For example, in what has been referred to as the "1-day rule," a pastor felt that he would be punished for 1 day following the commission of a sexual sin.

Sexually addicted pastors, who suffer from arrested adolescent theological development, may also believe certain delusional qualities about themselves. An addict's normal sense of entitlement may be enhanced by a narcissistic view of him- or herself. Pastoral sexual addicts' narcissism may also allow them to feel that they will not get caught, out of some sense of special protection by God from being discovered. The adolescent quality of their beliefs may cause them to think that they are being victimized by the people they serve and that they are being overworked and underpaid. Finally, this same type of thinking allows them to blame others, including seductive men or women, for various forms of sexual misconduct or offense.

Role and Identity

There are two factors to evaluate in sexually addicted pastors, concerning their role and identity. First, what is the identity they bring into the role of pastor, based on their personality and developmental history? Second, what aspects of the role of pastor contribute to the risk of sexual addiction?

---

1. See the treatment of moral and theological development in Fowler (1981).

Trauma leaves the sexually addicted pastor shame-based, narcissistically injured, developmentally arrested, and dependent. In a study of 25 pastors who offended against at least one victim, Irons and Laaser (1994) found that 6 of the participants demonstrated profound personality disorder, 3 with narcissistic personality and 3 with personality disorder not otherwise specified. Of the remaining participants, 11 were diagnosed with narcissistic personality traits, 9 with dependent personality traits, 8 with obsessive-compulsive personality traits, and 4 with histrionic personality traits (Axis II of the 4th edition of the *Diagnostic and Statistical Manual of Mental Disorders*; American Psychiatric Association, 1994). Only 3 of the pastors had major depression, and 6 had dysthymia. Fifteen pastors were diagnosed with sexual addiction, 9 with alcohol dependence or abuse, 1 with other drug addiction, and 1 with an eating disorder.

These findings support the picture of a well-liked, successful, and charismatic pastor who is able to function, but who leads a double life of sexual and other addictions, who is needy and chronically depressed, and who may react dramatically and defensively to being confronted.

Experience demonstrates that pastors may be hoping that the role of pastor will bring relief from their identity issues. One pastor said that she hoped to be "ontologically transformed" by her ordination. Laaser (1991) has referred to this as "ordination as a shame-reduction strategy." This pastor hoped that her sexual addiction would be arrested and that she would be a new person. Similarly, some pastors hope that the ordination vows they take will prevent them from performing acts of sexual immorality. Many Catholic priests, for example, believe that the rite of ordination and the vow of celibacy will stop them from indulging in inappropriate sexual thoughts and acts.

The role, status, and power of a minister may bring narcissistically injured people a sense of relief from their inferiority and woundedness. One pastor described the high he felt after preaching a good sermon and receiving affirmations from his people. The trappings of the pastoral role—robes, special clothing, access to people's homes and lives, and others' adulation and trust toward people of God—do create a vulnerability to grandiosity. It can be that pastoral sex addicts become as dependent on the role of pastor as they are to anything else.

Pastoral sex addicts come from families who assign them roles that can lead them into ministry. They are often heroes and are expected to be heroic. This role can be combined with the role of a saint, a role in which they are expected to be religious. Many Catholic priests, for example, tell stories about times in their childhood in which they somehow knew that they were meant to be priests. One of them referred to this as "being ordained by my mother and not by the Church." These pastors can also be caretakers or enablers, having learned how to care for others, doing lots of things, but not being able to care for themselves. This can lead to workaholism and burnout.

Another common role is that of lost child. Pastors who are lost children receive lots of affirmation for being independent and strong and without any noticeable needs. Lost children spend lots of time alone, seemingly self-sufficient, but really being lonely. Pastors can feel comfortable in this role, which may be part of the reason they have difficulty admitting problems to others. They can even theologically justify alone time as being part of their need for meditation and prayer. Meditation and prayer are valuable activities, but these pastors have no sense of a balance between participating in community and being alone.

The role and identity of a pastor become dangerous when people transfer great power and status to these, giving away a childlike trust to the pastor. The transference and trust blind people to the inappropriate nature of certain requests. These people may be willing to please the pastor in many ways, including sexual, and assume that if the pastor is asking, it must be all right. Conversely, wounded pastors who do not feel truly powerful may not be fully aware of the power their role has with poeple. Their own shame and dependence crave affirmation and may encourage the positive transference, even in unconscious ways. Some pastors consciously and unconsciously encourage sexually seductive behavior because of the affirmation and attention received.

Many situations in which a pastor becomes sexually inappropriate with a parishioner begin with the pastor being a warm and caring parentlike figure. When the parishioner responds with willing trust, the pastor can come to depend on and crave this adulation. His or her own needs may become more and more apparent in the relationship. Many victims have described a time when they felt that the relationship switched from one in which they were being cared for to one in which they were caring for the pastor.

All pastors have very demanding roles. People crave their time and attention. Sexually addicted pastors do not know how to balance their caregiving time with time of self-nurture. They may be starved for attention and nurture. Like all sex addicts, they interpret sex as equal to love and may seek to get their needs fulfilled sexually. There can be a certain adolescent anger to their interpretation of their neediness. They may complain about the demands of their people and project a martyrlike image of themselves. They may then also come to feel entitled to needs fulfillment. This angry, martyr-like entitlement is the fuel of self-delusion that can allow them to cross sexual boundaries.

Isolation

The pastoral role—at least, in most parish settings—is one in which there is very little accountability. A pastor may have elders, a church council, or a supervising pastor from the denomination (e.g., conference minister, bishop), but there is usually very little direct supervision. Many congregation members will put ministers on a pedestal, expecting them to be herolike. Atop this pedestal, clergy are expected to be self-sufficient and self-reliant, able to care for themselves. Clergy are expected to be alone and to not need monitoring.

There may also be many people around the church on a daily basis, but many of the pastor's normal daily activities afford the opportunity to leave. Pastors may have been isolated and alone as children, even experiencing the role of the lost child. As addicts, pastors will thrive on this aloneness. It affords them the opportunity to act out in private ways and maintain their double life, one public and honored, the other private and perverse.

Trust

Clergy are given, at least historically, a total measure of trust. This is the nature of the pedestal on which they sit. People transfer to clergy their need for a loving and nurturing parent and a direct link with God. God the father or mother often is personified in the role of pastor.

Unfortunately, for pastoral sexual addicts the trust and transference give them rather instant access to people's lives. This access may be abused. The priest whom we mentioned in the introduction to this article was trusted to be a surrogate father to boys in the parish. Parents did not worry that the boys were spending time with him. We worked with a congregation in which a priest had abused nine boys. Many of the members blamed the boys for the sexual activity; even one of the boys' fathers thought it must have been his fault. This is similar to those countless situations in which women are blamed for being sexual with a pastor.

The trust factor can allow a pastor to go unchallenged for years. People may ignore obvious symptoms of trouble because they need the pastor to be innocent and blameless. We worked with another church in which the general membership revolted against the leadership of the church for firing their beloved pastor. Historically, even church leaders have wanted to protect the role of pastor. This has led many to cover up sexual misconduct. The "geographic cure," in which a pastor is transferred to another situation, in all likelihood to repeat the same behavior, has sometimes been the result. Many have excused this behavior as being the quiet and loving thing to do for all concerned.

Consequences

Pastors, by the nature of their training, should know how to access help for themselves. Given a previously discussed dynamic, however, they know how to help others and not themselves. One of the excuses that we often hear as to why they do not go for help is "Who can I talk to confidentially?" There is often a built-in-fear of consequences in this question. If there is any inclination to reach out for help, it may be met with the knowledge that sinful sexual behavior is usually immediate grounds for loss of job and perhaps the privilege of ordination.

In the current legal climate, in which entire churches and even denominations have been sued for a pastor's sexual misconduct, the threat of immediate dismissal and inability to return to ministry is even more real. Legal liability has done much to prevent church leaders from even considering the question of restoration to ministry. It becomes harder to convince a pastor that it is better to be honest than it is to lead a miserable and secret life.

TREATMENT ISSUES

Treatment for a sexually addicted pastor is no different than treatment for anyone else. It may involve inpatient or intensive outpatient programs. Long-term care will require individual, marriage, and family therapy; attendance at support groups; and a network of accountability. Carne's (1997) model of recovery, containing educational, behavioral, and psychodynamic components, is the most effective form of treatment. This is because all of these areas need to be simultaneously attacked therapeutically. Pastors may otherwise tend to compartmentalize, theologize, or think in black-and-white terms about what they need.

It is often thought that clergy issues require special clergy support groups, that only other clergy will truly understand the issues involved. The factor of confidentiality may also be used by clergy to avoid general addiction groups. We have found, however, that although it may be occasionally helpful to provide clergy-only groups, it can be more helpful to participate in general recovery for sexual addiction. It may be just as important to recover from narcissism and dependence on the pastoral role as it is to recover from sexual addiction.

We suggest that sexually addicted pastors be given the time and opportunity to take a leave of absence from the pastoral role. This is obviously more difficult financially for pastors with families. This is true even for pastors whose sexual misconduct has not involved offending behavior. Offending behavior requires that for reasons of safety and legal liability, a pastor must leave at least the parish pastoral role. This time away from the role is important so that the addict can focus on recovery, both from sexual addiction and from the narcissism and dependence on pastoral role, and can learn how to care for self and not just others.

In addition, the pastoral role requires the following considerations.

Assessment

Pastors who are sexually addicted are impaired professionals. Chapter 19, by Richard Irons, discusses in depth the issues of impaired health-care professional. As such, we believe that they should be thoroughly assessed as to the degree of impairment. Such assessment will be important in determining a pastor's ability to continue to practice ministry or return to ministry after a period of rehabilitation. One of the key questions of assessment is whether it is safe for a pastor to practice ministry or whether there is a danger of further sexual misconduct. This will be particularly true if the pastor has sexually offended against a vulnerable person.

Richard Irons (1994) has been the pioneer in describing the nature of the assessment process. Irons stressed the importance of assembling a team of professionals that will participate in the assessment process. We have seen too many cases of clergy for whom an incorrect diagnosis has been made by one assessor trying to make a judgment after only a few hours of a one-to-one interview. Persons with narcissistic personality traits or characteristic addictive features of denial and delusion may easily be able to fool one person. In the Irons assessment model, however, psychometric testing, psychosocial interview, and addiction screening are administered by a variety of professionals, who can assemble a total picture from their individual diagnostic impressions.

The real goal of professional assessment is to recommend the appropriate forms of treatment that the diagnosis and level of impairment suggest. Clergy can be restored to the practice of ministry depending on the severity of their illness and the nature of the sexual misconduct.[2] A careful plan of ongoing rehabilitation and accountability can be designed, and ongoing sobriety or freedom from illness can be maintained (Irons, 1991). We feel that ministers who have received successful treatment may be 10 times less likely to sexually offend than the average seminary graduate.

Therapists working with clergy will find it helpful to use a third party to assess when and if a pastor is healthy enough to return to work. This takes the therapist out of the role of policing the client and helps to maintain the trust necessary in the therapeutic alliance.

Vocational Guidance

It is possible that sexual misconduct has created a situation in which it will be difficult for a minister to return to the practice of ministry or to certain forms of it. A minister who has offended against vulnerable members of a congregation will have difficulty returning to parish ministry. Some sex addicts have compared this with an alcoholic's being a bartender.

Clergy will need to reexamine their calling or vocation. There are dysfunctional reasons why a person may have chosen the ministerial role. Healing from this dysfunction must be found before a mature decision can be made.

---

2. In cases of sexual offending, the legal liabilities of denominational bodies may prevent them from being able to restore a minister to practice, even if the minister seems healthy enough to return.

Spiritual Direction

Another important facet of vocational guidance is spiritual direction. If a person is to find a true calling as a member of the clergy, that person's theology may dictate that this calling be heard from God. There has been a rich tradition of "soul care" for centuries in most faith traditions. In the 20th century, spiritual direction was often confused with psychological counseling. The field of pastoral counselor has vacillated back and forth as to whether a pastoral counselor provides psychological or spiritual counseling. We recommend that clergy receive spiritual direction from persons qualified in their faith tradition to provide it. Spiritual reflection, prayer, scripture study, theological study, and worship are the tools of the spiritual director. Meeting with this person can be a matter of daily or weekly activity and may coexist with counseling and support groups.

Spiritual direction can be an important component of the process of recovery from sexual addiction for all addicts. Resolution of early trauma demands that the trauma be recognized, felt, and grieved. Spiritual direction encourages efforts to forgive and reconcile. This may even include face-to-face meetings or symbolic written or spoken acts of forgiveness. This process may take years, but the goal of forgiveness is one that purely secular counseling often ignores.

Family Support

Clergy function in communities of faith. Their biological families are entrenched in these communities. In the process of intervening with clergy who have committed sexual misconduct, spouses and children are often ignored. The events of discovery of misconduct may be dramatic. Clergy have been asked to leave churches literally overnight. Family members have suddenly lost the ability to participate in their community, perhaps even being uprooted geographically. Public humiliation may be a factor in this process. Family members become the innocent secondary victims of the sexual misconduct. There have been too many situations, however, in which the wife's or children's needs have become secondary to the more urgent need to find help for a member of the clergy. Instead, family members have often been expected to "be strong" and to help emotionally, physically, spiritually, and financially to survive the crisis.

It is not uncommon for a spouse to be blamed for the sexual misconduct. If he or she had been more available emotionally and sexually, the clergy person would not have needed the outside sex. The herolike nature of the clergy role often prevents many from seeing where true responsibility for misconduct lies. This dynamic can make it even more difficult for family members to be seen as needing help.

It is also true that the same dysfunction that causes clergy to commit misconduct will create various forms of dysfunction in the family. Spouses may have their own backgrounds of trauma. Marriage issues may be very pronounced. Clergypersons may use this level of estrangement to justify their misconduct. It is important, therefore, for all members of clergy families to be assessed as to their own issues. Support and attention should be given equally to all members of the family.

Church Support

It is imperative to attend to the needs of the congregations served by sexually addicted clergy whose addiction or sexual misconduct has become public knowledge. The diagnosis of sexual addiction may or may not mean that a pastor has to leave his or her congregation. The presence of sexual offending behavior will usually be the determining factor.

For those pastors who remain in their churches, there will need to be a process of counseling between the pastor and the leadership of the church. This will not be unlike marriage and family counseling. A church is like any other system, and there can be just as many unhealthy dynamics as there are church members. If churches are places that reach out to wounded people, wounded people there will also project their issues onto each other. If the pastor's recovery can be used courageously as a model for others, more mature communities of faith can be built. Certainly, accountability for the pastor's recovery will be a vital part of this process.

In situations in which a pastor has to leave, it will be even more important to provide healing to the church congregation. There will be those who have been directly sexually violated (primary victims) and those whose trust and faith have been damaged (secondary victims).[3] It is important that congregants be allowed to voice feelings, whatever they are, during support groups or meetings set up by the church.

Countertransference

Working with pastoral sex addicts raises traditional countertransference issues that any professional might have. It is often challenging to deal with the narcissism, dependency, or addiction. The nature of sexual activity may be difficult to hear about. Working with sexual offending behavior is always a minefield, in how much it may get counselors in touch with their own trauma issues. In addition to these possibilities, working with clergy sex addicts also may raise issues of counselors' own faith. How do they see the role of pastoral authority? Have they

---

3. For a comprehensive treatment of working with congregations, see Hopkins & Laaser (1995).

been damaged emotionally, sexually, or spiritually by clergy in their past? What is the level of their faith in a God Who might allow these things to happen? It is not uncommon for faith and trust to be challenged by the sexual hypocrisy of those who call themselves clergy. Counselors' own level of maturity and spiritual support should be in some order before they try to deal with clergy.

If one is, however, able to bring healing to this group, it is rewarding work.

CONCLUSION

Sex addiction is about lust and the neurochemistry of lust. It is also about a search for intimacy. Sex addicts long for nurturance and acceptance. They are lonely and lack true community. In this search for intimacy, sex addiction is a confused spirituality. Much of what sex addicts experience is truly a matter of spiritual longing to be connected with God and with others. Sexual acts with self and others can be an attempt to find this connection, replacing real fellowship with fantasy or symbolic partners. If this is true, clergy are the most pronounced example of this type of spiritual confusion.

Working with pastoral sex addicts requires therapists to be familiar with traditional sex-addiction treatment, in addition to issues unique to the vocation. The vocation is often unconsciously chosen by the pastor to cover childhood trauma and sexual issues. Treatment must address this and include 12-step participation, behavioral and cognitive intervention, insight analysis, and expressive modalities designed to abreact the underlying trauma (Adams, 1997). Treatment should also include spiritual direction and assistance in values clarification. This allows the pastor to unearth the unconscious reasons for choosing the ministry and offers an opportunity to consciously choose the vocation from a position of spiritual and emotional maturity. Integrating sexuality into the whole of their selves, including their spirituality, is crucial to the prevention of sexual acting out.

Personality disorders and identity issues also need to be addressed in treatment. Entitlement, dependency, and narcissism are common themes. If the pastor returns to active ministry, an accountability program should be established. Getting an independent evaluation to determine the specifics of a return to work helps the therapist to maintain the trust and safety necessary in the therapeutic alliance.

Clergy who act out sexually with parishioners create primary and secondary victims: those who are directly violated and those whose trust and faith have been damaged by the pastor's addiction. The congregation is victimized by the projection of shame and the overmoralizing of sexual issues that the pastor's acting out causes. The pastor's family is also a casualty in the wake of sexual acting out.

Offering healing and treatment of pastors and their congregations are important steps in repairing communities damaged by sexual addiction. By bringing healing to this group, counselors assist in the transformation of sexually addicted pastors from those who can damage themselves or others to those who are truly wounded healers. Counselors also assist in building trust and maturity in members of faith communities who can positively affect the culture.

REFERENCES

Adams, K. M. (1991). *Silently seduced: When parents make their children partners, understanding covert incest.* Deerfield Beach, FL: Health Communications.

Adams, K. M. (1997). Case study. *Sexual Addiction and Compulsivity, 3,* 273–281.

Blanchard, G. (1991). Sexually abusive clergymen: A conceptual framework for intervention and recovery. *Pastoral Psychology, 4,* 237–246.

Carnes, P. (1991). *Don't call it love.* New York: Bantam.

Carnes, P. (1997). *Sexual anorexia: Overcoming sexual self-hatred.* Center City, MN: Hazelden.

Fowler, R. (1981). *The stages of faith.* New York: Harper & Row.

Friberg, N., & Laaser, M. (1998). *Before the fall.* Collegeville, MN: Liturgical Press.

Hopkins, N., & Laaser, M. (Eds.). (1995). *Restoring the soul of a church: Healing congregations wounded by clergy sexual misconduct.* Collegeville, MN: Liturgical Press.

Irons, R. (1991, Spring). Sexually addicted professional: Contractual provisions for reentry. *American Journal of Preventive Psychiatry and Neurology,* 57–59.

Irons, R. (1994). The breach of trust. In: *Sexually exploitive professionals* (pp. 350–379). New York: Sage.

Irons, R., & Laaser, M. (1994). The abduction of fidelity: Sexual exploitation by clergy—Experience with inpatient assessment. *Sexual Addiction and Compulsivity, 1,* 119–129.

Laaser, M. (1991). Sexual addiction and clergy. *Pastoral Psychology, 4,* 237–246.

Laaser, M. (1996). *Faithful and true.* Grand Rapids, MI: Zondervan.

Schwartz, M. F., & Master, W. H. (1994). Integration of trauma-based, cognitive, behavioral, systemic, and addiction approaches for treatment of hypersexual pair-bonding disorder. *Sexual Addictive and Compulsivity, 1,* 57–76.

CHAPTER 19

Sexually Addicted Health-Care Professionals

RICHARD R. IRONS

For medicine may be regarded generally as the knowledge of the loves and desires of the body and how to satisfy them or not; and the best physician is he who is able to separate fair love from foul, or to convert one into the other.
—Eryximachus in Plato's Symposium

The healing potential in the professional–patient relationship is facilitated by the inherent disparity in position, education, and power. Yet since its origin in prehistory, the healing profession has been shadowed by abuse of privilege. Sexual misconduct and offense are among the most common and egregious forms of abuse. Standards of conduct and ethical codes have been established to define ideals, expectations, and boundaries for health-care professionals. They sometimes fail to remain godlike and perfect in their discharge of duties, despite being held to these higher moral and ethical standards. For they are human and subject to the same maladies and shortcomings as the patients they serve.

Health-care professionals may or may not have multiple domains in which their sexual addiction is acted out. Some professionals are able to successfully compartmentalize their addiction, expressing it only outside professional practice or a committed relationship or only on the Internet. Although this compartmentalization is probably incomplete, the "rules" established by the narcissistic professional addict may preclude acting out within certain relationships because of the risk of significant harm and consequences for both the professional and the person under his or her care. Most sex addicts try to maintain the illusion of control by setting limits on their sexual fantasy or behavior. All health-care professionals have been trained to use delayed gratification of their own desires and to establish interpersonal boundaries with patients in order to serve as professionals in the service of patients. The large majority of sexually addicted health-care professionals in whom addiction was initially established before or outside of the professional workplace will try to maintain this limit until the late stages of their disease.

Each patient who comes to a health-care professional seeking help, relief, cure, or healing attempts to garner sufficient belief and trust in the professional, to implement the instructions and counsel given. Courage and faith permit the patient to surrender to the healing process beyond the boundaries of logic and sensibility.

IDENTIFICATION

The experience of seduction in a professional–patient relationship by either person takes on direct and immediate importance when events occurring between a professional and a patient lead to an allegation or formal complaint of professional sexual misconduct or offense. I have served as medical director of assessment programs that have formally evaluated more than 350 physicians, clergy, and lawyers who have been accused of such improprieties. Professional sexual misconduct and professional sexual offense present with a wide and diverse array of scenarios, as outlined in table 19.1. To precisely define the type and severity of professional impropriety, and to make accurate and appropriate diagnoses, it is important to gather as much information as possible about the events leading to assessment, including the specific nature of the thoughts, feelings, and actions that occurred between the physician and the complainant. A statement of the complainant(s)' description of events is crucial and should be obtained prior to beginning any evaluation or investigation. A sexually exploitive professional may utilize more than one scenario or may use variations on a given theme. The behavior in question is often ritualized and frequently compulsive in nature. Once an assessment team has been able to compare the physician's

Table 19.1. Common Sexual Impropriety Scenarios

- Patient's perception that therapeutic touch is erotic or sexual
- An extension of caretaking or emotional support beyond professional boundaries
- Romantic enmeshment with patient or coworker
- Use of power and position to advance sexual agendas
- *Fatal Attraction* enactment of a rescue fantasy
- Paternal or maternal nurturance of a patient
- Involvement with a family member of the patient
- Medical frotteurism, voyeurism, or exhibitionism
- Unnecessary or overextensive genital examination
- Rude/abusive/insensitive/verbally inappropriate solicitation
- Surgeon offering "sexually enhancing" procedures or offering sexual therapy for a patient's sexual or relationship problems
- Cultural dissonance between physician and patient becomes sexualized
- Molestation of patient who is physically, mentally, or emotionally unable to offer resistance or is under the influence of mood-altering substances
- Attempt by physician to resolve conflicts involving sexual preference
- Unconscious reenactment of incestuous desires or past sexual abuse

version of events with that of the complainant, it becomes possible in most cases to construct probable scenarios and to begin to establish a causal hypothesis on how and why impropriety may have occurred.

Professional sexual improprieties can generally be classified into one of three major categories: paraphilia, Sexual Disorder Not Otherwise Specified (NOS), or work-related problems. The essential features of a paraphilia, as defined in the *DSM-IV-TR* (American Psychiatric Association, 2000), involve recurrent, intense, sexually arousing fantasies; sexual urges; or behaviors generally involving (1) nonhuman objects, (2) the suffering or humiliation of oneself or one's partner, or (3) children or other nonconsenting persons, which occur over a period of at least 6 months. The diagnosis is made if the behavior, urges, or fantasies cause clinically significant distress or impairment in social, occupational, or other important areas of functioning (*DSM-IV-TR*, p. 566). A Sexual Disorder NOS is defined as "a sexual disturbance that does not meet the criteria for any specific sexual disorder and is neither a sexual dysfunction nor a paraphilia. Examples include (a) marked feelings of inadequacy concerning sexual performance or other traits related to self-imposed standards of masculinity or femininity, (b) distress about a pattern of repeated sexual relationships involving a succession of lovers who are experienced by the individual only as things to be used, and (3) persistent and marked distress about sexual orientation" (*DSM-IV-TR*, p. 582). Sexually addicted health-care professionals often fall into one of these two diagnostic categories. When the behavior, scenario, or both do not easily fit into either category and are not considered a direct symptom or manifestation of some other *DSM-IV-TR* Axis I diagnosis, then we have utilized the work-related problem (V62.2) descriptor for such professional sexual misconduct.

A more complete listing of possible Axis I diagnoses associated with professional sexual misconduct or offense is presented in table 19.2. Our assessment team members have found it helpful to complete the differential diagnosis on Axis I before considering Axes II and III. Psychosexual disorders and paraphilias, when identified, should be described as precisely as possible. If the NOS category is utilized, then it is important to use appropriate descriptors that define the features seen. In our program the most frequent features noted, in addition to specific paraphiliac behaviors, are those of addiction, exploitation, voyeur-

TABLE 19.2. Possible *DSM-IV TR* Diagnoses Associated
With Sexual Misconduct Other Than Sexual Disorders

- Organic Mental Disorder
- Erotomanic Delusional Disorder
- Bipolar Affective Disorder
- Obsessive Compulsive Disorder
- Atypical Dissociative Disorder
- Impulse Control Disorder
- Adjustment Disorder (with disturbance of conduct)

ism, predation, romance, and assault. The severity of the disorder, its duration, the current level of activity, and its amenability to treatment should also be defined to the greatest extent possible. Many cases involving professional sexual impropriety are associated with and at least partially attributable to characterologic pathology.

CONFRONTATION BY INTERVENTION

Intervention is the first action step in resolving allegations of professional sexual impropriety or misconduct. A successful intervention requires complete honesty and compassion on the part of those who are confronting the potentially impaired professional. A straightforward presentation of the allegation is almost always the best approach. Expression of concern on the part of concerned parties and authority figures who are present can help keep the accused from slipping into morbid despair and possible suicidal ideation or action, while nevertheless making it readily apparent that sexual harassment, abuse, and offense are intolerable and unacceptable. A good intervention reflects social justice by making the perpetrator of sexual exploitation accountable for the behavior and assuring the victim(s) that there will be no further misconduct. Experience suggests that professionals alleged to have engaged in sexual impropriety who are referred for formal assessment are a diverse, predominantly male population, who will commonly have one or more of a wide array of diagnosable illnesses. Although specialized professional assessment programs have found that many of these professionals have sexual disorders, significant numbers were found to have undiagnosed mental disorders. Some present with active substance dependency, acute mental illness, or acute psychiatric illness. The majority of these professionals can be helped, and it is possible for carefully selected professionals to re-enter professional life at some time in the future, with supervision and under carefully drafted and monitored recovery contracts.

Some will apply the philosophy of determinism to professional sexual misconduct. Others will consign offenders to exile, as examples for the public to see the wages of moral turpitude. Many will divide the lot into those who are "sick" and those who are "bad" (like the character Dr. "Hannibal the Cannibal" Lector in the film *Silence of the Lambs*). Through our choices, we will push professionals accused of sexual misconduct toward the medical model (assessment and treatment with potential rehabilitation) or toward the legal model, wherein they seek justice and a legal remedy to the allegations made against them. Whenever possible, professions dedicated to offering help and healing to others should extend the same services to peers who have encountered and experienced this occupational hazard. Table 19.3 outlines a general protocol that can be used to address allegations of professional sexual misconduct. Although treatment and therapy are often prolonged, many professionals experience personal healing and signifi-

TABLE 19.3. One Protocol for Confronting Allegations of Professional
Sexual Impropriety

1. Allegations of professional sexual misconduct should be carefully documented and
   serve as precipitating events in a peer review, licensure board investigatory process,
   or both.
2. When sufficient collateral information has been accumulated, then an independent
   multidisciplinary assessment by a team of experienced professionals is often useful,
   if the accused physician is cooperative.
3. If the accused professional is not willing to undergo independent assessment, then
   the concerned parties must decide whether due process or emergency action with
   due process is appropriate.

cant life transformation, especially when it is supported and encouraged. However, professional rehabilitation is possible for some, but not all, of those professionals who have been able to attain personal growth and genuine change. In
the hundreds of sexually exploitive professionals whom I have assessed, treated,
or known, only slightly more than one half of them have returned to their former
professional practice, and the mean time between intervention and professional
reentry is about 18 months.

Sexually inappropriate behavior by a professional involving a patient is illegal, as well as unethical. Professionals who engage in professional sexual misconduct are probably in violation of the state or provincial laws under which they
are permitted to practice. Some professionals who have committed professional
sexual offenses may be recurrent perpetrators. In some instances sexual exploitation will be reported to a professional board by a subsequent treating physician
or other therapist. It is generally perceived that licensure board actions are too
infrequent and too mild, but without timely reporting by victims and substantive information from other health-care providers, such cases continue to be
very difficult to substantiate to the point that definitive licensure board action
can be taken. In at least 15 of the 50 U.S. states, there are specific criminal laws
that define professional sexual misconduct as a specific felony. Professionals who
engage in predatory patterns of sexual exploitation do serve prison terms.

Victims who are able to overcome the trauma and pain associated with
sexual abuse may become empowered sufficiently to initiate and engage in criminal, civil, or administrative law (professional licensure board) actions that result
in other types of restitution, as well as revocation of professional licensure. In
most cases, victims do so because they wish to bring justice to the abusers of
power. Legal actions may require the victim to describe the specific behaviors
involved on multiple occasions and in public, which is often painful and traumatic. Witnesses often are understandably reluctant to testify, which compli-
cates appropriate prosecution. However, recurrent interludes of misconduct with
numerous patients will likely result in much more punitive action, including
revocation of licensure.

MULTIDISCIPLINARY ASSESSMENT

The professional entering an assessment becomes a patient and is requested to set aside the professional role and its attendant defensive armor. An assessment is usually a short-term residential or day process of 3 to 5 days that provides independent, objective, multidisciplinary assessment for possible mental illness and professional impairment. The assessment model presented here is based on 12 years of experience evaluating sexually exploitive professionals. It was developed in response to the need expressed by licensure boards, regulatory agencies, professional organizations, and the public for an objective forum in which allegations of sexual harassment, professional sexual misconduct, and professional sexual offense could be explored and considered independently from treatment, therapy, administrative due process, civil suits, and criminal legal proceedings. The crucial objective for the assessment team is to establish a causal hypothesis that helps explain the vulnerability of the victim(s) and the behavior of the accused professional. The ability to formulate such a hypothesis requires elaboration of the reality between the victim(s)', peers', and the professional's versions of events leading to the formal complaint(s). The degree to which this hypothesis can reconcile disparities in the multiple accounts of the events determines to a large measure the value, acceptance, and utility of the assessment conclusions and recommendations.

It is important to reiterate whenever necessary that the assessment is not a trial and that the team members are not being asked to sit as judges or jurors. Assessments are not intended to substitute for the finding of facts and adjudication inherent in legal proceedings, but rather as an alternative or supplementary means by which an impartial inquiry into the physical and mental health of the accused professional may be conducted. Possible personal vulnerabilities, mitigating as well as aggravating factors, cognitive distortions, and errors in judgment that may have substantially contributed to the allegations brought forward can be considered within the medical model. Diagnoses and recommendations made by team consensus during clinical staffing may be accepted and implemented as deemed appropriate by all concerned parties. Using this model, the team can agree about 95% of the time on conclusions and opinions regarding

- professional impairment or potential impairment
- diagnoses based on *DSM* criterion
- recommended courses of action
- whether professional rehabilitation appears feasible and realistic
- the ability of the professional to practice medicine under supervision and with corrective action, while maintaining and protecting public safety, at present or in the foreseeable future.

When the factual disparity between the complainant's and the professional patient's versions of events remains too great, then the assessment team should not advance a causal hypothesis, but instead should report the assessment as inconclusive and recommend that the matter be forwarded into formal legal process (Irons, 1994).

The assessment model described is comprehensive, but often very expensive. It has some other significant limitations as well. There is no uniform or standard nomenclature or definition of professional sexual impropriety, and standards vary from profession to profession and from one assessment team to another. Assessment professionals are often requested to do a comprehensive evaluation without a team of evaluators or will find that the only way they can complete an assessment requires component evaluations to be done independently and without the opportunity to arrive at conclusions and opinions by consensus. The expectations from an assessment and the type chosen commonly depend on the concerned party who has confronted the individual. Regulatory agencies (e.g., hospitals, managed care organizations, state or provincial licensure boards) will have a different perspective and agenda than do professional organizations or employers. And finally, individuals and organizations that do evaluation as a initial part of the treatment process have an inherent conflict of interest even if they offer other treatment alternatives, as most patients (including professional patients) will find it difficult, if not impossible, to choose an alternative. There is an inherent tendency to diagnose what you know and can treat.

In our published, peer-reviewed study (Irons & Schneider, 1994) of 137 consecutive health-care professionals referred for a formal multidisciplinary assessment of alleged professional sexual offense, 93% of the professionals were found to have work-related problems related to sexual conduct. At least 66% acknowledged sexual exploitation in their professional practice, and in 27% such exploitation was not found to be present, based on the information available. In 7% of the cases, the professional denied exploitation, although collateral information was believed to be credible; therefore, the assessment results were deemed inconclusive. It is of interest that 65% of these professionals were diagnosed with a sexual disorder, usually a paraphilia, whereas 30% did not meet diagnostic criteria. Even so, 86% of this subpopulation of 41 professionals without a defined sexual disorder were still believed to have work problems related to their sexual conduct. In the entire sample of 137, 58% were determined to be professionally impaired at the time, and 10% were found to be potentially impaired. We recommended inpatient treatment for 49% of these professionals and outpatient treatment for another 43%. No treatment was recommended for only 2% (3) of our study population. These 3 professionals presented with allegations that the assessment team believed were either false or grossly exaggerated. In 10 cases (7%), treatment recommendations could not be made because assessment results were inconclusive. Of the 88 patients in our study diagnosed with a sexual disorder, 73% were defined as sexually exploitive in their professional practice, 87% had work-related complications, and 85% were found to have addictive features associated with their disorder. Thirty-eight percent (33) were diagnosed with chemical dependency.

The lack of standard protocols for assessments, the problems with maintaining consistency even within a dedicated assessment program, and the reasons for conducting the assessment (e.g., punishment, rehabilitation, defense against a malpractice claim, or a last chance to reconcile a marriage when the spouse discovers she has been betrayed) make comparison of assessments from different providers difficult. Professionals with more financial and professional assets to lose are more likely to get sophisticated evaluations, in contrast to those who have leaner resources or who engage in limited or "general" professional practice.

TREATMENT, THERAPY, AND PROFESSIONAL REHABILITATION

Historically, most of the treatment provided for professionals who engaged in sexual violations was given through individual psychotherapy or as an adjunct to treatment for either a substance-related disorder or some other *DSM* Axis I disorder. A major area of controversy, as well as a conundrum to research that workers in this area have experienced, is in defining when an Axis I mental disorder (with or without Axis III medical conditions) has contributed significantly enough to be considered a mitigating cause for the sexual offense(s). Skeptics are eager to suggest that those facing consequences for sexual exploitation wish to "flee into illness or addiction" to avoid taking personal responsibility for engaging in unprofessional conduct. Some academic nimrods would rather wash their hands of the whole mess by concluding that most professional boundary violations (and particularly serial patterns of sexual misconduct) are a manifestation of characterologic pathology and will be found to be part of an unsavory personality disorder.

Often, initial treatment for professionals who are evaluated and found to have sexual disorders, other mental disorders, or both, associated with professional sexual misconduct, begins at residential sites or by using day intensive programs that adhere to one of the following models. Each model has its own strengths, weaknesses, limitations, and biases.

Cognitive/Behavioral (Including Community Offender Treatment)

Gene Abel, at the Institute for Behavioral Medicine in Atlanta, Georgia, has extensive experience in cognitive/behavioral treatment over more than 20 years of work. Two methods appear to be especially helpful for disrupting the cognitive distortions of professionals involved in sexual misconduct. First, in a group setting, members are able to confront and challenge the irrationality or rationalization within each other's justifications and beliefs. A second method is to have the professional perpetrator write a letter to one of his victims, explaining in detail all the ways the professional groomed and manipulated the patient-victim to encourage and seduce the patient into sexual activity. Such letters should never be mailed to the patient-victim, of course. Abel and colleagues focus on "developing skills to decrease arousal, including the development of safeguards to attempt to prevent the professional from ending up in a high-risk situation again," paralleling the authors' work with other types of sex offenders, but extending it considerably (Abel, Osborn, & Warberg, 1995). Abel believes that professional sexual misconduct has features in common with paraphilia, and that about 20% of sexually exploitive physicians in his treatment program have an actual paraphilia that extends into their medical practice, usually manifested as exhibitionism, voyeurism, frottage, or rape (Abel & Osborn, 1999). Psychophysiologic measures such as the penile plethysmograph and the use of the polygraph (lie detector) may be utilized in diagnosis or evaluation of treatment outcomes.

Typically, a period of evaluation and intensive treatment is followed by a structured aftercare program, including cognitive-behavioral therapy, reeducation, and a strong emphasis on relapse prevention. Examples of reentry plans and procedures are available in the literature (Abel & Osborn, 1999; Abel, Osborn, & Warberg, 1995; Schoener, Milgrom, Gonsiorek, Luepker, & Conroe, 1989). Abel states that of the physicians referred to his treatment program, 52% have returned to practice. Of the 18% who have not returned to practice, nearly two thirds were removed from practice by their medical board or as a result of criminal action. The number of patients victimized, the sex of the victims, and the extent of sexual involvement (voyeurism, frotteurism, frottage, oral or anal sex, intercourse, or extensive affairs) are not major factors in determining the acceptability of a physician returning to practice. Instead, assuming successful completion of treatment, it is primarily the ability to establish a practice plan that protects the public that determines the viability of professional reentry (Abel & Osborn, 1999).

ADDICTION MODEL

In our previous study of consecutive professionals presenting for assessment with allegations of professional sexual misconduct, more than half of those evaluated met the *DSM* criteria for addictive sexual disorders, active substance dependency, or both (Irons & Schneider, 1994). Many sexually exploitive health-care professionals have derived great and lasting benefits from completion of a formal addiction treatment program. Although some residential treatment providers have claimed high recovery rates for professionals with primary substance dependency, there exist few, if any, large-scale controlled studies. The treatment recovery rates

TABLE 19.4. Cognitive Behavioral Components of Treatment for Professional Sexual Misconduct

---

A. Cognitive-Behavioral Therapy
  - Identification and disruption of chain of events leading to sexual misconduct
  - Identification and correction of cognitive distortions supporting sexual misconduct
  - Building victim empathy
  - Behavior therapy techniques to decrease paraphilic interests
B. Treatment to resolve emotional conflicts contributing to sexual misconduct
  - Psychotherapy to treat chronic anxiety, depression, anger, stress, or personality disorders
  - Skills training to correct assertive and social skills deficits
  - Bibliotherapy
  - Required writing of a referenced paper on the relationship of his or her emotional problems to sexual misconduct
C. Methods to ensure patient protection
  - Practice of style alterations
  - Physical layout of medical workplace to allow monitoring
  - Specific patient education and protection
  - Staff and colleague surveillance systems
  - Polygraphs

(Adapted from Abel & Osborn, 1999.)

reported are usually either directly compiled by the treatment center marketing department or by a research organization that the center contracts to do the work. Few studies have used prospective study methodology. Many rely on responses without objective corroboration and do not take into account patients who did not complete treatment or who were administratively discharged. In some treatment centers, the psychoeducational part of the treatment program and the group therapy component contain patients with different types of substance-related disorders, addictive sexual disorders, or both and will at times have patients who are victims of professional sexual misconduct. This approach has the tendency to treat sexual boundary violations as secondary to the substance or sexual addiction. The profound impact of professional sexual boundary violations on victims and their families, and the cognitive distortions professionals have acquired, may not be addressed during primary treatment, when the emphasis is on abstinence and powerlessness over mood-altering behavior. Developmental and dynamic themes of individual patients may often not be fully explored or developed, especially if the patient is not comfortable sharing last abusive or traumatic shame-bound events in therapy groups. In the past decade, more sophisticated treatment providers began utilizing competency-based individualized treatment plans, which do provide both structure and a theoretic base that most patients can understand and apply.

Analytical/Dynamic

When professional sexual boundary violations are believed to primarily repre-sent a manifestation of preexisting characterologic pathology, long-term insight-oriented dynamic individual therapy is often recommended. This approach is particularly suited to patients who are considered "psychologically minded," meaning that they have the capacity for introspection and development of in-sight. The goals and objectives of such therapy are often vaguely or inconsis-tently defined and deemed accomplished. Therapy is traditionally based on the professional patient's perceptions, with little or limited emphasis placed on com-paring those with the victim's perceptions or depositions available from con-cerned parties or agencies. The latter groups may influence the initial goals of therapy, but seldom are able to monitor therapy effectively or provide their in-put on adjustment of goals or completion of primary treatment.

Despite more than 100 years of experience using this approach, it remains difficult to determine the effectiveness of therapy, because controlled studies would be extremely difficult, if not impossible, to construct. The variation in treatment between practitioners, as well as the variation an individual practitio-ner may exhibit in treating different patients, is very difficult to define and quan-tify. Dr. Glen Gabbard (1994) has acquired extensive clinical experience with professional sexual boundary violations in his years at the Menninger Clinic in Topeka, Kansas. He uses a typology of professional sexual misconduct, in which professionals fall into one of four groups with a roughly ascending order of frequency: (a) professionals who are "lovesick"; (b) professionals captivated by a romanticized masochistic surrender ("giving in" to a challenging or difficult cli-ent, hoping to mollify the client by being flexible with boundaries); (c) preda-tory psychopathy and paraphilias; and (d) psychotic disorders. Within the romanticized and especially the "lovesick"category, he has accumulated a signifi-cant number of professional patients whom he has evaluated and treated, which includes professionals with masochistic and self-destructive tendencies who pas-sively allow clients to intimidate or control them. He believes that delving in depth into issues or dynamics that are acted out through the sexual misconduct leads over time to healing and transformation.

Some of the more common and significant themes addressed in such dy-namic therapy include

- Unconscious reenactment of incestuous longings
- Wishes for maternal nurturance misperceived as sexual attraction
- Enactment of rescue fantasies on the stage of one's professional life
- Lonely patient perceived as idealized version of self or transformational object
- Confusion of therapist's needs with patient's needs
- Repression of rage at patient's successful thwarting of therapeutic efforts
- Patient's anger at organization, institute, or authority

- Manic defense against mourning and grief at termination
- Conflicts regarding sexual identity or orientation

Gabbard has written an analytic yet lucid book describing ways love and hate are replicated to some extent in the analytic setting through the externalization of internal object relations. Of course, the analytic situation is intended to be the stage for the analysand's externalization of object relations— not the analyst's (Gabbard, 1991). The principles he deftly expounds on loving relationships and romantic space are based on "the dialectical relationship and tension between the paranoid-schizoid and depressive modes of experiencing, with the ever-present potential to collapse in one direction or the other." He subdivides transference hate into two broad categories analogous to the distinction between erotic and erotized transference (Gabbard, 1991b).

> In the more benign variety, the patient recognizes that the hate is in part internally derived and therefore requires analysis. The hateful feelings are ego dystonic, so the patient maintains a therapeutic alliance with the analyst in pursuit of understanding the feelings rather than acting on them. In the malignant variant, the "as if" quality of the feeling disappears, and the patient views the analyst not as a figure similar to someone from the patient's past, but rather as a truly malevolent individual deserving of hatred, identical in that sense to the original object. Analytic space collapses so that the patient is operating in a world that seriously compromises the therapeutic alliance. (Gabbard 1996)

Professionals are often conflicted about the acknowledgment of anger, let alone hate. In rich commentaries over the years on physicians' internal dynamics, George Valiant reminds us that reaction formation is a pervasive form of defense and an expression of the resentment professionals feel when their labors in the service of others are not appreciated.

In my opinion, an eclectic combination of these models tailored to the needs and psychopathology of the professional being treated provides the optimal treatment and therapy necessary for personal healing and professional rehabilitation. Anger, based on resentment, bitterness, and hatred acted out through professional sexual misconduct, inflicts destructive consequences on many others beyond the perpetrator and primary victim(s). Commonly, the destructive anger harbored by professionals in treatment bears the mark of either resentment or envy. This caustic poison acts itself out through attacking, judgmental thoughts, and unconscious vindictive actions against themselves and others. The atonement of such anger is found in the exploitive professionals' determination to seek the roots of their own rage and past trauma. Through abreaction and insight, empathy for their victims can be found. Months or years later, another form of restitution may be possible. The offending professional might have the opportunity to accept and appreciate the need for those harmed to express their anger, indignation, and outrage without hiding behind intellectual defenses and rationalizations. When able to access the courage to endure confrontation of this poisonous anger, the wounded professional may discover that the anger is derived from an arrogant inflation of perceived duty (within his or her professional persona). Anger and self-pity can arise from witnessing innocent suffering or the experience of emotional, litigation-based, intellectual, or physical trauma in the course of professional service. At this juncture, true and genuine personal restitution is possible (Irons & Roberts, 1995).

Controlled studies that can look at these treatment models and compare their efficacy are needed. In the future it may be possible to assign professional patients to various subsets with specific type(s) of professional sexual misconduct and congruent personal psychopathology, then differentiate the effectiveness of each treatment model for that specific subset.

THE CRUNCH: IS THE PROFESSIONAL SAFE TO RESUME PRACTICE?

Following intervention and initial treatment, professional boundary violators who have not engaged in "egregious" professional sexual misconduct customarily will expect to return to work, even if they have not completed a full course of treatment or therapy. With a continuing trend toward criminalization of professional–patient sexual violations, many of these professionals and their legal advocates are becoming less concerned with early professional reentry. There is increasing recognition of the fact that through evaluation, primary treatment and continuing progress toward the achievement of personal recovery goals, such professionals may be able to take genuine responsibility for their unethical or unprofessional conduct or both, offer restitution, and demonstrate rehabilitation potential. It is difficult to predict how long a sexually exploitive professional may have to withdraw from practice when treatment is in the early stages. Professionals in treatment often feel that their inability to remain gainfully employed and the uncertainty about whether they may return to their previous practice only adds to their burden of guilt and shame. The expense of treatment increases the degree of negative cash flow and can make it difficult to concentrate on recovery, especially when accompanied by a fear of losing family and financial stability. Fortunately, many professionals have disability insurance, business overhead insurance, or other buffers against such adversity. In the last decade, it has become more difficult for professionals in treatment to maintain their long-term disability claims, especially if they have lost professional licensure. Professionals in treatment need honest responses to their questions regarding the length of expected treatment prior to gaining the opportunity to return to professional practice. Before it is possible to make a balanced and realistic determination of professional rehabilitation potential, documented progress on a number of fronts

TABLE 19.5. Prerequisites for Professional Reentry

1. Successful completion of primary treatment, as defined by the treatment program and also by concerned parties
2. Records from initial evaluation and treatment, which define the nature of the professional's sexual disorder and any other addictive disease, psychiatric disorders, or medical problems known to be present, as well as plans for continuing care
3. Assurance by the treatment team that its members believe, to the best of their knowledge, that the professional is able to practice his or her profession with reasonable skill and safety
4. Definition by the treatment team, regulatory bodies (when appropriate), and other concerned parties of specific boundaries within which the professional will be able to practice

---

must be attained. Table 19.5 outlines common prerequisites a professional should have before return to work can be safely and reasonably considered.

The time any professional may need to complete these prerequisites varies considerably. In my 15 years of experience, I have found that 6 to 12 months is not uncommon, and the mean time is probably greater than a year. As a result, many professionals must find nonclinical or nonprofessional work during this uncertain period until rehabilitation is complete, and it is possible to determine if professional reentry is feasible. Successful and effective treatment almost always requires at least some intensive group therapy within a therapeutic milieu. Self-diagnosis and self-disclosure are extremely important passages in the recovery process, albeit painful and difficult experiences for the professional who has exploited his or her patients (clients) and who feels guilt and shame about past personal and professional behavior. The task of acknowledging one's lack of control over the sexual behavior and the acquisition of a strong desire to heal, change, and grow are critical passages in the treatment process. Many professionals are able to return to a monitored practice, but the timing of the return must be carefully staged in the therapeutic process. In most states, relapse will lead to the loss of licensure and destroy hope of future return to professional status.

In some situations, especially when the completion of these prerequisites exceeds 2 years, a comprehensive reassessment by an objective team (or therapist) skilled in the management of professionals seeking professional reentry can be extremely helpful. In such a process, the assessment team should review treatment and therapy, confirm the working diagnostic impressions and treatment plans, and recommend practical steps the professional can take to professional reentry, professional rehabilitation, or vocational counseling that will help the health-care professional transition into a nonclinical career.

In the arena of professional sexual boundary violations that includes workplace sexual harassment, it is becoming increasingly clear that there is little, if any, tolerance for even minor levels of recidivism. Furthermore, there will be increased resistance to any professional admitting to sexual harassment, due to the severe potential consequences incorporated into federal employment laws. The use of chaperons or workplace monitors is commonly utilized, but has limitations as a deterrent against either professional sexual misconduct or sexual harassment. For health-care professionals who engage in direct patient contact, it is crucial for them to recognize that any patient encounter can evoke transference, countertransference, or both. In the early stages of professional reentry, limited trust and credibility, uncertainty, and even misunderstandings regarding boundaries or behavioral intent will have the potential of adversely influencing the fragile conditions under which the professional is permitted to resume professional practice. If chaperons do offer only limited protection of public safety, they at least reduce the risk of groundless allegations against a vulnerable reentering practitioner. This is why the use of a comprehensive and closely monitored professional rehabilitation/reentry contract is so important.

CONTRACTUAL PROVISIONS FOR PROFESSIONAL REENTRY

At this juncture, it is then possible to draft a suitable contingency contract specific enough to be useful in promoting continuing recovery. Prerequisites will vary from situation to situation and will need to be agreed on by all concerned parties. Concerned parties may include the employer, the professional's partners or business, the hospital in which the professional has practice privileges, or a state professional health or rehabilitation program. Any of the concerned parties may serve as the *contracting program*, as the term is used herein. If a professional licensing board is involved, its input and cooperation are crucial for this reentry tool to be effective.

The following 15 contractual elements have been found to be of value in drafting a contract for the returning professional (Irons, 1991). Each should be considered for inclusion individually, for all may not apply to a given situation.

For many behavioral boundary violations, attempts at behavioral modification and verbal or written warnings to address questionable behavior have been issued before. The goals now are to provide a mechanism for protection of the professional patient relationship, to allow restoration of credibility and trust, and to promote corrective action. Recovering sexually exploitive professionals who return to their community and their practice present a model of healing that can instill hope and optimism in others struggling with this addiction, their codependents, and the victims of this devastating disorder.

1. The professional acknowledges pain and suffering from a specific sexual disorder and attendant defects of character and agrees to abstain from certain specific behaviors in personal and professional life.
2. The professional establishes and defines a recovery network. Persons within this network may include family members, significant others, trusted friends,

mentors, sponsors, and individuals from the professional's workplace. The recovery network may meet initially and as needed to ensure that all participants understand the terms of the contract and the established boundaries.

3. The professional agrees to continue in treatment with a therapist experienced in treatment of the sexual disorder and any other relevant mental disorders, providing that the treatment is also acceptable to the directors of the contracting program or concerned parties. Both individual and group therapy should be considered. Regular, timely written reports (at least quarterly) should be provided to the contracting program or to a mental health professional who provides "oversight" of the clinical progress and who makes such reports to the contracting program and necessary concerned parties.

4. The professional identifies a primary care physician who is experienced and informed about the treatment of addictions and sexually transmitted diseases, including AIDS. The designated physician will see the professional for medical review on a regular basis and will agree to be part of the individual's recovery network.

5. The recovering professional agrees to respect, defend, and uphold specific practice boundaries established and supported by all concerned parties. These boundaries should be defined in this clause as precisely as possible.

6. The professional agrees to a precise and regular monitoring of practice boundaries through an established regular procedure. This may include:

    a. The use of a professional "clinical associate" for a professional–patient (client) interaction;
    b. Regular practice review by a peer professional;
    c. Random patient chart reviews;
    d. The use of patient satisfaction surveys, which are reviewed by the practice monitor;
    e. Regular reports by the designated practice monitor, usually a professional peer, to the contracting program and concerned parties at specified intervals; or any combination of these.

7. The professional agrees to provide body fluid samples on request for the purpose of determining the presence of any mood-altering substances, including alcohol. If the individual has a history of substance abuse or dependency, testing should be done on a random basis. If no such history exists, then testing should be done if there is reasonable cause to suspect substance use that may directly or indirectly be affecting professional performance.

8. The professional agrees to monitoring of compliance with prescribed psychotropic medication if determined necessary, with reports forwarded to the contracting program.

9. When appropriate for inclusion in the contract, there may be a provision in which the recovering professional agrees to participate actively in a 12-step program for sexual addiction recovery that promotes only healthy nonsexual relationships among group members.

10. The professional may also agree to encourage and support both treatment and 12-step program participation for family members and others with whom the professional has continuing social contact.
11. The professional agrees to complete professional education, or specific courses on professional boundaries, ethics, interpersonal communication, or anger management, if requested.
12. The professional agrees that the terms of this contract, and especially the professional practice boundaries, will be disclosed to others, including patients (clients) on a "need to know" basis. This provision needs to carefully and precisely define who needs to know and what they need to know.
13. The contracting program, members of the recovery network, and concerned parties outline their obligation to report sexual offenses, professional impairment, and sexual misconduct as defined by state law. Professional impairment, professional misconduct, and violations of this contract will be reported to the state licensing board as required by state law and by any stipulated agreement the professional may have with the state's licensing board. It is recommended that copies of these specific laws be provided to the recovering professional. The signed agreement needs to state that violations will be promptly reported.
14. The contracting program agrees to provide advocacy and continuing support for the professional. The program will regularly review the professional's progress in recovery and compliance with the provision of this contract. It will provide timely written reports to regulatory bodies and agencies that require them.
15. The professional agrees to continue participation in this recovery program for a defined period of time with annual review of contract terms.

A contract so constructed defines boundaries of acceptable personal and professional behavior. It provides a mechanism by which a professional can take responsibility for his or her conduct, while participating in a state professionals' program that provides a support system for complying with contractual requirements. The success or failure of the contract depends on the effectiveness of the monitoring provision. It is essential that a clear statement of the consequences for violating the contract provision sends an unambiguous message to the professional that the responsibility for maintaining compliance lies with him or her and not with the supporting professional program.

The provision determining disclosure of the terms of the contract (on a "need to know" basis) will vary from state to state and from situation to situation, but the policy is a critical feature of the agreement. Professionals in early recovery find disclosure difficult to accept because it potentially can result in discredit and rejection. Disclosure protects all involved parties—the professionals' patients (or clients), the public, the advocates for the professionals, and even the recovering professionals themselves. Resistance to this disclosure provision—

or attempts to minimize it—provides some evidence of how well the professional is handling the reentry process. Ongoing group therapy with other recovering professionals helps the individual deal with the powerful emotions that inevitably arise during implementation of contract terms. The spirit with which the professional accepts and facilitates monitoring will also vary. It is hoped that this set of recovery contract provisions for professionals will assist those who address the complex and challenging problems of sexual and characterologic disorders in this population. Continued growth in our understanding of the nature of sexual exploitation and further knowledge about treatment approaches and continuing care will help us rehabilitate professionals who truly are unable to help themselves. They have much to teach us if we are willing to listen and learn.

REFERENCES

Abel, G., Osborn, C., & Warberg, B. (1995). Cognitive-behavioral treatment for professional sexual misconduct. *Psychiatric Annals, 25,* 106–112.

Abel, G., & Osborn, C. (1999). Cognitive-behavioral treatment of sexual misconduct. In J. D. Bloom, C. C. Nadelson, & M. T. Notman (Eds.), *Physician sexual misconduct* (pp. 225–246). Washington, DC: American Psychiatric Press.

American Psychiatric Association. (1994). *Diagnostic and statistical manual of mental disorders (DSM-IV)* (4th ed.). Washington, DC: Author.

American Psychiatric Association. (2000). *Diagnostic and statistical manual of mental disorders, text revision (DSM-IV-TR)* (4th ed., rev.). Washington, DC: Author.

Eddy, D. (1990). Designing a practice policy. *Journal of the American Medical Association, 263,* 3077–3084.

Gabbard, G. O. (1991). Technical approaches to transference in the analysis of borderline patients. *International Journal of Psychoanalysis, 72,* 625–637.

Gabbard, G. O. (1994). Sexual misconduct. In J. Oldham & M. Riba (Eds.), *Review of Psychiatry* (Vol. 13, pp. 433–456). Washington, DC: American Psychiatric Press.

Gabbard, G. O. (1996). *Love and hate in the analytic setting.* Northvale, NJ: Jason Aronson.

Irons, R. (1991). Contractual provisions for working with physician sexual addicts. *American Journal of Preventive Psychiatry and Neurology, 2*(3), 48–50.

Irons, R. (1994). Inpatient assessment of the sexually exploitive professional. In J. Gonsiorek (Ed.), *Breach of trust: Sexually exploitive professionals* (pp. 163–175). Thousand Oaks, CA: Sage.

Irons, R., & Roberts, K. (1995). The unhealed wounders: Seductive and sexually exploitive clergy. In N. Friberg, D. K. Haskin, H. Hopkins, M. R. Laaser, & N. M. Hopkins (Eds.), *Restoring the soul of a church: Healing congregations wounded by clergy sexual misconduct* (pp. 33-51). Collegeville, MN: Liturgical Press.

Irons, R., & Schneider, J. (1994). Sexual addiction: A significant factor in sexual exploitation by health care professionals. *Sexual Addiction and Compulsivity, 1,* 4–21.

Schoener, G., Milgrom, J., Gonsiorek, J., Luepker, E., & Conroe, R. (1989). *Psychotherapists' sexual involvement with clients: Intervention and prevention.* Minneapolis, MN: Walk-In Counseling Center.

CHAPTER 20

The Homeless and Sex Addiction

KEN McGILL

INTRODUCTION

Homelessness in America is one of the most complex phenomena this country has ever attempted to address. The very mention of the word conjures disparate emotions, experiences, and issues for clinicians who endeavor to provide effective treatment and interventions with the population. Providing treatment of any kind for the homeless is challenging and complex, as the clinician must function as one of many team members in the "constellation" of providers who deliver integrated and comprehensive care, with the overall goal of seeing the homeless person become self-efficacious. Providing clinical treatment for the sexually addicted homeless person is complicated by the fact that at any moment, the clinician may have to switch from the role of the therapist, whose focus is on addressing important therapeutic goals with the client, to that of the coordinator, whose immediate focus is to intervene and access resources that will satisfy important biopsychosocial needs of the homeless person.

The purpose of this chapter is to examine what clinical case management looks like with the sexually addicted homeless person, highlighting practical strategies and clinical interventions that must be addressed and delivered in order for proficient treatment to occur with members of this underserved population. It must be noted, though, that the material presented in this chapter is not intended to be an exhaustive examination of the subject of clinical case management with the sexually addicted homeless person. In reality, there has not been much specific research done on this very deserving topic. The information presented in the next few pages attempts to provide the reader with a basic overview of the subject, as well as to demonstrate that further research is necessary to reveal how the correlation between traumas experienced in the lives of homeless persons, combined with chronic drug dependence, create a set of circumstances in their lives where sexually addictive behavior not only is present, but also results in what the literature calls sex addiction (Carnes, 1997; Greenblatt & Robertson, 1993; Griffin-Shelley, 1997; Susser et al., 1995). An integrative treatment model of sex addiction will be suggested, with specific applications made to the homeless sex addict. Before case conceptualization occurs, though, we must know who the homeless client is and, most important, the unique issues that homeless people are likely to present with in the counseling situation.

THE HOMELESS POPULATION IN THE UNITED STATES

In 1999, the National Law Center on Homelessness and Poverty (2000) estimated that 700,000 people in the United States experience homelessness on any given night of the year, and up to 2 million people experience homelessness during a 1-year period. Of these numbers, the National Law Center (2000) reports that 25 to 30% are mentally disabled, 30% are veterans, and 40% are drug or alcohol dependent. Given these numbers, it is estimated that the number of homeless people who are challenged with drug- or alcohol-dependency in this country is about 300,000 people. Although the demographics of the homeless population are diverse, research indicates that the homeless person is likely to be between the ages of 31 and 50, African American, and male, even though homeless families that are headed by single mothers are among the fastest-growing segment of the population (National Coalition for the Homeless, 2000).

What constitutes homelessness? According to the Stewart B. McKinney Act of 1994, a person is considered homeless who lacks a fixed, regular, and adequate nighttime residence and has a primary night residency that is (a) a supervised publicly or privately operated shelter designed to provide temporary living accommodations . . . , (b) an institution that provides a temporary residence for individuals intended to be institutionalized, or (c) a public or private place not designed to be, or ordinarily used as, a regular sleeping accommodation for human beings (National Coalition for the Homeless, 1999).

Causes contributing to homelessness are inadequate job skills and education in a changing job environment that requires technical skills; chronic unemployment and high levels of poverty among those unable to find work; decreases in government benefits; deinstitutionalization of the mentally ill without adequate follow-up services; and personal crises in families (Hopper & Hamberg, 1984; U.S. Conference of Mayors, 1995; Wallace, 1988). For the clinician, homeless people may present into therapy with the following health problems: liver disease, seizure disorders, drug-resistant mycobacterium tuberculosis infection, elevated rates of hypertension, pulmonary disease, arterial disease, nutritional deficiencies, respiratory and gastrointestinal infections, scabies and lice infestations, frostbite, and heatstroke, along with leg ulcers and chronic venous insufficiency (Harris, Mowbray, & Solartz, 1994; McCarty, Argeriou, Huebner, &

Lubran, 1991). In addition, homeless people may also present with alcohol and drug dependence; elevated rates of mental illness; trauma from accidents, as well as from physical and sexual abuse, both as children and as adults; various injuries and amputation of limbs or digits due to infection at injection sites; HIV; and especially, because of the crack cocaine epidemic, sexually transmitted diseases (Hoff, 1989; Howard, 2000; Morse & Calsyn, 1992; Pablos-Mendez, Raviglione, Battan, & Ramos–Zuniga, 1990; Raba, 1990; Redliner, 1994; Sgroi & Bunk, 1988; Torres, Lefkowitz, Kales, & Brickner, 1980). J. D. Wright (1989) states, "the homeless persons who abuse either alcohol or drugs are generally in the worst possible shape, more estranged, less intact, sicker and with the poorest prospects for the future" (p. 102).

Although substance abuse, psychiatric problems, and health problems, combined with the absence of safe and affordable housing, interrelate and exacerbate the distress on the homeless (American Public Health Association, 1990; Harris et al., 1994; McCarty et al., 1991), Goodman, Saxe, and Harvey (1991), Figley (1985), and van der Kolk (1987) use a construct of psychological trauma as a means of understanding the potential effects of homelessness on individuals and families. In defining psychological trauma, Figley (1985) and van der Kolk (1987) refer to psychological trauma as a set of responses to extraordinary, emotionally overwhelming, and personally uncontrollable life events. As a result, these events may cause the person to demonstrate many of the symptoms that are grouped to form the diagnostic entity post-traumatic stress disorder (PTSD), as recorded in the *Diagnostic and Statistical Manual of Mental Disorders* (*DSM III R*, American Psychiatric Association, 1987). Additional general symptoms of psychological trauma that are common among victims of chronic or ongoing trauma include substance abuse, self-mutilation, intolerance of intimacy, a general sense of helplessness, and a sense of isolation and existential separateness from others (Figley, 1985; Harvey, 1991; Sheehan, 1994).

It is critical that the clinician recognizes that the homeless person, who has been referred for treatment, has been exposed to traumatic events, many of which involve the rupture of interpersonal trust and a loss of a sense of personal control. The loss of interpersonal trust and sense of control not only serve to undermine and erode the homeless person's ability to cope, but may propel the homeless person to engage in drug abuse and sexually addictive behavior (American Psychiatric Association, 1994; Briere & Runtz, 1988; Carnes, 1991; Daniels & Scurfield, 1994; DuPont, 1997; Evans & Sullivan, 1995; Goodman, 1998; Howard, 2000; Lowinson, Ruiz, Millman, & Langrod, 1997; Morris, 1998; Rawson, 1990; Robinson, 1999; Schwartz, Galperin, & Masters, 1997; Taylor, Fulop, & Green, 1999; Tedesco & Bola, 1997; Washton, 1989; Wright, 1989). The "goal" of this behavior is to "self-medicate" or to regulate their internal emotional states, due to traumas experienced in their lives (Carnes, 1997; Clatts & Davis, 1995; Daniels & Scurfield, 1994; Griffin-Shelley, 1997; Heilakka, 1993; Herman, 1992; Robinson, 1999; Whitfield, 1998). As sexual behavior is compulsively utilized to detach from, deny, minimize, avoid, or survive both protracted and repeated traumas while they are occurring, as well as the painful reexperiencing of trauma, the homeless person, like others who have engaged in compulsive sexual behavior, demonstrates behavior that the literature calls sex addiction (Balswick & Balswick, 1999; Carnes, 1991, 1997; Daniels & Scurfield, 1994; Earle & Earle, 1995; Goodman, 1998; Griffin-Shelley, 1997; Kasl, 1989; Laaser, 1996; Schneider & Schneider, 1991). Having an awareness that these are some of the background issues and experiences that homeless persons may present into therapy with is important for clinicians to consider as they begin clinical case management with their clients.

CLINICAL CASE MANAGEMENT WITH THE HOMELESS PERSON

Before considering the specifics of clinical case management with the homeless person, clinicians must be aware of important therapeutic issues and the significance of their role as they interact with their clients in the treatment setting (Howard, 2000; Levin & Green, 2000; Nathan & Gorman, 1998). Exploring issues that are critical for cultural competence (Cross, Bazron, Dennis, & Isaacs, 1989; Locke, 1992), such as valuing diversity, making a cultural self-assessment, understanding the dynamics of cultural interaction, and adapting practices to the diversity present in the therapy setting, are crucial in the formation of a successful therapeutic alliance. In addition, successfully managing transference and countertransference as well as being aware of the possibility of secondary traumatization developing, indicate that it is a necessity for the clinician to access a group of peers for support and to discuss issues that could affect the therapeutic relationship (Howard, 2000; Koshes, 1992).

Case management is generally described as a coordinated approach to the delivery of health, substance abuse, mental health, and social services, linking clients with appropriate services to address specific needs and to achieve stated goals. With this in mind, it is essential that the clinician know the role that he or she is undertaking with the homeless client. Traditional case management focuses on the acquisition of resources for the homeless client, whereas clinical case management introduces and involves ongoing psychotherapy that focuses on intra- and interpersonal change (P. Cooke, 1992; Levine & Fleming, 1987; Levine & Greene, 2000; Nathan & Gorman, 1998; National Association of Social Workers, 1992; Swayze, 1992). Regardless of the different treatment modalities the clinician chooses to employ when working with the homeless client, it is important for the clinician to possess and demonstrate relevant skills and knowledge that are appropriate to the level of care and within his or her scope of practice with the client. The clinician should also seek and receive training, consultation, and supervision where ethically and legally required, always operating with the best interest of the client in mind.

As mentioned earlier, the clinician begins case management with the sexually addicted homeless person by practicing basic, core functions of traditional case management (Barrow, 1988; P. Cooke, 1992; First, Rife, & Kraus, 1990; Harris & Bergman, 1993; Levin & Green, 2000). These core functions, as applied with the sexually addicted homeless population, include:

Client outreach, identification, and engagement, which means that the clinician may need to rethink how clients are identified for therapy. Homeless people who are sex addicts are likely to be encountered in a variety of settings: from urban rescue missions and religious institutions with sobriety-based support structures to detoxification programs and day-treatment programs; in Skid Row intensive outpatient substance-abuse programs, as well as in drug-free therapeutic communities; in halfway houses, as well as on the street (White, 1998). It is suggested that the clinician contact any of these agencies to voluntarily provide psychoeducational training about sex addiction to staff and clients alike, with the goal of becoming a referral source or even an onsite provider of services to clients who seek therapy for sex addiction.

Client assessment consists of an in-depth, comprehensive evaluation of the biopsychosocial needs of the client, as well as a detailed, extensive gathering of the sexual history of the client. Standardized instruments such as the Addiction Severity Index (McLellen, Parkih, Braff, Cacciola, & Incmikoski, 1990), the Sexual Dependency Inventory (Carnes, 1999), and the Posttraumatic Stress Index (Carnes & Delmonico, 1997), as well as other clinical assessment materials the clinician may choose (MMPI-2; Butcher, Dahlstrom, Graham, Tellegen, & Kaemmer, 1989) are a few of the valuable tools to utilize in the interview process with the client to ensure accurate assessment of clinical issues. As traumatization issues are likely to surface in the assessment process, the clinician should exercise careful attention to proceed at a rate of inquiry that is comfortable for the client. As the clinician honors the resistance demonstrated by the client as a self-protective safety measure, he or she should also take steps to reduce shame and humiliation related to the disclosure in a safe and nonthreatening manner (Howard, 2000).

The bulk of the work the clinician will engage in with the client is in *service planning, goal setting, and implementation.* Based on clinician–client collaboration and the outcome of the case management assessment, the clinician and client have worked to identify relevant needs, goals, and services that are necessary for successful treatment to occur. At this point in the case conceptualization process, the clinician will need to determine the best approach to employ in order for service delivery to occur. Levin and Green (2000) and Gillespie and Murty (1994) suggest three different "interorganizational models" to consider as services are coordinated with the client. The first is *single agency,* where the clinician retains full autonomous control of the case and establishes separate relationships with other agencies on an as-needed basis. The second is *informal partnership,* where staff from different agencies work collaboratively as a team to provide multiple services to the client on a case-by-case basis. Finally, the *formal consortium* model entails that case managers and service providers operate to provide services to the client following a formal, written contract, with each agency being accountable to the consortium. All three models of engagement have advantages and disadvantages for interagency conflict to develop, and it is imperative that clear communication occur to meet the stated objectives for the client.

A second consideration in the service planning stage, especially if the client is dually diagnosed and substance-dependent with little or no sobriety, is to determine if treatment will occur in a sequential, parallel, or integrated manner (Ries, 1994). The *sequential* treatment model describes the serial or nonsimultaneous participation in both the mental health and the addiction treatment settings. In the sequential treatment model, one form of treatment would be engaged in and completed before treatment in the other setting begins. This model is used when it is determined that it is in the client's best interest to reach a period of abstinence from chemical abuse before psychotherapy about traumatic events commences. In the *parallel* treatment model, the client would simultaneously receive mental health treatment and addiction treatment in two different settings. In the *integrated* treatment model, elements of both mental health and addiction treatment are unified into a comprehensive treatment program. In the two latter treatment programs, psychotherapy begins concurrently with addiction treatment, as some clinicians may assess that the client will not achieve sobriety unless traumatic issues are addressed (Howard, 2000).

Linkage and monitoring means that the client will receive, either from the clinician or by referral service, access to the necessary components of treatment in order to achieve the stated goals. At this stage of case management, important interventions are implemented and monitored throughout the course of therapy. Key areas (A. Cooke, 1992) to address for the homeless sex addict are the economic area, the social area, the institutional area, and the psychological area, which will be addressed in greater detail further on. In the economic area, linkage is made for food, clothing, employment, transitional and permanent housing, and financial assistance. In the social area, personal hygiene, social skill development, and interpersonal skill development, along with family support and conflict resolution skills, are addressed. In the institutional area, education, legal, health, and other supportive services are engaged by the client, with the overall linkage process monitored by the clinician for the client's compliance to this flexible, but agreed-upon, treatment plan. These components of treatment are continually addressed in the early, middle, and late stages of treatment with the homeless client, with what is arguably the most important area of treatment with the homeless sex addict being the psychological area.

SEX ADDICTION TREATMENT WITH THE HOMELESS PERSON

In his research with sex addicts, Carnes (2000) utilizes an integrated, systemic treatment model in which critical individual, interpersonal, and environmental factors in the client's life are thoroughly assessed and addressed in the treatment of sex addiction. Using this multisystemic, ecological theoretical model (Boyd-Franklin, 1989; Bronfenbrenner, 1979; Earle & Earle, 1995; Harvey, 1991; Koss & Harvey, 1991) with the client allows for the detection and impact of trauma, as wide-ranging developmental influences, social contexts, and racial, ethnic, family, community, and psychological experiences are considered and examined in the therapy session. In this model, the clinician will need to determine how current maladaptive responses to post-traumatic stress experiences in the home-less client's family of origin, as well as recent past, have opened painful and lasting psychological wounds that the client is attempting to anesthetize through sexually addictive behavior (Carnes, 2000; Evans & Sullivan, 1995; Goodman, 1998; Myers, 1995; Robinson, 1999; Whitfield, 1998). This sexual behavior, crystallized into a reoccurring addictive cycle and usually fused with other compulsive behaviors (chemical dependency, gambling, eating, etc.), creates a powerful "addiction interaction" that affects every aspect of the life of the homeless person (Carnes, 2000).

Carnes's (2000) integrated treatment model, adaptable for individual, group, and family treatment in a variety of treatment settings, as well as with ancillary treatment, pinpoints 30 specific "competency" areas for the clinician and the homeless client to collaborate and work on to achieve successful recovery. Though not exhaustive, critical areas for the clinician to intervene with the homeless client in the early stage of treatment are centered around denial about the client's sex addiction, as some clients may not view their sexually addictive behavior as addiction, in addition to understanding the cyclical and systemic nature of the illness. Helping the homeless sex addict to surrender to the process of recovery by working Steps 1 through 3 of the 12-steps in this stage of treatment is also crucial, as well as helping the client to limit self-injurious behavior and to establish a period of sexual sobriety. One of the recovery tasks for the client to work toward is reducing shame, grieving losses, and creating opportunities to engage in a culture of support. See chapter 5 for more guidelines on shame reduction. Careful attention should be given by the clinician regarding the client's disclosure of HIV status, as case management issues and concerns may dictate that a higher level of care be effected in connection with the homeless client (Froner, 1988; Sorenson & Batki, 1997).

During the middle stage of treatment, it is essential for the client to work to resolve feelings and experiences surrounding traumatic conflicts and wounds, as well as to explore, define, and cultivate healthy sexuality in his or her life. In addition, the homeless client must do the important work of identifying elements of healthy relationships and begin the process of building and engaging in those relationships. Success in this area is crucial in order to rid the client from the two profoundly dangerous "landmines of loneliness," disenfranchisement and social isolation. These two areas alone could derail treatment effort and trigger relapses into addictive behavior (Rouff, 2000). Additional interventions during the middle stage of treatment will focus on establishing healthy exercise and nutritional patterns, working toward creating balance in the client's lifestyle, as well as connecting with family members and working to resolve issues and renew relationships with them (Heaton-Matheny, 1998). Significant attention will need to be given to the development and implementation of relapse prevention strategies throughout each stage of therapy. Refusal skills that focus on identifying high-risk relapse factors and understanding and dealing with social pressures, as well as learning and implementing methods to deal with negative cognitive and emotional states, are critical. Such skills will need to be continually rehearsed and practiced in order for the homeless client to function and feel competent when using these skills in everyday situations (Marlatt & Gordon, 1985; Price, 1999).

It is strongly recommended that the clinician and the client include in the treatment plan ancillary treatment in the form of attendance with one of the 12-step fellowships that welcome and support people who are recovering from sexual addiction, as well as any other addiction the client is challenged with. For successful recovery to be realized in the homeless client's life, attendance in Sex Addicts Anonymous, Sex and Love Addicts Anonymous, Sexual Compulsives Anonymous, or Sexaholics Anonymous groups is vital. The groups are based on the 12 steps and present a similar and helpful adjunct for treatment of the homeless sex addict, differing for the most part in each group's definition of sexual sobriety. Fellowship groups such as S-Anon and COSA are for partners of the sex addict, as their lives have been affected by the compulsive sexual behavior of the sex addict. Working with a sponsor to address and integrate recovery efforts will also enhance client work toward treatment success.

Late-stage treatment will focus on reviewing clinical and other biopsychosocial goals the client has accomplished in treatment, with important attention given to ensure that the client is practicing activities and managing responsibilities that are conducive for his or her economic, social, psychological, and relational success. A critical review with clients must be done to confirm that they have transferred their "cultural membership from the culture of addiction to the culture of recovery" (White, 1996). The clinician must address relevant elements of the client's culture, such as language, religion, morality, values, symbols, rituals, history, dress, food, recreation, music, and art, to ascertain that a transfer of loyalty and, it is hoped, a transformation has occurred in these important areas. Connecting the "graduate" with other "alumni" from the agency will assist the client further in the all-important transition to independent living. Finally, the clinician is encouraged to discuss with clients how they are developing and implementing activity for their spiritual growth and personal renewal.

CONCLUDING THOUGHTS

Additional research with the sexually addicted homeless population is needed, not only because it is almost nonexistent, but because clinicians in agencies across the country who work with the homeless are reporting they have to make sex addiction *the primary focus of treatment*, if they are to achieve any measure of success with their homeless clientele. At the same time, many are reporting about the need for integrated treatment approaches with the sexually addicted homeless, with a few providing practical and helpful suggestions for your consideration. The suggestions are

1. *Practicing clinical case management with homeless sex addicts who reside in residential therapeutic communities or who attend outpatient treatment facilities is meant to be done in collaboration with other clinicians or other chosen mental health providers.* Taking a collaborative approach will double the therapist's efforts and enhance overall clinical effectiveness; provide the clinician with peer support; lower the possibility of therapist burnout; and model healthy interpersonal working relationships to homeless clientele.

2. *Partner with an existing school of psychology at a local university to deliver* clinical services at established agencies and shelters for the homeless. Two existing projects have been developed and are currently being funded by community foundations in the Los Angeles area.

3. *Research, create, and offer supervision of a 12-week integrated-treatment program,* with a format that incorporates psychoeducation, group therapy, individual counseling, 12-step meetings, step studies, and bibliotherapy about sex addiction. Teach and involve counselors/case managers in the treatment and delivery process as skill development permits.

4. *Meet with members of the clergy or parachurch agencies that currently work with the homeless* (churches, parishes, "rescue missions") in underserved communities, offering outreach, education, treatment, and other traditional case management services to potential clients in that setting.

5. *Attend a Sex Addiction Intensive training conference at the Meadows or via the Internet,* in order to equip yourself and eventually your staff with the latest research and skill development in the area of sex addiction.

SUMMARY

Being homeless in America ensures that homeless persons will be exposed to harmful and dangerous situations that affect their physical and mental health, as well as jeopardize their safety and well-being. Experiencing chronic homelessness, as well as having previous exposure to traumatic situations, increases the probability that the homeless person may employ sexually addictive behavior, in addition to other harmful compulsions, to "anesthetize" or regulate internal emotional states, which is likely to result in behavior the literature calls sex addiction.

As the homeless person presents for services before the clinician, assessment and attention must be given to both traditional case management responsibilities, as well as to sex addiction issues, in order for successful treatment to be realized. An integrated treatment model of sex addiction adapted for clinical case management use with the sexually addicted homeless population is reviewed. Additional qualitative research is suggested to study and develop additional treatment models for the sexually addicted homeless population.

REFERENCES

American Psychiatric Association. (1987) . *Diagnostic and statistical manual of mental disorders* (3rd ed., rev.). Washington, DC: Author.

American Psychiatric Association. (1994) . *Diagnostic and statistical manual of mental disorders* (4th ed.). Washington, DC: Author.

American Public Health Association. (1990). Alcohol and other problems among the homeless population (position paper). *American Journal of Public Health, 80,* 243–246.

Balswick, J. K., & Balswick, J. O. (1999). *Authentic human sexuality: An integrated Christian approach.* Downers Grove, IL: InterVarsity.

Barrow, S. M. (1988). *Delivery of services to homeless mentally ill clients: Engagement, direct service and intensive case management at five programs.* New York: New York State Psychiatric Institute.

Boyd-Franklin, N. (1989). *Black families in therapy.* New York: Guilford.

Briere, J., & Runtz, M. (1988). In G. E. Wyatt & G. J. Powell (Eds.), *Lasting effects of child abuse.* Newbury Park, CA: Sage.

Bronfrenbrenner, U. (1979). *The ecology of human development.* Cambridge, MA: Harvard University Press.

Butcher, J. N., Dahlstrom, W. G., Graham, J. R., Tellegen, A., & Kaemmer, B. (1989). *MMPI-2 (Minnesota Multiphasic Personality Inventory–(2): Manual for administration and scoring.* Minneapolis, MN: Univesity of Minnesota Press.

Carnes, P. (1989). *Contrary to love: Helping the sexual addict.* Minneapolis, MN: CompCare.

Carnes, P. (1991). *Don't call it love: Recovery from sexual addiction.* New York: Bantam.

Carnes, P. (1997). *The betrayal bond: Breaking free of exploitive relationships.* Deerfield Beach, FL: Health Communications.

Carnes, P. (1999). *Sexual Dependency Inventory.* Wickenburg, AZ: New Freedom.

Carnes, P. (2000). *Counseling the sex addict: Intensive training.* Symposium conducted by the Meadows Institute in Scottsdale, Arizona.

Carnes, P., & Delmonico, D. (1997). *The posttraumatic stress index.* Wickenburg, AZ: New Freedom.

Clatts, M. C., & Davis, W. R. (1995). *The public health impact of street outreach to homeless youth in New York City: Implications for AIDS education and prevention.* Paper presented at the Third Science Symposium on HIV Prevention research: Current Status and Future Directions, Flagstaff, AZ, August, 1995.

Cooke, A. L. (1992). The role of helping professional: Developing strategies for intervention in homelessness. In C. Solomon & P. Jackson-Jobe (Eds.), *Helping homeless people: Unique challenges and solutions.* Alexandria, VA: American Association for Counseling and Development.

Cooke, P. W. (1992). Case management models and approaches for counseling and working with homeless people. In C. Solomon & P. Jackson-Jobe (Eds.), *Helping homeless people: Unique challenges and solutions.* Alexandria, VA: American Association of Counseling and Development.

Cross, T., Bazron, B., Dennis, K., & Isaacs, M. (1989). *Towards a culturally competent system of care: A monograph on effective services for minority children who are severely emotionally disturbed.* Washington, DC: Georgetown University Child Development Center.

Daniels, L. R., & Scurfield, R. M. (1994). War-related post-traumatic stress disorder: Chemical addictions and non-chemical habituating behaviors. In M. Williams & J. F. Sommer (Eds.), *Handbook of post-traumatic therapy* (pp. 205–221). Westport, CT: Greenwood Press.

DuPont, R. L. (1997). *The selfish brain: Learning from addiction.* Washington, DC: American Psychiatric Press.

Earle, R. H., & Earle, M. R. (1995). *Sex addiction: Case studies and management.* Levittown, PA: Brunner-Mazel.

Evans, K., & Sullivan, J. (1995). *Treating addicted survivors of trauma.* New York: Guilford.

Figley, C. R. (Ed.). (1985). *Trauma and its wake: The study and treatment of posttraumatic stress disorder.* New York: Brunner-Mazel.

First, R. J., Rife, J. C., & Kraus, S. (1990). Case management with people who are homeless and mentally ill: Preliminary findings from an NIMH demonstration project. *Journal of Psychosocial Rehabilitation, 13*(4), 87–91.

Froner, G. (1988). AIDS and homelessness. *Journal of Psychoactive Drugs, 20,* 197–202.

Gillespie, D. F., & Murty, S. A. (1994). Cracks in a postdisaster service delivery network. *American Journal of Community Psychology, 22*(5), 639–660.

Goodman, A. (1998). *Sexual addiction.* Madison, CT: International Universities Press.

Goodman, L., Saxe, L., & Harvey, M. (1991). Homelessness as psychological trauma. *American Psychologist, 46,* 1219–1225.

Greenblatt, M., & Robertson, M. (1993). Adaptive strategies, and sexual behaviors of homeless adolescents. *Hospital and Community Psychiatry, 44*(12), 1177–1180.

Griffiin-Shelley, E. (1993). *Outpatient treatment of sex and love addicts.* London: Praeger.

Griffin-Shelley, E. (1997). *Sex & love: Addiction, treatment and recovery.* London: Praeger.

Harris, M., & Bergman, H. C. (Eds.). (1993). *Case management for mentally ill patients: Theory and practice.* Langhorn, PA: Harwood Academic.

Harris, S., Mowbray, C., & Solarz, A. (1994). Physical health, mental health, and substance abuse problems of shelter users. *Health & Social Work, 19,* 37–45.

Harvey, M. R. (1991). An ecological approach to the treatment of trauma victims. Manuscript submitted for publication.

Heaton-Matheny, J. (1998). Strategies for assessment and early treatment with sexually addicted families. *Journal of Sex Addiction and Compulsivity, 5*, 27–48.

Heilakka, S. (1993). Integrating sex therapy and addiction recovery. In E. Griffin-Shelley (Ed.), *Outpatient treatment of sex and love addicts* (pp. 101–112). Westport, CT: Praeger.

Herman, J. L. (1992). *Trauma and recovery.* New York: Basic.

Hoff, L. A. (1989). *People in crisis: Understanding and helping.* New York: Addison-Wesley.

Hopper, K., & Hamburg, J. (1984). The making of America's homeless: From skid row to new poor. New York: Community Service Society of New York.

Howard, J. (2000). *Substance abuse treatment for persons with child abuse and neglect issues* (Treatment Improvement Protocol Series 36, Center for Substance Abuse Treatment). Rockville, MD.

Kasl, C. D. (1989). *Women, sex and addiction: A search for love and power.* New York: Harper & Row.

Koshes, R. (1992). Understanding the framework of homelessness. In C. Solomon & P. Jackson-Jobe (Eds.), *Helping homeless people: Unique challenges and solutions.* Alexandria, VA: American Association for Counseling and Development.

Koss, M. P., & Harvey, M. R. (1991). *The rape victim: Clinical and community inteventions* (2nd ed.). Newbury Park, CA: Sage.

Laaser, M. (1996). *Faithful and true: Sexual integrity in a fallen world.* Grand Rapids, MI: Zondervan.

Levin, S. M., & Greene, J. A. (2000). *Case management for substance abuse treatment: A guide for treatment providers.* (Treatment Improvement Protocol Series 36, Center for Substance Abuse Treatment). Rockville, MD.

Levine, S., & Fleming, M. S. (1987). *Human resource development: Issues in case management.* College Park: University of Maryland, Center of Rehabilitation and Manpower Services.

Locke, D. C. (1992). *Increasing multicultural understanding: A comprehensive model.* Newbury Park, CA: Sage.

Lowinson, J., Ruiz, P., Millman, R., & Langrod, J. (1997). *Substance abuse: A comprehensive textbook.* Baltimore, MD: Williams & Wilkins.

Marlatt, G.A., & Gordon, J.R. (Eds.). (1985). *Relapse prevention: Maintenance strategies in the treatment of addictive behaviors.* New York: Guilford.

McCarty, D., Argeriou, M., Huebner, R., & Lubran, B. (1991). Alcoholism, drug abuse and the homeless. *American Psychologist, 46*, 1139–1148.

McLellen, A. T., Parkih, G., Braff, A., Cacciola, A., & Incmikoski, R. (1990). *Addiction Severity Index, 5th ed.* Philadelphia, PA: Pennsylvania Veterans' Administration Center for Studies of Addiction.

Morris, K. (1998). Seeking ways to crack cocaine addiction. *Lancet, 352*, 1290.

Morse, G.A., Calsyn, R. J. (1992). Mental health and other human service needs of homeless people. In M. J. Robertson & M. Greenblatt (Eds.), *Homelessness: A national perspective.* New York: Plenum.

Myers, W. (1995). Addictive sexual behavior. *American Journal of Psychotherapy, 49*(4), 473–484.

Nathan, P. E., & Gorman, J. M. (1998). *A guide to treatments that work.* New York: Oxford University Press.

National Association of Social Workers. Case management's cost, benefits eyed. *National Association of Social Workers News, p. 12.* Washington, DC: NASW Press.

National Law Center on Homelessness and Poverty: 2000–Homelessness and poverty in America (Online). www.nlchp.org/h&pusa.htm

National Coalition for the Homeless: 1999 – Why are people Homeless? (Online). ww.nch.ari.net/causes.html.

Pablos-Mendez, A., Raviglione, M. C., Battan, R., & Ramos-Zuniga, R. (1990). Drug resistant tuberculosis among the homeless in New York City. *New York State Journal of Medicine, 90*(7), 351–355.

Price, D. M. (1999). Relapse prevention and risk reduction: Identification of high risk situations. *Journal of Sex Addiction and Compulsivity, 6,* 221–252.

Raba, J. M. (1990). Homelessness and AIDS. In Brickner, P., *Under the safety net* (pp. 214–233). New York: W. W. Norton.

Rawson, R. (1990). Cut the crack: The policy maker's guide to cocaine treatment. *Policy Review, 51,* 10–20.

Redliner, I. (1994). Healthcare for the homeless—Lessons from the front line. *New England Journal of Medicine, 331*(5), 327–328.

Ries, R. (1994). *Assessment and treatment of patients with coexisting mental illness and alcohol and other drug abuse.* (Treatment Improvement Protocol Series 9, Center for Substance Abuse Treatment). Rockville, MD.

Robinson, D. (1999). Sexual addiction as an adaptive response to post-traumatic stress disorder in the African-American community. *Journal of Sexual Addiction and Compulsivity, 6,* 11–22.

Rouff, L. (2000). Schizoid personality traits among the homeless mentally ill: A quantitative and qualitative report. *Journal of Social Distress and the Homeless, 9*(2), 127–144.

Schneider, J. P., & Schneider, B. (1991). *Sex, lies and forgiveness: Couples speaking out on healing and sex addiction.* Center City, MN: Hazelden.

Schwartz, M., Galperin, L., & Masters, W. (1997). Sexual trauma within the context of traumatic and unescapable stress, neglect and poisonous pedagogy. In M. Hunter (Ed.), *Adult survivors of sexual abuse: Treatment innovations.* Thousand Oaks, CA: Sage.

Sgroi, S., & Bunk, B. (1988). A clinical approach to adult survivors of child sexual abuse. In S. Sgroi (Ed.), *Vulnerable populations: evaluation and treatment of sexually abused children and adult survivors, 1* (pp. 137–156). New York: Lexington.

Sheehan, P. L. (1994). Treating intimacy issues of traumatized people. In M. B. Williams & J. F. Sommer, *Handbook of post-traumatic therapy* (pp. 94–106). Westport, CT: Greenwood Press.

Sorenson, J. L., & Batki, S. L. (1997). Psychosocial Sequelae. In J. Lowinson, P. Ruiz, R. Millman, & J. Langrod (Eds.), *Substance Abuse: A comprehensive textbook.* Baltimore, MD: Williams & Wilkins.

Susser, E., Valencia, E., Miller, M., Tsai, W.Y., Meyer-Bahlburg, H., Nat, R., & Conover, S. (1995). Sexual behavior of the homeless mentally ill men at risk for HIV. *American Journal of Psychiatry, 152*(4), 583–587.

Swayze, F. V. (1992). Clinical case management with the homeless mentally ill. In H. R. Lamb, L. L. Bachrach, & F. I. Kass (Eds.), *Treating the homeless mentally ill.* Washington, DC: American Psychiatric Press.

Taylor, J., Fulop, N., & Green, J. (1999). Drink, illicit drugs and unsafe sex in women. *Addiction, 94,* 1209–1218.

Tedesco, A., & Bola, J. R. (1997). A pilot study of the relationship between childhood sexual abuse and compulsive sexual behaviors in adults. *Journal of Sexual Addiction and Compulsivity, 4,* 147–157.

Torres, R. A., Lefkowitz, P., Kales, C., & Bricker, P. W. (1980). Homelessness among hospitalized patients with acquired immunodeficiency syndrome in New York City. *Journal of American Medical Association, 258,* 779–780.

U.S. Conference of Mayors. (1995). *A status report on hunger and homelessness in America's cities: 1995. A 29 city survey.* Washington, DC: U.S. Conference of Mayors, 1995.

van der Kolk, B. A. (1987). The psychological consequences of overwhelming life experiences. In B. A. van der Kolk (Ed.), *Psychological trauma* (pp. 1–31). Washington, DC: American Psychiatric Press.

Wallace, R. (1988) A synergism of plagues: Planned shrinkage, contagious housing destruction and AIDS in the Bronx. *Environment Restoration, 47,* 1–33.

Washton, A. M. (1989). Cocaine may trigger sexual compulsivity. *U.S. Journal of Drug and Alcohol Dependency, 13,* 8.

White, W. (1998). *Slaying the dragon: The history of addiction treatment and recovery in America.* Bloomington, IL: Chestnut Health Systems/Lighthouse Institute.

White, W. (1996). *Pathways: From the culture of addiction to the culture of recovery.* Center City, MN: Hazelden.

Whitfield, C. L. (1998). Internal evidence and corroboration of traumatic memories of child sexual abuse with addictive disorders. *Journal of Sex Addiction and Compulsivity, 5,* 269–289.

Wright, J. D. (1989). *Address unknown: The homeless in America.* New York: Aldine de Gruyter.

CHAPTER 21

Treatment Concerns for Gay Male Sexual Addicts

ROBERT WEISS

Although the most basic tenets of addiction assessment and treatment are minimally affected by gender and cultural concerns, an empathic understanding of the social and psychological values and experiences of specific populations helps the addiction specialist provide effective appropriate care. Homosexual men, having experienced developmental and social challenges related to both the cultural repression and vilification of homosexuality and the trauma of AIDS, require just such a specific understanding to provide appropriate addiction intervention and support. This chapter attempts to point out some of the developmental and cultural concerns unique to male homosexuals, as these concerns may affect treatment. Childhood repression of homosexual feelings, HIV and AIDS grief, gay activism, and substance abuse are some of the concerns this chapter attempts to consider in relationship to the provision of effective treatment for sexual addiction.

The provision of outpatient treatment to sexually addicted homosexual men differs qualitatively from the clinical process provided for heterosexual men. Although the overall methodology and structure of cognitive-behavioral addiction treatment remains consistent across sexual orientation and gender lines, clinical intervention with gay male sexual addicts requires familiarity with a specific knowledge base of terminology and relational concerns. A working understanding of the cultural norms intrinsic to the gay male population, along with a nonjudgmental and nonpoliticized therapeutic patient alliance, allows the clinician to effectively confront the denial underlying the active addictive process and to work toward effective recovery.

DEVELOPMENTAL ISSUES

The treatment clinician must be aware of the specific developmental and societal obstacles that can hinder the recovery process for sexually addicted gay men.

Many of these issues relate to the specific maturational challenges endemic to growing up as a gay male in a culture not only hostile toward homosexuality, but, moreover, completely unaware of childhood and adolescent homosexual development. From early childhood, most prehomosexual children and adolescents learn to hide the parts of themselves that may not be acceptable or rewarded. First in the family, and later in the social environs of school and peer play, men learn that it is disadvantageous to openly exhibit androgyny or demonstrate interests or behaviors that lie outside of culturally supported male patterns of behavior.

> Boys called "sissies" often have few ways to express their distress about being different and about being teased. Some respond to social pressure by increasing gender conforming behavior . . . others respond with some lowering of self-esteem, depression and lowered ability to interact with, enjoy and learn from peers. Not infrequently, the people to whom such boys would turn for adult support and comfort—their parents—may also be uncomfortable with, and lack understanding of, the child's being different. . . . These effects can be carried forward into adulthood as a lifelong view of interpersonal relationships consisting of some kind of transference wariness or distrust of self or others that the young man will bring into future relationships. (Hanson & Hartmann, 1996)

For many male homosexuals, the learned survival skills of disavowal and suppression of central parts of the self, coupled with reduced social interaction and isolation, may later serve to underscore any addictive process. Thus, typical addict characteristics of isolation, poor self-concept, secrecy, and compartmentalization may have more firmly established developmental roots in the gay male sexual addict population. A treatment tool that is useful toward effecting reduction of this type of internalized shame and self-disconnection involves the writing and treatment-based disclosure of a meticulously complete, written sexual addiction history. Recovery is promoted as the addict faces shameful feelings related to sexual behavior in the supportive, nonpejorative, reality-based environment of treatment. Complete disclosure helps to reduce the shame perpetuated by sexual secrets and helps raise self-esteem. More important, disclosure provides the opportunity for a lived experience of acceptance and support in the face of a shaming and disavowed sexual history.

> Mark, a 29-year-old Caucasian gay male, entered outpatient sexual addiction treatment after being asked to separate from a 5-year primary relationship by his significant other, Jeremy. The spousal relationship was shattered when Jeremy, arriving home early from a business trip, found Mark having sex with a male prostitute. Early in treatment, Mark admitted that he had been acting out with other men frequently throughout his relationship, a behavior later revealed as part of a much larger historical pattern of anonymous sexual en-

counters. In group therapy Mark stated, "Growing up, I certainly knew better than to talk to anyone about being gay, and being gay to me meant having sex with men. My parents would have had me committed if they had known. Later when I came out, it seemed natural to continue to keep my sexual life to myself. I figured it wasn't anybody's business. When I met Jeremy and fell in love with him, I wanted to talk about it, but the more important the relationship became, the less possible it was for me to admit the truth; I had no idea how to even start talking about it and just felt that he would leave me if he knew. The addiction group is the first place where I have felt completely known, *all of me*, and cared for anyway."

HOMOPHOBIA AND SEXUAL ORIENTATION CONCERNS

Negative core cognitions, an integral component of the addictive process, help to support a shame-based, distorted view of the self. These nonaffirming views of the self are often magnified for gay male sexual addicts, many of whom carry additional burdens of self-hatred for being homosexual. The treating clinician must recognize the potential for these men to have an internalized contempt for their own homosexuality, intertwined with feelings of self-abasement specific to sexual acting out. The exploration of shame throughout the therapeutic process must attend to the often-entangled concerns of sexual addiction and internalized homophobia.

A challenge to directive addiction treatment can arise if a patient views the containment of his sexual acting out as being the resolution to concerns regarding sexual orientation. Sexually addicted bisexual or heterosexual men who addictively act out with other men, particularly those patients with an identifiable history of sexual abuse, will often place an immediate focus on the "resolution" of their sexual orientation (Hunter, 1990). They can be confused about their sexual desires, the addictive process, societal/family expectations, and long-term relationship goals. Clients may hold a distorted concept of the treatment process, concluding, "My problems would be solved if I'd only stop sleeping with men" or "the real problem with my sexual acting out is my attraction to men." In early treatment, the sexual orientation question may actually serve as a block or smokescreen to the more immediate concern of containing the addictive behaviors themselves. "Why am I like this?" or "How do I figure out whether I want to be with a man or a woman?" are questions best to be superficially explored at first, with the primary focus of treatment on containing the addictive process. Once a significant period of sexual sobriety is obtained, social supports created, and sexual shame reduced, the patient may then be ready to address longer-term sexual orientation concerns.

Henry, a 38-year-old first-generation Korean American man, had been in a heterosexual marriage for 7 years. He first attended treatment after having been arrested in a local park restroom for engaging in a sexual act in a public place. The patient's sexual acting-out history was found to be entirely related to anonymous sexual conduct with men, though he remained an active sexual partner with his wife. Henry expressed that he had always been intensely sexually attracted to men, a feeling that was unacceptable to him and outside of any acceptable principle in his family of origin and cultural roots. Immediate initial treatment concerns related to the containment of illegal sexual activity and assessment of any potential STD transmission to his wife, who was unaware of any of Henry's extramarital sexual behaviors. Once sexual sobriety was established in individual treatment, Henry entered an outpatient addiction group where, over time, he was able to fully disclose his sexual history, including several incidences of childhood sexual abuse by an adolescent male neighbor. After several months in group and individual treatment he was able to have full disclosure to his wife, who also entered outpatient individual and co-addiction group treatment. Two years after group graduation, having been regularly involved in 12-step meeting attendance, the patient voluntarily returned to treatment to address his evolving interest in separating from his wife in order to openly explore the possibility of an intimate primary male partnership.

COMMUNITY POLITICS VERSUS DENIAL

A broader cultural issue that can impinge on sexual addiction treatment of gay men is the gay activist political stance toward societal equality and acceptance that has evolved in the American gay community over the last 25 years. Antidefamation groups, political action committees, parades, marches, and economic clout have all worked toward this cause. This necessary work, employed to challenge a homophobic and often hostile culture, can also become an obstacle for the recovery of gay male sexual addicts if these issues are utilized to further deny the realities of sexual addiction. Clinicians faced with such politicized arguments run the risk of not going far enough in appropriately confronting and intervening in the behavior of a gay male sex addict, due to fears of being branded homophobic or prejudiced.

  A recent clinical sexual addiction training at a major urban HIV program was frequently interrupted by several men in the audience adamantly expressing their anger at sex being viewed as an addiction. They stated that this view seemed to "pathologize" gay male culture while promoting the "traditional heterosexual values of single partnership and marriage." They expounded that open, frequent sexual choice was "the birthright of gay men who had been shamed long enough for their sexual choices."

  A substantive counter to the previous argument is a clear focus on the necessity for *all addicts* to have appropriate boundaries regarding their behaviors. That is, though alcohol consumption is an acceptable activity in our culture, those who are alcoholic cannot drink due to their inability to consume alcohol in a way that is healthy and nondamaging. In a similar view, though it may be appropriate and healthy for some gay men to make sexual choices that are not subject to predefined boundaries or that may exist outside of ongoing relationships, gay male sexual addicts cannot engage in such activities without risking the activation of negative patterns of shaming and self-defeating behaviors. A clearly defined *sexual sobriety* for the recovering homosexual or heterosexual sexual addict does not underlie any moral, religious, or political tenet, any more than does alcohol sobriety for the recovering alcoholic.

LANGUAGE AND CLINICAL OBJECTIVITY

The treating therapist must become comfortable with the exploration of *the language and experience of gay sexual behavior*, remaining open to previously unknown terminology or sexual behavior choices. Words like *tearoom, sex club, glory hole, chicken,* and *fisting,* common expressions in the world of a gay sexual addict, may require the clinician to explore unfamiliar and potentially uncomfortable sexual experiences and practices. At all times the therapist must maintain an open, nonjudgmental stance and response to intimate disclosures, as this will be a deciding factor in building a trusting therapeutic alliance with this shame-based population. It is not unusual, for example, for some homosexual male sexual addicts to disclose histories of anonymous sexual liaisons numbering in the thousands. Treating therapists should not view this behavior as pathological beyond its obvious implications for addiction treatment. Greater numbers of partners may have more to do with the accessibility of male sexual liaisons than with any particular level or type of pathology.

HIV AND AIDS

The numbers of gay men seeking relief from sexually dependent behaviors have clearly risen with the advent of HIV and AIDS. Long-term illness and death, relating in part to sexual behaviors, have vitalized the sexual recovery movement and brought forward tragic realities to the gay community. Unquestionably, exploration of the ramifications of unprotected sex can be a primary intervention tool in sexual addiction treatment. Thus the direct and nonshaming use of such terms as *violating to others* or *abusive* may effectively help to convey to an addict in denial the reality of unsafe sexual practices. Thanks to the proliferation of invaluable programs and literature, the concept of *safe sex* is now almost universally known in the gay community. However, despite these efforts, safer sexual practice is actually on the decline. Overall, safer sex practices among gay men may be declining, possibly due to boredom with safe sexual practice. HIV-prevention training materials and messaging rarely acknowledge sexual addiction, but clearly, there are many men who will engage in potentially life-threatening sexual behavior related to the intensity of the moment and possibly may later risk a partner's health (male or female) in order to protect their own sexual secrets. It is imperative for any clinician treating sexual addicts to ask direct questions about safe sexual practice and be aware that unknowing partners could be infected due to the addict's behavior. See chapter 14 for specific guidelines for treating HIV-infected clients.

GRIEF AND LOSS

In addition to working through the anticipated grief of surrendering active sexual addiction, patients may have additional emotional burdens in relationship to HIV and AIDS health disorders, which have devastated the gay community. Many have lost friends, partners, and acquaintances to AIDS, though many addict patients will not have not fully grieved these losses, as the addiction process can preempt healthy grief resolution. A primary function of the treatment process is to help provide patients with the safety to grieve partner loss, survivor guilt, and the sequelae of trauma of having cared for the sick. HIV testing itself can often be a defining intervention treatment issue, helping to break down a sexual addict's denial system. Gay sexual addicts who are HIV-positive have their own personal mourning to confront, as well as hidden guilt and shame about the possibility of having infected others with the virus. The HIV-positive sexual addict who feels despair about his status may no longer believe there is any reason to bother with safe sexual practice. This kind of denial regarding the victimization of self and others is open to confrontation, behavior modification, and affective release.

> Alex, a 27-year-old single homosexual male, had in his early 20s been diagnosed as HIV-positive. Depressed and isolated regarding his own HIV status, the possibility of his own declining health, and the loss of several friends due to AIDS, Alex increasingly turned for comfort and distraction to anonymous encounters in the sex clubs, along with the use of crystal meth. Several weekends a month he would check into a sexual bathhouse or sex club, do drugs, and have anonymous sex, often with 15 or more partners. When he entered addiction treatment, Alex admitted that he had not been having safe sex in those situations and had to face the realities that he may have infected others with the virus, as well as reinfecting himself. At the time Alex stated, "I just figured they were there for the same thing that I was and that if they were concerned about HIV they would have asked or pulled out a rubber. Since they didn't do that, I figured they must be positive, too. Besides, what difference does it make who I did or how? I went because I knew that no one would want me now that I have AIDS, so why even try having a relationship or dating?"

SEXUAL RECOVERY AND BOUNDARIES

Like any sexual addict, the homosexual man who is sexually addicted needs help in defining clear boundraries toward creating intimacy and healthy sexuality. The determination of these guidelines is an essential part of early treatment. Although a period of initial celibacy is recommended to help extinguish specific sexual behaviors, a committed, written sexual plan should be established as a basic prescription for evolving romantic and sexual behavior (see *sample plan that follows*). Structure is put in place for dating to encourage the exploration of shared interests, peer status, and mutuality before having sex. Clinicians should keep in mind that homosexual men do not have the traditional heterosexual sanction of legally approved marriage, and many homosexual couples come together without the blessings of conventional religious organizations or family. This should be acknowledged as recovering couples are encouraged to seek out alternative methods for maintaining partnership stability.

SAMPLE SEXUAL PLAN

Behaviors I Wish to Be Free of (Defines Sobriety)

- Anonymous sex (parks, gym locker room, restrooms, etc.)
- Unsafe sex
- Sex prior to 30 days of acquaintance
- Compulsive masturbation to pornography—videos, magazines, online materials
- Phone sex
- Hooking up online for sex
- Sex with former boyfriends
- Sex with men who are in a relationship

Recovery Behaviors I Want More of (Rewards of Recovery)

- Healthy intimacy with friends
- Increased creativity
- Financial security
- Playing with my dog
- Going back to school
- Nonsexual massage
- Regular exercise
- More movies and fun evening activities

Warning Signs (Potential Warnings of Relapse)

- Overeating
- Going out to the bars alone
- Seeing old boyfriends
- Going to bed too late
- Procrastination
- Family visits
- Poor self-care (unmade bed, house a mess, etc.)
- Smoking
- Not getting exercise
- Overworking (more than 45 hours in a week)

CONCURRENT ADDICTIONS

Many sexual addicts suffer from multiple addictions, the phenomena of more than one substance or behavioral addiction or both operating at the same time. According to Carnes's survey of male sexual addicts in treatment (Carnes, 1989), approximately 87% reported more than one addiction in their histories. It is a reasonable hypothesis, though scientific research is clearly needed, that homosexual male sexual addicts would report even higher occurrences of multiple addiction than do heterosexual sexual addicts, as a significantly higher incidence of substance abuse exists in the homosexual population than in the general population. Current data estimates an incidence of substance abuse of approximately 30% in the homosexual population, contrasting with 10%–12% for the general population (Cabaj, 1992). Theories regarding the higher rates of chemical dependency in the gay community are multiple and complex—ranging from biological/genetic to the socio-cultural. Most likely, some combination of these factors contributes to this phenomena. "The use of substances can be associated with identity formation, coming out and self acceptance for many gay men . . . Internalized homophobia and societal homophobia combine to reinforce the use of alcohol and drugs" (Cabaj, 1996).

CYBERSEX

Increasingly over the past several years, the Internet has taken over as the preferred method for men to meet up for anonymous sexual contact. In chat rooms or through personal ads, locally or across nations, men can find each other and hook up for sexual encounters of all kinds without any words exchanged in the actual physical encounter. James tells the story of his typical Internet sexual activity.

Getting home for work I would immediately go online to find someone for sex. Sometimes it would take a few minutes, sometimes I would be online for several hours, but inevitably I would find what I was looking for. Unlike the bars or even the sex clubs where I would have to chance that the person I was seeking might not be into my type of sexual behavior, with the computer I knew in advance that my chosen person would be into exactly what I was seeking. I would tell them over the computer that I wanted them to be undressed and waiting for me when I got there with the lights off and their door unlocked. If I got what I wanted then they would be waiting there for me, ready to have sex right away without conversation or having to know them at all, sometimes I wouldn't even fully see what they looked like until after it was over.

The built in anonymity, affordability, and accessibility of internet sex (Cooper, Delmonico, & Burg, 2000) has added fuel to the fire of sexual addiction for the gay community which is seeing the inevitable problematic result played out in an increase of sexually transmitted disease and challenges for those seeking to create personal intimacy rather than sexual intensity.

In what health officials believe is the first time a disease cluster has been traced to cyperspace, the department of public health here has tracked an outbreak of syphilis cases to an America Online chat room. Officials from the San Francisco Department of Public Health said six men who had contracted syphilis in the last three months have traced their last sexual encounters to partners they met through a chat room. Officials said, "These men represent a sizable number of the 17 syphilis cases reported in San Francisco this year, and the cluster has provided a frightening glimpse of a potentially larger public health risk, as more and more people use computers to find sex partners. (*San Francisco Chronicle*, August 24, 1999)

CRYSTAL METH

Methamphetamine use is by far the most dangerous and troublesome of the more recent addictions to have affected the gay community. Known as "the sex drug," crystal meth is the drug of choice for anonymous sexual activity in bathhouses, in sex clubs, and over the phone sex lines. Users describe the drug's effects as allowing them to be sexual for 24–48 hours at a time without coming down, sleeping, or eating. Safe sex is often not even considered by drug-addicted men who have continuous multiple anonymous partners, often for days at a time. One recovering drug and sexual addict stated, "When you take crystal meth, you can have sex continuously for hours, even days . . . the sex just goes on forever." Another stated, "There was no love, no caring, no emotion involved. I didn't even care who they were, what their names were." Effective treatment for multiple addictions that fuse the drug use and sexual activity must address not only the substance use, but also the addictive, intensity-based nature of these anonymous sexual encounters. Recovery for this type of multiple addiction requires a reintroduction of human relatedness into the patient's sexual interactions, helping patients reestablish ties to intimacy and healthy sexuality.

CULTURAL REINFORCEMENT FOR ADDICTION

For many within the urban gay community, public social activity remains tied to a great degree to the use of alcohol and the seeking of sex, romance or both. It is no coincidence that many of the most consistently successful private local businesses in the urban-American gay community remain the bars and bathhouse/sex clubs. Many popular regional gay publications would not survive without the surfeit of advertising focused on corporeal perfection, sexual massage, prostitution, and sexual partnering/romance. As homosexual men have become more open regarding sexual orientation, there has been an evolution of choice for gay social experiences and involvement. Today, there are ever-expanding numbers of volunteer groups, dating clubs, supportive churches, and recreational organizations, yet despite this phenomena, dance clubs and bars remain as popular and accepted as ever as primary places to socialize or find a sexual/romantic partner. Though ever-increasing numbers of gay men are engaging in creating stable, long-term relationships, the gay bathhouses and sex clubs continue to thrive on men who seek anonymous, casual sexual encounters. These broadly accepted communal activities, immersed in experiences that nourish chemical and sexual addiction, profoundly speak to the ongoing need for effective addiction interventions and experienced treatment professionals who are sensitive to gay culture. Recovering gay men need to be informed as to where they can go for entertainment and social interaction, outside of situations that may encourage relapse. Recovering male sexual addicts need role models and support for creating healthy integrated sexual and romantic relationships. A treating clinician, familiar and comfortable with the gay community, will be able to provide the activities and resources that promote an active stance toward recovery.

SUMMARY

The basic principles of addiction treatment, sound intervention, confrontation of denial systems, containment of self-destructive behavior, shame reduction, affective release, and the introduction of healthy coping skills and relationships fully apply to the treatment of homosexual male sexual addicts. Many underlying elements of early neglect, family dysfunction, and abuse are also the same, though they may manifest differently in homosexual child/adolescent development and in ensuing adult behavior. Overall, there are more similarities to the general population than differences in treating gay sex addicts. Thorough scientific research and study are lacking, with little factual information available regarding the relationship of homosexual male sexual addicts to HIV/AIDS and safe sexual practice, multiple addictions, and primary relationship recovery. The increasing fusion of substance abuse, cybersex, and sexual addiction requires a unique understanding of the dynamics of these multiple addictions in a subculture that is vulnerable to addictive disorders. One area that distinguishes clinical treatment of this population is the degree of acceptance and empathic understanding required of the treating clinician. Working with homosexual sexual addicts requires a unique understanding of this distinct cultural subgroup, with its own dialect, traditions, and cultural beliefs. Successful treatment must recognize and account for these dynamics, while at the same time maintain focus on the addictive process.

REFERENCES

Cabaj, R. P. (1992). Substance abuse in the gay and lesbian community. In J. H. Lowenson, P. Ruiz. & R. B. Millman (Eds.), *Substance abuse: A comprehensive textbook* (2nd ed., pp. 852–860). Baltimore, MD: Williams and Wilkins.

Cabaj, R. P. (1996). Substance abuse in gay men, lesbians and bi-sexuals. In R. P. Cabaj & T. S. Stein (Eds.), *The textbook of homosexuality and mental health*. Washington, DC: American Psychiatric Press.

Carnes, P. (1989). *Contrary to love*. Minneapolis, MN: CompCare.

Carnes, P. (1992). *Out of the shadows*. Minneapolis, MN: Hazelden.

Centers for Disease Control. (1992). Hepatitis A among homosexual men—United States, Canada, and Australia. *Morbidity and Mortality Weekly Report (MMWR)*, *41*, 155–164.

Coleman, E. (1981–1982). Developmental stages of the coming out process. *Journal of Homosexuality*, *7*, 31–43.

Cooper, A., Delmonico, D. E., & Burg, R. (2000). Cybersex users, abusers and compulsives: New findings and implications. *Sexual Addiction and Compulsivity*, *7*, 5–20.

Hanson, G., & Hartmann, L. (1996). Latency development in prehomosexual boys. In R. P. Cabaj & T. S. Stein (Eds.), *The textbook of homosexuality and mental health*. Washington, DC: American Psychiatric Press.

Hunter, M. (1990). *Abused boys*. New York: Fawcett Columbine.

Schneider, J., & Weiss, R. (2001). *Cybersex exposed: Recognizing the obsession*. Center City, MN: Hazeldon.

BIBLIOGRAPHY

Finnegan, D. G., & McNally, E. B. (1987). *Dual identities: Counseling chemically dependent gay men and lesbians*. Minneapolis, MN: Hazelden.

Gonsiorek, J. C. (Ed.). (1982). *Gay and lesbian clients.* New York: Harrington Park.

Green, R. (1987) *The sissy-boy syndrome and the development of homosexuality.* New Haven, CT: Yale University Press.

Harry, J. (1982). *Gay children growing up: Gender, culture, and gender deviance.* New York: Praeger.

CHAPTER 22

Adolescent Sex and Love Addicts

ERIC GRIFFIN-SHELLEY

In a report published in the first year of the new millennium, the United States Surgeon General's Conference on Children's Mental Health (2000) reported that more than 7 out of 10 American adolescents with mental health problems are getting no care. These are the adolescents with obvious difficulties like depression, panic and anxiety disorders, and substance abuse. The story for adolescent sex and love addicts is much worse. Very few of them are identified, and fewer are receiving any type of care or counseling for a disorder that is overwhelmingly shameful and tremendously painful to the sufferer.

Most sex and love addicts trace their initial acting out to adolescence or before. One individual whom I worked with stated that he "never remembers a time when I was not sexual." His fourth-grade teacher noted that he was "touching himself," his peers teased him about masturbating, and he exposed himself at home. His sex addiction was firmly in place by the time that he entered puberty. Then, it escalated to adult bookstores, prostitutes, and phone sex. A woman indicated that she was sexually abused as a preteen. When she became an adolescent, she tried to "turn the tables" on men and boys and would have casual sex with anyone who approached her because it gave her a feeling of power over them. Now, she is involved in sadomasochistic sex, euphemistically called "dominance and submission" (or "D/S"), which is an unconscious reenactment of her abuse, as well as an attempt at mastery over her sexual difficulties.

Working with teenage sex and love addicts is extremely difficult because of the resistance of the adolescents themselves, as well as of their families, other concerned adults, and the community. Much like teen gambling and substance-abuse problems, no one really wants to believe that someone so early in life can be struggling with such overwhelming and shameful problems. I can identify strongly with this point of view. Thirty years ago, I began my career in drug-abuse prevention, working in the community, especially the schools, to help

343

stop the aggressive expansion of chemical abuse in the early '70s. It was not until I actually worked on an adolescent, inpatient unit in the mid-'80s that I came to believe that teens could be addicted to drugs. I knew that they could have drug "problems," but I did not see it as rising to the severity of addiction. Only when I met 16-year-olds who had been using heroin intravenously for over a year, 17-year-olds who had been "tripping" on psychedelic drugs for 3 years and were almost psychotic, and 15-year-olds whose alcohol and marijuana abuse caused them to flunk out of school, get thrown out of their homes, and get arrested, did I see clearly that adolescents could indeed be addicted to drugs and alcohol.

Education is needed to enable people, including teens, parents, teachers, counselors, clergy, and police, to begin to ask the question "Could this teen be addicted to sex, love, or both?" Is this person pathologically dependent on sex or love? Is this adolescent "hooked on" sex, relationships, or both? When I worked on the adolescent unit, that staff knew that I had written a book on adult sex and love addicts. Consequently, they began to refer teens to me who had obvious problems with sex or love. These cases form the bulk of the illustrations in *Adolescent Sex and Love Addicts* (Griffin-Shelley, 1994).

On the unit itself, I began to educate the staff, the teens, and their parents about compulsive sexual and relational behavior. The adolescents themselves, except for those suspected of being addicted, picked up the idea the most rapidly, especially the idea of relationship dependency. They were given ongoing education about substance dependency, and they quickly made the switch to sex and love. In fact, they began to identify peers who were "male dependent" or "female dependent." The area of sexual dependency was more difficult to examine because most people are more secretive about their sexual thoughts, feelings, and behaviors. Even in this regard, the teens themselves were less judgmental of peers who had sex addiction issues than were the adults who knew these children.

The adults had more blinders and were more resistant to the thought that someone "so young" could already be dependent on sex and love. Counselors and teachers were a bit more open. Probably not surprisingly, the most resistance came from parents. The home environment, obviously, contributed to the development of sex and love addictions. An example of this is a middle-aged professional who came to me for treatment of his compulsive use of pornography, including adult videos, magazines, and the Internet, and an obsessive need to both please and humiliate women. In his family, he had been exposed to a dominant mother and a submissive father who had a pornography collection that focused on humiliating sexual acts with women. My client had been exposed to his father's collection at age 8 by his older brother. His obsession with sadomasochistic sex and compulsive masturbation were firmly established in his adolescent years, although they did not come to light until he sought treatment in his late 30s.

Adolescent sexuality and love relationships are challenging to adults. Some of this, obviously, has to do with their own unresolved issues around romantic and sexual relationships. Clearly, due to hormonal changes, boys and girls go through dramatic physical maturation starting from age 10 (or earlier). Different rates of growth can have profound effects on teens. A girl who develops breasts or begins her menses at age 10 will have few peers to relate to and may be overwhelmed by these early developments. Likewise, a boy who does not have secondary sex characteristics like facial hair or a hormonal-induced growth spurt until he is 15 will have difficulty adapting to his rate of development. Both are likely to be teased and ostracized by their peers. Their parents, teachers, and other adults in their lives may not be able to assist them in these normal challenges of development.

What happens to teens who become obsessed with love or are driven to be sexual? Who will understand them? Who will help them? Counselors and therapists, teachers and coaches, community leaders and parents are all likely to be confused, frustrated, embarrassed, and angry with sex- and love-addicted adolescents. Sex and love addiction is still highly stigmatized among addictions and mental health problems for adults. Efforts to reduce stigma do not address sex and love addiction specifically. The medical establishment has resisted ongoing efforts to include sex and love addiction in the ultimate arbitrator of diagnoses, the *Diagnostic and Statistical Manual of Mental Disorders*, 4th Edition (*DSM-IV*, 1994), of the American Psychiatric Association. The statistically sound, standard screening test for sex addicts, Patrick Carnes's Sex Addiction Screening Test or SAST (1989), has not been normed for adolescents. Love addiction screening tests have been presented, but none have been statistically tested, nor have they been tested on teens.

Without screening tests and with the desire to recognize normal adolescent experimentation and development, how can professionals determine if a teenager is a sex and love addict? Following the path of assessing adolescent chemical dependency is the most logical direction. Initially, before more sophisticated and reliable screening tools and interview techniques were developed, clinicians used the diagnostic criteria applied to adults, with flexibility built in to account for age and developmental factors. Once a professional is open to the idea that some teenagers could be addicted to sex and love, he or she is at this stage of realization with adolescent sex and love addiction—that is, applying adult criteria with open-mindedness.

Definition of Addiction

Although there is still debate about the definition of addiction, most professionals in the field seem to agree with the World Health Organization, which defined addiction as "a pathological relationship with a mood altering experience or thing that causes damage to the person and/or others." There are three important elements in this definition. A "pathological" relationship is a sick, imbalanced relationship. For teens, this may be somewhat more difficult to determine, due to sexual and relational experimentation and occasional abuse. However, standards for healthy sexuality and relationships apply for adolescents, as well as for adults. For example, healthy relationships involve mutuality, equality, and respect for each other. Sex or love (or both) that fails to meet this standard should at least raise the question of whether it is addictive.

Sex and love qualify as "mood-altering" experiences for all of us. As with chemical use, early experience with sexuality and relationships may involve significantly more risk taking that the naive person expects. The difference between healthy people and addicts is that when sexual or relational experiences cause pain, normal people seek to alter their sexual or relational activities in ways that reduce and preferably eliminate pain. Sex and love addicts, because they are "hooked on" mood alteration, seek to change everything else but their sexual or relational experience. Consequently, a teenager who is masturbating compulsively to the point of self-injury will find ways to adapt the activity—for example, use creams or gels, in order to continue to masturbate. A normal nonaddict would simply wait until the injury heals before resuming the action. Likewise, an adolescent who is hurt in a love relationship would hold back from involvement in another relationship until he or she feels capable of interacting safely again. A love addicted, or "male/female dependent," teen will hop from relationship to relationship, never being without one. Often, these individuals have two or three flirtations and previous relationships "simmering" or waiting in the wings. As they say in Sex and Love Addicts Anonymous, these are "rain checks" in case something happens to their current relationship. Intrigue is part of the active searching for potential partners. Love addicts are never far from their next mood-altering experience.

Furthermore, the sexual or relational activity (or both) needs to cause pain to self and others. Obviously, in healthy relationships and sexual activity, there is pain. Most of us struggle with the fact that "we always hurt the ones we love." Because of our society's sexual hangups, sex can be a source of embarrassment and pain even in couples with strong mutual care and respect. The pain that we are addressing in the addiction is the pain that comes from its obsessive/compulsive nature. A pathological attachment to sex, love, or both means that the mood-altering experience is the addicts' priority in life—not the people who populate their world. Consequently, partners of sex addicts feel "used" by their sexual partners. Often, partners of sex addicts try to be more sexual than they feel comfortable with, in order to please their partners. Partners of love addicts can feel stalked, possessed, and smothered by the attention of their love-addicted partners. For adolescents, these reactions to pathological attachments need to be considered with a "grain of salt" for developmental issues. Is the difficulty in a sexual relationship because one or both of the partners are naive, victims of abuse, or immature? Typically, relationships have intense periods of sexual activity. Sometimes, this occurs initially. For others, the sexual height is during the "honeymoon" after a commitment is made. Normally, the passion wanes after the "honeymoon" or initial engagement. A sex and love addict seeks this level of intensity at all times in his or her sexual or romantic relationships (or both). For teens, initial experiences with sex and love are new and, consequently, intense. Nonaddicted teens will enjoy this passion, but when it fades and relationships and sexuality mature, they accept these changes with understanding and appreciation. A need for intensity may signal an addiction to sex and love.

SYMPTOMS OF ADDICTION

Just as with the definition, there is no universally accepted list of symptoms of sex and love addiction. However, nine characteristics are generally accepted as part of addictions: pursuit of the "high," tolerance, dependency, withdrawal, cravings, obsession, compulsion, secrecy, and personality change (Griffin-Shelley, 1991). With adolescent sex and love addicts, these symptoms have not had 30 years to develop, but the sex addict who started masturbating at age 6 has 10 years of habituation and reinforcement by the age of 16, and the love addict who was falling for pretty girls in first grade (usually age 6) likewise has 12 years of addiction by age 18.

As noted previously, sex and love can be intoxicating. It would be "sex negative" and prudish to suggest that people should avoid these feelings. Sex and love are essential to life and to reproduction of the species. Problematic sexual or romantic involvements are characterized by the pursuit of sexual or relational activity solely for the "good feeling," the "high," and not for the interpersonal rewards of physical and emotional intimacy. In fact, sex and love addicts have an unhealthy attachment to the euphoria and pleasure that they experience, without regard or need for an attachment to the other. They are attached to their fantasies, not to reality. Consequently, a sex addict can compulsively masturbate to Internet pornography and have only superficial relationships with peers. Love addicts can be "in love with love" and not care to really know the people in their fantasy world. Clinicians and others need to be open to observing whether the romantic and sexual involvements of an adolescent are with the people themselves or with the good feelings that the activity generates. One question to ask is, "Is sex [or love] the organizing principle around which this teen's life revolves?"

Tolerance means that the person needs more and more to get the same result. Addictions are often described as progressive, potentially fatal diseases. Tolerance addresses the progressive nature of the disorder. A sex addict teen may have discovered masturbation, but the activity became increasingly frequent from once a week to daily, perhaps numerous times each day. There may be a progression from fantasy, to pornographic magazines, to adult videos, to Internet chat rooms, to phone sex, to making pornography. A love-addicted adolescent may idolize one person and gradually develop a collection of pictures, letters, diaries, and memorabilia around the love/obsession object. The love addict teen may move from relationship to relationship when the romance fades (1 to 3 months), leaving a string of "broken hearts." This teen may not be able to stop flirting, "intriguing" (as they say in the Sex and Love Addiction program), and cruising for a new relationship, even when he or she is in what appears to be a committed relationship.

Relationship dependency, or "I can't live without him or her," seems commonplace in adolescent romances. Because there is no apparent physiological *dependency* that occurs as there is with some drugs, the dependency here is primarily psychological. A sex- and love-addicted teen cannot imagine life without sex or love. One sex-addicted teen used fantasy and masturbation as a nightly ritual and was convinced that sleep would be impossible without using orgasm as a "sleeping pill." A love-addicted teen attempted suicide, rather than living without love. Depression and suicide are more common than people thought 30 years ago. In fact, the U.S. Surgeon General reported that "For young people 15–24 years old, suicide is the third leading cause of death, behind unintentional injury and homicide. In 1996, more teenagers and young adults died of suicide than from cancer, heart disease, AIDS, birth defects, stroke, pneumonia and influenza, and chronic lung disease *combined*" (http://www.surgeongeneral.gov/library/calltoaction/fact3.htm). Despite our growing awareness of the risk of suicide in teens, do we ask what's behind that desire to die? Do we consider sex and love dependency as an answer to what might drive teens to harm themselves? If not, why not?

Physiological *withdrawal* from some chemicals, especially alcohol, can be life-threatening. However, the physical symptoms can be managed safely under medical supervision. The usual cause of relapse is the psychological withdrawal from the "drug of choice." Sex and love addicts go through a withdrawal period that is typically 1 to 3 months. They have the usual symptoms—that is, irritability, anxiety, depression, tension, difficulty sleeping, disturbed appetite and energy levels, problems with concentration, and preoccupation. The reality of the question "Can I live without this [sex or love] in my life?" stares them in the face. Activity, distractions, and encouragement that "This, too, shall pass" help the addict survive this difficult time. Sex and love addicts are encouraged, sometimes even contracted, to abstain from sexual activity and new romantic involvement for at least 90 days. Sex is appropriate in the context of a committed relationship, according to Sex and Love Addicts Anonymous.

Adolescents are not used to withdrawal, so it is an unusually difficult experience for them to go through. Mutual support from other addicts can be essential to adolescents' surviving this phase of recovery. Older addicts have often had more than one previous attempt at sobriety, so they have some idea what is in store for them in withdrawal.

Addicts usually experience *cravings*, which are intense desires to act out sexually or romantically. Cravings are usually the strongest when sobriety or abstinence is the weakest, often in early recovery. Learning to cope with cravings is key to successful relapse prevention. Addicts need to plan in advance a coping strategy for dealing with cravings. Often, they are encouraged to call another addict and share with them their current struggles. Sharing at meetings is also a frequent suggestion. Similar to withdrawal, teens have not had much training in dealing with resisting cravings successfully. Adolescence typically is a time of experimentation and "trying on" new roles and persona. Teens rarely have the life experience to distinguish between giving in to a self-destructive impulse, a craving to act out on their sex and love addiction, from trying something that does not have serious, potentially lifelong consequences. Is it normal teen exuberance and experimentation, or is it addiction being cemented in place?

A key element of addiction is *obsession*. An obsessive thought is one that does not go away. In gestalt psychology, our attention is described as having a foreground and a background. If you look at your finger, the finger is the center of your awareness, but the rest of reality fills in the background. In normal experience, something comes to our attention, to our foreground, gets resolved, and moves to the background. An obsession is a thought that is stuck in the foreground. No matter how a person tries to resolve it, avoid it, become distracted from it, it remains central in his or her mind. Addictions become central in this way. When sex and love addiction is central, the sex and love addict obsesses about sex, love, or both. The obsession may take the form of planning sexual acting out or a romantic escapade, sexual or romantic fantasies, or euphoric recall of past sexual or relational experiences.

Sex and love obsessions in teens "leak out" in the form of sexual jokes or innuendo in conversation, flirting, intriguing, cruising normal contacts for sexual or romantic partners, poetry, doodling, writting in journals, letters focused on sex or relationships, or any combination of these. Often peers, adults, and parents notice these obsessions—for example, "Can't you think or anything else but him or her?" or "Can't you think of anything else but sex?" but they dismiss these warning signs as "normal" and "a phase" and do not intervene, explore the issue, or suggest getting help.

Not surprisingly, obsessive thoughts lead to *compulsive* behaviors. Some clinicians prefer the term *sexual compulsion* to *sexual addiction*. I use the two interchangeably. Sometimes, the term *relationship dependency* is used, rather than *love addiction* (because people "don't want to give love a bad name"). I've not yet seen terms like *compulsive love* or *love compulsivity* used like *sexual compulsivity*. In any case, compulsive behavior is driven. To the person, the compulsion feels unstoppable, inevitable, like a freight train without brakes. Obviously, as with the other aspects of addiction, teens have little or no experience with trying to stop a compulsion. Some sex addicts report that from their first masturbatory experience, they were sexually compulsive. Similarly, some love addicts get "hooked" from their first love experience. One sex addict said that he was swooning for girls in fourth grade and compulsively looking for that "one true love" who would take away his shame, self-hatred, and loneliness. The compulsion fuels the progression of the addiction. One adolescent found himself moving rapidly from fantasies, to pornographic magazines and stories, to adult videos, to finally making his own pornographic videotapes.

Secrecy is an element in every addiction, but due to the intense shame around sex and love addictions, sex and love addicts are even more secretive. They began their double lives as children. Their compulsive sexual and romantic involvements were too risky to reveal to others. One sex and love addict refused to go on a family trip because he did not want to be far from his obsessive love object. He was ridiculed and humiliated for this for years afterward. Another sex addict took mental pictures of the other boys in the showers after gym and compulsively masturbated to these secret fantasies throughout high school.

Finally, addicts often develop a *personality change*, especially as their addiction progresses. Friends and family members of addicts often describe them as Dr. Jekyll/Mr. Hyde types; that is, they can be nice, warm, responsible people, but when they are "under the influence of" their addiction, they are irritable, self-centered, impulsive people who seem like they "don't care" about others. Addicts learn to develop their capacity for dissociation to the point where they can live double lives, where they are split between their addict self and their nonaddictive self. One adolescent was the ideal student, always helpful, hardworking, and pious in front of others, but in the privacy of his bedroom, he wrote sadistic pornographic stories for his own gratification. A love-addicted teen was one person when she was "in love" and another when she was not; for example, she was pleasant and reasonable when in love, but irritable, overly demanding, and inconsiderate when looking for love.

TYPES OF ADDICTIVE BEHAVIOR

Because so many people seem to have trouble with the idea that adolescents can become addicted to sex and love, some concrete examples of addictive behavior may shed light on this concealed problem. The first have to do with general addictive thoughts, feelings, and behaviors about sex and love. Patrick Carnes developed a Sexual Addiction Inventory (1989) that identifies may of these problem areas. These difficulties elaborate the previous definition—that is, the "pathological relationship" with sex and love as "mood-altering experiences." For sex and love addicts, this "sick" relationship is the "central organizing principle" in their lives. Everything else revolves around sex and love.

Consequently, there are many distortions in their thinking, many apparently irrational feelings stemming from these distorted thoughts, and obviously hurtful behaviors emerging from these twisted thoughts and illogical feelings.

At times, these unusual thoughts, feelings, and behaviors may be due to immaturity, inexperience, and insecurity, all of which are typically adolescent, but teens, parents, and others involved with these adolescents would be most helpful to these teens if they did not so readily dismiss these problems with the assumption that time, personal growth, and life experience will change them. If these are the budding signs of a sex and love addiction, time will allow only for reinforcement of the addictive process because growth has been halted, at least in these areas, and experience seems to drive the addiction forward.

Obsession, preoccupation, and spending excessive amounts of time related to sex and love are key elements of the addiction. For adolescents, their obsessive love will probably be easier to observe than their constant thoughts about sex. However, one sex addict teen's frequent visits to the men's room to masturbate were noticed by his peers, and he became the object of their ridicule. This humiliation by his peers, of course, fed the compulsion because he had no alternative coping skills and was too ashamed to ask for help.

Probably the most common cognitive distortion is thinking that "sex is love" or that obsessive/possessive love is love. Obviously, the need for unconditional love is underneath both of these distorted thoughts. Before you can get to that level, however, you need to explore what these thoughts really mean and how the person learned them. One teen sex addict learned to think "sex is love" from observing his older sister have sex with her boyfriends. One love-addicted adolescent saw her parents' emotional distance and decided that love meant enmeshment—in other words, the opposite of what she felt and observed in her family.

A rather wise member of Alcoholics Anonymous must have observed that the "insanity" of the addiction mentioned in the 2nd Step meant "doing the same thing over and over again and expecting different results." Most 12-step fellowships have absorbed this wisdom and pass it on to newcomers. Repeating compulsive sex and love behaviors with the distorted thought that "This time things will be different" is the hallmark of the addiction. Every addict can relate to this concept. However, in an active addiction, the cycle repeats itself endlessly. The defenses of denial, rationalization, minimization, and projection operate to preserve the sex and love addicts' status quo. The love addict says, "This relationship will be different." The sex addict says, "This time I will only look at online pornography for 15 minutes."

Teenagers have less perspective on this repetitive pattern, which is one reason that the possibility that they are addicted is dismissed. Remember the teen who by 15 had been masturbating for 10 years. Remember the teen who has had anonymous sex with more than 100 partners. Remember the teen who is on his or her third suicide attempt after a failed love relationship. These adolescents may be ready for the diagnosis of sex and love addiction and, in fact, they may be greatly relieved that finally someone knows what is wrong with them and offers them some hope for recovery.

Sex and love addicts feel that they have to have sex even when they do not want to, that they have to follow through once they have seduced someone with their intrigue, that they feel depressed or worthless after having sex, and that they find periods of abstinence to be extremely difficult. Confusion about sex and love abounds. Is sex love? Can you use love to find sex? Adolescents are confused about these things just due to normal developmental issues. Add in a history of neglect or abuse, and there is even more confusion. Abuse issues and normal developmental tasks seem to sidetrack most clinicians from considering sex and love addiction. However, therapy without an addiction perspective does not usually work for obsessions and compulsive behaviors. One of my clinical rules-of-thumb is that if normal therapy is not working, look for an addiction. So, if clinical work around abuse issues and developmental tasks is not working, then consider a hidden addiction. The most hidden addiction will be sex and love addiction.

Often, when working with adolescents, clinicians do not get a detailed history of their relationships and their sexual education and development. In this history, the role of masturbation and the fantasies used for arousal may be significant. Experimentation and exploration with masturbation are normal for teens of both sexes. Masturbation once or twice a week, usually when they do not have an active sex life or a willing partner, is common. However, masturbatory behavior can be problematic, especially if there are deviant fantasies as part of the arousal pattern. In an effort not to be "sex negative," clinicians can unwittingly overlook or even encourage compulsive masturbation. A number of clients have told stories of confession to priests or revelations in therapy about their out-of-control sexual behaviors, only to be told, "It's normal," "Don't worry about it," or "It will go away." Unfortunately for some, it not only did not go away, it escalated into a much more damaging form of sex and love addiction.

Involvement with pornography is another area of concern, especially with the easy access and availability through the Internet. Many sex addicts report that their sexual addiction started with preadolescent exposure to their father's pornography collection. Typically, the involvement escalates from pictures and magazines, to written stories, to videotapes and movies, to live shows and adult bookstores. Some advance to making their own stories, pictures, and videos. Often, they keep a collection. Their overstimulation leads them to looking for stimulating pictures or suggestive moments in newspapers, magazines, on television and the Internet, and movies. Again, there is the question, Is this normal sexual exploration and education, or is this sexual addiction? The degree of obsession, compulsion, secrecy, and withdrawal should point to the extent of the onset of addiction. A teenager in residential treatment was identified as an addict because he bored holes in the wall in his room in order to observe the females in the next room. When questioned in more detail about his sexual activities, he indicated that he was all ready to the point of making his own pornographic movies and that he "had to have sex every day."

Adolescents are involved in purchasing and selling sex in person, on the phone, and on the Internet. Both male and female prostitution are known to be related to drug-addiction because drug addicted teens need money. Often, people fail to consider the possibility that these adolescents became addicted to sex and love, as well as to chemicals. A boy who was sexually abused by his father discovered during his teen years, as his sex addiction flowered, that he could get paid to have sex with older men as a "hustler."

Instead of various forms of prostitution, some sex addicts confine their acting out to one-night stands, casual sex, and anonymous sex. Others, those who could be called love addicts, have a series of relationships one right after the other. One 16-year-old said that she had sex with numerous boys at a time, but that she could not have sex with them if she knew their names. Some look to swap partners or to get their partners to have sex with others. Others cruise beaches, parks, gyms, malls, public bathrooms, and baths to find sex partners. Sex addicts advertise in personal columns and on the Internet. Some seek sexual highs with sexual activity outside their orientation, or with transvestites, or with different racial or ethnic groups. A sex-addicted teen was "thrilled" to find that he could "score" at the mall, the park, and the gym. Another found that he could never be faithful to one girlfriend. He "always cheated on them," which created guilt feelings that in turn drove him to numb the pain through more acting out. In Alcoholics Anonymous, they say, "One drink is too many and 1,000 is not enough." He was learning that in sex addiction, there are never enough partners.

Adolescents are keenly aware of the double standard for men and women regarding exhibitionism in America. Essentially, men are arrested and jailed for exposing themselves, whereas women are rewarded for taking off their clothes and exposing their genitals. Exhibitionism can take many forms, which include being in a car or in public places, but it can also be found on stage; in one's home; through pictures or videos; in bathrooms, showers, and locker rooms; and by one's choice of clothing. One adolescent sex addict discovered that he could expose himself at a bookstore coffee shop by wearing loose shorts and no underwear. Another addict found that she could supplement the sexual high of stripping with the "rush" of having power over men at bars and clubs where she danced. Adolescent sex and love addicts may appear to be going through the normal developmental issues of establishing an identity, of being "known," with these behaviors, but there is an underlying loss of control, powerlessness, and unmanageability that is not present in healthy maturation.

Voyeurism is also a major issue for adolescent sex and love addicts. Some find that this was their initial involvement in the addiction and may have even predated their teen years. One reported "looking for love" in fifth grade, compulsive staring at the opposite sex, and obsessively reviewing the "mental pictures" of the day each evening, followed by masturbation. Another teen, after observing his father masturbating while looking out the window at the neighbor, exposed himself to a sunbathing neighbor whose police officer husband threatened to have him arrested. One teen found herself driven to buy and read romance novels and obsessed about love objects whom she encountered during the day. Again, many teenagers have similar behaviors, but they are not as driven and do not suffer from the same consequences as sex- and love-addicted adolescents.

The addicted teens are in a great deal of emotional pain, which gets acted out in all of these various ways. The active addiction actually interferes with accomplishing the developmental tasks of this stage of life. Hours spent looking through peepholes, binoculars, and windows, hoping to see a sexual incident, or cruising Internet websites and chat rooms for "cyber sex," produce lonely, isolated adolescents lacking in self-confidence and social skills. Sexualizing people in public places like malls, beaches, and parks or in gyms, locker rooms, and restrooms instills shame and eventually despair, the feeling of being "an outsider looking in" on life.

Frotteurism, taking "indecent liberties," or rubbing up against people in public places in order to feel sexually stimulated, occurs with adolescent sex and love addicts. One teen love addict "cruised" television and movies for beautiful women to swoon for. A sex-addicted teen rubbed up against women at church, despite obvious comments about his inappropriate and sexualized contact. Another teen found that she could find sex partners by touching men and boys in sexual ways.

Many adolescents experiment with more subtle sexual contacts, such as flirting, sexual innuendo, sexual jokes and humor, and using explicit sexual stories or language as part of their identity development. They may be imitating adults or discovering what is effective in creating sexual and romantic encounters. Sex and love addicts use these behaviors to expose their sexual interest and assess the responsiveness of others. One teen openly joked about being a "sex addict" to see who would be intrigued and willing to explore more overtly. Another teenager's constant flirting earned her the label of "male dependent" from her peers.

Adolescents are not free from having paraphilias such as fetishes, sadomasochism, or transvestitism. The diagnostic dilemma is, again, what is an experiment and what is an addiction? Does a teen with a fascination for feet, curiosity about bondage, or intrigue with cross-dressing automatically become labeled perverse? Societal shame tends to cause people to react strongly to abnormal sexual interests and activities. These intensely negative feelings are more vestiges of our puritanical past than appropriate responses to normal developmental curiosity and experimentation. With this in mind, it is also important not to minimize, excuse, or deny the possibility of sexual addiction when such behaviors and interests surface. One teen was introduced early to bondage from his father's pornography. As it was with his father, this quickly became an addictive outlet for his repressed rage at his mother. Another adolescent experienced intense shame at being caught in a neighbor's home, attempting to steal underwear for cross-dressing. He attempted suicide, but the counselors never asked for details about his sexual activity and what drove him to invade someone else's home to satisfy his sexual addiction.

Some adolescent sex addicts make obscene phone calls, others engage in phone sex. The Internet has given sex addicts the opportunity to engage in "cyber sex," where partners engage in explicit sex chat while masturbating. Sometimes, this leads to phone sex and in-person meetings. Often, people who would not otherwise engage in overt sexual acting out will experiment with it on the Internet. Cooper, Delmonico, and Berg (2000) suggested that these people fell into an "at-risk" group and that "anonymity, access, and affordability" facilitate their deeper involvement. Although there is no research yet, it is quite likely that the "cyber generation"—that is, adolescents who have grown up with access to the Internet—may be using this medium for sexual education, experimentation, and addictive acting out.

TREATMENT

Effective treatment of sex and love addiction usually involves psychoeducation, psychotherapy, and support (Griffin-Shelley, 1994). Education takes the form of bibliotherapy (reading about the topic), written work (keeping journals, writing assignments), and individual and group discussion. Psychotherapy includes individual and group therapy with counselors experienced in sex and love addiction and, especially for the adolescent patient, family therapy whenever possible. Support comes from peers, informed adults, and people in recovery (12-step meetings, online resources). Resources for adults are growing significantly; for example, there are over 50 books written about sex and love addiction, but sex and love addiction in adolescents remains "in the shadows" (the title Carnes used in 1983 for the first book on sexual addiction). There are major barriers for adolescents who want or need treatment for their sex and love addictions.

BARRIERS TO TREATMENT

Diagnosis

A large hurdle to the recognition of sex and love addiction by treatment professionals is its lack of inclusion in the *Diagnostic and Statistical Manual of Mental Disorders* (DSM), the "bible" of classification of psychiatric disorders. Addiction medicine is a relatively new specialty. Alcoholism was not recognized as a disease until 1955, and cocaine addiction was not included until 1980. The term *sexual addiction* was actually used in the 1987 edition of the *DSM (III-R)* in an example of "Sexual Disorder, Not Otherwise Specified (NOS), but the words were dropped in the 1994 edition (*DSM-IV*). That edition, as an illustration of "Sexual Disorder, NOS," did include "distress about a pattern of repeated sexual relationships involving a succession of lovers who are experienced by the individual only as things to be used [i.e., sex objects]." This could be the beginning of a diagnostic category for sex addiction and, if "love" was substituted for "sexual," the foundation for love addiction would be present. Not surprisingly, in all of this, no mention is made of adolescents.

Parents

In terms of treatment, the main obstacle can be the adolescent's parents. There are many reasons for resistance to identification and treatment of sex and love addiction by parents. First, most carry shame about sexual and relational issues from our culture. They and their children are somehow supposed to know about healthy sex and relationships, often without adequate models or education. They do not want to be labeled "sick," especially with any addiction and even more so with sex and love addiction, nor do they want their children to carry such a stigmatized diagnosis. For most parents, having a mentally ill child, by implication, means that they are "bad parents." Shame and self-blame need to be processed in order to overcome this barrier. Parents and teens need to understand that ignoring, minimizing, or avoiding an addiction will have major lifelong consequences and that, no matter how devastating the diagnosis, it is much easier to change at this point than later in life.

The second major barrier to treatment is parents' fear of looking at themselves. Not only do they not want to be seen as "bad parents," but, even more so, they do not want to be identified as "bad" people, nor do they want to examine their own sexual attitudes and behaviors. The family lives of sex and love addicts vary from enmeshed to disengaged, from rigid to chaotic (Carnes, 1989). Sex and love addicts describe high levels of emotional (98%), sexual (80%), and physical (75%) abuse in their upbringing (Carnes, 1989). Consequently, adolescents who are in these families are dealing with extremely difficult situations. It is not surprising that one of their coping skills might be to escape into sexual or romantic fantasies and behaviors (or any combination of these). Their parents are wounded people, and, as they say in A.A., "hurt people, hurt people." Family therapy not only brings up issues of appropriate parenting and family dynamics, but it also taps into the parents' own family histories and their own hurts from the past. Because these parents have not healed their own wounds, they have passed on their woundedness to their children. In addition, they usually are living in denial, rationalization, or minimization of their hurts, so they have given their children defensive styles of coping and will activate this defensiveness in therapy.

Another problem with the parents of a teenage sex and love addict is codependency. Codependency is an idea that grew out of alcoholism treatment. Some alcoholics' partners seemed to "enable" the addicts to drink. They made excuses for them, overlooked their problematic behavior (ignoring what is referred to as the "elephant in the living room"), and saw themselves as "only helping" when, in fact, they were contributing to the problem by softening or alleviating the negative consequences of drinking. They seemed to be overly dependent on the alcoholic, hence the term *codependency*, or a dependency coexisting with alcohol dependency. The parents may be emotionally dependent on the adolescent and may unconsciously "enable" their sexual and romantic acting out.

The parents of one teen thought that they had hidden their homosexuality from the world by living as a heterosexual couple while each had a same-sex partner. Their need to remain hidden allowed them to ignore their daughter's out-of-control sexual acting out, even when "cars of boys" came to the house, honked, and took their teen to the local park for anonymous sex. A mother's dependence on her husband was so strong that she could not enforce her demand that he remove his pornography collection because she knew their sons were all ready involved.

Other difficulties that parents face in bringing their sex- and love-addicted teens into treatment include intellectual, financial, and spiritual limitations. Some have difficulty grasping the "big picture," in thinking abstractly, and understand only concrete explanations and interventions. Some are poor, have little or no health insurance, and cannot afford the costs of psychotherapy. Some have not been exposed to healthy spirituality or may even have been harmed spiritually in their past. Each of these barriers needs to be recognized, processed, and resolved for the treatment to go forward. Finally, although there is a strong "taboo" against this, some parents vicariously get off on their children's sexual acting out.

Other Adults

As noted earlier, other adults who interact with adolescents often are reluctant to see or identify sex and love addictions in children "so young." Relatives, teachers, coaches, ministers, and counselors usually only see the "tip of the iceberg" because of the sex- and love-addicted teens' efforts to maintain secrecy and stay "in the shadows." If these adults have "blind spots" or resistance to acknowledging sexual addiction and love dependency in adolescents, the addicts will collude with them to keep their shameful thoughts, feelings, and behaviors hidden. In addiction terms, this blindness is the basis for codependency, which occurs with other adults as well as with parents. Codependency in adults comes from ignorance, their own woundedness, or, even worse, perpetrator tendencies.

Ignorance about sex and love addiction is understandable, but changeable. Other adults have much the same difficulties in dealing with their own hurts as do parents. Sayings like "Put it behind you," "Get over it," "Move on," and "It happened," carry a lot of weight in American society. The value of working through past wounds is greatly underestimated. At times, it seems there is a need to rush to forgiveness without full expression of the feelings associated with the violation. Unfortunately, this blindness to the influence of the past creates blindness to the problems in the present. Worse, avoiding the resolution of past wounds can lead to perpetrating new victims. About 80% of sexual offenders have histories of sexual victimization as children, a similar percentage as those adults who identify as sexual addicts as adults. So, an adolescent who was molested by his uncle and "never told anyone" grows up to compulsively molest teenage boys who were the same age as he was when he was molested. His sexual addiction grew from fantasy and masturbation to sexual victimization.

Sometimes, adult sex and love addicts who are in recovery are reluctant to even talk to, let alone get involved with, adolescents who are seeking help for sexual addiction. This is usually because of their own vulnerability to acting out with teenagers, but it can also be a fear of being labeled a child molester if they pay attention to teens who attend 12-step fellowship meetings. This barrier can be misinterpreted by adolescents who attend meetings as rejection and a message that they are not welcome in the fellowship.

A fellowship for teenagers like Alateen would be extremely helpful for children of sex and love addicts. In the process of dealing with their parents' addictions, so adolescents would self-identify their own addictive behavior as people do in Alanon and Alateen. This sometimes happens for adults in the S-fellowship partners' support groups, S-Anon, COSA, and Co-SLAA.

Peers

As with parents and other adults, peers can be a barrier to help and treatment out of their own shame, embarrassment, or lack of understanding about sex and love (their own woundedness), as well as codependency. As I indicated before, with education, teenagers can learn what addiction to sex and love is and how to identify it in others. Very few adolescents have been exposed to the concept of sex and love addiction, but most teenagers do have a general understanding of chemical dependency. They see both experimentation and dependency in their peers. They usually know who is abusing drugs and alcohol, and almost a third have directly experienced nicotine dependency by the end of high school. Most have known peers who are obsessed with something, such as Pokeman cards, and who exhibit compulsive behaviors—for example, video game fanatics. They need to be exposed to the idea that sex and love can be dangerous not only in terms of pregnancy and sexually transmitted diseases, but also in the potential for life-threatening addiction. They need to be educated about where to draw the line between experimentation, abuse, and addiction. They need to know that addicts don't "learn from their mistakes" and what behaviors and patterns can be symptomatic of addiction.

Clearly, adolescents do not have the same life experience or perspective that an older person has. Teens are ambivalent about this because they want to grow, learn, and be independent, while not getting hurt in the process. Many teenagers have already been hurt in sexual and love relationships. Anywhere from 30 to 50% of women and 10 to 25% of men report inappropriate sexual contact before they were 18. So, adolescents may be blind to sex and love addiction out of their own desire to ignore what happened to them. Their woundedness may not be the result of direct sexual or romantic abuse, but they may have been harmed by parental and societal attitudes about sex and love. In either case, the unresolved hurts can create barriers to the identification and treatment of sex and love addiction in their peers. Adolescents are more likely to listen to their peers; this is why many outreach and prevention programs use "peer counselors." Silence from peers about their out-of-control sex and love lives will allow addicts to tell themselves that they are "okay" and don't need help.

Teens can also be codependent. Their need to be liked or loved may lead them to reassure partners that their behaviors are acceptable. An insecure teenage girl may be flattered by the online attention and flirtation of a male peer. Her intrigue could lead her to experience phone sex. As the addiction progresses, she may rationalize that she feels "grown up" and "liberated" and may blind herself from the progression of her acting out. Once engaged in a relationship, her need for love may codependently lead her to violate her own values and integrity, perhaps by participating in three-way sex. The initial excitement has become fear, but she feels unable to let go of the relationship because, now, she "can't live without it."

Naivete or codependency may lead teens to tragic sexual assaults by perpetrators who victimize children in what appears to be a compulsive pattern. Sexually addicted adults may seek out teenagers as part of their sexual acting-out ritual. Likewise, sexually addicted teens may victimize other teens. In fact, among adults, it is not unheard of for two sex and love addicts to find each other and engage in an intense relationship. Confusing intensity for intimacy, they foster addictive behavior much as chemically dependent partners—for example, "drinking buddies"—can enable the progression of addictions.

Lack of Training and Research

Another significant barrier to better help for adolescent sex and love addicts is the lack of professional training and research in the field. Most training for professionals who want to learn about sex and love addiction comes from the literature, attending professional conferences, and supervision or consultation with a more experienced therapist. Dr. Carnes at the Meadows in Wickenberg, Arizona, offers week-long trainings and certification in sexual addiction treatment. Trauma bonds and unhealthy relationships are addressed in his curriculum and writings (Carnes, 1998). Generally, love addiction gets much less attention, although it may be more prevelant. Professional schools may include sexual addiction in an overview course on addictions, but they rarely refer to love addiction.

Obviously, there is much to learn about sex and love addiction and a great deal to know about adolescents who become addicted to sex and love. Research is desperately needed to establish more objective, scientifically based diagnosis, treatment, and prevention efforts. We know from the United States Surgeon General's Conference on Children's Mental Health (2000) that most American adolescents with mental health problems are not getting care. Sex- and love-addicted teens are one of the most stigmatized and ignored subgroups in this population.

BIBLIOGRAPHY

American Psychiatric Association. (1994). *Diagnostic and statistical manual of mental disorders*, 4th ed. Washington, DC: American Psychiatric Association.

Carnes, P. (1983). *Out of the shadows: Understanding sexual addiction*. Minneapolis, MN: CompCare.

Carnes, P. (1989). *Contrary to love: Helping the sexual addict*. Minneapolis, MN: CompCare.

Carnes, P. (1998). *The betrayal bond: Breaking free of exploitive relationships*. Deerfield Beach, FL: Health Communications.

Cooper, A., Delmonico, D. L., & Burg, R. (2000). Cybersex users, abusers, and compulsives: New findings and implications. *Sexual Addiction and Compulsivity: The Journal of Treatment and Prevention*, 7, 1–2.

Griffin-Shelley, E. (1991). *Sex and love: Addiction treatment and recovery*. New York: Praeger.

Griffin-Shelley, E. (1994). *Adolescent sex and love addicts*. Westport, CT: Praeger.

Surgeon General. (2000). Surgeon General's conference on children's mental health: Developing a national action agenda. http://www.surgeongeneral.gov/cmh/default.htm

CHAPTER 23

Classifying Problematic Sexual Behavior

A Working Model Revisited

DAVID L. DELMONICO
ELIZABETH GRIFFIN

A variety of factors have long separated the fields of sexual addiction and sexual offense behavior. Recent literature has examined the similarities and differences between clients from both fields and has suggested that there may be more overlap between the two populations than once thought. The barriers that have kept the fields from working together on assessment and treatment issues are being replaced by bridges that provide promise for clients suffering from these problematic sexual behaviors. This chapter proposes a four-quadrant model of conceptualizing clients with problematic sexual behaviors. These four quadrants represent the (1) sexually addicted sex offender, (2) the sexual offender, (3) the sexual addict, and (4) the sexually concerned. Characteristics, assessment, and treatment of these populations are discussed to emphasize the similarities and suggest categorical differences. This chapter is based on previous literature and anecdotal clinical information. The authors attempt to synthesize previously discussed concepts into an integrated model for clinical application and future research.

INTRODUCTION

The sexual addiction and sexual offender fields historically viewed themselves as unique entities that treated unique populations. Only recently have professionals from both fields examined the similarities between these groups. Research has suggested that there may be an alternative group of subjects with problematic sexual behavior: the sexually addicted sex offender (Blanchard, 1990; Irons & Schneider, 1994). Although the authors use the term *sexual addiction, sexual dependency, sexual compulsivity,* and *hypersexuality* have also been used. Regardless of terminology, most clinicians agree that sexual addiction/compulsivity is present within a distinct group of sexual offenders. One way to improve treatment outcomes is through the use of specific assessment and treatment techniques. This article addresses some of those interventions for four distinct groups: (1) the sexually addicted sex offender; (2) the sexual offender; (3) the sexual addict; and (4) the sexually concerned.

Wolf (1988) proposed a model of sexual aggression and addictive behavior. It was suggested that childhood history, personality, precipitating events, and the addiction cycle are components of the "Aggressive Developmental Sequence" (p. 138). Although there have been long-standing barriers of disagreement among professionals in the sexology, addictionology, and criminal justice fields, this article proposes that a combination of understanding and training in all these fields will ultimately benefit the clients served. It is hoped that placing professional judgments aside and attending to the contributions of each of these fields will expand current assessment and treatment models that are available and reduce recidivism in all quadrants.

Some professionals hesitate at the sexually addicted sex offender diagnosis. Many offender and criminal justice professionals believe that such a label provides an excuse for an individual's problematic sexual behavior. They worry that individuals who molest children or rape may use the label of sexual addiction to minimize their crime and divert the system that imposes consequences for such behavior. Addiction professionals challenge the sexually addicted sex offender diagnosis, assuming that the term *offender* contributes to the unnecessary guilt and shame and ultimately impedes progress in therapy. However, this model suggests that it is possible to hold clients accountable without detriment to treatment progress. Appropriately identifying an individual as a sexually addicted sex offender is neither shaming nor a license to perpetrate, but rather an alternative that can provide avenues for treatment and ultimately affect long-term treatment and recidivism.

Lennon (1994) and Earle and Earle (1995) supported the recent movement toward an integrated approach to assessment and treatment for the sexual addict–sexual offender paradigm. Addiction approaches offer the 12-step model and other systemic ways of conceptualizing inappropriate sexual behavior; offender treatment has contributed with components from the cognitive-behavioral approaches and ways to understand deviant arousal patterns. Incorporating the strengths of these two theoretical models may be the next step in finding appropriate and helpful treatments for those with problematic sexual behavior. The integrated model incorporates a variety of techniques from addiction and offender therapy to address relationships, intimacy, communication, sexual behavior, and childhood trauma. This multimodal approach provides a more comprehensive picture of the individual, rather than focusing exclusively on the problematic sexual behavior.

In the conceptualization of sexually addicted sex offenders, it is equally important to understand that not all sexual addicts are sexual offenders or vice versa. Mutually exclusive groups of sexual offenders or sexual addicts exist. The proposed model discusses the similarities and differences between the sexual addict, the sexual offender, the sexually addicted sex offender, and the sexually concerned.

The model presented consists of four quadrants to conceptualize those who present in therapy with problematic sexual behavior. Figure 23.1 provides a graphical overview of the model and demonstrates how the offender and addict groups may be mutually exclusive, but can combine to create a separate category known as the sexually addicted sex offender. The fourth quadrant is represented by those who do not meet criteria for either sexual offender or sexual addict, but present with other problematic sexual behaviors in therapy.

Assessment is the essential piece to working within this model. In order to determine the appropriate placement of a client within the four quadrants, a thorough assessment must be conducted by a professional with knowledge of offense and addictive behaviors. This model operates under the premise that the differences in treatment between the four quadrants are critical to the success of the client.

ASSESSMENT

Assessment is essentially the same for all clients who present with problematic sexual behavior. The first and foremost assessment tool is a well-conducted clinical interview. The interview questions need to be direct, but not leading, and presented in a manner that makes the client feel comfortable and safe to answer honestly. It is important to review confidentiality of disclosure prior to conducting the interview. Clinicians must always keep in mind that clients are not going to feel comfortable discussing sexual thoughts and behaviors, especially if the assessment is a one-time interview. In addition, individuals who have engaged in illicit behaviors are less likely to voluntarily disclose information, due to the possible legal consequences of their behaviors. The most effective assessment allows time for relationship building between the clinician and client. It is essential to obtain a detailed report from the client regarding family history, school history, sexual history, abuse history, relationship history, criminal history, and health history. It is not uncommon for individuals in the first three quadrants to have multiple diagnoses, including Axis I, Axis II, or Axis III disorders, or any combination of these. Most notable are conditions such as major depression and anxiety-related disorders. It is important to refer for a medical or psychiatric evaluation, depending on these other comorbid conditions. Psychological testing is one way to assess for these other diagnoses that may require further assessment and treatment.

	Sexual Addict	Nonsexual Addict
Sexual Offender	**Quadrant I** *Characteristics:* • Higher Frequency of Less Intrusive Offenses • Ritualized Sexual Behaviors • Report Sexual Memories at Very Young Age • Comorbid Addictive Behaviors • Shame Regarding Offense Behaviors • Ritualized Use of Pornography • Feelings of Frustration, Rejection, Powerlessness, Shame • History of Neglect, Sexual and Emotional Abuse • Clear Progression of Fantasy and Behaviors *Treatment Techniques:* • Accountability & Responsibility (second order change) • Relapse Prevention (offense & addictive behavior) • Addiction–Offender Relationship • Victim Empathy Training (impact on victims) • Pharmacological Intervention (for treatment of obsessive thinking, depression, or both) • Trauma Work (mid-treatment) • Sexual Health Education (intimacy and love; positive and negative sex) • Couples & Family Intervention (addiction education; relationship issues; safety) • Multiple Addiction Treatment • Participation in 12-Step Fellowship	**Quadrant II** *Characteristics:* • Sexual Behaviors More Intrusive • Less Ritualized—More Impulsive • Sexual Fantasy/Behavior Begins in Late Adolescence or Early Adulthood • Lower Frequency of Addictive Behaviors • Narcissistic/Shameless About Offense • Feelings of Anger, Frustration, Hatred • History of Physical Abuse • Minimal Use of Pornography *Treatment Techniques:* • Accountability & Responsibility (first order change) • Relapse Prevention (offense behavior) • Victim Empathy Training (narcicism) • Deviant Arousal Reconditioning • Pharmacological Intervention (anger, impulse control, testosterone reduction) • Cognitive-Behavioral Interventions • Anger/Stress Management • Trauma Work (late in treatment) • Sexual Health Education (power, control, and sexual behavior; gender equity issues) • Couples & Family Intervention (offender education; safety issues; reunification issues; family roles)
Non-Sexual Offender	**Quadrant III** *Characteristics:* • High Frequency of Nonintrusive Sexual Behaviors (e.g., masturbation, affairs, one-night stands, etc.) • Highly Ritualized and Cyclical Behavior • Repeated Effort to Stop Fantasies/Behaviors • Ignore Consequences of Behavior • Feeling Hopeless, Helpless, and Despair • Early Sexual Memories • Heightening Risk of Sexual Behavior to Achieve Same Level of Pleasure. • Obsession With Obtaining, Being, or Recovering From Sexual Behaviors • Double Life • Few Nonsexual Relationships *Treatment Techniques:* • Addiction Cycle Education • Ritual Recognition and Re-Training • 12-Step Involvement • Relapse Prevention • Sex Offender Prevention • Sexual Health Education • Trauma Work (mid-treatment) • Pharmacological Intervention (obsessive thinking) • Couples & Family Intervention	**Quadrant IV** *Characteristics:* • Frequent Masturbation Concerns • Sexual Affairs • Mixed Sexual Drive Couples • Fetishes • Sexual Dysfunctions • Nocturnal Emissions • Other Sexual Concerns *Treatment Techniques:* • Human Sexuality Education • Bibliotherapy • Sex Therapy • Couples or Family Counseling or Both

FIGURE 23.1. Four-Quadrant Model of Problematic Sexual Behavior

Psychological testing can provide a composite picture of a client's overall mental and emotional health. If available, the test results can serve as an avenue to begin dialogue around specific areas of concern for the client.

Standard psychological tests such as the Minnesota Mutiphasic Personality Inventory (MMPI-2; Butcher, Dahlstrom, Graham, Tellegen, & Kaemmer, 1989) and the Millon Clinical Multiaxial Invnetory (MCMI-II; Millon, 1992) can help the clinician understand a client's defense patterns, as well as overall psychological health. The Shipley Institute of Living Scale may be used to assess verbal and abstract reasoning and to screen for possible organic concerns. The Test of Variable Attention (TOVA; Greenberg, 1996) is a useful tool in screening for attention deficit disorder (ADD) in adults. ADD is often an undiagnosed problem for many offenders and addicts. An undiagnosed ADD client can often appear unmotivated and a "failure" in a treatment setting.

Instruments that have been developed more specifically for sex addicts and sex offenders include the Sexual Addiction Screening Test (SAST; Carnes, 1989), the Sexual Dependency Inventory–Revised (SDI-R; Carnes & Delmonico, 1997), and the Multiphasic Sex Inventory (MSI; Nichols & Molinder, 1984).

The Sexual Addiction Screening Test (Carnes, 1989) is a brief screening tool designed to detect the presence of sexual addiction. High scores on this instrument warrant further investigation into the presence and extent of sexual addiction.

The Sexual Dependency Inventory–Revised (SDI-R; Carnes & Delmonico, 1997) is a more comprehensive assessment of the various forms of sexual dependency. There are 10 subscales representing the 10 subtypes of sexual addiction: fantasy, seductive role, voyeuristic, exhibitionistic, intrusive, exploitive, paying for sex, pain exchange, anonymous, and trading sex. The SDI-R can be used to detect the presence and extent of sexual addiction; however, the instrument is detailed and lengthy and should be used only if sexual addiction is suspected.

The Multiphasic Sex Inventory (Nichols & Molinder, 1984) was designed and normed on adjudicated sexual offenders. It measures level of responsibility for offense, level of denial, sexual knowledge, degree of sexual obsessive thought, and motivation for treatment.

Current trends also indicate that it is necessary to assess for compulsive or illegal behaviors on the Internet. Although instrumentation is limited at this point, clinical interviews should not neglect to inquire about such online behavior as part of the comprehensive assessment. In order to screen for online sexual problems, screening instruments such as the Internet Sex Screening Test (ISST; Delmonico, 1999) are available. Carnes, Delmonico, and Griffin (2001) discuss ways to assess and treat individuals with compulsive cybersex behaviors. Other researchers report common characteristics of the users of online sexual activity that may be useful in the assessment process (Cooper, Delmonico, & Burg, 2000).

Other assessment procedures might include phallometric testing and polygraph testing.

Phallometric testing is a physiological method of assessing sexual arousal patterns. Sex addicts and sexually addicted sex offenders typically have polymorphous sexual arousal patterns. They will often respond to any and all sexual stimuli. This does not necessarily indicate that these behaviors are problematic, but simply that these clients are easily aroused in the presence of any sexual stimuli. Caution must be used when employing the plethysmograph for assessment purposes because sex addicts and sexually addicted sex offenders are often easily triggered by the sexual material used in the assessment. The phallometric assessment needs to be performed by an individual who is sensitive to the difficulty that sex addicts and sexually addicted sex offenders have in containing their sexuality after such an assessment.

Phallometric results for the sex offender often indicate specific arousal patterns, as compared to the polymorphous results discussed previously. There are also clients who are nonresponders on a phallometric assessment. Nonresponse patterns can occur for a variety of reasons, including anxiety, deception, sexual dysfunction, health problems, and medication side effects. A follow-up phallometric assessment may be in order 3 to 6 months after the onset of treatment if a nonresponse pattern is found. If specific arousal patterns are present, the assessment can be used as part of the treatment planning process. Scores on phallometric testing can serve to begin honest dialogue about the client's sexual arousal patterns that he or she may not have otherwise disclosed.

Polygraph testing can also be used as part of the assessment process. It is imperative that the polygraph be done as a therapeutic process and not as a police interrogation. The polygraph examiner needs to have experience working within therapeutic environments and to understand the concept of the therapeutic polygraph. The possible consequences should be fully disclosed to the client prior to polygraph testing.

We see the use of phallometric and polygraph testing as a last resort to the internal honesty of the client. It is also thought that these assessment tools are best utilized as part of a comprehensive treatment plan and not as the sole source of information for an accurate depiction of a client's diagnosis or clinical status. Furthermore, these forms of assessment are best used therapeutically, rather than punitively, and can be extremely helpful in developing a positive and honest relationship with clients if used properly.

Figure 23.1 provides an overview of the characteristics and treatment suggestions for each of the four quadrants. The following sections examine these quadrants more thoroughly by discussing the common characteristics and treatment approaches.

QUADRANT I: THE SEXUALLY ADDICTED SEX OFFENDER

Characteristics

Sexually addicted sex offenders typically report early and extensive memories of sexual behavior or fantasy that have developed into a ritualized pattern of behavior throughout their lives. Those found in this quadrant usually have a high frequency of sexual violations against others, especially in Level 2 behaviors (e.g., voyeurism, exhibitionism, sexual harassment, etc.) and less often in Level 3 behaviors (child molestation, rape, and incest) (Carnes, 1983). The sexually addicted sex offender typically reports a history of multiple forms of child neglect, emotional or sexual abuse, or any combination of these. Sexually addicted sex offenders may also change their form of sexual acting out (e.g., compulsive masturbation, pornography, multiple affairs, etc.); however, this change should not be viewed as treatment success because it often represents different aspects of the same addiction cycle. The viewing of pornography often begins at an early age and progresses in frequency and intensity as the addiction develops. This "progression" noted in pornography use is often a common theme among behaviors for the sexually addicted sex offender. Progression can include both frequency of a behavior (increases over time) and intensity of the behavior (moving toward higher-risk behaviors). Not all individuals progress at the same rate; however, progression is often evident when viewing the history of acting-out behaviors in this quadrant. Sexually addicted sex offenders often show remorse, guilt, and shame about their offense behavior and struggle with feelings of unworthiness, frustration, rejection, and powerlessness (Blanchard, 1990). Clients in this quadrant often want to please their therapist and manipulate the outcome of their treatment, which often leads to the underreporting or misreporting of the frequency and types of sexual behaviors in which they engage.

It is not unusual for individuals in this group to experience multiple addictions with other substances or behaviors. At times, these addictions occur simultaneously to the sexual addiction. However, alternate addictions may surface when the client addresses the sexual addiction. Most common collateral addictions include alcohol, drugs, and gambling/spending.

TREATMENT GOALS AND APPROACH

The sexually addicted sex offender presents the most complex array of treatment issues, often a culmination of many years of personal issues and perpetration against others. All aspects of addiction, history, and offense behavior must be addressed to promote long-term success in treatment. Following a thorough risk assessment, the first step in treatment involves the development of risk-prevention strategies to stop any current intrusive behaviors and prevent future acting out. As a result, the sexually addicted sex offender often requires multiple modalities for successful treatment (e.g., individual therapy, group therapy, 12-step groups, etc.). A common goal in the first three quadrants is to encourage accountability and responsibility for past, present, and future behaviors. This accountability includes clients' stopping negative acting-out behaviors and therapists' providing victim empathy training to educate sexually addicted offenders or the impact of their inappropriate behavior. Because addictive patterns and offense behavior exist in this quadrant, it is important to intervene with both addictive-cycle treatments and offense behavior interventions. Treatments for the sexually addicted sex offender include relapse prevention techniques, offense cycle aware-ness, other cognitive/behavioral strategies, victim empathy training, and trauma work. In addition, participation in a recovery support group (e.g., 12-Steps, etc.) is essential to ensure honesty, accountability, and a sense of support for the client. Most addiction treatment professionals believe that individuals struggling with sexual addiction will need some form of group support throughout their lives. Although the frequency of their attendance may change over time, sexual addicts must always remain cognizant that the addiction may resurface.

One critical issue in effectively treating the sexually addicted sex offender is a pharmacological assessment. Some research (Sealy, 1995) has suggested that the use of certain medications can be extremely helpful in certain clients. The use of various pharmacological agents can assist clients in reducing depression, anxiety, obsession, and so forth. Once the biological system is functioning cor-rectly, various treatment concepts can be more easily understood and imple-mented in the client's recovery plan.

Another important consideration is the timing and appropriateness of each intervention. For example, although deviant arousal reconditioning may be ap-propriate for the offender quadrant, it may not be appropriate in treatment of the sexually addicted sex offender because the stimuli used may jumpstart the addiction cycle. Another example is therapy with past trauma issues. Although examining past trauma issues is often useful for addicts and offenders, the tim-ing of this intervention is extremely important. As an early intervention, sexu-ally addicted offenders may see this as an excuse for their behavior and use it to minimize or justify their sexual offense. Timing is also a consideration in refer-ral to 12-step support groups because these groups can also become an excuse for behavior. For that reason, we suggest that sexually addicted sex offenders be ready to accept full responsibility for their behavior prior to starting such a group and prior to examining past trauma issues.

The treatment of the sexually addicted sex offender is particularly depen-dent on the idea of "second order change" (Watzlawick, Beavin, & Jackson, 1967). Second order change involves not only modifying or stopping behavior, but also promoting introspection to encourage a change in lifestyle, underlying beliefs, and attitudes. Clients who stop their sexual behavior based solely on possible consequences are more likely to relapse than those who can stop behavior based on a shift in their attitude and beliefs about themselves, oth-ers, and the world. Second order change is always the goal of treatment; how-ever, for some, stopping based on fear of consequences may be all that can come about.

Case Example

Chad is a 34-year-old voyeur. He recalled that his window peeping starting as early as age 10, when he was aroused by looking into neighbors' windows. His childhood history included a sexualized environment where his father openly viewed pornography and encouraged his children to do the same. There was often sexualized conversation and humor in his household and multiple sexual affairs for both his mother and father. Chad often felt isolated from his peers and used his father's pornography as an escape from reality. As an adolescent he had been caught many times peeping into windows, but it was always dismissed as "boys will be boys" behavior. At age 35 he was court ordered to treatment. Although he continued his peeping and compulsive sexual behaviors (e.g., pornography, adult bookstores, paying for sex, etc.), he reported to his therapist that he was not sexually acting out. After 1 year, probation had ended and Chad chose to end his therapy. Chad's behavior rapidly got worse, as indicated by several arrests over the next 12 months. He voluntarily entered an integrated treatment program that addressed his sexual addiction and sexual offense behaviors, including his childhood and social issues. Chad was held accountable for all forms of his sexual behavior and began to build a support system that valued his recovery. Chad's treatment included Luvox, a medication to decrease obsessive thinking, in conjunction with individual and group therapy and 12-step support.

QUADRANT II: THE SEXUAL OFFENDER

The nonaddicted sexual offender category consists of individuals who engage in illegal, paraphilic offense behavior without underlying evidence of sexual compulsivity. Although legal terms are helpful in determining offense behavior, it is not necessary for an individual to have been arrested or charged with a sexual offense to be considered a sexual offender. In fact, Abel et al. (1987) studied nonincarcerated paraphiliacs and reported that a large number of self-referred paraphiliacs have engaged in offense behavior that had not yet been discovered. This quadrant represents the historic view of the typical sexual offender, without underlying sexual compulsivity issues (Abel, Osborn, Anthony, & Gardos, 1992). The literature describes a variety of characteristics and treatment techniques used to assist this quadrant of individuals (Laws, 1989; Maletzky, 1991).

Characteristics

The sexual offender often reports a lower frequency of offense behaviors than the sexually addicted sex offender quadrant. The age of onset for sexual fantasy and behavior is often in late adolescence or late adulthood, as compared to the addicted offender, who reports very early memories of sexual fantasy and behavior (Blanchard, 1990). Prominent underlying feelings may include depression, loneliness, stress, anger, and frustration. Incarcerated sex offenders often report the highest levels of anger, frustration, and hatred, which may stem from higher reporting of violent forms of maltreatment in childhood (Blanchard, 1990). This assertion regarding incarcerated sex offenders is supported by our clinical experience, in that sexual offenders often report physical abuse in childhood, as opposed to sexual abuse. Although pornography may be present, it is not typically used in a ritualization cycle as the fuel to promote the offense (Blanchard, 1990). Finally, individuals in this quadrant may not experience significant amounts of guilt or remorse about their behavior. They often fail to see the damage that they have caused others and focus only on their own inconvenience of dealing with therapy, legal systems, and so forth. The repeat sex offender will often have a criminal history unrelated to sexual behavior, but this points toward an overall propensity for antisocial behaviors. However, it is important to remember that there are many types of sexual offenders. Some individuals may have offended on only one occasion as a result of lack of judgment and boundaries and do not exhibit a pattern of sexual offense behavior. All of this must be taken into account during the assessment and treatment planning phases.

Treatment Goals and Approach

Initially, the primary focus for treatment is to stop current acting out and to prevent future relapse. In this initial phase of treatment, various cognitive and behavioral techniques may be useful for all aspects of therapy, including the incorporation of accountability, responsibility, and relapse prevention. However, cognitive behavioral techniques alone may not address important issues necessary for long-term relapse-prevention planning. In order for genuine victim empathy to occur, clinicians should explore past childhood trauma issues for individuals in this quadrant. It is often through this understanding of the client's own victimization that true empathy can be attained. It must be noted that the timing of past trauma work is crucial and must not serve as an excuse for behavior. A strong foundation in accountability and responsibility training is often necessary for trauma work to be useful in this quadrant. Solid relapse prevention plans and skills are needed because the past trauma therapy can cause old coping strategies to resurface, which in this quadrant includes the sexual exploitation of others.

The penile plethysmograph is useful not only in assessment, but also in treatment of sexual offenders. Plethysmography involves measuring the level of sexual arousal by placing a strain gauge around the penis and physiologically measuring the intensity of arousal. A female version is also available, but rarely used. Sex offenders often show arousal to specific scenarios that match their acting-out behaviors. Arousal reconditioning techniques can be an effective way of redirecting deviant arousal patterns. The plethysmograph becomes a way to monitor treatment of the sexual offender.

Case Example

Joe is a 40-year-old sexual offender. He molested his 14-year-old stepdaughter. Joe came from a home where he witnessed a great deal of violence between his mother and father and had, in fact, been emotionally and physically abused by his father. Joe presented in treatment as an angry individual who had a low tolerance for frustration and poor impulse control. Joe reported no history of sexually compulsive behaviors (no pornography, bookstores, prostitutes, etc.). He did, however, have a history of physical assault behavior. He felt little shame or remorse for his behavior and justified his molesting behavior by blaming the victim for her promiscuous behavior. Joe was angry that he was court ordered to therapy because he had no emotional or behavioral problems. Treatment focused on impulse control and anger reduction. Joe also was educated about the cycle of abuse and taught various relapse-prevention techniques. Communication skills were discussed as a possible way to express his anger toward his father for past abuse. No 12-step or pharmacological interventions were required.

QUADRANT III: THE SEXUAL ADDICT

Individuals in Quadrant III meet the criteria for sexual addiction/compulsivity, but have not engaged in a sexual offense behavior. Often, the strength of the therapeutic relationship and the honesty of the client are the only ways to ensure accuracy in assessing the presence of offense behaviors. Many untreated sexual addicts are often in this quadrant for a short period of time before the desire for higher-risk behaviors places them in the sexually addicted sex offender quadrant. However, a percentage of sexual addicts use fantasy, compulsive masturbation, pornography, and multiple affairs behaviors throughout their lives. It is these individuals who occupy the sexual addict quadrant.

Characteristics

The sexual addict often reports problems with fantasies or excessive sexual behaviors such as masturbation, pornography, multiple affairs, anonymous one-night stands, and so forth. Although none of these behaviors alone constitute sexual addiction, the history, frequency, sense of loss of control, obsession, and consequences help ascertain if the behavior has become problematic (Schneider, 1994). We acknowledge that sexual fantasy is not necessarily unhealthy or addictive, but addicts report intrusive, unstoppable thought patterns that repeatedly interfere with their social, occupational, and intimate lives. Memories of sexual experiences are often from very young ages and show a pattern of highly ritualized and cyclical behaviors. Even after the most severe consequences and repeated efforts to stop their behavior, sexual addicts continue to engage in these behaviors, which often fosters feelings of hopelessness, helplessness, despair, and shame. The excitement-seeking behaviors continue and increase over the course of the addiction, as clients attempt to maintain a secret life visible only to themselves. It is important to note that because of this "tolerance effect" in sexual addiction, the sexual addict always runs a close risk of crossing a line that is illegal and intrusive of others. The crossing of this line then places the addict into Quadrant I, the sexually addicted sex offender. Individuals can remain in the sex addict quadrant for many years without crossing into offense behavior, but it is important to remember that these sex addicts often use their behaviors to cope with stress and anxiety. If the stress and anxiety reach peak levels, crossing the boundary is always one behavior away.

As mentioned in Quadrant I, multiple addictions are often present either simultaneously or consecutively with the sexual addiction. Again, it is important to assess the presence of other addictions to successfully treat this quadrant.

Treatment Goals and Approach

The emphasis in the treatment of the sexual addict includes educational sessions about addiction models, addiction cycle recognition, ritualization behavior, sexual health, and support groups. In addition, relapse prevention techniques should be developed to help addicts feel more in control of their behaviors and curtail future acting-out behaviors. This relapse prevention should have components of sexual offense prevention that may include issues such as progression of behaviors, responsibility, accountability, victim empathy, and objectification of others.

Pharmacological intervention may also be necessary for depression or obsessional thinking patterns. Refer the client to an appropriate medical physician who is familiar with pharmacological intervention for addictions, because medications and dosages may vary greatly in addiction treatment. It is also important to closely monitor clients for "switching addictions," as the medications may become their new drug of choice to replace the sexual behaviors they are reducing.

Case Example

Sherry is a 29-year-old sexual addict. Sherry has sexually acted out with as many as 100 different men, all of whom she met in singles clubs and bars. Sherry's father left the family when she was only 5, and she has had no contact with her father since then. Her uncle sexually molested her when she was 10 years old. She reports a positive and healthy relationship with her mother. Sherry began going to bars and singles clubs on weekends to meet other people. She soon found herself seducing men and engaging in one-night stands. The weekends soon expanded to weekdays and Sherry was consumed by sex with men. She would often have shame and remorse about her behavior, but would find herself unable to control the urge to escape reality by seducing another man. Sherry had been treated on multiple occasions for sexually transmitted diseases and each time promised she would not return to her sexual lifestyle—she always did. Sherry finally sought treatment from an outpatient therapist, who began to address the sexual addiction and encouraged her to attend a 12-step fellowship for Sex and Love Addicts. The combination of individual therapy and the support of a 12-step group has been successful in helping Sherry manage her life.

QUADRANT IV: THE SEXUALLY CONCERNED

This final group of clients seeks treatment for specific sexual concerns. These clients are neither sexually addicted/compulsive nor sexual offenders. They may present in therapy at the urging of a partner, self-concern, or sexual dysfunction. It is important for the clinician to conduct a thorough assessment, because many times clients minimize their behavior for fear of being shamed or judged. A thorough assessment will help clients be rigorously honest with themselves and with their therapist.

Characteristics

Clients in this quadrant may have concerns about frequent masturbation, sexual affairs, sexual drive, fetishes, paraphilias, or sexual dysfunction. It is important to conduct a thorough assessment of individuals presenting these issues because there may be underlying concerns or issues with sexuality. Although none of the behaviors alone are indicative of sexual addiction or offense, it is important to address the concerns directly and focus on the clients' motivation for seeking treatment, when they first became sexually concerned, and their history of sexual behavior.

Treatment Goals and Approaches

Treatment for this quadrant may include human sexuality education, sexual therapy, or couple's therapy. Many times, bibliotherapy can be used to educate clients in this quadrant as to common sexual practices. If sexual dysfunction is present, the therapist may employ specific techniques to address the dysfunction, or, if not trained, the therapist should refer the client to a qualified sex therapist for appropriate treatment of the dysfunction. Finally, clients in this group may have other relationship issues outside of their sexual concerns, and these issues could be addressed in the context of couple's or family sessions.

Case Example

Aaron was a 19-year-old college student. He was concerned because he felt he masturbated too often—about three times per week. Aaron was raised in a religious home where he was taught that masturbation is not acceptable sexual behavior. He often felt guilty for masturbating in his parents' home and felt ashamed of his behavior. Aaron described his childhood as typical and denied any suggestions of emotional, physical, or sexual abuse. Aaron was hoping that he would be able to stop masturbating when he became involved in a serious relationship with a female. However, he reported that his masturbation increased slightly as he fantasized about sex with his new girlfriend. After a complete assessment, treatment involved sexual education about typical sexual practices among 19-year-old males. Focus was also on the guilt Aaron felt when he did masturbate and how he may be able to process and reframe his feelings.

Common Treatment Considerations

Although each quadrant has individual considerations for assessment and treatment issues, several factors must be taken into account for all four quadrants. For example, family and couple's treatment are important aspects in all quadrants. Sexually problematic behaviors often occur inside a system that helps to sustain them. The problematic sexual behavior will continue to resurface in a family that does not understand the dynamics that enable it.

Second, sexual pathology is often the focus of the four quadrants; therefore, it is important to help clients develop their understanding of healthy sexuality to place them on a road to recovery. After all, clients can make little movement forward unless they understand their direction. The discussion and development of healthy sexuality are often overlooked and can be critical for successful recovery.

Finally, spirituality and sexuality are often paired for individuals. A discussion of an individual's spiritual life will help that person gain insight into his or her self-understanding sexual behavior. Spirituality cannot be overlooked in assessing or treating any of these four quadrants.

DISCUSSION

The purpose of this chapter was to present a model that elaborates on the characteristics, assessment, and treatment of those who present with sexually problematic behavior. This model includes the sexually addicted sex offender, the sexual addict, the sexual offender, and the sexually concerned client. We hope that discussion of the sexually addicted sex offender will provide impetus for further research and clinical data. Future studies could examine this model, in either qualitative or quantitative designs, and expand upon its basic premises. We believe that certain quadrants may be larger than others in the general population; however, future studies would need to confirm or dismiss this assumption. As the awareness of sexual addiction and sexual victimization grows, it is vital for treatment professionals to find a common ground and work cooperatively in the assessment and treatment of those with problematic sexual behavior. Furthermore, it is imperative that professionals understand the similarities and differences both among and between sexual addicts and sexual offenders. Support and criticism of this model are necessary to increase awareness of those suffering with problematic sexual behavior.

REFERENCES

Abel, G. G., Becker, J. V., Mittelman, M., Cunningham-Rathner, J., Rouleau, J., & Murphy, W. D. (1987). Self-reported sex crimes of nonincarcerated paraphiliacs. *Journal of Interpersonal Violence, 2*(1), 3–25.

Abel, G. G., Osborn, C. A., Anthony, D., & Gardos, P. (1992). Current treatments of paraphiliacs. *Annual Review of Sex Research, 3*, 255–290.

Blanchard, G. T. (1990). Differential diagnosis of sex offenders: Distinguishing characteristics of the sex addict. *American Journal of Preventive Psychiatry and Neurology, 2*(3), 45–48.

Butcher, J. N., Dahlstrom, W. G., Graham, J. R., Tellegen, A., & Kaemmer, B. (1989). *Manual for administration and scoring: MMPI-2.* Minneapolis, MN: University of Minnesota Press.

Carnes, P. J. (1983). *Out of the shadows.* Minneapolis, MN: CompCare.

Carnes, P. J. (1989). *Contrary to love.* Minneapolis, MN: CompCare.

Carnes, P. J., & Delmonico, D. L. (1997). *Sexual Dependency Inventory–Revised.* Wickenburg, AZ: Gentle Path.

Carnes, P. J., Delmonico, D. L., & Griffin, E. J. (2001). *In the shadows of the net: Breaking free from compulsive online sexual behavior.* Center City, MN: Hazelden Foundation.

Cooper, A., Delmonico, D. L., & Burg, R. (2000). Cybersex users, abusers, and compulsives: New findings and implications. *Sexual Addiction & Compulsivity: Journal of Treatment and Prevention, 7*(1–2), 5–29.

Delmonico, D. L. (1999). *Internet sex screening test.* (Online). Available at: http://www.sexhelp.com/internet_screening_test.cfm

Earle, R. H., & Earle, M. R. (1995). *Sex addiction: Case studies and management.* New York: Brunner/Mazel.

Greenberg, L. (1996). *Test of Variable Attention.* 4281 Catella Ave #215, Los Alamitos, CA: Greenberg.

Irons, R. J., & Schneider, J. P. (1994). Sexual addiction: Significant factors in sexual exploitation of health care professionals. *Sexual Addiction and Compulsivity: Journal of Treatment and Prevention, 1*(3), 198–214.

Laws, R. D. (1989). *Relapse prevention with sex offenders.* New York: Guilford.

Lennon, B. (1994). An integrated treatment program for paraphiliacs, including a 12-step approach. *Sexual Addiction and Compulsivity: Journal of Treatment and Prevention, 1*(3), 227–241.

Maletzky, B. M. (1991). *Treating the sexual offender.* Newbury Park, CA: Sage.

Millon, T. (1992). *Millon Clinical Multiaxial Inventory–II.* Minneapolis, MN: National Computer Systems.

Nichols, H. R., & Molinder, I. (1984). *Multiphasic Sex Inventory.* 437 Bowes Drive, Tacoma, WA: Nichols & Molinder.

Schneider, J. P. (1994). Sex addiction: Controversy within mainstream addiction medicine, diagnosis based on the *DSV-III-R* and physician case histories. *Sexual Addiction & Compulsivity: Journal of Treatment and Prevention, 1*(1), 19–44.

Sealy, J. R. (1995). Psychopharmacological intervention in addictive sexual behavior. *Sexual Addiction & Compulsivity: Journal of Treatment and Prevention, 2*(4), 257–276.

Watzlawick, P., Beavin, J. H., & Jackson, D. D. (1967). *Pragmatics of human communication.* New York: Norton.

Wolf, S. C. (1988). A model of sexual aggression/addiction. *Journal of Social Work and Human Sexuality, 7*(1), 131–148.

SECTION IV

Clinical Practice
and Resources

CHAPTER 24

How to Build a Sex Addiction Practice

MARTHA TURNER

The interested and addiction-trained professional can start an outpatient practice for recovering sex addicts, providing there is commitment, a nonjudgmental attitude, and appropriate supervision. This chapter describes a multilevel model of a successful sex addiction practice that I developed. Volunteering to give presentations on the disease and writing articles are useful ways to market. Six patients are enough to make a group (the most cost-effective way to treat addicts). When one's genuine interest for treating sex addicts is known, many referrals will come from the recovering community. Pitfalls are discussed, as well as things that work well. Groups for different levels of recovery can then be developed to meet most of the needs of the patients. First, there is a "basics" group for those starting to want recovery. Getting patients to come and talk is the goal. The next level is "Phase 1" or "Beginnings," a 6-week focus group for individuals and couples starting recovery. It is designed to explore the causes and consequences of sexual addiction and codependency. Couples are helped to equalize their dynamics by coming in together. The next level is "Phase 2," which focuses on relapse prevention, involvement in the 12-step programs, and getting a sponsor. Finally, there is "Phase 3," the long-term group intended for trauma work, learning healthy coping mechanisms, and solving problems of daily living. Here, developmental delays are addressed and social skills are taught. With consistency and quality treatment, the practice and patients will thrive.

Sex addiction is a fascinating and terrible disease (Carnes, 1991). Not everyone can or ought to treat it. However, for the practitioner who is familiar with the disease concept of chemical dependency and has had training in addictions, treating sex addiction can open a whole new vista. Not only is understanding this disease pioneer work, which often includes other addictions and their various neurotransmitter responses, but the treatment delves deeply into childhood trauma to find the origins of the disease.

THERAPISTS' CHARACTERISTICS AND QUALIFICATIONS

Because of the exquisite sensitivity to rejection, judgment, and sexual shame experienced by sex addicts, the people treating them need to be knowledgeable, committed, consistent, supervised, and nonjudgmental toward these patients and be comfortable with their own sexuality. One cannot be moralistic about how a child found a way to survive. Likewise, when that child becomes an adult and the survival mechanism has evolved into behavior that is now dangerous, life-threatening to self or others, and must be stopped, there is still no place for judgment or anger in the treatment process around these behaviors. The other necessary ingredients are patience, respect, and positive regard for the valiant souls who are trying to trust, hoping for help, and truly wanting a better quality of life. It is a tall order, but entirely possible. Some of the preparations for a therapist to treat sex addicts are

1. Read the books and articles referenced here, as well as subscribe to *Sexual Addiction & Compulsivity: The Journal of Treatment and Prevention.*
2. Attend workshops and training sessions on sex addiction, as well as the annual conference sponsored by the National Council on Sex Addiction and Compulsivity (NCSAC).
3. Find a supervisor who is familiar with addictions and sexual dynamics.
4. Do an internship with an established program that treats sex addicts.
5. Become familiar with state guidelines about reporting.
6. Learn how to do interventions.
7. Apply to the American Academy for information on certification in multiple addictions.

When I began to work with sex addicts, I had already been treating chemically dependent patients for 8 years, including 4 years as assistant director for a drug and alcohol rehabilitation program. One of my alcoholic patients, after over a year of treatment, cautiously shared that there was another addiction—sex addiction. I was open to learning about it and, as the saying goes "When the student is ready, the teacher appears." Soon another sexually addicted person came to see me and said that the recovering community needed professional help. I offered to run a group specifically for sex addicts and had the great fortune to find a cotherapist* who was willing to take a risk with me.

We started with six people who had been able to put a few weeks of sobriety together. They then told me we needed to read Patrick Carnes's book and go to his workshop. They told me when the next one was and I went. Thus we helped each other. In those early days, the disease seemed so difficult and powerful that we were not sure recovery was possible. Commitment and faith kept

---

*I gratefully acknowledge Victor J. Malatesta, PhD.

us going, along with more education from Carnes (1991) and the study group he formed. Slowly, we began to see some progress.

THE MULTILEVEL SEX ADDICTION PRACTICE MODEL

More people came for help, mostly self-referred from the 12-step program SLAA (Sex and Love Addicts Anonymous). We started another group and began to build up the practice. We found that if people felt safe and were able to put time together free from their addictions, their trauma wounds would begin to present themselves (Turner, 1990). Naturally, this would also generate more psychic pain, which would call up the addiction to medicate it. If their support system (group, 12-step program, good friends, hobbies, creative outlets, spirituality, exercise, nutrition, and other self-care habits) was strong, they could tolerate the pain without relapsing and could experience healing (Turner, 1996). We taught and promoted balanced living, social skills, relapse prevention, and trauma work (van der Kolk, 1987), as people could handle them.

The success of our groups generated referrals. Recovering people in the 12-step groups saw that those in our program were moving along faster and more thoroughly than those going to meetings alone. Before long, there were invitations to do presentations locally. We were delighted to have opportunities to educate other professionals, especially from rehabilitation programs where chemical dependency was the only focus and sex addiction was unknown, but was contributing to relapses. There were interviews for magazines, radio, and television talk shows, which gave us the opportunity to mention our program and telephone number. A few very brave recovering people risked their anonymity for the purpose of educating the public. All of these brought referrals.

We added more groups and a group for spouses of sex addicts. Because of our interest in childhood sexual abuse as a generator of later evolving sex addiction, we also began to see incest survivors without sex addiction, but with PTSD and other addictions. We started a group for incest survivors, too.

After a couple of years, our groups became more advanced. We found that newcomers often were not ready for the level of intensity or intimacy that the established groups were now experiencing. We then designed a 6-week focus group called "Beginnings." For 3 hours once a week, both individuals and couples could attend this intensive, but safe, psychoeducational class. They could ask any questions. We taught them what the addiction is, where it comes from, how addicts and codependents find each other, how to stop the addiction, and what are the promises of recovery. Those who were unable to stop their dangerous behaviors were referred to specialized inpatient facilities for more intensive treatment. Medications were offered when deemed appropriate. Most people, however, were able to finish the group with relief, hope, and an interest in going further and were now going to 12-step groups for sex and love addiction.

For couples who attended Beginnings together, there was the realization that sex addiction was a family disease and that the spouse had a definite role, as well as a similar background. This helped them to speak the same language and have a more cooperative spirit in recovery. We strongly encouraged couples to do their individual tracts (meetings, group therapy, individual therapy, or any combination of these), so that the spouse's progress could parallel and complement the addict's. If they could do this, it would greatly diminish ongoing abuses and power plays. The level of cohesion and good feelings that develops in 6 weeks is remarkable. This is due, in part, to the skill of the leaders and also to the great relief from isolation, shame reduction, and hope that are felt by the patients.

Some could go into the advanced groups from Beginnings, but others were still not ready. To protect the stability of the advanced groups, we started Phase 2, an 8-week focus group for relapse prevention. Here, we could introduce the concept of a therapy group and concentrate on the tools to prevent relapses. This gave people time to make their support systems more solid, find a sponsor, and start using the telephone to connect regularly with other recovering people.

The advantage of these three phases is that they can be tailored to meet the patient's needs. The safety and integrity of the advanced groups can be protected from chronic relapsers. If people in the advanced groups begin to have regular slips because of the pain of their trauma, we invite them to repeat Phase 2 to reinforce the tools and then, if back on track, return to the Phase 3 group they were in. When patients reexperience the raw but delicate childhood traumas, they may need medication, referral to one of the few treatment programs that specialize in sexual addiction, or both. Their places in their groups would be reserved for them upon their return.

At each phase we ask people to make a commitment. They must attend all of the Phase 1 and 2 groups. For Phase 3 they must commit for at least a year. Most find their advanced group so helpful that they stay for several years until ready to let life teach them. For addicts who prefer to be unaccountable and fuzzy, committing to a year may be too frightening to think about. They may stop for a while or repeat Phase 2. Because Phases 1 and 2 run in sequence, they may repeat both. Some have repeated both a couple of times before moving on to Phase 3.

These options enable patients to keep coming to their "anchor" group of the week, which they know they can handle, until they are ready to make that long-term commitment. This is all done without shaming them and with the knowledge that people are in different stages of readiness. They are impatient to move forward as rapidly as possible because of their shame, remorse, and awareness of time lost in the addiction. What they do not know is that they cannot proceed faster than their ability to sustain sobriety. We want the same successes that they want and try to teach them how to pace themselves. We want to avoid setbacks as much as possible because their sense of failure is high.

Some people decide to leave the program for a while. We try to keep our relationship with them through telephone calls and letters. It is not unusual to receive a call a year or two down the road from one of them, in relapse, wanting to come back. This time they may be ready to do "whatever it takes" to recover. We celebrate their return.

MARKETING STRATEGIES

It is important to put the word out on a regular basis that the program exists. Some of the ways one can market include

1. Accept all reasonable requests to give presentations. Take brochures, bibliographies, and business cards with you. The best places are counseling programs, treatment centers, professional trainings, and educational centers (colleges and graduate schools).
2. Offer to give workshops for the recovering community. Some attendees will be therapists who may refer patients.
3. Have caution when the media call. The media's perspective may be rushed and sensational in order to tie into a recent story. Reporters may request "live" patients. In these cases, the motive is to sell the show and it will *not* be worth it. Protect the patients and yourself from these predators! The producers do not care if they ambush or shame someone. In other cases, if the media person has done some reading on the subject and is respectful and interested in educating, the therapist's contribution can be valuable.
4. Develop a mailing list and send out brochures and an announcement of the next Beginnings class date two to three times a year.
5. Attend the annual conference of the NCSAC to learn the latest on treatment issues, to network, and to market your program.

PROGRAM INTEGRITY

A program's success depends on the quality of the staff. In addition to treating individuals and running a couple of the groups, I do supervision and in-service training for my staff. Sometimes people who refer often are invited for a closer look at our program, plus some free education. In-service is a way to get everyone together because some group leaders are independent contractors and will come in only to do one group.

All groups, except Beginnings, are held in the evenings for 90 minutes once a week. Patients sign a confidentiality clause and agree to group rules and to payment of group 1 month in advance. Bills are given out the last group of each month. Payment is expected the next week. For those who are more financially limited, a weekly group payment is acceptable as long as they stay current. Most people pay by cash or check and often do not want their insurance companies involved because of the nature of their illness. If they do use insurance, they wait until the end of the month to submit and collect whatever their insurance coverage allows. Diagnoses are made with discretion to help with confidentiality. A word of caution here is to watch for those who have compulsive spending or debt problems. They may fall behind in payments and must be confronted.

Any rules that are breached are group issues. Although everyone is treated equally, the integrity of the group comes before the individual. For those who never had a voice in their families of origin, they feel valued. Those who want special treatment as a compensation for childhood neglect must learn to get needs met in other appropriate ways. Subgroups, talking about group issues outside of group, liaisons, and other secrets are destructive to the integrity of the group and must be addressed as soon as they are known.

Groups are very rich and often energizing. Therapists with training, commitment, honesty, and consistency find it a privilege and an honor to be a part of these people's journey. I am also very fortunate to have an excellent program coordinator** who has the commitment, enthusiasm, understanding, training, and good-heartedness to give to STAR (Sexual Trauma and Recovery) the true spirit of recovery. She designed Phases 1 and 2. A good coordinator keeps track of everyone, does intakes and interventions, markets, runs groups, mentors, and models what happens when one chooses freedom from addictions and trauma.

Because Phases 1 and 2 are run in sequence, new referrals may have to wait a few months until the next Beginnings. In order not to lose these patients, should their courage fail them, we added a holding group called "Basics," which is nonintensive and aimed at just getting people to come once a week and break their isolation by talking. There are no other expectations. They are encouraged to go to meetings, but not required to do so until Phase 1. They are introduced to the first step (Powerlessness) and made aware of Patrick Carnes's book *Don't Call It Love* (1991).

In preparing them for Phase 1 (Beginnings), we gently inform them that this is a long process and that they are not expected to know much about sex addiction or intimacy, for that matter, and that no questions are considered silly or inappropriate. It is like "prekindergarten," in that people are in a confused, lost state. They are emotionally developmentally arrested at an early stage and need to ease into the process of recovery. This is not to demean them, because many of them are exceptionally bright and successful, but to understand how battered they feel and how much shame and self-loathing is going on. They want to cover up for their harshly negative core beliefs and will demonstrate all kinds of defenses. If the therapist knows the disease, he or she will know what the

---

**I gratefully acknowledge Mary Jo Porreca, CAS.

patient needs more than the patient does at this time. Consistent encourage-ment to go slower, without judgment, will bring the results desired.

The previous groups are intended for the majority of people with sex addic-tion classified as Level 1 behaviors (Carnes, 1989), which include compulsive masturbation, multiple partners, pornography, telephone sex, computer sex, prostitutes, and affairs. These behaviors are excessive, but still acceptable by the general public. There have also been referrals for Level 2 sex offenders. These include exhibitionists, voyeurs, or those who make indecent telephone calls or liberties. Occasionally, we will see Level 3 offenders such as pedophiles. They are all assessed to see if they will fit into our program or need a more specific treat-ment facility geared just for offenders. An addicted sex offender group is struc-tured differently than the other groups. It must focus on responsibility, accountability, and victim empathy *before* doing trauma work. If these individu-als can accomplish the first three things, they could then come into a Phase 3 group to do their trauma resolution.

Another idea to be implemented in the future would be a group for couples. Sometimes the 12 steps can, unintentionally, be divisive of couples because so many of them are trauma-bonded. The survival behavior familiar to them is to perpetuate chaos, which undermines sobriety. If couples first do their own indi-vidual work, they can then benefit from Recovering Couples Anonymous (a 12-step meeting), couple's counseling, and a therapy group for couples. They will need a lot of help with communication skills and intimacy. They need to learn how to disrupt trauma bonds and to stop power plays (positions of victim, perpe-trator, and rescuer). Then their lives will have a quality beyond their wildest expectations. Best of all, a multigenerational legacy of addictions, child abuse, and neglect will have ended for each of them. A truly worthy cause!

SUMMARY

A sex addiction practice can be rewarding, satisfying, and endlessly interesting for a therapist with appropriate training, commitment, love, respect for his or her patients, good boundaries, supervision, and a spiritual openness. Be pre-pared to learn a lot about yourself because your own issues around sexuality are certain to come up. Sexuality is so personal, so sensitive, so easily misunder-stood, and so easily wounded throughout our lives that we cannot help being affected. With the right attitude and patience, one will find that sex addicts, once committed to recovery, are very motivated, grateful, and rewarding to work with. Although it may take months or years to engage them in the recovery process, it is worth the effort. A multilevel approach has been described to help reduce failure rates and promote a graduated, flexible treatment plan that will meet the needs of most patients with sex addiction. This is a disease about relationships and disordered intimacy that is relevant to us all. It is treatable in the vast majority of patients and extremely gratifying. Take a chance!

REFERENCES

Carnes, P. (1989). *Contrary to love: Helping the sexual addict*, Minneapolis, MN: CompCare.

Carnes, P. J. (1991). *Don't call it love: Recovery from sex addiction*. New York: Bantam.

Turner, M. (1990). Long term outpatient group psychotherapy as a modality for treating sexual addiction. *American Journal of Preventive Psychiatry and Neurology*, 2(3), 23–26.

Turner, M. (1996). A self-care program for recovering people. *Sex Addiction & Compulsivity*, 3(4), 282–288.

Turner, M. (1995). Couples in addiction. In G. Weeks & L. Hof (Eds.), *Integrative solutions: Treating common problems in couples therapy* (pp. 124–147). New York: Brunner/Mazel.

van der Kolk, B. (1987). *Psychological trauma*. Washington, DC: American Psychiatric Press.

Resources

COSA (Partners)
9337-B Katy Freeway
Suite 142
Houston, TX 77024
612-537-6904

NCSA/C National Council for Sexual Addiction and Compulsivity
1090 Northchase Parkway
Suite 200 So.
Marietta, GA 30067
770-989-9754
www.ncsac.org

RCA Recovering Couples Anonymous
PO Box 70
Chesterfield, MO 63006
510-336-3300
www.recovering-couples.org

SA Sexaholics Anonymous
PO Box 111910
Nashville, TN 37222-1910
615-331-6230
www.sa.org

SAA Sex Addicts Anonymous
PO Box 70949
Houston, TX 77270
713-869-4902
www.saa-recovery.org

S-Anon (Partners)
PO Box 111242
Nashville, TN 37222-1242
615-833-3152

SCA Sexual Compulsive Anonymous
PO Box 1585
Old Chelsea Station
New York, NY 10011
www.sca-recovery.org

SLAA Sex and Love Addicts Anonymous
The Augustine Fellowship
PO Box 338
Norwood, MA 02062-0338
781-255-8825
www.slaafws.org

SRA Sexual Recovery Anonymous
PO Box 73
Planetarium Station
New York, NY 10024
212-340-4650
www.sexualrecovery.org

www.sexhelp.com
www.sexaddict.com
www.onlinesexaddict.com

Contributors

Kenneth M. Adams, PhD, a licensed psychologist in clinical practice in Royal Oak, Michigan, is the author of *Silently Seduced: When Parents Make Their Children Partners, Understanding Covert Incest* and clinical director for the Program for Sexual Health and Addiction.

Maureen Canning Fulton, MA is in private practice specializing in sexual compulsivity, sexual trauma, and related addictive disorders. She is also the past president of the Arizona Council on Sexual Addiction and Compulsivity and Advisory Board member for the National Council on Sexual Addiction and Compulsivity.

Patrick J. Carnes, PhD, is the clinical director for sexual disorder services at The Meadows in Wickenburg, Arizona. He is the author of many books on recovery including the classics *Out of the Shadows: Understanding Sexual Addiction, revised edition (1992), Contrary to Love,* and *Don't Call It Love.*

M. Deborah Corley, PhD is the Director of Research and Family Services at Sante Center for Healing in Argyle, Texas. She and Jennifer Schneider are co-authors of *Disclosing Secrets: When, to Whom & How Much to Reveal* (Gentle Press, 2002).

David L. Delmonico, PhD, NCC is an Assistant Professor in the Counseling Program at Duquesne University, Pittsburgh, Pennsylvania, and a nationally known author and speaker on the topic of sexual compulsivity and cybersex. Dr. Delmonico is the coauthor of *In the Shadows of the Net* and *Cybersex Unhooked.*

Ralph H. Earle, PhD is president of Psychological Counseling Services, Ltd., and author of numerous books including *Come Here, Go Away: Stop Running From the Love You Want* and *Sexual Addiction: Case Studies and Management.*

James Fearing, PhD, is a nationally known expert in intervention and President/CEO of National Counseling Intervention Services, Inc., in Minneapolis, Minnesota.

Marnie C. Ferree, MA, is a licensed marriage and family therapist with the Woodmont Hills Counseling Center in Nashville, Tennessee, where she is the coleader of Bethesda Workshops, an intensive workshop program for sex addicts and their spouses.

Brenda Garrett, RN, MC, is affiliated with Psychological Counseling Services, Ltd., and specializes in sexual addiction, boundary issues, and codependency.

Elizabeth Griffin, MA, is a licensed marriage, family, and child therapist with over 17 years assessing and treating individuals with sexually compulsive and/or sexual offending behaviors.

Eric Griffen-Shelley, PhD, is a licensed psychologist in Pennsylvania who has worked with sex addicts for over 15 years and authored *Sex and Love: Addiction Treatment and Recovery* (Praeger, 1991) and *Adolescent Sex and Love Addicts* (Praeger, 1994).

Diana Guest, MA, MFT, is a psychotherapist in private practice in San Diego, California, an adjunct faculty member at National University, and coauthor of the book *The Clinician's Guide to 12-Step Programs: When and Why to Refer a Client*.

Richard R. Irons, MD, was the foremost authority on impaired health care professionals and director of the Professional Renewal Center in Lawrence, Kansas. Sadly, he passed away while this book was in its final stages.

Mark R. Laaser, PHD, CAS, is a writer, teacher, and counselor and has authored a number of books about sex addiction. He and his wife work with individuals and couples around the country.

Ken McGill, MA, MFT, a licensed Marriage and Family Therapist with over 16 years of counseling experience in his work with the homeless population in Los Angeles, California, is a doctoral candidate in Clinical Psychology at Azusa Pacific University and is employed by the University Counseling Center at APU.

Judith C. Heaton Matheny, MSSW, ACSW, is the clinical director of the Family Care Center in Louisville, Kentucky where she specializes in sexual health, sexual addiction/compulsivity, and sexual trauma.

Alyson Nerenberg, PsyD, is a nationally known clinical psychologist specializing in the treatment of addictions, sexually compulsive clients, and trauma survivors. She trains therapists throughout the country on how to conduct psychotherapy with these populations.

Jan Parker, PhD, MFT, is a psychotherapist in private practice in Poway, California, an Associate Professor at National University in San Diego, and the co-author of the book *The Clinician's Guide to 12-Step Programs: How, When and Why to Refer a Client.*

Shannae Rickards, PhD, is a licensed psychologist in private practice in southern California where she specializes in the treatment and research of trauma, eating disorders, and borderline personality disorder.

Donald W. Robinson, MA, LPC, is a therapist in private practice in Royal Oak, Michigan, author of peer reviewed articles for national publications, and national lecturer on various aspects of addiction and recovery.

Jennifer P. Schneider, MD, PhD, practices internal medicine and addiction medicine in Tucson, Arizona, and is the author of several books on the impact of sex addiction on the family, including *Back From Betrayal: Sex, Lies, and Forgiveness,* and *Cybersex Exposed* (with Robert Weiss).

Mark F. Schwartz, ScD, MSW, is a licensed psychologist and adjunct professor in the department of Psychiatry and Obstetrics at St. Louise University School of Medicine, and Clinical Co-Director of the Masters and Johnson outpatient program. He has achieved international recognition for his contributions in the treatment of intimacy disorders, marital and sexual dysfunction, sexual compulsivity, sexual trauma, and eating disorders.

John R. Sealy, MD, is the Medical Director of the Sexual Addiction Recovery Program- Del Amo Hospital and Assistant Clinical Professor of Psychiatry at the UCLA School of Medicine.

Stephen Southern, PhD, a nationally recognized clinician and consultant with 26 years of experience in treating individuals, couples, and families, is a consultant to the Masters and Johnson Treatment Programs and director of the Center for Relational Therapy in Hattiesburg, Mississippi, where he maintains a private practice.

Timothy M. Tays, PhD, is affiliated with Psychological Counseling Services, Ltd. in Scottsdale, Arizona, and specializes in sexual addiction and image management.

Martha Turner, MD, is a board certified psychiatrist and addictionologist in private practice in Bryn Mawr, Pennsylvania, and founder of the STAR program.

Robert Weiss, LCSW, CSAT, is Clinical Director of the Sexual Recovery Institute of Los Angeles, California, coauthor of the Hazelden publication *Cybersex Exposed: Simple Fantasy or Obsession,* and a national speaker on sexual addiction treatment.

Marie Wilson, MA, ATR-BC, CSAT, LPC, is an Associate Professor and Coordinator of Art Therapy Programs at Caldwell College and has authored several articles on using the creative process with sex addicts.

Permission Acknowledgments

Chapter 2.   Copyright © 1998. *Intervention and the sexually addicted patient* by James Fearing. Reproduced by permission of Taylor & Francis, Inc., http://routledge-ny.com

Chapter 3.   Copyright © 1999. *Breaking through defenses* by Maureen Canning. Reproduced by permission of Taylor & Francis, Inc., http://routledge-ny.com

Chapter 4.   Copyright © 1998. *Strategies for assessment and early treatment with sexually addicted families* by Judith C. Matheny. Reproduced by permission of Taylor & Francis, Inc., http://routledge-ny.com

Chapter 6.   Copyright © 1999. *Manifestations of damaged development of the human affectional systems and developmentally based psychotherapies* by Mark F. Schwartz and Stephen Southern. Reproduced by permission of Taylor & Francis, Inc., http://routledge-ny.com

Chapter 9.   Copyright © 1996. *Recovery for couples* by Mark R. Laaser. Reproduced by permission of Taylor & Francis, Inc., http://routledge-ny.com

Chapter 13.   Copyright © 1995. *Psychopharmacological intervention in addictive sexual behavior* by John R. Sealy. Reproduced by permission of Taylor & Francis, Inc., http://routledge-ny.com

Chapter 14.   Copyright © 1999. *Dual and triple diagnoses: addictions, mental illness, and HIV infection guidelines for outpatient therapists* by John R. Sealy. Reproduced by permission of Taylor & Francis, Inc., http://routledge-ny.com

Chapter 17.   Copyright © 1999. *Sexual acting-out in borderline women: impulsive self-destructiveness or sexual addiction or compulsivity?* by Shannae Rickards and Mark R. Laaser. Reproduced by permission of Taylor & Francis, Inc., http://routledge-ny.com

Chapter 18.   Copyright © 1997. *Pastors and sexual addiction* by Mark R. Laaser and Kenneth M. Adams. Reproduced by permission of Taylor & Francis, Inc., http://routledge-ny.com

Chapter 21.   Copyright © 1997. *Special populations: Treatment concerns for gay sexual addicts* by Robert Weiss. Reproduced by permission of Taylor & Francis, Inc., http://routledge-ny.com

Chapter 24.   Copyright © 1998. *How to build a sex addiction practice* by Martha Turner. Reproduced by permission of Taylor & Francis, Inc., http://routledge-ny.com

Index